Mystic Universe

Other Books by Ashish Dalela:

The Science of God
Time and Consciousness
Conceiving the Inconceivable
The Balanced Organization
The Yellow Pill
Cosmic Theogony
Emotion
Moral Materialism
Signs of Life
Uncommon Wisdom
Gödel's Mistake
Quantum Meaning
Sāṅkhya and Science
Is the Apple Really Red?
Six Causes

Mystic Universe

An Introduction to Vedic Cosmology

Ashish Dalela

SHABDA
PRESS

Mystic Universe—An Introduction to Vedic Cosmology
by Ashish Dalela
www.shabda.co

Cover Design: Kit Foster
Interior Design: Ciprian Begu

Published by Shabda Press
press.shabda.co
ISBN 978-93-85384-06-6
v1.13(02/2021)

Dedicated to His Divine Grace A. C. Bhaktivedānta Swami Prabhupāda. I have been trying to understand your instructions and emphasis on cosmology for two decades now, but I understood it only after I finished writing this book. Every aspect of Vedic philosophy has a place in the structure of the universe. The universe is the best map of Vedic philosophy we can draw. If one can understand the structure of the universe, then one can understand how the different facets of Vedic philosophy are connected. To the extent that we don't understand the universe's structure, we also don't understand Vedic philosophy. The inverted tree is a scientific model of the universe— of everything, in fact. Scientists will discuss it for centuries to come.

Now our Ph.D's must collaborate and study the 5th Canto to make a model for building the Vedic Planetarium. My final decision is that the universe is just like a tree, with root upwards. Just as a tree has branches and leaves so the universe is also composed of planets which are fixed up in the tree like the leaves, flowers, fruits, etc. of the tree. I am sending this letter to you, and you can make photocopies of it and send to our other Ph.D.'s and begin serious research into the matter in detail. But one thing, I am convinced that the universe is just like a great tree as described therein.

— A. C. Bhaktivedānta Swami
Letter to Svarūpa Dāmodara, April 27, 1976

Contents

List of Figures

List of Tables

Preface

Cosmology has been one of the most fascinating subjects in the history of human knowledge. People have looked at the skies and asked themselves: Are we alone in the universe or is there someone out there, in this apparently endless vastness of space and time? How did we get here? How did all the planets, stars, and galaxies come about? What explains the existence of all this?

The questions in cosmology spawned a bitter rivalry between science and religion in the days of Copernicus and Galileo, over whether the solar system was geocentric or heliocentric. The geocentric model that prevailed before Copernicus and Galileo had led everyone to believe that we are at the center of the universe and therefore the chosen beings, overseen, administered, and judged by the heavens above. The heliocentric model proposed by Copernicus and Galileo suggested that ours is just one of the many planets, and the centrality of our existence in the universe is just false. With that, we also lose the meaning, purpose, and importance that religion attributes to our lives.

At the heart of the debate about cosmology lies the problem of giving our lives meaning. If we are special, then we can talk about the purpose in our lives, give meaning to our existence, and organize society around that meaning and purpose. If we are merely accidents, then providing that meaning and purpose seems pointless; it would seem that we are simply governed by physical forces and we have no ability to decide and choose, let alone give life meaning.

Notwithstanding the considerable problems that arise from adopting the heliocentric scientific view, the enormous amount of empirical evidence seems to suggest that it is *true*. Whether or not we *want* to seek meaning in our lives, no such meaning would seem to exist, if scientific theories are true. Therefore, if the key purpose of adopting a geocentric model was to conclude that humans are part of God's grand strategy, then such a premise would seem a human concoction. Indeed, as people become aware of the conflicts between modern science and religion, the sense of purpose and meaning in our lives is undercut, and even the materialists are now worrying about how to supplant the resulting vacuum with a "theory" of morality and responsibility without God.

That this entire problem began in the cosmological models of science and religion now seems too distant, but it is also obvious that if there were a non-materialistic solution to the problem, it would also bring the age-old cosmological conflict back onto the front stage of intellectual debate. It is considering this fact that this book undertakes an analysis of the Vedic cosmic model.

In the Vedic model, too, we are in the "middle" of the universe but in a completely different sense than in Christian theology: we are neither the best, nor the worst kinds of life forms. We are neither the chosen ones, nor are we the most condemned. Our world is neither too perfect, nor the most imperfect. We are not the best endowed in terms of bodies, senses, minds, and intellects, nor are we the worst in all these departments. Our joy and pain are neither the greatest nor the worst. We are in the "middle" of the universe in quite the same sense that the large mass of people lies in the middle of the Bell Curve. In other words, we are mediocre. Our lives are boring, because we are surrounded by mediocrity: mediocre knowledge, beauty, wealth, power, and pleasure.

If religion was the opiate of the masses, then the Vedic view doesn't support any happy delusions. In contrast to the Christian outlook, which tried to "motivate" people by telling them they are the chosen ones, because they are at the center of the universe and thus have God's greatest attention, the Vedic view tells us about our mediocrity. It talks about perfection too, but achieving it needs a lot of hard work, perseverance, and commitment. Only a few are motivated by that plan. In particular, if you are truly interested in improving the quality of your life, you must develop new kinds of perception, new ways of thinking, renounce sensual pleasures, and develop new forms of morality.

The connection between religion and the "centrality" of our material existence in the universe is therefore rather obtuse in Vedic philosophy (if you are used to this centrality from the Christian perspective). Vedic philosophy does not coddle your hopes about any kind of universal human privilege. If anything, it asks you to develop knowledge, renounce enjoyments, and give up attachments to this body, which are not for the faint-hearted, or for those looking for a quick solution to their material problems. This contrast may be instructive to those who put all religious views under the same blanket of preposterous illusions. In particular, if the scientific goal is to prove that we are piddling fragments within a gigantic cosmos, then that is completely taken for granted in the Vedic view. The difference only lies in how the Vedic view also describes the resurrection out of this irrelevant existence, through the discovery of why the present life form one has isn't their only possible life form.

Due to unfamiliarity with the Vedic viewpoint, a misunderstanding of what its philosophy really depicts, and due to the mindset to study the Vedic literature unguided by the masters who live its teachings, Vedic descriptions too have come under attack in the last few centuries, especially from those who have commented on the Vedas from a Western viewpoint. Those critiques have indeed swayed several people against the Vedic philosophy, but they have also brought many people closer to it in the quest for understanding its real meaning and implication. Such critiques have therefore had a polarizing effect: most people today are either for or against it, and seldom neutral about it.

This book is targeted to the people in both groups. The sheer detail and sophistication of the Vedic cosmological model, backed by an equally detailed and sophisticated theory of matter called *Sāñkhya*, has often intrigued even the most skeptical among us. Part of the reason for this interest is the sheer level of consistency and resonance between the theories of matter and cosmology and the day-to-day practice of *yoga*, *Ayurveda* (the Vedic science of health and healing), *Jyotiṣa* (the Vedic exposition of astrology), and *Vāstu-Shāstra* (the theory of architecture), which continue to be widely practiced by many people as complements or substitutes to the dominant scientific practices today. The close links between these and Indian classical music, dance and art, the relation to the *Sanskrit* language, and the enormous amount of classical literature in India, make for compelling studies even in Western universities.

But it is one thing to study and practice Vedic knowledge for medicine, music, art, literature, astrology, and architecture, and quite another to see its cosmological and material theories in light of modern astronomical evidence. The practical utility of Vedic methods of healing and health, the aesthetic value in traditional Indian music and art, and the widespread use of Vedic astrology even in the Western world, need not detract us from the differences between Vedic and modern cosmologies and the theories of matter. When you live in a polarized world, it helps to understand the reasons why some people disagree with you, so long as those reasons are rational and not dogmatic. But to even engage in this discussion, one first needs to understand the conceptual and theoretical differences between the Vedic and the modern outlooks. How else can we even disagree, if the *languages* of disagreement are different?

I have on numerous previous occasions argued that the Vedic and the modern scientific theories are based on two mutually incompatible descriptions of the world. The Vedic model is hierarchical and cyclic while the Western model is flat and linear. By hierarchy I mean that, in the Vedic model, matter is described not just as objects, which can be perceived by our senses, but as several tiers of realities that cannot be tasted, touched, seen, smelt or heard, but can be "seen" by the mind, intelligence, ego, and moral sense. The portions of reality that are invisible to the senses, but visible to our deeper modalities of sensations, are, in Vedic philosophy, *logically prior* to the visible objects. In contrast, in modern science, material objects are the fundamental reality, and our bodies, senses, mind, intellect, and moral sense *logically follow* from material objects. This difference between science and Vedic theories leads to numerous other differences in their viewpoints. For instance, a direct consequence of this difference is that space and time in modern science are flat and linear, while they are hierarchical and cyclic in the Vedic viewpoint.

I have also described the usefulness of this difference to modern science, especially regarding unsolved problems in mathematics, computing, physics, chemistry, and biology. The books that detail these applications are listed at the end of the present book. I have no doubt that this viewpoint will revolutionize science in ways that we cannot foresee right now, creating new kinds of technologies, a deeper understanding of things we presently fail to understand, and far more robust predictions than those possible in science today.

My effort to explain the Vedic viewpoint to the modern audience has taken one of two forms—breadth and depth. By breadth I mean taking Vedic philosophy and applying it to a newer domain of study, such as mathematics, computing, physics, or biology. By depth I mean taking an unsolved problem in science—e.g., the measurement problem in quantum theory, or a particular paradox in set theory—and proposing a solution based on the Vedic ideology. This work clearly lies in the "breadth" rather than the "depth" category.

In an earlier book *Six Causes: The Vedic Theory of Creation*, I described the *principles* of creation, leaving the actual created entities (e.g., stars, planets, etc.) to a later effort. This book fills the gap. It expands upon some of the principles of creation, but importantly, it identifies different parts of the Vedic cosmos with those principles. For instance, the coverings of the soul are identified as the coverings of the Vedic universe, the domain of possibility is identified with the *Garbhodaka Ocean,* the different tiers of material reality in *Sāñkhya* are identified with planetary systems, etc. The readers may treat this book as a companion to *Six Causes* and may read them one after another.

Vedic cosmology is so different from the modern worldview that before specific depth problems can even be discussed, a broad understanding of how the Vedic viewpoint describes the cosmos is necessary. And even before we can truly appreciate the Vedic theory of matter, a good understanding of the problems in modern science is important. One of these problems is that modern science employs numerous kinds of logical and conceptual entities, while not considering them materially real. Unless the ontological status of these entities is clarified, the foundations of science itself will remain unclear.

Common examples of such entities are sets, numbers, structure, and order. We cannot "see" any of these things, although we can see them demonstrated through material objects. For instance, we cannot see numbers, but we can count objects. If therefore numbers would follow the creation of objects, then objects should not be described using numbers (we would be hypothesizing that numbers are real *after* objects are real, although our science would indicate that numbers are real *before* objects are real). Similarly, we cannot use set theory, probability, trajectories, structure, order and many other concepts that we currently use in science because their use represents a logical fallacy of using a derived entity to explain the entity from which it was derived. Science commits itself to a pragmatic use of many conceptual entities that we cannot observe through our senses (although we can "think" about them) but tends to deny that there is anything beyond the things that we can "see".

In Vedic philosophy, the things that we cannot see, but which we can think, judge, intend, and value, are prior to the things that we can see. That is, the stuff that we can see is developed based on things that we cannot see. This is true of modern science as well; for instance, we must have a theory of geometry and numbers before we can use it to describe the world. The difference, however, is that Vedic philosophy explains how matter emerges from the ideas, while science claims that the ideas emerge from matter. If this were indeed taken to its logical conclusion, then we must be able to reduce numbers and geometry to objects, but such a task has proven to be logically impossible: attempts at such reduction have resulted in logical contradictions.

To truly understand the foundations and origins of what we see, we must understand that which we cannot see. The stuff that we cannot see, however, isn't necessarily "non-material". Matter isn't just the things that we perceive; indeed, ideas, judgments, intentions, and morals can also be material.

There is hence, in Vedic philosophy, a lot more matter in the universe than what we can perceive through our senses, and while this matter has *effects* on what we can see, we cannot *model* these effects based on the things that we can see. In essence, our theories of matter—when these theories are based upon the generalization of the things that we can sensually perceive—would always be incomplete: they would fail to predict many of the observations.

Modern cosmology has already encountered this problem. The gravitational theory fails to account for two key observations—(1) the rotational speeds of galaxies, and (2) the expansion of the universe—leading cosmologists to postulate ideas such as "dark matter" and "dark energy", which are "dark" because we cannot see them. These aren't "minor" problems in cosmology, either. Dark matter and dark energy are estimated to be over 95% of the universe, while the visible matter is under 5%. And we are only talking about the large-scale structure of the universe, not the many details within it.

There is nothing in our sensual observation that will help us formulate theories about this "dark" reality, although theories about it can be based on things that can be thought, judged, intended, and valued, although not perceived by the senses. The study of the Vedic material theories therefore has significant scientific importance, besides historical and cultural value. The importance is that it helps us formulate theories about what we cannot see, although it exists. Since science has so far been done based only on things that we can see, practicing this alternative science has proven incredibly difficult for established scientists. All their training in formulating new ideas fails when they must think about what they cannot perceive through the senses.

This scientific value, in particular, is what motivates this work. My goal is to describe how Vedic theories view matter and the cosmos quite differently than modern science, and why this viewpoint is scientifically valuable in formulating theories that explain the phenomena current theories cannot. Much of the consternation in these types of approaches stems from a bias against anything unfamiliar and a sense of prejudiced preference for what we have done so far. Overcoming that fear and prejudice is probably harder than understanding a novel viewpoint. Our acceptance of a novel approach, however, depends not just on understanding what it claims, but also overcoming prejudice and fear. I don't expect either of these tasks to be easy, but I do believe that the outcomes of spending effort on them will be fruitful.

This book covers a vast ground in the attempt to help us understand the Vedic cosmic view. Beginning with an overview of the space-time theory, the book dives into the material ideology upon which this theory is based. It traverses questions about material causality, and how the laws of nature are different in modern science and in the Vedic view, and why the present scientific notions of lawfulness will forever remain predictively incomplete. Once we have grasped some of the fundamental ideas in the Vedic theory of matter, we are now prepared to interpret the observations in astronomy in a new way. Science, for those who understand it well, is an act of interpreting the experimental data. This interpretation creates models, and when the models are generalized, theories are created. The Vedic viewpoint gives us a new way to interpret experimental data, and you will see that the problems of "dark matter" and "dark energy" do not arise in this approach because we begin in the abstractions rather than in the contingent details of the things we can see.

As we begin to see why the current cosmological model is inadequate in explaining observations, we can also see the value in an alternate viewpoint. The discussion of this view again involves the description of models and theories, and their interrelation. After laying down some fundamental concepts around the differences between the nature of space-time within a universe and in between the universes, the book describes the present universe.

In Vedic philosophy, the material universe is developed through numerous layers of objectifying the properties of consciousness. Accordingly, the universe too can be described at several levels of abstractions. All these abstractions are real, but they are "dark" for our sensations. We cannot see them with our eyes, but we can see *effects* of their presence which we would be unable to explain using the matter we can see. Such deeper levels of reality, therefore, become *theoretical necessities* in science. That is, to explain the observations, you must postulate something that you cannot see. If we deny that thing's existence, our theories would also remain predictively incomplete.

The book ends with a detailed discussion of astrology, and why astronomy and modern cosmology differ so starkly from astrology. The basic difference is that astrologers attribute *meanings* to planets and stars, whereas astronomy and modern cosmology treat them as physical objects. The problem of meaning is central to all divisions of modern science and arises when a collection of objects has properties that cannot be reduced to the sum of independent parts. This problem can be solved if the parts have meanings in addition to physical properties. Much like the words on this page have meanings in addition to shape, size, and color, all material objects have meanings, but modern science attempts to reduce those meanings to physical properties. In the Vedic description, material objects have meanings, which then produce physical properties when those meanings are *objectified* or *represented* as signs.

The planets and stars too therefore are material symbols of meanings. That they have a material existence need not necessitate a physical description, if those material signs are viewed as a representation of a deeper level of reality that we generally call meanings. Astrology is therefore emblematic for a new class of sciences in which causality would be described based on meanings rather than physical properties. Common properties such as "distance" in space would no longer represent the physical length between two points but the extent of semantic difference between two objects. Similarly, the "duration" in time would no longer represent the physical period, but the amount of interval it takes to transform one meaning into another. Accordingly, causality is not the amount of "force" or "energy" transferred from object to another; it is rather the type of meaning exchanged in a communicative act.

Current attempts to overlay astrology upon astronomy are mistaken because they involve a leap from one way of thinking to another. Essentially, we jump from measuring lengths, times, and angles, to discussing the "meaning" of a planet, house, or star sign, and the causality leapfrogs gravity and other physical forces to discuss the interaction of types. There is no way we can construct the typed description of the world from the physical description. However, we can construct the physical description from the typed description. In that sense, the physical description is forever incomplete, but the semantic description can span both typed meanings and physical measurements.

In the Vedic model of the cosmos all the entities are not of the same *type*. Their effects in our sensual observation, too, are not identical. Specifically, some things we can directly see, while other things cause changes we can see, although the cause of change remains hidden. Only when we understand the theory of causality, and the way it causes changes, will we understand that even things that we cannot see can be said to exist, if these things are necessary to explain observations. Reality doesn't have to be completely visible to our eyes, as long as there are some effects of that reality that are visible.

The modern scientific descriptions of the cosmos primarily rely on gravitational theory, which is based on the distance between objects, when this distance is measured physically. There is, however, another method of measuring distance based on the similarity between meanings. For instance, by the semantic distance, two tables are "closer" to each other than a table and a chair, even though the table and the chair might be physically closer to each other. There is hence another description of space and time in which things that are physically close by are semantically very far, and things that are semantically very far are physically very close. Accordingly, the things that we currently consider very far based on their physical distance may be quite close, and the things that we consider quite close may be quite far. The distance now must be measured in terms of the "effort" it takes to *transform* an object into another, rather than simply move one object in another's *physical proximity*.

Think of two trees—mango and apple—that are so close to each other that the branches, leaves and fruits of one tree have intermingled with those of the other. In the part of our vision where the trees intermingle, the mango and the apple fruits seem to be physically close to each other, but they are on different branches, trunks, and roots of different trees. Despite this proximity, it is very hard to convert a mango into an apple. From a physical standpoint, we could swap the locations of the apple and the mango because all spatial locations in a physical theory are identical in the sense that they can be swapped. But in a semantic space, we cannot swap the location because it would require you to convert an apple into a mango. Therefore, when space is treated semantically, the physical notions about motion must also undergo a dramatic overhaul.

In Vedic cosmology, different planetary systems[1] are like different fruits on a gigantic tree. One cannot go to a planet unless one *becomes* that type of fruit. That means that one must "grow" on a different branch, not move from one location to another, remaining attached to the old branch. When a Frenchman travels to England, he doesn't become an Englishman. Rather, the Frenchman remains French while living in England. The Frenchman is like a fruit attached to his roots in France and moving the fruit amidst a different kind of fruit doesn't change the *type* of the fruit. Converting a Frenchman into an Englishman involves more than moving from one country to another. If the motion of a Frenchman is confused with the motion of the Englishman within England, and this ideology of change is extended to the entire universe, a mistaken account of change is created. By the modern account of space and time, there is no difference between a Frenchman and an Englishman in England. In the semantic account, there is a difference. The basis for a new description of space and time therefore exists in our present world although it has been disregarded in science by treating all objects as the same *type*. If all apples and mangoes are replaced by *particles,* then swapping them seems quite unproblematic. From this unproblematic account of motion, we can construct a physical notion of space and time, and then think of the entire universe in the same way. But that description would not work even in the present world if we had to swap apples and mangoes, and their type differences were accounted for.

The Vedic description of the cosmos is a sophisticated picture of reality, based on a different set of concepts which are intuitively available in the present world and can be made scientifically rigorous. Understanding Vedic cosmology requires a fresh look at everyday notions of space and time, rather than viewing them through the lens of gravity and material particles, which are limited caricatures of the present world, produced by discarding the type differences between objects. That they have partially worked so far doesn't mean that they are true, in the same way that swapping the locations of an apple and a mango does not mean that we indeed transformed one into another.

In current theories of cosmology, changing the location of an object doesn't change that object. We use this model to suppose that there are indeed objects whose properties are independent of their location in space-time. That, in turn, leads to the idea that the universe is *uniform* and that it has the same *type* of material objects, governed by the same laws, and properties of space-time. In Vedic cosmology, instead, the universe is described as a tree, and the fruits on that tree are not identical types. The tree is fixed (like space is fixed), but the soul can move from one branch to another. In this motion, the bodies may bear a similarity to each other, but the successive bodies are not the same. On the other hand, we can also keep the body the same but change the interaction between the various bodies thereby creating a greater sense of proximity or distance, which then appears like motion, although nothing is changing. The Vedic view is thus more encompassing; it allows what we call "motion" in science, but also describes a new kind of change that cannot be called motion because it involves changes in the type of object, in changing locations.

This is important because astronomy and cosmology involve the motion of celestial entities. This motion is physical in modern science, and it is semantic in Vedic cosmology. That is, the motion of a planet involves a change in the type of the object. A more generic theory of change is needed to explicate this idea of change, and under that theory our cosmic models would also differ vastly. In that sense, we need a new formulation of a terrestrial motion theory, before we can understand the true nature of the celestial motion.

Vedic and modern astronomies are based on different ideas, even though both describe the motion of celestial objects. The details of these differences are covered in this book to the extent that this understanding is necessary to comprehend Vedic cosmological theories. For a more detailed discussion, the readers can refer to the titles listed at the front of this book. I'm confident that you are beginning a journey into the exploration of a fascinating topic, which will be exciting due to the novel way in which it will be described here.

1

Studying Vedic Cosmology

Those who are in control of the external energy of the Lord, or in other words those who are in the material world, must first of all know how the external energy of the Lord is working under the direction of the Supreme Personality, and afterwards one may try to enter into the activities of His internal energy.
—Śrimad Bhāgavatam 2.4.6 Purport

Models vs. Theories

In studying cosmology, we come across two approaches. The first and most dominant approach draws a "model" of the cosmos—describing the structure of the universe as planets, systems of stars, sizes of and distances between planets—which essentially represents a *description* of what the current universe looks like. This description can also be viewed as the *explanation* of what we experience–e.g., the light received from different planetary systems, stars, etc. Clearly, the construction of the "model" requires an interpretation of observations to create a view of reality that explains our observations, and there can be potentially many models of the universe that explain the observations equally well.

A second, more encompassing approach, formulates a *theory* of the universe to then explain the *model*–i.e., why the universe has a structure. In any interpretation of data, we must assume a theory of nature: e.g., that space and time are linear, that light moves in a straight line, that the same laws of nature apply everywhere, etc. If we do not make those assumptions, we cannot even create a model from the observations. In a physical theory of nature, several equivalent models of observations can be created[1]. Given this fact, the creation of a model of the universe that explains all our observations does not *justify* the truth of that model. Similarly, even if your model was indeed correct, you still cannot confirm the truth of the theory, because another theory may explain that model equally well. Thus, data underdetermines models, and models underdetermine theories. Nevertheless, we need both theories and models, and science aspires to overcome the problem of underdetermination seen above[2].

The study of cosmology needs both a theory and a model. In modern physics, for instance, the theories are General Relativity, Quantum Mechanics, Thermodynamics, etc. and the models are structures such as galaxies, stars, solar systems, planets, etc. The models are constructed from observations, and the theories from the models. Just as many models can explain a given observation, many theories may explain a model. The complete theory of the universe depends on a complete model, which in turn depends on the completeness of the observational data.

The Vedic Approach to Cosmology

Unlike modern scientific cosmology where attempts to connect the models to the theories are made, modern studies on Vedic cosmology[3]have tended to describe the model without constructing the model from a theory. In fact, most Vedic cosmologists tend to separate these problems, often providing detailed information about the Vedic cosmic structure, although with little relationship between this structure and the underlying theory of matter. This approach to cosmology is not a sustainable one, nor is it indicative of the method employed in Vedic literature. As a contrast, the *Śrīmad-Bhagavatam* describes the theory of matter called *Sāñkhya* in the 3rd Canto before it describes the cosmological model in the 5th Canto. I take this to mean that it is essential to understand the theory of matter before we describe a specific *distribution* of matter.

In scientific cosmology, the cosmic structure is explained by gravitation theory. Gravitation theory, however, is consistent with infinitely many matter distributions, and why the cosmos has a specific distribution cannot be explained or predicted. To select a particular structure from infinite possibilities, additional information is required. How the actual universe is formulated is missing from the current theory.

For Vedic cosmology to be a better approach, the disparity between theory and model must be resolved; the theory must predict the model, and this means that the *Sāñkhya* theory would be required to predict the Vedic model of the cosmos, which would then be required to explain the observations. Both the theory and the model are described in the Vedic scriptures, but their interrelation is not well-understood today. This interrelation is the central goal of this book. To achieve it, we must develop an understanding of both *Sāñkhya* and the Vedic cosmic model.

Before the differences between Vedic and modern cosmic models can be understood, those between their material theories must be grasped. In fact, since a cosmic model is based on assumptions about the nature of space and time, which are viewed differently in modern and in Vedic models, the Vedic cosmological model cannot be understood unless the underlying theory of space and time is understood prior.

In modern cosmology, there are exotic objccts such as black holes, white dwarfs, baby universes, baby giants, supernovae, etc. which must be explained based on gravity, quantum theories, and thermodynamics. Similarly, in Vedic cosmology, there are "higher" and "lower" planetary systems, oceans, islands, and mountains, inhabited by different kinds of living beings, which must be explained based on the *Sāñkhya* theory of matter. Ultimately, models and theories can be described individually, but they cannot be understood independently. A proper understanding of cosmology therefore requires a prior understanding of the theory of matter, before that theory is used to explain the cosmic model.

An Analogy to Biology

The study of cosmology can be seen analogously to the study of different species in biology. The different species are the "models" used to explain observations, but these models need to be explained by a fundamental theory of nature. This means, in the context of modern biology, that the creation of different species must be explained by an even more fundamental theory of nature—i.e., physics, computing, and mathematics.

Unfortunately, this principle is not well-understood today, and when it is understood, it is not applied correctly. While biologists understand that living bodies must be reduced to chemistry and physics, they induct principles such as "natural selection" which are themselves never reduced. I have previously shown[4] that such a reduction cannot be performed because selection operates on larger wholes rather than the molecular parts, and reductionism becomes contrary to holism.

Fortunately, modern cosmology does not suffer from this problem as acutely as modern biology since cosmological models—e.g., expanding, contracting, or stable universe, and various kinds of exotic objects such as black holes, supernovae, white dwarfs, etc.—are expected to be explained based on more fundamental theories of physics such as gravitation, thermodynamics, and quantum physics. Nevertheless, since physics does not have a complete theory of all phenomena, the explanations of the models are inadequate. For instance, to explain the revolution and expansion of galaxies, we must postulate "dark matter" and "dark energy" which are models although not yet theories. The ideas of "dark matter" and "dark energy" are to cosmology what "natural selection" and "random mutation" are to biology. In both cases we don't have the ability to explain the models based on a proven theory, and therefore we induct additional ideas in our "model" which can't be reduced to the theory.

The gap in modern science therefore arises from a gap between models and theories. The model is supposed to explain the observation, and the theory is supposed to explain the models. When science fails to explain observations based on theories, it postulates models, and it appears that there is a "natural" explanation, although these models have no grounding in a fundamental scientific theory. Those who don't understand science too well, don't see the difference between models and theories, and take the models themselves to be scientific theories.

Models and Theories in Modern Cosmology

The current physical view in science also provides a model of the cosmos but it is impossible to explain this model based on current theory because there are innumerable alternate possible models. How do we select a model out of the innumerable possibilities of different models?

In gravitation theory, this selection is achieved by providing a set of initial and boundary conditions—i.e., the total number of particles and their individual masses. As the particles interact, they are not expected to coalesce and split, because the mechanical laws apply only when the number of particles remains invariant (called *elastic dynamics*). When the particles merge or split, the laws become indeterministic and the future of the universe cannot be predicted[5]. Not only is the current gravitational model inadequate in terms of requiring the initial input to the equations (who provides this input at the beginning of the universe?) but also undetermined subsequently if the particles merge and split. Similarly, how do we construct boundary conditions when boundaries themselves are not physical constructs? In classical physics, boundaries enable us to focus on limited parts of the universe, but what if the focus of study is the entire universe? Where would we draw the boundaries in that case?

The discrepancies between the theory, model, and observation, and the problems of indeterminism, in a sense, set the yardsticks for an alternative cosmological model. That is, any alternate cosmic model should be explained and predicted by the theory without requiring an infinite amount of information at the beginning, and the theory should not become indeterministic under ordinary interactions such as object merge and split. The theory may demand boundary conditions, such as if the universe is bounded, but in such cases, we would have to acknowledge that the universe is finite rather than infinite. Vedic theory of matter addresses these issues in modern theory and cosmology, and therefore it is a worthy model for scientific exploration even though it is based on scripture rather than speculation. The theory and cosmic model obviously have empirical touch points such as the prediction and explanation of passing days and seasons, the changing situations on the present planet, based on the motion of celestial bodies. There is, hence, no dearth of empirical validation, provided the theory and model are understood.

The Vedic View of the Universe

In Vedic philosophy, all objects big and small are *models*—i.e., conceptual and not physical entities, because to describe and explain them we must use concepts, which must exist prior to the objects. The method of describing these objects is also the method of their *production*; the objects are conceptual because they are produced from concepts. These entities must therefore be placed in what I call a "semantic space-time" rather than a physical space-time. The semantic space-time is closed, hierarchical, and cyclical, while the physical space-time is open, flat, and linear. The universe, in Vedic cosmology, is described at various levels of abstraction, and all these descriptions are real from the standpoints of different observers. The problem for cosmology is not just to explain our viewpoint, but to explain how all the viewpoints are produced.

Each model abstracts some details from reality, thus creating a limited picture of it. For instance, when we describe a forest, we neglect the trees in that forest; when we describe a tree, we might neglect the leaves. In this way, models are created by removing different details, and such models are always abstract. For the models to be "real," the abstractions themselves must be real. For instance, there must be something called a planet, a forest, or a tree, apart from the details in these objects.

Vedic philosophy treats numerous abstractions of the same phenomena as being equally real. Thus, if you see a leaf closely, you can see cells and their molecular mechanisms. If you abstract these details, you will see the leaf. If you abstract more, you can see a tree, and if you abstract even more you can see a forest. Which of these visions is real? In modern science, only the sub-atomic particles are real, and all other abstractions are false. In Vedic philosophy, all these abstractions are *potentially* real. They exist as *models*, which may be true or false, depending on whether they truly depict the reality or not. If the model only exists in an observer's mind, then it is false. The model is true if the abstractions we see in the world are also the real abstractions existing "out there".

The Semantic Space-Time

The universe is described as an "inverted tree" in the *Bhagavad Gita*. The "root" of this tree is the most abstract view of the world, from which more contingent pictures of the same world are produced as trunks, branches, twigs, leaves, and fruits, by dividing the abstract picture into details. Similarly, the abstract is produced from the details when those details are disregarded. Both the abstract and the contingent are materially real *entities,* but the contingent is produced from the abstract. The space-time in the universe, therefore, has a *tree* rather than a *box* structure.

In modern science, space-time is a very large "box". In Vedic philosophy, space-time is a "tree". Each node in the tree is a "perspective" about the universe and corresponding to each perspective is a conscious being. The observations of the universe in a very abstract form are performed by forms of God (Who is also a conscious being, although capable of more abstract observation), while the observation of successive contingent details is performed by other living beings (just like us) who have developed their perception to directly experience the details. The different levels of abstract descriptions of the cosmos are therefore real in Vedic cosmology because there is a specific type of living being observing them.

Thus, for instance, Lord *Śeṣa*—a form of God Who creates many "universes" in matter—sees each universe like a mustard seed–i.e., highly abstract–because He is not involved with the details of each universe. *Garbhodakaśāyi Viṣṇu* (another form of God) then observes each of the universes more closely and the same "mustard seed" is transformed into a very big "lotus flower", which (as we will see later) is the description of space. At the center of this lotus flower are the stigma and the style, the observation of which creates Lord *Brahma* (and his consort *Sarasvati*), who is said to reside on top of the lotus. As Lord *Brahma* observes the lotus closely, he produces the planetary systems, living species, and demigods (*deva*). The demigods then see the universe even more closely and become the "presiding deities" of various subtle types in all material objects. The humans and the animals in these planets see the world, take a subset of this variety and produce their mental and bodily experiences. For viruses, bacteria, and other living forms, the variety gets smaller and smaller. Unlike humans who abstract the molecular details or nerve impulses, the viruses and the bacteria focus upon molecular exchanges.

Thus, the universe is gradually divided into smaller and smaller parts, by some living entity who observers the universe ever more closely, until we arrive at the smallest parts in the universe. A form of God called *Kṣīrodakaśāyī Viṣṇu* accompanies all such observations, and He is thus said to be the "second bird" sitting on the branches of the material tree (the "first bird" being the soul). It doesn't matter whether you are on the material tree closer to the root or closer to the leaves. The extent to which you see the details are the "atoms" of your observation because you are not seeing anything more detailed. If these observations are *true,* then *Kṣīrodakaśāyī Viṣṇu* is in them. If these observations of details are only in your mind, then *Kṣīrodakaśāyī Viṣṇu* is still in your heart.

Thus, a true yogi sees *Kṣīrodakaśāyī Viṣṇu* in the external world *and* in his heart because he sees the true division of abstraction into details. The living being under illusion neither sees *Kṣīrodakaśāyī Viṣṇu* in their heart nor in the external world. Vedic philosophy therefore teaches us that if we simply knew the details of the present world, we would see *Kṣīrodakaśāyī Viṣṇu* in everything. As we become advanced, we would see the entire universe just as a mustard seed on the head of Lord *Śeṣa*. Ultimately, this vision of many mustard seeds (many universes) on the heads of Lord *Śeṣa* would be understood as the dream of Lord *Mahā-Viṣṇu*[6]*,*Who is another form of God that creates the space-time called *kārana samudra* in which Lord *Śeṣa* creates the innumerable universes. Like ordinary objects reside in the space-time in the universe, the many universes are also objects embedded in a deeper kind of space-time created by Lord *Mahā-Viṣṇu*, who then is the observer of the space-time of all the universes, and therefore transcendent to them. Lord *Mahā-Viṣṇu* resides in this deeper space-time and dreams that Lord *Śeṣa* is creating the universes, which even to Lord *Śeṣa* appear to be just like mustard seeds on his head.

This description of the Vedic cosmos can be summarized as the idea that the material creation is just like a tree, whose root is the origin of the space-time in which many universes are created, each universe is then again a branch of that tree, which then divides into numerous other branches, creating many planetary systems, which then divide into numerous planets, and the process continues over many tiers. Each such tier is produced by a different kind of observer, who, in the process of observation, creates a reality *within* the domain of their observation.

Zoom In, Zoom Out

In Vedic philosophy there isn't a single description of the universe. Rather, depending on the viewpoint from which you see the universe, you may see the forest, the trees, or the leaves. How you model the universe depends on the extent to which you have zoomed in or zoomed out. This creates many difficulties in understanding the cosmological models because the same thing may be described in a different way, using a different model. These models are nodes on the semantic tree, and you can move from the root towards the leaves, or from the leaves towards the roots, thereby zooming in and out, respectively. To reconcile these apparently contradictory models of the universe we must see them as parts of the single tree, which represents different visions of the world. To create the universe, all the viewpoints must be created. The world is physical if only the smallest details are real, and the larger abstractions are illusions. The world is semantic if all the levels of perception are potentially real.

The Vedic view differs from modern science because the leaf, the tree, and the forest are equally real (potentially). If you pluck a leaf, the tree still exists, and if you cut a tree, the forest still exists. In this way, the reality of the tree does not depend on the leaf, and the reality of the forest does not depend on the tree; rather, the leaf is produced by the tree, and the tree is produced by the forest. Similarly, the different models of the cosmos are produced from an even more abstract model of the same cosmos. Before we can understand any specific cosmic model, we must understand from whose "viewpoint" we are describing the cosmos.

The Vedic and the scientific cosmic models appear contradictory because they are pictures of the same world painted from different viewpoints—the scientific model is described from the viewpoint of humans, when humans are incapable of perceiving anything beyond the senses, while the Vedic model is described from the perspective of the creator, Who perceives not just the bodies, but also the minds, intellects, egos, and moralities of the different souls. A different type of consciousness is involved at each level of the various details that can exist.

The semantic tree approach can explain the diverse models of the universe as branches of a single tree. In one sense they are all "real" because they exist. In another sense, the more abstract descriptions are more "real" because they are logically prior to the details produced from the abstractions. After all, if the cosmos is different viewpoints of different observers, then the viewpoint that explains the production of various viewpoints is more valuable than any individual viewpoint.

This brings us back to the distinction between models and theories. The individual viewpoints are models based on the individual observer's perceptions from their unique standpoints, while the semantic tree as a whole—of which these models are parts—is the theory that explains all the models. In asking for a theory, thus, we are not denying the reality of the individual models but seeking their *explanation*. Quite specifically, even the current scientific model of the universe must be *explained* as arising from the limited perception of the world through a particular kind of limited perceptual process. This model would be overridden by a model that explains not just this model, but even the other models.

Trees and Fractal Geometries

The semantic view can be understood through the notion of *fractal geometries* in which a singular pattern is recursively applied to produce complex structures. Of course, in the semantic view, each branch of the tree structure represents a model of the world, and therefore these branches have to be treated as ideas rather than things.

Nevertheless, some key properties of the universe can be understood from this approach.

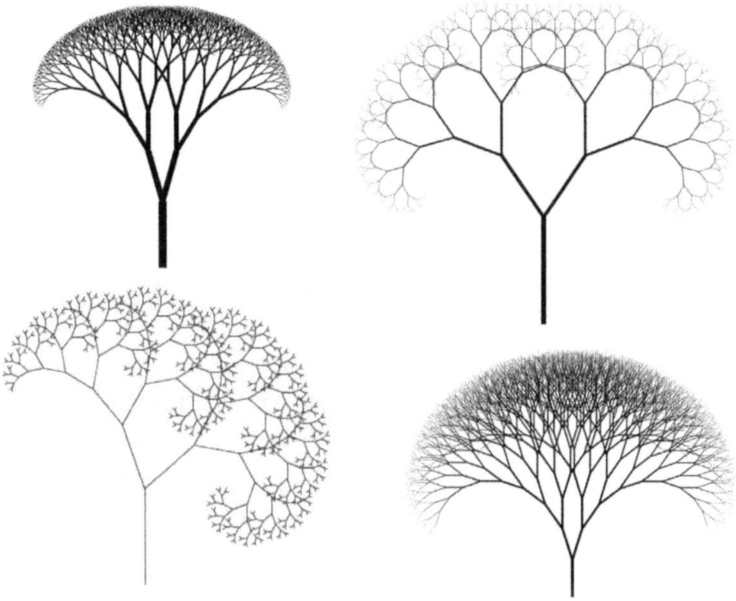

Figure-1 Trees and Fractal Geometries

Figure-1 illustrates how different trees can be produced by repeating patterns. Such patterns represent the *ideal* model of the universe, not the actual one. If the ideal model is applied, the structure of the universe at different levels of abstraction would be identical, creating a "hologram" in which the big structure is repeated and replicated inside the parts. In the ideal model, just knowing the structure of the universe would suffice to know the detail at every level of abstraction, and every living being who observes the universe at any of the levels of abstraction would form identical theories. The ideal model, therefore, would eliminate the differences in our theories, as everyone would describe the world using the same *theory* even though they experience the forest, the tree, and the leaves. This ideal model is, of course, not *actual* because different living beings do construct individual models of the experiences they have.

To create different experiences, the process of tree formation cannot be identical, although the experiences still exist as trees. In Vedic philosophy, this is achieved by material nature, called *prakriti*[7], which distorts the perception of the world. *Prakriti* hides some branches of the tree from our vision, even when the information about these branches is presented to us. Modern science is produced from *prakriti* due to which our vision of the world is "covered" in a way that we have formalized *simplification* of perception as a *methodological tool* in science. Essentially, when a scientist encounters some observations, she begins by ignoring some facts to begin formulating a theory. If a scientist is later reminded that some facts were ignored in theory formation, she would defend that those ignored facts can be "reduced" to the facts that were included.

As an *effect* of this simplification, some parts of the world are excluded in the process of theory formation, even though they exist, and are presented to the observer for inclusion. As a *consequence* of this simplification, *karma* is created which puts us in situations where we cannot see all the parts of the world. Both *karma* and *prakriti* produce an identical effect—i.e., the inability to see some parts of reality—but these are produced in different ways. Under the influence of *prakriti* we have the *option* of considering all the facts, but we neglect them deliberately. Under the influence of *karma,* we don't have the option of seeing all the facts, although they exist. The latter kind of illusion is produced when the world does not *communicate* with our mind or senses, although it exists.

Note that to even see all the parts of the world, the world must exchange information with our perceptual apparatus. If this information exchange is suppressed, then we cannot see the whole reality even though it exists. This unavailability will cause our theories to fail. That failure can in turn prompt us to revise our theories and methods of observation.

The key point is that the universe is ideal although we may not see it either because our vision is covered by *prakriti* or the communication to this ideal world is suppressed due to *karma*. Since *karma* is created due to *prakriti,* the living being passes through many cycles of changing his *prakriti* and then *karma* and alters his theories and experiences.

As our perception is corrected to include all presented facts in theory formation, the production of *karma* is halted, and even more facts are presented to us, which are then incorporated into our understanding, and this process repeats until the world is seen as *ideally* being produced by a kind of tree formation process. To see the parts missing from our perception, we must learn about these parts from some *revealed source* because we don't know what we don't know. Such perception is called *jñāna-cakṣu* or the vision of knowledge where we seek to find the truth after learning about that truth from someone who knows it. As our seeking becomes stronger, we begin to see the truth, thus reducing *karma*, which then creates the domino effect of even more truth revelation.

The Vedic view of reality is founded on an epistemology in which the world is hidden from our perception due to innate habits of simplification (called *prakriti*) and due to the consequences of these habits (called *karma*), which suppress the communication to certain parts of reality. The fact that there is money in the world does not mean that I am rich, because I may not have access to that money. Similarly, the fact that something exists in the world does not mean that I will know about it, unless I can interact with it. If nature works in such a way that what I can know depends on my previous habits of knowing, then I will not know what I don't know. This necessitates the revealed sources of knowledge.

Universes and Semantic Trees

In Vedic philosophy, there are numerous "universes", each of which is created as a tree, which in the overall picture of reality, is a branch of the single cosmic tree. The theory of all the universes is the same—i.e., that they are semantic trees—but the exact shape and form of these universes vary depending on the exact steps involved in creating that tree.

As shown in Figure-1, different trees can be created by changing the number of branches that emanate from the root, and the angle at which they are placed in relation to each other. These two things—the numbers of branches and their angles—can be treated as fundamental ideas from which a universe is created. All these ideas are in turn produced from three fundamental modes of nature—called *guna*—but they are modified in many ways through successive combinations to create a tree.

The original material reality is called *Pradhāna*, which represents the three modes in "balance" due to which the distinction between the modes is not visible. From this *Pradhāna* the distinction between the three modes is created when the "balance" is disturbed. The disturbed state of primordial matter is called *prakriti* and it represents our desires or what we seek in the world. When the modes of nature are disturbed, desires about pleasure are created. The further development of these desires is called *mahattattva* and it is the basis of the space-time within a universe. Thus, *Pradhāna* is the space-time in which all the universes are contained, *prakriti* is the different 'locations' in *Pradhāna* at which different universes are created. The space-time in each of these universes is *mahattattva.* Successive divisions in each universe are produced by dividing *mahattattva* and they produce other categories of *Sāñkhya* (which I will discuss later). The key import of this view is that the space-time within each universe is not identical. Rather, through the mixing of the three modes in *prakriti*, different kinds of space-times for each universe are created. The *mahattattva* is an intermediate result of this mixing, and it produces a fundamental set of ideas that we might call the *axioms* underlying that particular universe. From those axioms, even more complexity is produced, just like many theorems can be created from a set of axioms, or many statements can be produced by combining alphabets.

Thus, Vedic philosophy describes how matter in the balanced state is *Pradhāna*, in the distinguished state is *prakriti*, and in the state of mode mixing is *mahattattva*. Once the modes of nature have mixed, the fundamental *ideas* underlying the universe have been produced. From these ideas even more complex ideas are produced, and the universe begins to develop from the root to the branches, to the leaves, repeating the process of division and diversification. The successive stages of development involve the observation from different kinds of living beings, who create more variety by expanding on the previous abstractions via details.

All the universes are in one sense identical as they are comprised of the three modes. In another sense, they are different because the relative proportion of the three modes and their combinations differs. The *theory* that describes all the universes is therefore identical. However, the *models* that pertain to each universe are different. In these models, different fundamental ideas are emphasized, and these ideas are then taken to be the *axioms* of the universe since we cannot know anything more fundamental than these ideas unless we step outside that universe.

In that sense, perfect knowledge of the universe cannot be obtained from the observation of any universe, even if the model of that universe were perfectly drawn. Since each universe is only part of the total reality, and reality is expressed diversely across the universes, a complete understanding of any universe requires transcending its experiences. This is just like the truth of the axioms used in a formal system cannot be judged from within that system. To test the axioms, we must compare them to other axioms, and to find the basis of axiom formulation itself.

It is therefore stated that even Lord *Brahma*—who is the creator of the details in each universe—doesn't know the complete truth about the universe, because he is within that universe. Only when one transcends the material creation itself does one truly know its nature perfectly.

The Problem in the Parallax Method

The study of the cosmos requires distance measurement to luminaries. Once these distances are known, one constructs the *model* of the cosmos. If a sufficiently detailed model has been constructed, we can aspire for a theory that explains this model. One of the fundamental problems in all modern theories of the cosmos is that the procedure by which we measure the distance to a luminary is flawed. This procedure is called the *parallax method* and it relies on a flat, linear, and open space-time.

The essence of this method of distance calculation is drawn from our method of depth perception by two eyes, which relies on an object that you are seeing and a "background" against which you see. Suppose you are looking at a book in front of you, and you shut the left and the right eye one after another, you will see the object move against the background. This movement can then be used to calculate an angle relative to your eye position, which can then be used to compute the distance to the object. The scheme relies on your left and right eye being a certain distance apart. If the distance to the measured object is comparable to the distance between the eyes, the parallax method holds true. For distant celestial objects, these two distances are not comparable. So, astronomers enact the left and right eyes by going on the two opposite sides of Earth.

Figure-2 illustrates this process in which we measure the parallax of a foreground star against the background star at two points in time—e.g., June and December. The method assumes that foreground and background stars haven't moved during the time we do the measurement.

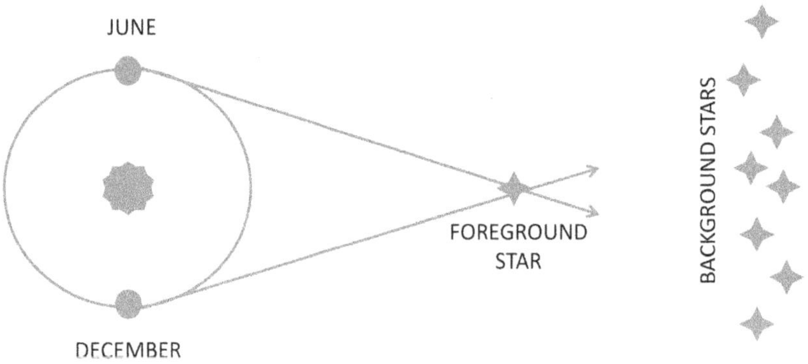

Figure-2 The Parallax Method of Depth Perception

Aside from the fact that the luminary itself may have moved during this time, which would render the depth perception inaccurate, there are deeper conceptual issues in the parallax method which arise when meanings are incorporated in nature. The problem is that space and time are no longer linear. So, we cannot define the real distance between two points based on the straight-line distance between two points, because light itself does not "travel" on this straight line. When space and time are hierarchical, light must go up the tree and then downwards, and the distance on this tree is the real distance between the two points, rather than the straight-line distance between them. This idea has an everyday counterpart in the construction of roads between two points in space. The shortest path between two cities is certainly a straight line, but the road on which you can drive to that city need not be a straight line. Should we measure the "distance" between two points by the straight line that joins the two cities? Or should we measure the distance by measuring the length of the road that must be traversed to reach the destination? What do we really mean by "distance" when roads are not straight lines?

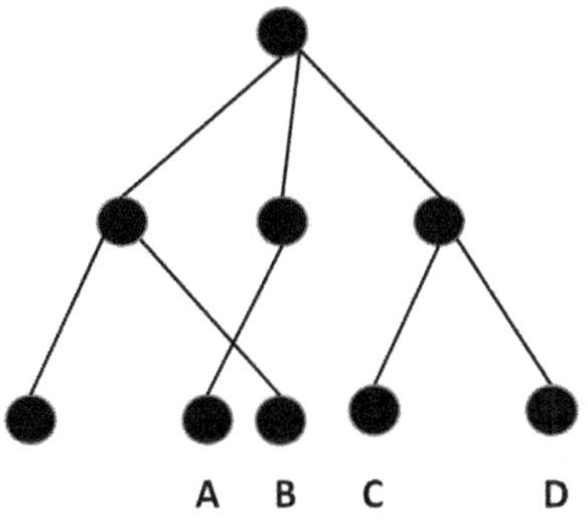

Figure-3 Two Kinds of Length Measurements

This idea is not entirely new and has been previously used in general relativity as curved space-time. When space-time is curved, then the shortest path between two points is longer than if space-time were flat. Accordingly, it takes a longer time to travel between two points, quite like it would take you longer to reach a destination if the roads were windy. The curvature of space-time, however, still assumes that the universe is just one space-time. In the hierarchical view, however, space and time are segmented into hierarchical domains: the spatial domains are closed, and the time domains are cyclic. Since this space-time is structured as a tree, to go from one leaf to another, we must traverse upwards from the leaf to the branch or trunk where the destination leaf is attached. We cannot go on a straight line that joins the leaves, because there is no "road" between the leaves except through the branch and trunk attachment.

Clearly, when you have to traverse the hierarchy in a tree, the distances between two points may be larger or smaller than if you based this measurement on the straight-line path parallax method. This can be easily illustrated through an example shown in Figure-3. The straight-line distance between A and B is smaller than the distance between C and D. But the hierarchical distance between A and B is greater than between C and D. Therefore, by the parallax method, we will deduce that A and B are closer as compared to C and D, because we are trying to deduce the distance based on the parallax shift and this shift will appear lesser, even though light takes much longer to go from A to B. Since we have no way of knowing when the light from a distant luminary originates, we also have no way of knowing how long it took to reach our eyes, and therefore the actual distance between the source and destination. If light takes a longer hierarchical path, but we *project* it as a smaller distance against a background, then the distance calculation method will produce inaccurate results. The flaw in the parallax method is therefore that we have assumed a theory of space-time and light in determining distance: the assumption is that space-time is flat and light travels in a straight line along this path. The curved space-time theories make adjustments by slightly elongating the distance depending on the visible matter, but they don't account for the conceptual hierarchical structure of space-time.

Therefore, if space and time are hierarchical then *all* distances measured using parallax are wrong. The real distance can be shorter, or longer, just as the distance between C and D appears to be longer but it is shorter than between A and B. If the universe has meaning, then we cannot calculate the distance between two points using parallax. We must rather know about the *conceptual construction* of the world to understand how information traverses up and down a hierarchy, because this hierarchy is the "road" on which information travels. When we see light, and if we are unaware of the conceptual structure of the universe, we will make up some values for the distance based on parallax, but we cannot go to that destination in the time predicted by such a calculation. The real distance to a destination must be based on the time it takes for information to go to that destination regardless of how close or far it seems to us. In a hierarchical scheme, all perception (especially that of cosmic distances) becomes an illusion if we are unaware of the space-time structure, which, by definition, is not always sensually perceivable because many tiers of that information are more abstract than what the eyes can see.

The flaw in the parallax method has another problem, namely, that time taken to transfer information depends on how conceptually *similar* or *dissimilar* the source and destination are. For instance, a teacher and a student may be close to each other, but the teacher cannot impart his knowledge to the student quickly. The knowledge in the teacher and in the student makes them semantically different, and for the student to learn everything that the teacher knows, the student's mind must be *transformed* into a mind like that of the teacher, and this process depends on their semantic difference rather than their physical distance. Accordingly, the time taken to transfer the information from a teacher to a student may be more, even though the distance appears to be small.

If the student and the teacher are semantically similar, then information can be transferred quickly, regardless of their physical distance. This is the basis of "telepathy" in which similar minds can instantly communicate with each other although they are at a great physical distance from each other. The communication appears to violate the requirement for *locality* when this locality is defined physically, although there is no violation because similar minds are indeed very close in space because distance in space is defined semantically rather than physically; these minds might be, in fact, overlapping with each other semantically.

This indicates how we might communicate with those who are no longer physically visible to us: e.g., the spiritual master who has disappeared from our physical vision. If our mind is semantically like that of the spiritual master, the two minds overlap, and what the spiritual master is thinking will appear as thoughts in our minds. There is, hence, no need for the physical presence of the spiritual master, if the disciple is developing his mind like that of the spiritual master. The master does not have to drill ideas into the disciple's head through physical presence. Rather, if a disciple has molded his mind to think like the spiritual master, then ideas in the master's mind will automatically appear in the disciple's mind, and vice versa. This idea may appear far-fetched to many people, but the understanding of semantic space makes it very apparent.

In current material science, distance to an object is how far it is in front of us. In a new material science, the distance to an object would be based on how long it takes for information to be transferred to it, when that information is semantic rather than physical. Physical information is supposed to travel in a straight line, but semantic information must travel hierarchically. The modern physical picture of nature is actually a construction from the semantic picture where we flatten the hierarchy into a linear space-time, and this flattening results in incompleteness. In the context of cosmology, the direct outcome of this flattening is that the real distance to a luminary is computed incorrectly using a parallax.

The Flaw in Euclid's First Postulate

In so far as the study of the cosmos is the study of the structure of space, one is compelled to ask some basic questions about the nature of space. One of the central dogmas in science, from early Greek times, is that space is a collection of *points*, and you can join any point to any point to construct a *path*. The parallax method is based on this dogma because we suppose that the straight-line path is the simplest path joining two points. When Euclid created his geometry, he made five postulates:

1. A straight-line segment can be drawn joining any two points.

2. A straight-line segment can be extended indefinitely.

3. Given any straight-line segment, a circle can be drawn having the segment as radius and one endpoint as center.

4. All right angles are congruent.

5. If two lines are drawn which intersect a third in such a way that the sum of the inner angles on one side is less than two right angles, then the two lines must intersect each other on that side if extended far enough. This postulate is equivalent to the parallel postulate.

When Non-Euclidean geometry was created, Euclid's fifth postulate (also called the "parallel postulate") was discarded, creating hyperbolic and elliptical geometries, which are used in the theory of general relativity. However, to understand the Vedic view of space, we must discard the first postulate itself. That is, we cannot "draw a line from any point to any point". Each point in space is a destination which cannot be reached unless we know exactly how that destination was produced. Thus, we cannot reach these points through arbitrary paths. Rather, a path is the *process* by which one point (an abstract concept) is elaborated to produce another point (a contingent concept). The tree topology helps us envision this idea: the points are nodes at which the tree branches join, and leaves lie at the ends of a branch. The leaf does not exist if the branch connecting it to the trunk, and ultimately to the root, does not exist. Therefore, the paths are logically prior to the points, and produce the points. We cannot join an arbitrary point to another arbitrary point through a line because that line represents the path to a destination, and that path has to be defined and constructed before the destination point is created.

In a semantic space, all locations are different types, and to create a new type we must add information to an abstract type. If a chair exists at one location, and a table at another location, we cannot transform the table into a chair, and vice versa, by moving them in straight lines. The physical view of space discards the type differences, and when all points are identical, we can draw a line between any two points, resulting in Euclid's first postulate. In the Vedic view, this postulate is incorrect, and everything resulting from this postulate is therefore flawed. Space has to be defined as a set of procedures or paths that construct objects. The procedure represents the mode of nature called *rajo-guna* and the object constructed by that procedure represents *tamo-guna*. The abstract idea to which that procedure is applied to create its instantiation or object represents *sattva-guna*. Everything in the universe, in Vedic philosophy, is produced through a combination of these "modes" of nature.

A given procedure can produce many objects (but not arbitrary objects). Similarly, an object can be created by many procedures (but not arbitrary procedures). To completely know an object, we must know what it *is*, and *how* it was created. If we only describe an object, we are uncertain about the procedure of its creation. Similarly, if we specify the procedure, we are uncertain about the object it produced. This uncertainty, as I have discussed elsewhere[8], underlies the uncertainty principle in atomic theory where the *same* object has two pictures (what it is, and how it was created) and specifying one of them does not fix the other. Thus two "dimensions" —one denoting objects, and the other denoting procedures—are required to completely specify anything in space.

Unfortunately, when we see an object, we don't know the method by which it was produced unless we develop a subtle vision. Therefore, the *path* by which an object was created remains invisible to the senses. Furthermore, when the type differences between the objects is discarded, it appears that an object could be anywhere in space. Through a succession of approximations and oversimplifications, the everyday semantic world is reduced to a physical world. When we perceive this *interpretation* of the world, the real distances between objects are misunderstood. What appears close to our sensual perception isn't necessarily close, and what appears far in our sensual perception isn't necessarily far. The real distances can only be known when we see the type differences between objects and include the procedures by which they were produced. Just because I can touch something with my hand doesn't mean it is close, and just because I cannot see something doesn't mean it is far. The distance to an object is the length of the *path* it would take an observer to *become* that object, which is not necessarily the straight line to that point. In fact, in a semantic space, the path to a point is *never* a straight line unless the points represent a parent-child relationship between two nodes.

There are hence two ways to describe space. First, space can be described based on sensual perception, which draws straight lines between points; these lines can be (in the semantic view) compared to lines that join the leaves of a tree. Everything in modern science is based on this idea about space and it is false because there are no real lines directly joining the leaves. Second, space can be described based on object construction methods, which corresponds to the branches and trunks that constitute the path between two points. This is the real path between any two objects, although it remains invisible to sensual perception.

With a semantic definition, we can also construct the physical definition, but the reverse is not possible. As seen above, if we have a tree, then we can also measure the distances between the leaves. But if we only have distances between the leaves, we don't know the tree. In a world that has both matter and meaning, the physical view is incomplete; the physical view can describe the states of individual objects, but not how matter is distributed in a system. However, if we replace this view by the semantic tree, then we must alter our *definition* of distance: distance is not about the metric between visible objects, but the metric between contingent and abstract objects. The physical distance that we measure by our senses is simply irrelevant to the description of nature because that distance represents neither *object type* nor *procedure type*.

The conflict between the Vedic and the modern scientific viewpoints stems from a disagreement on the nature of space. However, once we understand the properties of space and how its points are created, we can also relate it to a different kind of geometry that will discard most of Euclid's postulates. The construction of that geometry is a mathematical project, out of the scope of this work. But even without a formal theory of that geometry, we can discuss the tenets of Vedic cosmology, if we understand why we are discarding the tenets of Euclid's geometry.

Book Overview

In this book, I will try to describe Vedic cosmology in the context of the Vedic theory of matter, space, and time. This theory is called *Sāñkhya* and it results in a hierarchical and closed view of space and time. If you are unfamiliar with *Sāñkhya*, or curious about how its relation to the inverted tree view of the universe, the next two chapters cover this in more detail. Once we have gathered a better understanding of *Sāñkhya*, it becomes easier to understand the Vedic cosmological model. We can then see why matter is intertwined with our process of observation, why the creation of matter is related to the study of concepts, and why these revisions entail a new view about space and time. Following this, the book discusses the Big Bang theory of the universe, and its problems. By the time we finish this discussion, you would have seen why many fundamental concepts in science such as force, matter, energy, and motion must be revised, and why they produce misinterpretations of observations.

Until these revisions are properly understood, it is pointless to compare the Vedic cosmic model with that in modern science. The differences in cosmology are generally apparent to most people, but the underlying theoretical differences are not. The book therefore delves into the rationale for a different theory of matter before it describes the differences in cosmology. How this description of matter overcomes the problems in current science is also discussed wherever necessary or appropriate.

A few words must be said about why I wrote this book. There are already many works on Vedic cosmology: the *Purāna* such as *Śrīmad Bhāgavatam*, and *Jyoti Śāstra* such as *Surya Siddhānta*, which provide descriptions of the Vedic cosmic model. Why then write another book, when English translations of these already exist? I had two main reasons: (1) while both the theory of matter and the cosmic model are amply described in Vedic literature, their connection is not apparent to most people, and elucidating that connection is quite valuable to understanding the model, and (2) in the modern world where most people have grown up learning scientific theories and seeing their technological achievements, seeing the differences between the Vedic and the modern theories of matter, and understanding why those differences are important, is extremely valuable to grasping the value in the Vedic cosmic model.

The key purpose of this book is to *connect* the Vedic model of the cosmos to the theory of matter that pervades Vedic literature, and explaining why that theory of matter (and the resulting cosmic model) is superior to that in modern science. For that purpose, a discussion of the key scientific concepts, and why they are incorrect is essential. It is also imperative to realize how these concepts are used to interpret scientific observations, when a different theory would produce a completely different understanding of the universe. Most people do not recognize how cosmic models are produced from assumptions about scientific theories, and how these theories play a crucial role in interpreting empirical data.

A key problem in describing *any* model is: Why this model? Could the universe be different than what it is said to be? What necessitates the universe to have a specific structure? In *Sāñkhya*, it is possible to see why there are certain tiers of matter, as they arise necessarily out of the nature of experience. The same is true of the Vedic cosmic model, although unless we see its connection to *Sāñkhya* the necessity is not apparent.

In our attempts to understand Vedic cosmology, we often come across contradictions with modern cosmology, which are outcomes of a fundamental difference in the theoretical differences in modern scientific theories and in the Vedic theory of matter. Unless these differences are grasped, their consequences for the cosmic model remain hidden.

A common example of this conflict is the flat vs. spherical models of the Earth, or the heliocentric vs. geocentric descriptions of the planetary motions. While many people may accept the description of the Vedic texts based on faith, equally as many would reject it due to the conflict with accepted modern scientific dogmas, because unless the theoretical preliminaries are grasped, the reasons for the conflict seem to lie in a preference for faith rather than reason or experience. This results in a flawed notion about the Vedic system: the system is expected to foster the ability to verify after the knowledge is gained via faith. Without verification, there is no difference between blind faith (where verification is not required), and faith used as a method of inquiry from those who know.

There is a long history of Western scholars assuming the responsibility of translating Vedic texts into English simply based on knowledge of Sanskrit, when the greatest teachers of Vedic knowledge have trodden this path with utmost caution, undertaking a commentary only when ordered by their teachers, and preserving the meanings received from them. The scholars who undertake such translations are epitomes of the popular saying: fools rush in where angels fear to tread. Their efforts are as laughable and mischievous as an attempt to translate a book on modern science into another language without a firm grasp of the science.

When someone embarks upon a translation without mastering the subject, he is bound to produce a misrepresentation. While this seems obvious to anyone who undertakes any other translational exercise, it doesn't seem to have deterred Western scholars from undertaking the journey anyway. Their sole aim in producing these translations appears to be to malign, ridicule, and mock the Vedic culture, and its scientific practices, by pretending to know the science described in these texts, when all they can claim to know is Sanskrit vocabulary and grammar. This book hopes to correct that misadventure to a small extent, by illustrating how the viewpoint from which they interpret is itself incorrect.

2

An Introduction to Sāñkhya Philosophy

This verse is the potential basis of great scientific research work, for it explains how subtle forms are generated from the ethereal element, what their characteristics and actions are, and how the tangible elements, namely air, fire, water and earth, are manifested from the subtle form.

—Śrimad Bhāgavatam 3.26.34 Purport

The Problem of Counting

The term *Sāñkhya* is etymologically related to the word *sankhyā*, which means numbers. *Sāñkhya* is thus a theory of numbers, and to understand this philosophy it is convenient to begin with a discussion of the nature of numbers, the problems that arise in defining numbers, how the problems lead to paradoxes in modern mathematics, and how these paradoxes are addressed in *Sāñkhya*. This approach casts a traditional viewpoint in a new light and helps us grasp some of its key tenets. I will therefore undertake a quick overview of the problem of numbers, connect them to the general problem in the understanding of universals, relate these problems to key issues in epistemology, and then draw some important conclusions about the nature of concepts and truths.

Once these ideas have been clearly grasped, the fundamental ideas in *Sāñkhya* can also be easily understood. If, however, the problems in universals and epistemology are not understood, many false notions about the nature of concepts and truth continue, as they have, in the last few centuries. The erroneous notions hinder our understanding of perception and conception, and how we know reality. With this background, let's dive right into understanding the problem in defining numbers.

Russell's Theory of Numbers

What is a number? Is it an idea or a thing? This question has been debated since Greek times, and it remains unanswered. Bertrand Russell and Alfred North Whitehead—two famous British logicians—attempted to answer these questions in the early 20th century through a mammoth three-volume work, *Principia Mathematica*. They proposed a simple scheme drawn from an everyday intuitive fact about collections—they claimed that numbers are properties of *collections*. They are not therefore individual objects, nor are they purely ideas (supposing that ideas were in our minds and therefore could not be objectively defined).

A collection of five horses has the property of *fiveness*, although this collection is not alone in possessing that property. The same property of *fiveness*, would, for instance, be observed even in the set of five cats, five dogs, or five mice. Russell and Whitehead therefore proposed that the number *five* is the property of all sets that have five members, and to delineate this property of fiveness, we would have to form a set which contains all those sets that in turn have exactly five members.

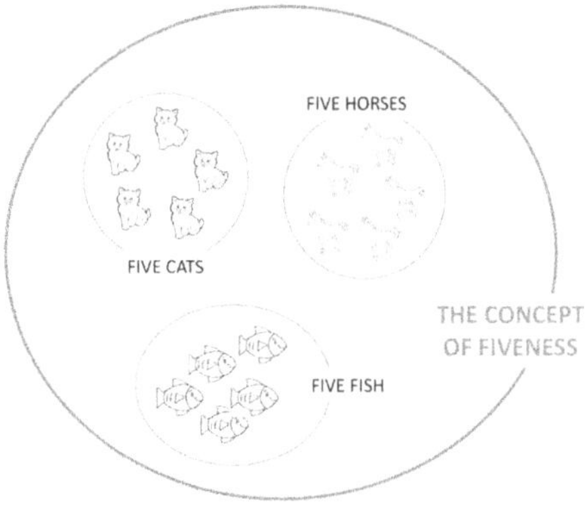

Figure-4 Russell's Theory of Numbers

To arrive at this definition of fiveness, we would have to create a set of all sets that have exactly five members each. This requires us to divide all the objects in the universe into groups of five, before we could define the idea of *fiveness*, which presents a difficult *practical* problem of finding all the objects before dividing them into groups of five. However, mathematicians aren't concerned with such practicalities. They are more interested in theoretical definitions. For instance, mathematicians frequently deal with infinite sets—e.g., the set of all rational numbers—which is an infinite set, too. So, the fact that this process of defining a set could potentially involve infinite steps did not concern Russell and Whitehead.

There is, however, another *theoretical* problem in the definition, namely, that to make a set of five cats, we must first count them as 1, 2, 3, 4, and 5 and before you can have a set of five cats, you must have the definition of the number '5' already available. This definition of fiveness is precisely what we were trying to arrive at through the procedure of collecting objects into sets of five, and if this definition is assumed in constructing the set of five objects, then the approach assumes what it is trying to conclude! You can see that to define *fiveness* we must have defined the idea of five[1], because otherwise we could not form a set of five members, and therefore collect these sets into a larger set called *fiveness*.

Ideas and Things

This problem in the definition of a number presents a classic divide between *ideas* and *things*. We generally suppose that ideas are only in our minds—i.e., they are not real things in the external world. Through science, we suppose that our mind would one day be reduced to the chemistry in the brain, which would then prove that the mind is nothing but *matter*. Once this reduction has been achieved, we would then prove that matter results in chemistry, which then creates the mind (through evolution and such processes), which then comes to have ideas.

Russell and Whitehead were trying to perform such a reduction for only one such idea—the idea of number—and their method shows that to derive the idea of *fiveness* from objects, the objects themselves would have to have been individuated as distinct entities using the idea of *fiveness* even prior. In short, we cannot derive fiveness (or any other idea) from things without using that idea to *classify* and *identify* that thing.

For instance, if you were trying to define the idea of *cat* through a collection, you must first collect all the cats. This might be practically difficult, but let's assume that you can do it. However, you still have the problem of distinguishing a *cat* from a *horse*. If you cannot distinguish the two, then your cat collection may also include horses, and the definition would be wrong. The collection of all cats requires the definition of what we mean by cat, and the distinction between cats and horses requires you to have the *ideas* of cat and horse even before you collect them into the sets to arrive at their definition! The definition of ideas through collections therefore ends up requiring the definition to exist even prior.

In short, the problem is not unique to numbers, but for any kind of idea whatsoever—if you try to derive the idea from things. To define an idea from a set of things, you must first collect the objects to which that idea can be applied, and therefore the idea must exist even prior.

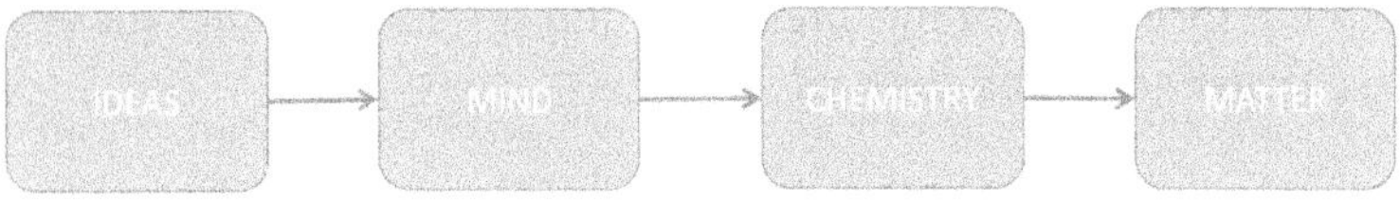

THE REDUCTION OF IDEAS TO MATTER IN SCIENCE

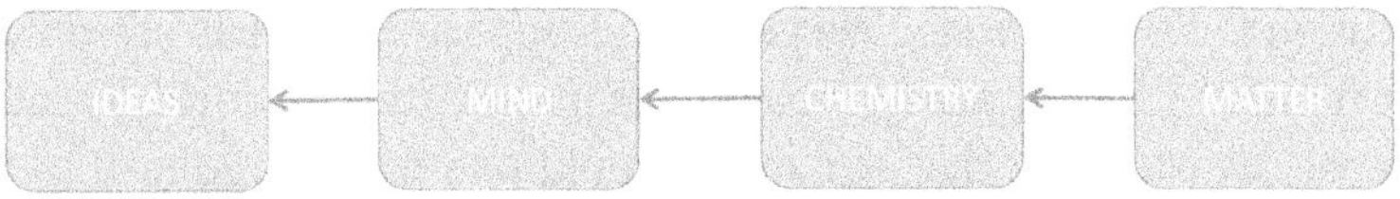

THE CREATION OF IDEAS FROM MATTER IN NATURE

Figure-5 The Materialist Notion of Mind and Ideas

This is called the problem of *recursion*: to know something you must know it beforehand. If there were only things in the world, and ideas were only collections of those things, then such a definition would be impossible as we could not distinguish the things to collect them into idea-specific collections. It follows that if our minds were byproducts of the chemistry in the brain, then we could not know anything because whatever material state in the brain represents the ideas would require some preexisting ideas. Similarly, when a brain state becomes a representation of an idea is impossible to explain unless that idea preexisted in us.

To know any concept from the world of things, *someone* must know it *a priori*–i.e., not from the world of things. Then, that person can apply that concept to the world of things—i.e., use it to classify and divide the world of things—and designate those things by the chosen concept. Once things have been identified using concepts, others can learn these concepts using language and observation of things to which the ideas are attached. When the others learn about such concepts, they too can *see* the world of things in terms of those ideas which were previously imparted to them. Those who receive the knowledge of the idea must also potentially have the ability to grasp the ideas independent of the things before they apply those ideas to the classification of things. And they must accept the ideas thus received simply as a matter of *faith* in the teacher.

Counting = Distinguishing + Ordering

The above problem in numbers arises from the fact that counting involves two mechanisms—(a) for distinguishing things from one another, and (b) for ordering them into a sequence. Furthermore, these methods become interdependent if ideas are derived from things. As we saw above, before you can count horses as 1, 2, 3, 4, 5, you must be able to distinguish the horses from one another. If you could not distinguish these horses, you could not know if there were 5 horses or just 4, 3, 2 or 1. To distinguish these horses, you must have the idea of horse as distinct from a zebra or a donkey. Once you have identified the individual horses, you must have another *method* of ordering them into a sequence. For example, you might sequence the horses by their height, age, color, etc. which in turn requires even more concepts—height, age, and color.

Thus, in the simple act of distinguishing and ordering, you must possess the concepts required to distinguish and order *a priori*. This *a priori* knowledge need not be innate in you; it can also be derived through education from a teacher, but the teacher suffers from the same problem of having learnt the idea from his or her teacher, and the process of learning seems infinite. The only resurrection out of this infinite cascading sequence of teachers, is a person who did not need to learn the ideas from someone else. He or she must have created these ideas out of their innate ability to create. Furthermore, this original person who creates these ideas could not have derived them from the observation of objects. The origin of the ideas must therefore rest in the originator's mind, and this mind too cannot be conceived materially because then the problem of converting the material object-like mind into ideas returns to haunt us.

Therefore, in Vedic philosophy, God is said to be the origin of all ideas, and He creates these ideas through His person, which is comprised of six original ideas—knowledge, beauty, renunciation, fame, power, and wealth. All knowledge—i.e., concepts—is manifest from the idea of knowledge; all beauty is manifest from the idea of beauty, and so forth. These ideas then *descend* through a succession of teachers, each of whom has acquired these ideas from their teacher, all the way to God, Who is the original teacher and creator of the ideas. Indeed, even the world of things is produced from these ideas, which is why we can associate ideas to things, without committing a mistake of tying objects to ideas.

Even if it seems premature to introduce the notion of God so early in the discussion of numbers, what is indisputable is that the problem of concepts is not unique to counting, but exists for any perception and cognition, because in the simple act of distinguishing and ordering things (upon which the rest of science rests) you must have a rich repertoire of ideas before you can apply them to the objects. In fact, the diversity of things that you see in the world would depend upon the diversity of ideas by which you can categorize it. For instance, if the conceptual distinction between a horse and a donkey did not exist *a priori*, then nobody could make that distinction, and if that distinction can never be made then two separate species of life itself could not exist. Therefore, the diversity of the world depends on the diversity of concepts. If you were born a blank slate such that the slate is written upon by the encounters with the world, the beginning of this encounter must be with the teacher who can impart you the diversity of concepts. To learn from the teacher, you must have *some* fundamental innate concepts so that you can learn language. In short, you must be born with some innate ideas using which you can learn a language and use it to acquire the multitude of ideas, which can then be used to distinguish, divide and organize the world in your mind.

This fact presents a vital challenge for empiricism. John Locke—another famous British philosopher—had claimed that our minds are blank slates at birth. Over time, as we encounter new facts, we acquire new ideas. In other words, Locke believed that all ideas are derived from things, and can therefore—in principle—be reduced to things. The problems seen above, which arise in distinguishing and ordering things (and in any cognition whatsoever) show that we cannot derive ideas from things, unless we already have those ideas in us beforehand. It is possible to learn new ideas, but some ideas must preexist in us to learn.

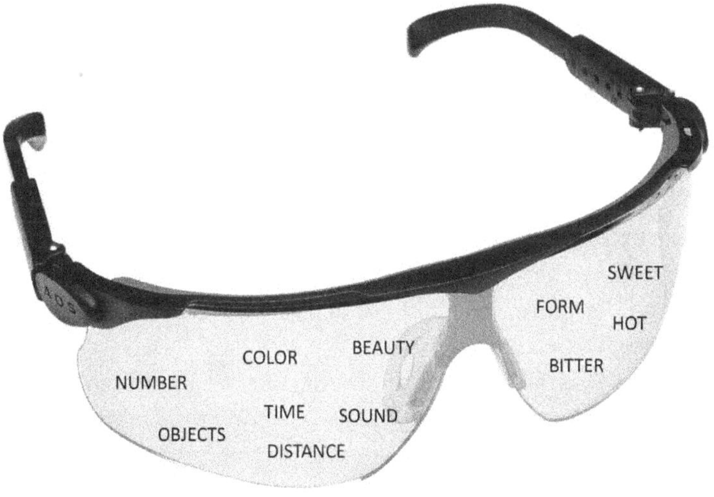

Figure-6 Ideological Goggles Shape Perception

It follows that to know the world, we must be wearing ideological goggles of some fundamental ideas and categories to even learn more ideas. At least, before you apply the ideas to the world of things, you must have those ideas acquired through another process. In other words, the fact that we see ideas in the world is because we already had these ideas present in us (as our goggles) to classify the world before we saw it. A mind that is a blank slate at birth will never see anything at all.

The fact is that we are already born with many ideas, which include sense perception distinctions such as color vs. form, yellow vs. red, sweet vs. bitter, proximity vs. distance, past, present, and future, and the notion of objectivity and individuality. These ideas exist in us because the perceptual apparatus through which we perceive *is* those ideas. The senses, mind, intellect, etc. are not blank slates. They have innate properties by which we can make fundamental distinctions. If these properties did not exist within us *a priori* then we could not learn any new ideas.

The Role of Synthetic A Priori

Immanuel Kant—an 18th century German philosopher—had a sophisticated name for this claim: he called it the *synthetic a priori*. The term *synthetic* denoted that all these ideas that exist beforehand are not trivialities—they represent the essential foundations of our knowledge. The term *a priori* denoted that these were not derived from the external world, but were somehow innate in us, even before observation. We had to have them if we were to know anything in the world, and therefore, we could not derive them from the world *a posteriori*—from experience.

Common examples of such synthetic *a priori* abound in our everyday world. For example, some people are tone deaf while others are musically savvy. A tone-deaf person cannot appreciate music; to appreciate music you must have the tonality in you. The tone deaf and the musically savvy therefore don't view music in the same way: one sees music in tones while the other doesn't. Music teachers will tell you: you must have some music in you before you can be taught more music. You cannot start as a blank slate and be taught music because if that were the case, then every person on Earth could be a great musician by going to music school. In fact, we could then correlate the musical abilities of a person to the number of years he or she spent in a music class learning about music, which is contrary to the fact that many musicians never went to music school. Some of us are born wearing the goggles of music, while others are not. In some people, the goggles of music are crystal clear, while in others they are hazy. Accordingly, they can be great or average musicians.

How Many Goggles?

Once we recognize the importance of ideological goggles, the next question is: How many such goggles must we possess *a priori* before we see them in the world (cognize, divide, and classify the objects in the world in terms of those ideas)? The answer to this question is the more the merrier. These goggles constitute your perceptual and conceptual apparatus and having more such goggles just entails that you have sophisticated senses, mind, intellect, etc. So, there is no limit to the number of goggles one can have; there is however a minimum on the number of goggles if you want to acquire more goggles. Thus, the human senses, mind, and intellect are more advanced, which makes us capable of vast amounts of learning. In contrast, the animal senses, mind, and intellect are less advanced, and that limits their ability for future learning. If you don't have the goggles of tonality in you, you won't be able to distinguish between the tones and hence you can never be taught music. Similarly, if you don't have a refined understanding of color and form, you cannot be taught painting. So, there is no limit to the number of goggles we can have *a priori* but there must be a minimum of goggles to learn new things.

This fact is embodied in all *languages*: we use the symbols of a language to communicate and we must therefore learn how the physical states of symbols encode meanings. If all we could grasp from the symbols were physical states, then we could never acquire ideas. To even understand that some token symbolizes an idea, we must have that idea in us beforehand, as the ability to comprehend language. Similarly, the creator of that symbol must possess the ideas before he or she objectifies them as symbols, from which others can learn those ideas. Ordinary ideas like shape, color, taste, sound, smell, etc. are already innate in us, which is why children begin education by learning about these ideas. As one acquires the words denoting the sense perceptible ideas, the education proceeds into more abstract constructs such as object-concepts—e.g., table and chair. The development of the mind and the intellect need the acquisition of complex ideas from primitive ones, but one must have the primitive ideas in their perceptual and conceptual apparatus to begin with.

In short, we might not know everything that exists in the universe, however, we must know a *language* of physical-state-to-meaning mappings innately, which can be used to comprehend the meanings encoded in a symbolic expression. Everyone must possess some innate language if they are to ever interpret the world of things into ideas and transform ideas into a world of things. If we have some innate language, then using it we can learn other languages–i.e., physical to semantic mappings. Using the native or learnt language, we can then interpret the world of things also into meanings. If the native language does not exist, then we cannot be taught any other language, and we may then have senses, but we would not be able to cognize the individual things with these senses.

If an elementary set of ideas and their mappings to things exists within us, then we can use this mapping to learn about more mappings. Over time, as more and more ideas are acquired, abstract or primordial ideas can also be converted into detailed ideas. Take the preliminary idea of a *car*. This idea is very abstract, and it can be refined to create other concrete ideas such as an SUV, a hatchback, a sedan, a truck, a sports car, etc. Once a new variation of an idea has been created, others can look at it, and acquire the idea for themselves too, because they also have a primordial basis of ideas-to-things mappings within their minds.

Figure-7 Detailed Ideas from Abstract Ideas

It is therefore correct to assume that we acquire ideas from the external world. But that acquisition is only due to two reasons. First, someone had that idea in their mind *before* that idea was *represented* in a thing. Second, we ourselves had a primordial basis of ideas to even acquire new ideas and then used it to distinguish an object. The object you see is a *vehicle* or *carrier* of that idea, but the idea would exist (or could exist) even when all these vehicles did not. The fact that we can create new ideas, and then convert them into physical things, indicates that ideas can exist even before the things embodying them do. The ideas must be logically and temporally prior to the objects in which they are embodied. In fact, the objects must be created from those ideas.

We also cannot *reduce* the ideas to individual instances of those ideas. For instance, we cannot reduce the idea of a hatchback to an instance of the hatchback because upon that reduction, nothing else (apart from that specific instance) could be a hatchback. We might claim that the idea of a hatchback is a property of all the hatchbacks (past, present and future) but this claim not only presents the practical difficulty of knowing everything that exists in the past, present and future, but also the conceptual problem that to even apply the idea of a hatchback to anything we must have that idea beforehand. We cannot therefore reduce the idea to a specific instance, nor to a collection. We simply cannot reduce it. We must accept that the idea exists even when the thing does not, and the idea is logically prior to the things in which it is embodied.

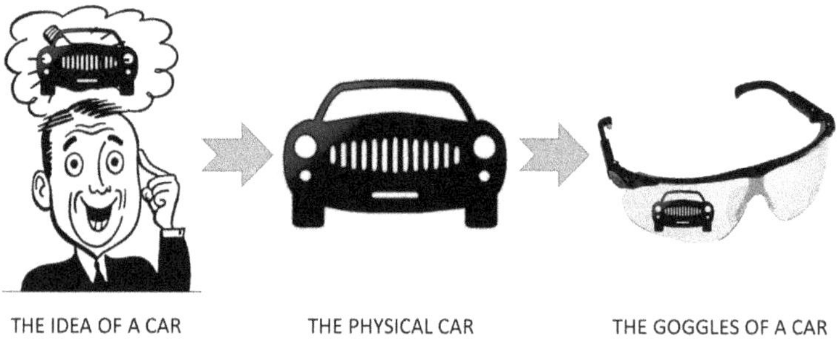

Figure-8 The Three Forms of an Idea

It follows from here that every idea that we see in the world must exist in *someone's mind* before it exists in the world as a symbol, object, or representation of that idea. When we see something, we interpret it according to the goggles we currently wear. Upon seeing those things, we might also acquire a new set of goggles, which allows us to see more things in terms of the newly acquired idea. The ideas therefore transform into things, which then convert into goggles. Every idea that can exist in a creative person can also become goggles in another person. We first think of ideas, then we create things from ideas, and then we disseminate those things so that other people can see the world in the same way as the creator originally saw it. Ideas become successful when they have been transformed into goggles in other people. There is an infinite number of goggles—just as there is a potentially infinite number of ideas.

The World is a Message

The conversion of our ideas into things, the conversion of ideas into goggles, and the reverse conversion of what we have in our goggles can be converted into ideas, and those ideas can then be seen in the world, implies that the world, our perception, and the languages in which the ideas are encoded objectively in any communication are very similar. This similarity can be understood if the world exists as the *embodiment* or symbolic representation of ideas. This would imply that the objects we see as things originally existed in our minds as ideas, but were then embodied into objects as representations, before they became goggles.

Just as we express our thoughts through sentences—spoken or written—and these sentences are material objects (i.e., they are encoded using paper and ink, or uttered using sound vibration), similarly, other material objects—like cars, houses, watches, etc., are also *messages*. To create the message, the *meaning* must exist beforehand. Similarly, to decode the message, a *language* of matter-to-meaning mappings must exist in us prior. The meaning that exists prior is the idea in our heads, and the ability in others to understand that meaning is the goggles by which they can perceive the encoded meanings. Before we can communicate to each other, we must have the meanings and the goggles to read them.

If we know some language, we can use it to transform our ideas into things—e.g., words—and the listeners can then grasp those words to convert them back to meanings. The relation between the external world of objects and our mind is like that between words and meanings. The meanings exist before the words, and the meanings can be transformed into the words, and then grasped by a correct interpretation of those words. Our ability to encode meanings in words, and then decode them from the words, does not imply that meanings *are* words. Rather, we must have the meanings before we speak words, and we must have the ability to comprehend the meaning before we listen to the words. The ability to create and understand meanings is prior to the embodiment of meanings in things, and these meanings are then transformed into the symbols or representations of meanings. The world is not created as meaningless things which we *interpret* as meanings. The world is created as a symbol of meaning which we can understand depending on our goggles of comprehension. How well we comprehend the world depends on whether the speaker and the listener are wearing the same goggles.

To know the world, therefore, we don't need to possess every possible idea, but only the *language* in terms of which it is encoded. The knowledge of the language is simpler than that of everything encodable in that language. We also create ideas using a language and the listeners comprehend them if they know how to understand the language. The fundamental ingredients of the world are therefore not things; they are the symbols and grammar of language. This idea is sometimes also called *semiotics* and it has generally been popular in continental Europe.

Not All Messages Are True

Not everything you see on TV or read in a newspaper is true. You might have the perfect understanding of language to grasp the meanings, but you don't necessarily have a way of knowing if those meanings are also true, simply by looking at the statements themselves. How do you know if some statement is also true versus another one that is false?

You can approach this problem in two ways. First, you can try to logically prove the claim based on some *axioms,* but the truth of the claim would depend on the truth of the axioms. Second, you can try to empirically validate the statement based on its conformance with the facts, but if the world is a message then you cannot simply compare two statements and infer that one is wrong and the other is right, without *a priori* assuming that one of the two statements is true. This assumption is like an axiom. Therefore, in both cases—empirical verification and rational confirmation, the problem reduces to knowing if our assumptions are true. Even if you have two mutually consistent messages, their consistency does not entail their truth because there can be other contradicting statements that you haven't yet encountered. How do we know that we will not encounter future refutations of what we presently hold true?

This problem is fundamentally unsolvable. We can *confirm* that our theories are compatible with experience (i.e., some other messages), but we cannot know if they are *true, if that experience constitutes a statement.* In this case, *confirmation ≠ truth.* In a logical proof, we can show that *if* the axioms are true, then the conclusion must be logically true, but we don't know if the axioms are true. This is hence a fundamental problem in all forms of knowledge: we can prove (logically) and confirm (empirically), but we cannot know if the claims are indeed true.

For instance, if all the politicians in your country were lying, and the TV and newspaper reports simply repeated those lies verbatim, all the statements that you can see and hear would appear to be mutually consistent. You could confirm that the statement reported in the newspaper is *true* because the politician indeed made that statement. But that doesn't mean that that the politician is telling the truth. If one politician agrees with the other politicians, the agreement would be quite like the newspaper reporting what the politician said, and that agreement still doesn't say if what they said is true. If the politicians disagree, you still have no way of knowing which one of the politicians is being truthful, because you would only try to find agreements (or disagreements) between those politicians, which may be a confirmation of what one (or the other) is saying but as we saw above, confirmation is not equal to truth.

Truth is also A Priori

We are now led to a peculiar problem: you cannot know the truth by comparing different things to each other. You can only know the truth if you *postulate* something to be true. These postulates become our *a priori* truths; we call them *axioms or assumptions.* When you see a politician speaking, for instance, you somehow—*a priori*—believe that he or she is lying. Your beliefs might be wrong, but you must have some beliefs—i.e., a point of view—to even judge. We have no way of being sure by comparing our beliefs to facts in the world. This point is similar to the problem of meanings we saw earlier: we noted that to see an idea in the world, you must know that idea beforehand. Similarly, to know the truth of something, you must already somehow know the truth beforehand.

René Descartes—the founder of Cartesian geometry—struggled with this problem quite a bit. He acknowledged that he could not trust his senses, because he might be hallucinating. He could not trust his mind, because there might be an evil genius controlling it, leading him to false thoughts. But he argued that he could not doubt his own existence because even if he was under illusion, he still existed. Descartes concluded—*cogito ergo sum*—I can think therefore I must exist.

Descartes went on to claim many things based on the supposed truth of his existence. Of course, Descartes is not *alive* anymore. If therefore we identify Descartes with the body that was born in 1596 and died in 1650, his existence is now false, in the narrow sense of his thoughts. Accordingly, if you take away the truth of his existence *now* then all that he said previously (and which was supposedly based upon the truth of his existence) would also be rendered false after his death. The only way that what Descartes said at that time could be true now is if his existence were true even now, although it couldn't be his body or mind. Alternatively, you could take the same type of reasoning and accept Descartes' conclusions assuming that at least your existence is true, even if everything else can be doubted, and then derive other truths from the first axiom.

The key point is that you could not know any truth unless you blindly accept some truths. Which axioms you accept to be true are your *choice*. We cannot reduce this choice to other claims, because there is no way of knowing if those claims are true. This collapse of knowledge is so fundamental that its importance cannot be overstated. It entails that your knowledge begins in *a priori* assumptions. If you cannot assume, you cannot judge the truth. However, this collapse gives us a very important starting point—namely that we have *choices* to decide what we accept to be true. These choices constitute our *assumptions* about reality.

Each of us begins in some ideas and assumes them to be true. These assumptions are then used to *judge* the truth of things that other people say. If everyone opposes your idea, then you might suppose that your idea is indeed false. But you might also believe that you are correct, and everyone else is wrong. In fact, some people have taken such lonely paths and proven over time that they were correct. How strongly can you hold on to your beliefs in the face of contradictory evidence or criticism? When should you give up your beliefs and until when should you hold on to them? When some people oppose, or most people oppose, or when everyone opposes? Should you just stick to your beliefs even in the face of all contradictions and try to prove yourself right against all odds?

The same problem of sticking to your beliefs exists even for observation of facts, when these facts are statements (like those made by your friends and family). If you could stand the opposition of your friends and family, then you might as well doubt the facts in the world, because, after all, they are also propositions. Common examples of such steadfastness include those people who continue to struggle despite many failures, sticking on with their innate beliefs although the real-world experiences seem to contradict their beliefs. You tend to think that my ideas may not always work, but I will find those situations in which they will work, and that would then become my picture of reality about the world.

This approach is not fundamentally wrong because if you were to give up your beliefs at the first instance of a contradiction, nobody would ever be able to hold on to any personal belief. If on the other hand, you never give up your beliefs, then you potentially run the danger of believing in false things. We all seem to give up beliefs at some point, but that point is not clearly defined. This is a problem for epistemology because depending on what beliefs you hold on to, some facts would be deemed true and others would be false. You have no way of knowing which is *actually true* except in reference to the beliefs you actually tend to hold.

Which Theory is Correct?

Once you realize that there are many possible axioms that you can choose, you need to ask: Which of these axioms must I choose? Each axiom set obviously works for some facts, because, starting with those axioms, we can derive and therefore explain those facts. The axioms would therefore appear to be sound *explanations* of those facts. However, every axiom set does not work for all facts. Rather, some axiom sets explain a particular set of facts adequately, but not the other facts.

If we combine the axioms that adequately explain different axiom sets, the axioms themselves become logically inconsistent. This leads to a problem which is called the contention between *consistency* and *completeness.* Most axioms are separately consistent, but incomplete as far as explaining phenomena outside those axioms. If we try to complete our axioms by combining the axioms that work well for different phenomena, then the combined set of axioms becomes logically inconsistent. Modern science indeed explains many phenomena, but the axioms involved in those phenomena are mutually inconsistent. Each such theory is therefore individually incompletely and collectively all such theories are mutually inconsistent. This inconsistency is illustrated in Figure-9 below.

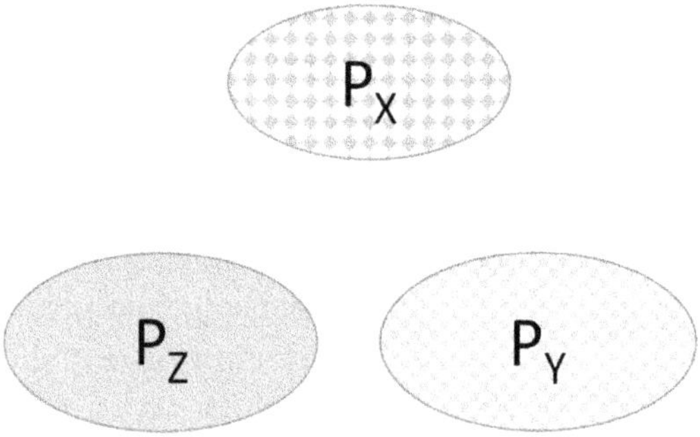

Figure-9 Axiom Reduction Fails for Exclusive Data

Assume that there are three theories—X, Y and Z—that use different axioms. Assume that the theory X explains some phenomena P_X, the theory Y explains some phenomena P_Y, and the theory Z explains some phenomena P_Z. Neither theory explains all the phenomena—P_X, P_Y, and P_Z, therefore each theory (X, Y, and Z) is *incomplete* by itself. Together, all these theories are *inconsistent* because they are based on different (mutually contradicting) axioms. If P_X was a subset of P_Y, which was a subset of P_Z, then we could reduce all the theories to just Z, because that theory would explain all the observations (Figure-10). However, this reduction is not possible if each axiom set explains different domains of data (Figure-9). For example, reduction will not work if P_X, P_Y, and P_Z were exclusive phenomena explained by a exclusive set of axioms X, Y, and Z.

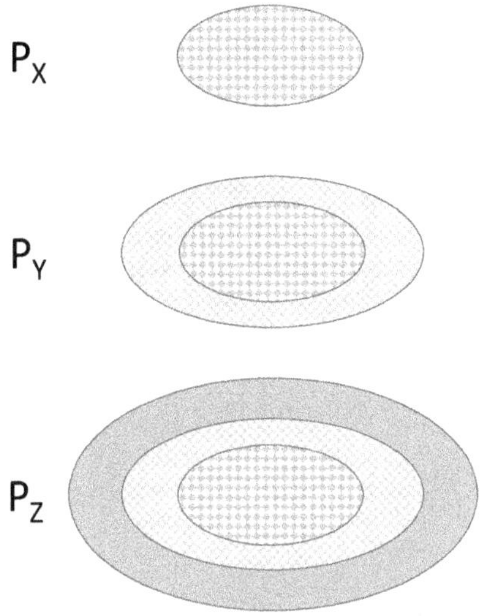

Figure-10 Axiom Reduction Works for Subsets of Ideas

Now, there are many independent axioms (X, Y, and Z) which explain exclusive phenomena (P_X, P_Y, and P_Z). Each axiom set is by itself *incomplete*. Put together, all the axiom sets are *inconsistent*. Each of the theories that employ an incomplete axiom set is ultimately false even though it can be empirically confirmed, because there are other phenomena where it doesn't work. The truth of the theory has therefore nothing to do with its empirical confirmation. This problem is called *underdetermination* where the same phenomena can be explained by different axioms. It follows that if we make a choice—e.g., for an axiom set—these choices will be false, even though they will work in certain limited number of scenarios. To know that these choices are false, we would have to find the phenomena where they don't work. If you have found those phenomena, you must discard the theory as being empirically confirmed and yet conceptually false because it doesn't always work and fails for some phenomena.

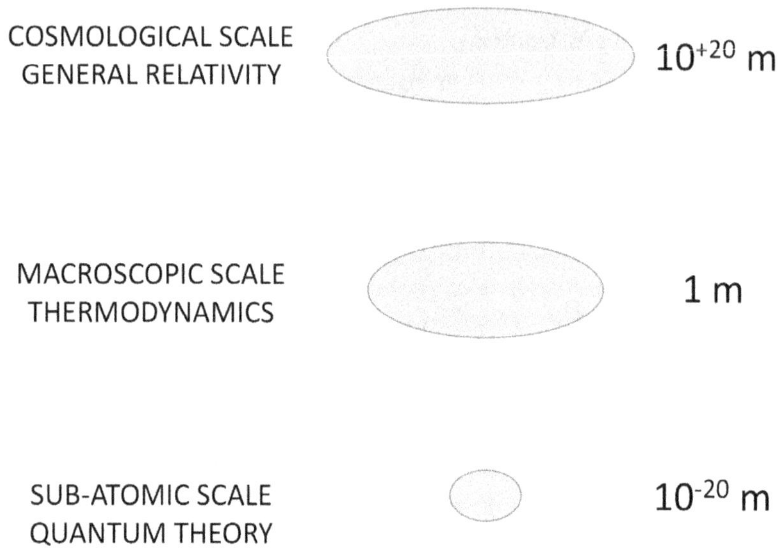

Figure-11 Different Theories for Different Scales

Common examples of such theories exist in modern science. For instance, quantum theory works for atomic objects, general relativity works for cosmological scales, and thermodynamics works for everyday objects. These three domains pertain to different levels of abstraction about the world, but since no theory works for all the domains, they are all empirically confirmed and yet conceptually false. Given this problem, the reduction of cosmology to a theory of macroscopic objects, and the reduction of macroscopic objects to a theory of atomic objects cannot be achieved because the different theories depend on different *axioms*. Reduction works only when the *same* theory is used to describe various phenomena. Reduction cannot work if different theories are involved at different *scales*—e.g., atoms, macroscopic objects, and the universe.

The Semantic Viewpoint

Modern science is characterized by a diversifying set of fields, which use mutually incompatible axioms. The problem for science is not merely how we find the axioms suitable for a given phenomenon, but how we combine the axioms across diverse phenomena. Clearly, if a more generic theory outmodes the less generic theories, then the previous theories were false, while the new theory is true. However, given the diversity amongst axioms even among the present theories, unifying them presents a problem. This unification entails finding a new, more generic theory for which the other theories are special cases. Such a generic theory would employ more abstract concepts than the concepts used in the current theories. In other words, the new theory *explains* the production of other theories, which in turn explain the phenomena themselves.

This understanding of the process of theory unification presents us with a hierarchy of theories that form an inverted tree. The root of this tree is the theory that explains all other theories. The trunks explain a fewer set of theories, while the subsequent branches, an even smaller set of theories. Finally, the stems connecting the leaves and fruits to the rest of the tree are theories that explain only the individual phenomena.

The diversity of phenomena is therefore like the leaves and fruits of a tree. The individual, mutually inconsistent theories are like the diverse branches of the tree. The theories that unify many inconsistent theories are like the trunks of the tree, while the ultimate theory that explains all phenomena is the root. There are hence many relative grades of truth. The leaves are individual truths. The stems connecting them to the tree are more general than these phenomena. The generality grows, as does the truth of the theory, as we move toward the root. The root is the most general and the absolute truth, while the trunks, branches, and stems are only relatively true. The tree is developed from the root to the leaves, and myriad theories and phenomena are also developed in that process. All of them exist, but they are not universally true. Therefore, only by tracing the leaves back to the root, we can know how these were produced.

Since the tree is inverted (i.e., roots above and the leaves below), the modern scientific process can be called bottom-up (from the leaves to the root), while *Sāñkhya* describes the world top-down (from the root to the leaves). The central issue in modern science is thus the unification of diverse theories, while the central issue in *Sāñkhya* is the diversification of a single theory. In *Sāñkhya*, any theory specific to a particular kind of scientific domain, therefore, brings with it all the assumptions of the higher-level theories, and adds only a small number of additional postulates, unique to that particular domain. The development of new theories and phenomena is therefore fairly easy in this approach.

Since the phenomena are also part of the tree, they are treated just like theories—i.e., both phenomena and theories are conceptual. In modern science, a phenomenon is a theory plus some initial and boundary conditions; each individual phenomenon is a different initial and boundary condition on the theory that explains the phenomenon. If you know the theory, then creating the phenomenon is very easy: you just set a different initial and boundary condition. The separate initial and boundary conditions thus *diversify* the theory. Nevertheless, modern science treats theories as conceptual entities and phenomena as physical entities. This approach is problematic and leads to the question of why a logical and mathematical theory is so effective in describing the natural world[2]. Previous variations of this problem are the Platonic divide between the material world and the idea world, and the mind-body dualism of Descartes. The divide between matter and ideas has existed since the inception of Western philosophy and has been carried forward in science.

In *Sāñkhya*, this divide doesn't exist. A 'horse', for example, is the instance of the idea of an animal, produced by refining the idea through additional conditions. Similarly, even the individual horses are instantiations of universal ideas, although they combine the universal with an individual; the individual makes each horse a unique instance of the universal. The idea of the horse exists in each horse, although each horse is an individual. This means that the idea of a horse is materially real, and exists *within* that horse, not in a separate world (as Plato claimed), and not just in our minds (as Descartes claimed). The idea of a horse in fact represents the conceptual definition of the 'species of the horse'; this definition constitutes the horse's *mind*. The idea of a horse is therefore not just in our minds, but in the horse's mind as well; in fact, the idea in our mind is only a representation of the ideas that constitute the horse.

Thus, the gross body of the horse is produced from the horse's mind, in the same way that a theory is instantiated into a phenomenon by adding initial and boundary conditions to it. The theory is materially real as information, and further information is added to this theory to produce a phenomenon. Similarly, the mind is real, and further information is added to this mind to produce the body. The mind and the body are distinct as abstract and detailed information, not as idea and substance. At a certain point in the refinement of ideas, the idea becomes perceivable, which constitutes the 'gross' body. The mind, and other abstract aspects of the living being, are called the 'subtle' body. The gross and subtle bodies interact as abstract and contingent information. In fact, all causal interactions in *Sāñkhya* are interactions between abstract and contingent information, never between two objects with the same level of abstraction. For instance, in modern science, the effect of gravity is explained as the interaction between two *masses,* which are conceptually the same kind of object (they are only quantitatively different in terms of their mass). This viewpoint creates a problem of how the mass is transformed into a *cause* which produces an *effect.* In *Sāñkhya,* instead, an object interacts with its theory, which then interacts with another object. The conversion of cause into effect (which are two phenomena) is mediated by the theory.

This mediation is always presupposed in science, although never explained. We just assume that nature is governed by a mathematical law, which exists in another world of ideas. In *Sāñkhya*, the theory exists in this world, and interacts with the objects to produce causes and effects. There is never, therefore, a *direct* interaction between two objects (e.g., two masses). Rather, the interaction is always mediated by a subtle object (and there can be many tiers of subtle objects, or theories).

The gross object is a symbol of the subtle object because the subtle object is converted into the gross object through addition of information. The material world we see, taste, touch, smell, and hear, therefore, is a world of symbols, which have meanings. We can measure them through physical instruments, but we cannot see the meanings in this way. To perceive the meanings, we must *interpret* the physical states, and that interpretation requires a linguistic mapping between the physical state and how it is perceived and understood. Once the interpretation is created, it must be judged to be true or false. Then it must be attributed usefulness for some purpose. Finally, those purposes must be evaluated according to our values. The subtle body is therefore not merely the ability to interpret but also to judge, intend and value the world. Each of these abilities constitutes a different kind of material 'element' in *Sāñkhya*. These 'elements', however, are not substances. Rather, each higher element is the theory of the previous lower elements. The highest element (the root of the universe) is the theory of everything. Conversely, the lowest element is only a material object and never a theory of anything else. The elements in between the highest and the lowest are both objects and theories. Modern science studies the world as if it were only studying the lowest element, because the world is always modeled as objects.

To advance modern science, we must begin to study things that are both theories and objects. Of course, before such a study is possible within science, the definition of objects themselves must be changed (they must be viewed as *refinements* of theories, that causally interact *through* the theories). Modern science, in effect, flattens the tree of hierarchies into a single tier of matter. It might suppose that there is another world which comprises abstract or contingent of ideas, but so long as the idea world remains separated from the material world, the hierarchies of the idea world can never be understood as some material reality.

The Tree of Material Knowledge

The material world is created hierarchically—starting from the most abstract existence of God. God has six qualities—knowledge, beauty, power, fame, wealth, and renunciation—which are objectivized in the material creation. The first representation of these qualities is called *Brahman.* When *Brahman* is mixed with the three modes of nature, the result is called *Pradhāna,* in which the three modes of nature are in "balance". The "balance" indicates that no mode is higher and lower, and therefore the hierarchical tree of knowledge is not created. When the "balance" is disturbed, the three modes are distinguished, and we can then distinguish between the six qualities. In this distinguished state, the same thing is called *prakriti* and in this state, different branches of the material tree are formed as possibilities of material existence. Once a living entity desires one such type of material existence, the *prakriti* produces an instance of that possibility resulting in a certain type of mind and body.

The *Brahman representation* of God is called "OM", and meditation on this sound can help us understand the nature of God just like we can understand the object intended in a *representation* or *symbol* by interpreting the symbols correctly. The following conversation with A.C. Bhaktivedānta Swāmi Prabhupāda illustrates this idea clearly.

Doctor: And the word Om has been praised in the Upanishads, but...

Prabhupāda: Om, Veda, pranavah sarva-vedesu. Kṛṣṇa says that raso 'ham apsu kaunteya prabhasmi sasi-suryayoh pranavah sarva-vedesu [Bg. 7.8]. Pranava is omkara. Sarva-vedesu, "That pranava I am." That is sound representation of Kṛṣṇa.

Doctor: Then that one word as a mantra, is it not...

Prabhupāda: Yes.

Doctor: ...the highest sort of word?

Prabhupāda: No. If you keep Kṛṣṇa, that "This pranava is the sound representation of Kṛṣṇa," then it is all right. If you think it is separately powerful than Kṛṣṇa, that is nama-aparadha.

Doctor: I understand.

Prabhupāda: Yes. If you accept it as Kṛṣṇa says, that "I am pranava," if you do remember Kṛṣṇa by chanting omkara, then it is all right.

Doctor: Otherwise, Om is only given to sannyasis?

Prabhupāda: Not necessarily. It is not mentioned there. Anyone chanting Vedic mantra, he has to begin with omkara.

Doctor: All mantras begin with Om.

Prabhupāda: Yes, omkara. So sarva-vedesu. Pranavah sarva-vedesu. This is beginning. Just like we take Bhagavata, Om namo bhagavate vasudevaya.

Doctor:

etad aksaram brahmaetad aksaram parametad aksaram jnatva yati ceti...(?)

Prabhupāda: The difficulty is that we consider Kṛṣṇa is different from omkara.

Doctor: That is a mistake.

Prabhupāda: That is a mistake.

Doctor: But then Kṛṣṇa is not different from Brahman.

Prabhupāda: If you take this omkara as Kṛṣṇa's sound representation, then it is all right.

Doctor: Then it is as good as chanting Kṛṣṇa.

Prabhupāda: Yes.

From the *prakriti, mahattattva* is produced. It represents the ideals like the conceptions of morality, the different notions about ideal knowledge, and different ideas about what real happiness is. From the *mahattattva*, the element of Ego is produced. From the Ego, Intelligence, from the Intelligence the Mind, from the Mind the Senses, from the Senses the Sensations, and from the Sensations, Sense Objects. These elements are not substances. They are more abstract forms of matter, akin to theories that are more abstract than the phenomena they explain. Each of these elements is some combination of the three modes, but the successive elements are produced through greater subdivision of the previous modes. This process of subdivision constructs a *tree*, the root of which is *Brahman*, whose trunks are the various universes, whose branches are various planetary systems within the universe, whose leaves are the living beings, which are further subdivided through numerous steps in the same way to produce the smallest atomic particles in the universe.

The entire material creation is therefore just like a book. The title of the book is the sound OM. The table of contents is the *prakriti*, the *mahattattva* is the title of each individual chapter, the different planetary systems are sections within the individual chapters, the sentences are macroscopic objects in the planets, and the alphabets are the atomic particles. The book is organized and developed as a tree from concept to implementation, and the material creation is also organized and developed like a tree—from roots to leaves. The entire book is a description of God—i.e., His symbolic representation—and by reading this book correctly we can know the nature of God or the Ultimate Reality perfectly.

The pantheists believe that the material world is itself God, which is like saying that a map is the territory. The impersonalists believe the sound OM is the ultimate reality which is like saying that the world is meaningless because it exists as sound but does not describe anything. The voidists claim that the universe is ultimately nothingness, which is like saying that the book was produced automatically without a preexisting source of knowledge, therefore while it exists it cannot be a description of anything (the object being described must exist prior to writing the book). The materialists suppose that there are only physical things, which is like saying that the book has weight but no meaning.

Numerous misconceptions about the nature of the world exist today, and these misconceptions arise because we only study a small part of the universe and extend that study to the entire universe, thinking that the whole is just like some of the parts. In Vedic philosophy, these misconceptions are called *māyā* or illusions which are produced when some parts of the material tree are covered from our vision. *Māyā* is also *prakriti*—i.e., comprised of the three modes—but it covers the living being's consciousness due to which he is unable to perceive the true nature of reality. The law of nature is that if our understanding is imperfect, then we are implicated in consequences of our experience; if, however, the understanding is perfected, then the material laws cease to act on the soul. Therefore, *māyā* or *prakriti* leads to *karma* which then puts the living being in many situations where he can correct his misunderstanding, by exposing him to things that he had previously failed to understand.

Scientific Knowledge of the Material Tree

The scientific study of this world requires a shift from flat and open space-time to a hierarchical space-time in which locations can be abstract or contingent. Furthermore, locations are not "points" in a flat and open space. Rather, the entire universe is a location, although more abstract than the planets, which are locations more abstract than the things in that planet. This kind of space-time is best understood as postal addresses and clock times. Like a country is a location on a postal address, which is divided into states, which are divided into cities, streets, and houses, similarly the space in the universe is divided into smaller parts. Time too is hierarchical and does not flow linearly like in modern science. Rather, there are cycles of time called *kalpa*, *yuga*, years, months, weeks, days, hours, minutes, and seconds, which are embedded in the higher cycle.

Material objects in this universe, situated at some space and time location, are *symbols* of meanings. Each object is a representation of the next higher (more abstract) object, and the correct meaning of that object can be obtained only when we know what the next higher object is. Therefore, objects cannot be studied independently; rather, before we can understand an object, we must know the next higher object. Thus, whether a room in the house is understood as a bedroom, kitchen, living room, or study, depends on the house as a whole. Each part of the house can be described physically as length, height, breadth, etc. but that is not the key point. The key point is that that physical entity has a *meaning* which can be understood only in relation to the next higher entity.

Ultimately, nothing can be understood unless seen in connection to Kṛṣṇa—who in the Vedic view is the highest entity. Meanings play an important role in science when we interpret the observations. For instance, when I see the shape of an object, I interpret it to be a "table". Another shape is called a "chair", and so forth. In cosmology, observations of light are interpreted as planets, stars, etc. Modern science and Vedic descriptions are *methodologically* different in the sense that when scientists interpret that sensations in isolation, while in the Vedic view, sensations are interpreted in the context of the next higher sensation. Some of these higher sensations may not actually be perceived by the senses; i.e., they need to be sensed by a higher type of sense—mind, intellect, ego, or moral sense. Interpretations are necessary to arrive at a *model* of our observation—i.e., the description of what *caused* the sensation—and the Vedic and scientific cosmology interpret the same sensations differently.

The model construction in turn depends on the theory, and the theory in modern science and Vedic cosmology are as different as chalk and cheese: the scientific view is physical (meanings are given to sensations in isolation) and the Vedic view is semantic (meanings are given to sensations in relation to the next higher sensation). To include higher entities into our theory of reality, we must have a clear role for concepts in science, such that we can talk about "higher" and "lower" concepts. That in turn needs a dramatic shift from physical to semantic views.

Sāñkhya is a valuable theory of nature because it describes the different *tiers* of the tree from root to leaves. The root of this tree is God, and the leaves are material objects. The connection between matter and God is established through numerous tiers—both material and non-material. These tiers represent the gap in understanding the role of God in the material world. We cannot connect God directly to the material objects, just like we cannot relate the leaves to the root without passing through the branches. All such attempts are not only futile, they are also false.

With this background about Vedic philosophy and its theory of matter, we can now dive into discussing the nature of causality in Vedic philosophy, and how it differs from that in modern science. After this, I will discuss the key issues in modern cosmology, and why they arise out of a flawed understanding of the material world. Following this, the subsequent chapters will discuss how *Sāñkhya* entails a certain type of cosmic structure, the nature of the different "universes", and then the details about the present "universe". The themes we have discussed so far will recur over and over, but as you go along this journey, you will gradually develop a richer and nuanced understanding of Vedic cosmology.

3

The Vedic View of Causality

At a time when material science predominates all subjects—including the tenets of religion— it would be enlivening to see the principles of the eternal religion of man from the viewpoint of the modern scientist.

— *Easy Journey to Other Planets*

The Substitute for Force

Science began in the preoccupation with gravity, and the large-scale structure of the universe is presently modeled through gravity. In Vedic cosmology, there is no such thing as gravitational *force*, although there is the gravitational *phenomenon* of objects falling. This phenomenon has an alternate explanation in Vedic cosmology, which must be understood before we can understand the cosmology. Indeed, the Vedas don't consider any change to be caused by physical forces although the attractions and repulsions between material objects are considered real. The difference arises from what *causes* the attraction or repulsion. In modern science, it is the physical properties like mass and charge. In Vedic philosophy, the same attraction and repulsion are caused by semantic principles like consistency, complementarity and completeness of meanings (which cause attraction) and inconsistency and incompatibility (which cause repulsion). This idea about attraction and repulsion is totally different, and it must be understood before we discard the Newtonian theory.

The semantic substitute for force is the idea of a conceptual *system* comprised of parts that represent different *compatible* functions. If an essential function is missing from a system, its preservation must generate an "attraction" that inducts the missing function. If, however, a system contains a part inconsistent with the whole, the system must generate a "repulsion" to eject the discordant function. Attraction and repulsion are thus phenomenal behaviors, but they arise out of the same requirement to maintain system *coherence*. Sometimes, to achieve coherence, a system must induct missing parts; at other times, it must eject incompatible parts. The injection or rejection may appear to be physical "forces" but they are not causes in themselves. They are instead *effects* of another cause in the system to maintain system integrity and coherence.

Of course, this coherence is only desirable, not necessary. Sometimes, it becomes essential to break a system into pieces, and to utilize its components as building blocks of other systems. Incompatibilities may therefore be injected in the system to cause its collapse. If the system is living, these incompatibilities are called 'diseases'. The host that receives a disease tries to destroy and eject the incompatibility to maintain its integrity, but it may not succeed. The host will, however, in general, engage in repulsion and attraction for its preservation. Similarly, there may be hosts that inject inconsistencies in other systems to destroy them.

All these phenomena are well-known in the case of living beings, as well as in higher abstractions such as society, organization, and ecosystems: all these entities engage in preservation, thereby causing attraction and repulsion of material entities that aid in their preservation. The question really is: Is the tendency for preservation an *effect* of what physical sciences call "natural forces", or are these forces in turn the effects of the natural tendency for preservation? If the forces are fundamental, then their effects of preservation must be epiphenomenal. If, however, the systems are fundamental then the forces are epiphenomena. At the level of causality, either mechanism can be fundamental. The resolution of this question therefore requires us to step outside the question of change and look at *meanings*. As we have seen, a physical system cannot have meanings because collections themselves are epiphenomena. Without such meanings, we cannot have names and concepts, and without names and concepts, there cannot be knowledge. Indeed, if there is knowledge in nature, then physical descriptions of nature will always be incomplete.

The key point is that the dynamics currently explained by the physical forces can also be explained differently in a semantic view of nature, where these forces would be *phenomena* rather than *reality*. In fact, the phenomena that physical forces cannot explain (e.g., living beings, organizations, and society) can also be explained succinctly in the semantic view in a way similar to the explanation of atoms and molecules.

This background can be used to understand why material objects fall towards the Earth: the reason is that the material object rising from the surface of the Earth is entering a region of the universe incompatible with its own nature. It is also exiting a region of universe which it is compatible with. Both systems—i.e., the one that is losing an object and the one that is gaining it—will apply a "force" to counterbalance the changes.

The force and the counterforce are called *prāna* in Vedic philosophy, and these are responsible for all changes. Vedic texts describe several kinds of *prāna* of which five (called *prāna*, *apāna*, *udāna*, *vyāna*, and *samāna*) are prominent. *Prāna* injects useful matter into a system, *samāna* digests the ingested matter into useful ingredients, *vyāna* circulates the digested matter within a system, *apāna* ejects waste from the system, and *udāna* causes the expression of meanings into symbols of those meanings. These symbols are generally viewed as purposeful activity in living beings, where we might write a book, compose a song, paint a picture, or organize a meeting. These five kinds of forces are used in Vedic philosophy to explain all kinds of activities or changes.

When an earthly object moves beyond the Earth's surface, *prāna* will try to absorb it back, while *apāna* will try to eject it from the receiving system. The resulting attraction and repulsion is called 'gravity' in science. The force in Vedic philosophy is an outcome of trying to preserve the integrity of a system. To become part of a new system, therefore, an object must be 'digested' and 'assimilated'. The nature of digestion and assimilation depends on the receiving system. Inanimate objects too, therefore, follow the same kind of process that is used to describe living beings, or the process by which a country permits foreign immigrants: they must leave the previous system, and be properly assimilated into the new system, without being a threat to the new system's integrity and functioning. The previous system either does not need the ejected functions (if the system has been redefined) or must find the means to replenish their departure (if they are still necessary). If these adjustments are made, both systems regain their stability; if these changes cannot be made, both systems become unstable, disintegrating in other ways.

In the semantic view, therefore, a falling object has a more complex explanation than gravity, but this explanation is identical to that for a variety of other phenomena (e.g., organizations) which cannot be explained by gravity. The problem with the gravitational explanation is therefore not that it doesn't adequately explain some chosen phenomena, but that the choice of phenomena it explains is very narrow. As we broaden the phenomena, new theories must be postulated, which will be conceptually inconsistent with gravity, and the unification of these theories becomes a new kind of problem. The semantic explanation appears to be more complex than a simpler physical theory. But it is far simpler than the *sum* of the many mutually inconsistent theories for various phenomena.

The apparent theoretical simplicity in modern science has been created by ignoring many phenomena; we forget that there are many apparently simple theories that cannot be reconciled. And if their reconciliation is somehow achieved, the complexity grows dramatically. For instance, general relativity is a far more complex than Newton's theory because it tries to reconcile the previously inconsistent theories of object motion and light. Similarly, quantum theory is a far more complex theory of change because it tries to reconcile the previously inconsistent theories of particle motion and radiation. The history of science shows that scientific theories become more complex as diverse theories are reconciled, although the complexity of the combined theory is lesser than the combined complexity of the individual theories. The semantic explanation too is more complex than the gravitational theory, but it is also one that demystifies numerous diverse aspects of the phenomenal universe.

The Working of Prāna

We earlier discussed how abstract ideas must be expressed in contingent details, and that this process creates the body from the mind. The method for the creation of the body involves the intake of food, air, and water, which is called *prāna*. When matter is ingested into the body, it must be analyzed into parts that can be used in the construction of the body, which his called *samāna*. The food must then be circulated to different parts of the body, which is called *vyāna*. The waste produced in the process must be ejected from the body, which is called *apāna*. And the existence of the body in a system of other bodies involves work of exchanging entities that are useful for other living entities, which is called *udāna*.

The analysis of the ingested parts depends on the nature of the whole body, and the matter that is ingested can be broken down into parts in many ways, although for a given type of living being, it would be broken down in a specific manner. The function of analysis is called *samāna* and performs what we call 'digestion'. This digestion includes not just food, but also speech and sensations—e.g., sight, touch, sound, smell, and taste. When we receive information from the external world, we analyze it into parts before we can integrate the new knowledge with the existing knowledge. How the new information is 'understood' thus depends on how it is broken down and integrated with the existing information. A similar process of ingestion, digestion, and integration occurs in all parts of the body, and therefore *samāna* should be seen as a force not just in the digestive system but in all parts of the body. Digestion, in fact, is a multi-stage process, which begins with chewing the food. The food is then partially digested in the stomach, and then in the intestines. Even this digestion in the alimentary canal should be viewed as a type of "pre-processing" which is then successively refined as the pre-processed food (or sensations) are sent to other parts of the body for further processing. The *samāna* therefore resides even in the senses, and in the organs. For instance, our eyes analyze the color perceptions into Red, Green, and Blue, and separate signals for each type of color are transmitted to the brain about the relative proportion of these colors. Similarly, all the senses perform different levels of pre-processing, which is then analyzed and integrated further in the brain, or other body parts.

Once the 'food' intake has been analyzed to fit into the body, it must be transmitted to the other parts of the body, senses, mind, intellect, etc., and this transmission is called *vyāna* or circulation, and it represents the circulatory and nervous system in the body. The circulatory system transmits the digested food, and the nervous system carries the cognitive and conative impulses. Upon circulation they are assimilated in the different parts of the living system. If they hadn't been digested for assimilation, their circulation would result in disease in the system.

The living body is like a factory in which materials are processed at different stages. In a petrochemical factory, for instance, crude oil is first separated into gasoline used in engines, and the residue is then further separated into various types of heavy oils such as those used in lubricants. This separation of the parts of crude oil is similar to the process call *samāna*. As the parts are separated, they are sent to different parts of a factory for further processing, and that transmission is a representation of *vyāna.* Each stage of processing discards some 'waste' products, which must then be eliminated, and the process of elimination is *apāna.*

The four types of forces (*prāna*, *apāna*, *vyāna*, and *samāna*) are therefore different processes in a multi-stage processing engine that ingests, digests, circulates, and eliminates matter. The *udāna*, however, converts the body into useful activities. The *prāna*, *samāna*, and *apāna* are the essential processes of ingestion, digestion, and elimination, which must exist in all parts of a system that processes matter. Since this processing is multi-stage, such parts must be interconnected through *vyāna*. And to then utilize this complex system for useful ends, *udāna* is necessary to externalize the meanings in the mind and the body. The five forces therefore exist in all parts of the body, and indeed in all functional systems, although they are prominently visible in some specific parts, such as *prāna* in breathing, *samāna* in digestion, *apāna* in excretion, *vyāna* in the nervous and circulatory system, and *udāna* in speech. Accordingly, they are sometimes identified with these prominent manifestations, which is a partial understanding of the working of these forces.

The *prāna* body is a force-based description of the gross and subtle body, and the object and process descriptions of the body are mutually complementary in the sense that the specification of the force reduces the possibilities of its material structure but does not fix that structure. Similarly, the specification of the material structure reduces the possibilities of forces that can be enacted within that structure but does not fix the exact reality. The objective and force descriptions are thus complementary and are said to be manifestations of *tamo-guna* (objects) and *rajo-guna* (forces). The force in question here is not *produced* from matter as in the case of modern science (where forces like gravity are produced by material properties like mass). Rather, force is a separate material reality that organizes matter into coherent and stable systems. When a person dies, the body is left behind, but the force of five *prana* is carried to the next body where it again organizes the new body suitable for living.

This ability to separate matter from force entails that matter and force are different. This idea is more consistent with atomic physics where matter (fermions) and force (bosons) are treated as separate realities, rather than one dependent on the other. Certain types of forces such as *udāna*—which clone the ideas for expression—are absent in modern science which is why it cannot describe the creativity in us. Similarly, how society and ecosystems circulate meaning to create stable systems is also missing in modern science, leading to separation between physical sciences and humanities. By incorporating all these forces in the description of a living system, and then extending them to all of nature, the Vedic system describes even societies, ecosystems, and living beings.

Prāna and Time

The five types of forces are not autonomous, and four additional factors—called *chitta, guna, karma* and time—also play an important role in the working of *prāna*. The *chitta* comprises unconscious impressions from the past, and these impressions drive the working of *karma*. Similarly, *guna* represents our emotional center, which can manifest in feelings such as fear and happiness, and they drive the working of *prana*. *Karma* represents the consequences of previous actions, and they automatically take the person toward circumstances where the person can enjoy or suffer. Finally, each of these—*guna*, *karma*, and *chitta*—constitute our unconscious which lies dormant unless activated by time.

Time constitutes the events that will occur irrespective of the individual actors; it constitutes the script of the drama unfolding in the universe. The participants in this drama are selected based on the unconscious *chitta, guna,* and *karma.* The Vedic theory of matter therefore describes the world at many levels. The force-based description of the objective body is subordinated to the *karma, guna,* and *chitta* description, which is further subordinated to time. Time selects the events in the universe, which then select the impressions, desires, and consequences lying dormant, which then selects the force, which is then converted into material activities. The preeminent role of time entails that the universe of events is independent of individual observers who participate in these events; that is, we can participate in different events based on our *guna, karma,* and *chitta* but we cannot change the destiny of the universe.

The role of *karma* entails that the events we participate in are caused by our previous illusion and choices, and therefore we are responsible for our choices. The role of *guna* entails that the personality of likes and dislikes we have developed in the past drives our future experiences. The role of *chitta* entails that the impressions acquired in the past filter what we consider true or false and focus our consciousness in different ways. The role of *prāna* entails that consciousness can be abstracted from the forces and a material system can *appear* to work automatically due to forces and without conscious intervention, which a materialist can take to be the ultimate description of the world. Similarly, since material objects are involved in the changes caused by the force, we can create the illusion matter is the true cause of forces and change in nature.

The current dogma in science (that material particles produce force, which then causes changes, which then appears as consciousness) is thus produced via four levels of oversimplifications: (1) the role of cosmic time in deciding the events in the universe is ignored, leading to the impression that we can change the world, (2) the role of the unconscious produced as impressions, personality, and consequences is discarded, leading to the impression that only the present decides the future, (3) the fact that force acts under the control of the unconscious is rejected, which gives the impression that bodies are working automatically without consciousness and therefore we are not truly responsible for our actions, and (4) the forces are reduced to material objects, creating the illusion that these objects are creating the material body, which then creates consciousness. Each of these oversimplifications creates a type of indeterminism or incompleteness in the predictions, but if you perform these oversimplifications, then you can construct the materialist ideology.

Scientists recognize that a theory that is more generic is naturally more encompassing. When constraints are applied to a generic theory, specific systems are produced. The material ideology is a specific type of theory produced by applying simplifications to the Vedic ideology. Those simplifications may sometimes appear to be true, but in the general case, they also fail to explain many phenomena. The contradiction between Vedic theory and modern materialism is therefore produced by discarding parts of reality described in the Vedic theory of matter (consciousness, *guna*, *karma*, *chitta*, and time), and the Vedic theory is therefore more encompassing and generic than modern materialism. We might say that Vedic materialism is a superset of modern materialism, although Vedic materialism is consistent with the existence of soul, God, choice, and responsibility, which create numerous problems for modern materialism.

The key conclusion is that the force-based description of the body is superior to the object description, the cognitive and conative description is superior to the force description, the *karma*, *guna*, and *chitta* description is superior to the cognitive and conative description, and the time theory is superior to all. The force-based description is necessary because the body is inert, objects by themselves remain in stationary states, and to cause changes, forces are necessary[1]. The mental description is necessary because the forces of change can be controlled by our mind. The *karma, guna,* and *chitta* description is necessary because the future is influenced not just by the present but also by the past. The time description is necessary because which specific aspect of *karma, guna* and *chitta* will be activated when cannot be predicted unless there is an agency which fixes the evolution of the cosmos. Each successive description thus arises because the previous description is in some way incomplete. In *Sāñkhya* philosophy, the object and the force descriptions are often merged together and called the 'body', although this 'body' is not just the limbs, organs, and internal functions we can see, taste, smell, touch, and taste, but also the force that moves the body. Even the 'body' in *Sāñkhya* is thus far more complex as compared to the body in modern science.

The Theory of Mode Interactions

Modern science postulates the properties of objects and the laws of their interactions. The object properties are defined in terms of their effects, which must be computed according to some natural laws, but the laws themselves are defined in terms of properties. There is hence a circular dependency between properties and laws. In the theory of gravitation, for example, the law of gravitation is defined in terms of a property called 'mass', but this property is not defined independently of the law. Rather, to measure mass, we must use the law of gravitation. Thus, mass is defined by gravity, and gravitation is defined in terms of mass. To measure mass, we must use the law of gravitation. And gravitation is only defined in terms of the property of mass. Mass is therefore only a theoretical construct in science and has no basis in observation or in reality.

The Vedic approach to causality avoids this circular dependence between laws and properties. There are only three properties in nature, called the three modes of nature (*sattva*, *rajas* and *tamas*), which are combined over and over to create all phenomena. Their interaction constructs a semantic tree, in which the higher node in the tree represents an abstract concept, and the lower nodes are details of that abstraction.

Thus, when the modes of nature are combined, there isn't a law that describes the effect of that combination. Rather, in this interaction, two (or more) trees are combined to produce one tree. The higher nodes in the interacting trees are generally fixed, since most objects may have many material commonalities. The lower nodes are, however, rearranged to construct a new tree. The tree resulting from the combination of individual trees depends on which mode dominates, and therefore which becomes the higher or more abstract node, while the other nodes become the detailed instantiation of the abstraction and refine it. Thus, when two qualities are mixed, they don't exist in equal proportion, side-by-side. Rather, one quality dominates and becomes the higher node in the tree, while the other qualities become the details. This can be understood by an example. For instance, to create a 'black shirt', you cannot mix the ideas of 'black' and 'shirt' and expect them to reside side-by-side in equal proportion, even though you need both ideas. The correct way to produce a 'black shirt' is to take the idea of 'shirt' and make it the abstract notion that will be refined by the idea of 'black'. Thus, both 'shirt' and 'black' exist in a 'black shirt' but the idea of 'shirt' dominates as the abstraction while the notion of 'black' is subordinate to the abstraction as a detail.

Sāñkhya describes that when the modes of nature are mixed, there is always one mode that predominates as the overarching tendency which covers the other modes. The dominating mode is slightly 'more' as compared to the mode that is dominated which is slightly 'less'. The effect of that mixing is that if the modes are in equal proportion, then no mode will ever dominate, and the semantic hierarchy would never be constructed; as a result, the world would never manifest. Thus, in the state of the universe called *Pradhāna* the modes of nature are in balance, and the universe is unmanifest. The manifestation begins when this balance is disturbed, and as one of the modes dominates, a hierarchy is produced in which the dominating mode is the abstract principle detailed by the dominated mode. Thus, in the *prakriti* stage, numerous such trees are constructed as possibilities that an observer can participate into.

As mentioned, the three modes of nature are *sattva* (goodness), *rajas* (passion), and *tamas* (ignorance) and different realities are produced out of their combinations. The method of combination entails that if we have good qualities in a greater proportion, then the bad qualities become undercurrents of goodness, and since goodness is dominating, it can overcome the undercurrents. For instance, if we have the good quality of truthfulness, we might sometimes hold back some of the truth due to ignorance, but we will not outright lie. If, however, ignorance dominates, then goodness is the undercurrent, and ignorance overwhelms goodness; i.e., even our good qualities would be used to instantiate ignorance: we will use our goodness to make our lies logically consistent and give them the appearance of truth. Thus, even thieves and crooks have some goodness, but they use this goodness to systematically spread crime[2].

The key point is that when the modes are mixed, one of them dominates, and becomes the main trend and the other trends are subordinated and used to create details. The modes are therefore never side-by-side, like equal peers. Rather, the dominating mode goes 'higher' and the overwhelmed mode goes 'lower'. The result of that domination is that the dominating mode will appear to be bigger in space, and longer in time, while the overwhelmed mode will appear to be smaller in space and shorter in time. However, these short and long durations in time can be altered as time passes, and a different mode manifests. When a mode that was previously subordinated slowly grows in strength, the master-slave relationship between the modes is inverted. There is hence a 'tipping point' at which the undercurrent becomes the overcurrent, and the slave who was earlier serving the master, becomes the new master.

The manifestation of the higher node into lower nodes creates a division of the abstraction into contingent parts. The *type* of the living entity is the whole, and its detailing creates the division in that whole. Of course, each part in a whole can itself be further divided into parts. Thus, in a sufficiently complex system, the whole is divided through several tiers of parts, and the relationship between part and whole is only relative to the next higher whole, and the entire semantic hierarchy must be considered to understand the true meaning of any individual part.

The Theory of Balance

Vedic philosophy describes how nature must exist in the "balance" of the three modes. This is because of the dominant-subordinate structure in the three modes. This structure creates a conflict between the three modes, where one mode cannot remain dominant for a long time and must give way for another mode to dominate. *Ayurveda* describes how a living body becomes diseased when any of the three modes predominates, and these modes are therefore now called *dosha* instead of *guna*.

Those familiar with *Sanskrit* terminology will recognize that the word "guna" is commonly used to denote "good qualities" and the term "dosha" similarly denotes "bad qualities" or "faults". Therefore, in balance, the three modes of nature are "guna" or good qualities, while under imbalance, the same three modes become "dosha" or bad qualities. This fact underlies the common adage that everything in moderation is good; anything in excess is bad. The above model of description can be applied to anything in nature, not just to living bodies, because it is a description of conscious experience, and everything material is in our experience.

For instance, the desires of the soul are produced from the *ānanda* and they constitute the judgment of good. The sense of responsibility is produced from the *sat* of the soul, and it constitutes the judgment of right. The abilities of the soul are produced from *chit* and they constitute the judgment of truth. The three aspects of the soul—*sat, chit,* and *ānanda*—often conflict. Sometimes you want to fulfill your duties, but you don't have the ability. Sometimes you have the ability, but it is not your duty. And sometimes you have the ability and it is your duty, but you don't enjoy it. The conflicts must be resolved through prioritizing. One of the three—*sat, chit,* or *ānanda*—will become dominant and the others will be subordinated. By this dominant-subordinate relation, the contradiction is temporarily solved; one aspect wins and the others become subordinate. However, the conflict will likely return again at a later time.

Common examples of such conflicts are visible every day. For instance, sometimes desire rules over ability and opportunity—e.g., I can digest milk, and I can drink milk, but I hate milk; so, despite milk being available, and my ability to digest it, I'm not going to drink it. At other times, opportunity rules over desire and ability—e.g., I want to drink milk, and I can digest it, but I have no access to milk; therefore, my desire and ability are meaningless because the opportunity determines the outcome. Finally, sometimes ability rules over opportunity and desire—e.g., I want to drink milk, and I have access to milk, but I have a bad stomach due to which I can't digest milk; now, my desire and opportunity are futile because the outcome is determined by my ability. When the three aspects of the soul are perfectly balanced, then what gives you pleasure is identical to what you are capable of, which is identical to your duty. The state of balance is called self-realization in which the soul can fulfill himself, has the duty to satisfy the self, and enjoys that product of that ability and duty. This is not very straightforward, as it might seem at first sight.

This stability is predicated on the assumption that the priority between the three facets doesn't change. But as we saw before, different aspects can dominate at different times. Sometimes you let your desires drive you to a new situation, sometimes you subordinate your desires to the situation, and sometimes you want to change the situation to fulfill your desires. Each such change involves an internal imbalance, and it drives the soul to change its relationships, abilities, and desires.

Apart from the fact that *sat*, *chit*, or *ānanda* can dominate the other at different times, each of these three aspects has many subdivisions, and they can also become dominant and subordinate. The *chit* for instance, is six qualities of knowledge, power, beauty, wealth, fame, and renunciation; there are as many types of responsibilities (*sat*) as there are types of relationships; there are as many pleasures (*ānanda*) as there are unique types of emotions. Each of these create further conflicts. You may not be sure if knowledge is always better than beauty, or power is more important than wealth. You may not be sure if you should prioritize love over anger, or anger over love. And you may not know if it is always better to be a father and take responsibilities for your children, or you should also be a child and act unreasonably in relation to a father. Given all the possible internal contradictions, the soul can try to be everything—changing his or her state in order to resolve all the contradictions.

The Theory of Elements

Sāñkhya describes nine tiers of material hierarchy, which are called *mahattattva*, ego, intelligence, and mind (which constitute the subtle body of the living being), followed by five elements called Earth, Water, Fire, Air, and Ether (which constitute the gross body). While terms such as mind, intelligence, and ego are generally understood (although imperfectly) in modern times, terms such as Earth, Water, Fire, Air, and Ether are generally not understood at all, or confused with something else. One reason for the confusion is the use of the same words in Greek philosophy, which viewed the above mentioned as "substances". The substance view of the world was then complemented with the idea of "form", and the present world was supposed to be a combination of both substance and form. How that combination occurs, and how the substances interact with the forms, was however never clarified within Greek philosophy.

In *Sāñkhya*, Earth, Water, Fire, Air and Ether are not substances. Rather, they are *objectifications* of sensual properties, and as such, they are forms rather than substances. These elements are produced from perceptual properties called *tanmātra* which include sight, sound, touch, taste, and smell. These perceptual properties are in turn produced from the senses—eye, nose, skin, ear, and tongue (these senses are not the organs in the body). The senses are in turn produced from the mind, which is produced from intellect, and so forth. The correct way to understand the senses is that they are objectifications of meanings. For instance, the idea of an apple is a meaning, which can be comprehended by the mind, but for it to be perceivable, it must have the property of being seen, tasted, touched, smelt, and heard. Similarly, for something to be seen, it must have a form, color, size. For the color to be perceivable, it must have a hue, intensity, saturation, etc. For the hue to be perceivable, it must be a combination of some primitive colors, such as red, green, and blue. Thus, in the attempt to make something perceivable, we must undergo a hierarchical process of objectifying the meaning in numerous distinct ways.

Sāñkhya describes this hierarchical process. The property of being seen, tasted, touched, smelt, and heard, is called the 'sense', and it has three parts: subjective (*ādiatmika*), objective (*ādibhautika*) and their connection (*ādidaivika*). The subjective part is responsible for the sensation of sight, taste, touch, smell, and sound; the objective part is the property of sight, taste, touch, smell, and sound in objects; and their connection is the causal agency (*chitta, guna, karma* and time) that produces the sensation. Thus, material objects have properties; the observers have the corresponding subjective ability to perceive; and the objects and the senses are connected by a causal agency to produce the sensations.

The division of each of these 'senses' produces the properties that subdivide each type of sensation. For instance, sight is divided into hue, brightness, saturation, form, size, etc. All these are collectively called *tanmātra* (which literally means 'form only'), and they are produced from the 'senses' through subdivision. That is, color and form cannot be defined unless seeing has been defined, and seeing cannot be defined, unless meanings have been defined. When the *tanmātra* are further objectified, the *values* of these properties are produced. For instance, color can have the value of red, blue, or green (or their various combinations). These values are produced from the *tanmātra* and they are now called the 'gross' material elements: Earth, Water, Fire, Air, and Ether. Each element objectifies the sensations of one type of sense (Earth for smell, Water for taste, Fire for sight, Air for touch, and Ether for sound).

Sāñkhya also divides each of the above material elements into three further parts called *manas*, *prāna*, and *vāk*. Everything we have discussed above regarding the *properties* is *vāk*. This *vāk* has subjective, objective, and connective divisions, which essentially means that the property of perceiving sight is different from the property of being visible. Similarly, all other properties have subjective, objective, and connective counterparts. These properties, however, lie inert unless activated by *prāna* or the life force that causes changes. The senses therefore are not the cause of vision; the *prāna* is the cause of vision, although it depends on the property of perceiving sight. The *prāna* is however also subordinate to the desire for vision, which is called *manas*. The term *manas* here represents the desire or need for sense gratification. This means that there isn't one universal type of eye or ear. Rather, each eye or ear can be defined by the kind of sights and sounds it desires to see or hear. Since the sights and sounds are objectified from the meanings in the mind, this desire essentially represents the visual objectification of that type of meaning. The key import of this idea is that our senses are themselves impelled towards certain types of objects, and they drag the mind with them. For instance, if the nose smells a specific desired type of smell, the mind's attention is automatically diverted to the cognition of that smell.

The material objects, in Vedic philosophy, are thus described in terms of *values* of sensation similar to modern science where matter is *values* of physical properties. Science postulates properties such as length, mass, momentum, energy, etc. and material objects have numerical values for these properties. For instance, objects have the property of mass, and each object is given a value of this mass. *Sāñkhya* instead uses properties such as color and form, which have values such as yellow and square. Unlike science where "values" are counted as *quantities*, Vedic philosophy describes the world in terms of *qualities* or *types*.

In *Sāñkhya*, material elements have a hierarchy and a complete understanding of an object requires the understanding of the higher (abstract) objects. For instance, if we can hear something, there is already a meaning because the mind which perceives meaning is higher than the sense of hearing. If we can touch something, it can also be heard. If we can see something, we can also touch it. If we can taste something, we can also see it. And if we can smell something, we can also taste it. The first gross element in *Sāñkhya* (called Ether) objectifies the meanings into a sound that can be heard. This isn't the beginning of matter, or of space, because the mind too has a location in space, although that location is a subtle object which is abstract for the senses, and hence cannot be heard.

The locations in the Ether are not points; they are rather extended forms, and the vibration represents the meaning encoded by them. Due to vibration, the space is never actually empty; rather even the so-called empty space has energy, due to which it represents meanings. These meanings are given simply by the location of space, and therefore, each location in space can be distinguished as a certain type of meaning.

The gross material elements should be thought of as objects, although their properties aren't the cause of changes. Rather, the cause is a deeper material cause called *prāna*, which is controlled by the subtle body, which is in turn controlled by *chitta, guna, karma*, and time. The subtle body is an evidence for the unconscious, the *prāna* is an evidence for the subtle body, and the gross body is an evidence for *prāna*. Thus, if someone doesn't believe in the existence of *prāna*, then they can study the gross elements, and try to explain their working. As science attempts to do that and finds that even after exhausting all material properties, we still cannot completely predict the gross material behaviors, it would have to discard the idea that causality lies in the gross matter. Then *prāna* will become a scientific construct. As *prāna* is found to be inadequate, the subtle body will become a scientific construct. When even the subtle body is found inadequate, then *chitta, guna, karma*, and time would be considered scientific causes. And when even this causality is found to be inadequate, the soul and God would be scientific causes. In Vedic philosophy, the causality of the soul and God is consistent and complete, so no further causes need to be searched for. The theory of elements, therefore, is only an *evidence* for subtle forms of reality, not the complete reality itself.

Atoms and Macroscopic Objects

When a living being has a perception, such as the sight of a color, it is not because light is traveling from one point in space to another and the observer just happens to be in the path of that light. Rather, the vision of light is information gain in the observer, *correlated* with the loss of information in another object, and the loss and gain of information is due to the *karma* in an observer who is either being rewarded or punished for past deeds. Unlike modern science where this transfer of information is the "transport" of some material object, in the semantic view, such transfer involves the correlation of material objects in space and time.

In *Sāñkhya* when information disappears and then appears at some other location, it is not *transferred* to or from another object. Rather, the disappearing information becomes *unmanifest* and the appearing information becomes *manifest.* Both appearance and disappearance are caused by *karma,* which lies as the possibility of an event and is actualized by time into an event. Furthermore, the universe is being manifest from the unmanifest at every instant of time, since the state of the universe is defined as a whole, and not by the states of the individual objects[3]. Therefore, the appearance and disappearance of information are correlated by the choice of the next state of the universe, not by information transfer. There is, hence, no information transfer from one object to another, although when we see information appearing and disappearing, we tend to imagine that information must have been transferred. Thus, scientific causal models are constructed based on the notion that information is being exchanged, when, in fact, there is no exchange. Information disappears in one object and appears in another, because the next state of the universe has less information at one location and more at another.

The mystery of information exchange is therefore not in a transfer of information but in the next state of the universe being defined such that objects have more or less information. This state then selects the appropriate *chitta, guna* and *karma* due to which experiences are automatically created. The source of information thus emits due to *karma* and the sink of information absorbs that information due to *karma*. The correlation between source and sink is established by the nature of space-time. The loss of information and the gain of information are fixed by the *karma* but which particular pair of objects would be involved in the exchange is not fixed. The gain and loss of information represent two separate *events* while the objects involved in these events are the *trajectories* that connect the events. The universe as events is fixed and evolves independently of all observers (governed by the space-time structure), while the observers are overlaid on these events due to their *karma*.

In this Vedic causal model, as seen, light does not "travel" from one object to another like classical physical particles are supposed to, and cause a change by colliding with another object. The change is rather caused by time, which converts *karma* into manifest experiences by adding information. So long as this information is not added, the *karma* remains invisible to sensory or mental observation. It is the "unconscious" which becomes "conscious" under the effect of time. Our pain or pleasure is therefore not the effect of something that lies "outside" but due to something that lies "within" the observer and covers his consciousness.

The smallest *macroscopic* object in Vedic philosophy is called the *trisarenu*. The *trisarenu* is sometimes termed as the "atom" not because it is the smallest possible thing in the world, but because it is smallest object that we can *see* with our naked eyes without magnification (the *trisarenu* is the particles that we can see when light pours in through a window). Clearly, this "atom" is not the atom of modern science, which, in any case, cannot be seen with the naked eye. The "atom" of Vedic philosophy is, however, the smallest *macroscopic* object that we can perceive through our senses, such as the eyes. We might say that the *trisarenu* is the "atom" of the realm of macroscopic objects, which is also called *bhūloka*.

However, the universe is not limited to such macroscopic "atoms", as science has shown. While our senses can only see macroscopic objects, each such object can be detailed even further, although these details are not seen by the senses. In scientific experiments the details are "created" by adding energy into the measured system, such that the senses can observe. For instance, particle accelerators produce sub-atomic particles by adding energy into the system. This energy acts upon abstract meanings to produce contingent meanings. Such creations are then magnified with more energy to bring them to a level where our senses can observe them.

The key point is that the atoms exist as *karma* in an unmanifest form. We will see later how there are different types of *karma* corresponding to the five elements, Earth, Water, Fire, Air, and Ether. When *karma* is converted into a manifest form due to time, an event is created (which may or may not be experienced), and this is then called the collapse of the wavefunction in atomic theory, which produces a measurement outcome. Which event would be experienced next cannot be predicted in current science because we are trying to predict the events based on the manifest properties of matter, when the event is actually produced from the unmanifest reality called *karma.* Our experiences are therefore not produced due to what we call matter, neither is the event caused by our consciousness. Events are rather outcomes of the actions performed in the past, which are effecting 'state preparations' of the present. These state preparations may be long past in history, and we may have no memory of these actions. Unless science recognizes that causality is the connection between events long past and the present, it cannot explain the occurrence of events, as seen in the problem of quantum physics.

The Explanation of Illusion

Sāñkhya explains that illusions are created by the interaction between our ideas and the world. This is no longer a mind-body interaction of Western philosophy because both body and mind are ideas. Furthermore, illusion is not merely an epistemological problem, but also a moral one. That is, if you are misperceiving the world, you have *chosen* some ideas as the axioms of your worldview, and this choice will have *consequences*. These consequences are different from the *effects*. For instance, the effect is an illusion and the consequence is the creation of *karma* that may correct the illusion by falsifying the previously chosen axioms.

Every cause-effect relation terminates after each interaction—e.g., if you mix sugar and water, after the mixing, the effect has been realized and nothing more needs to happen. However, the cause-consequence relation does not end with the effect and creates another experience—i.e., cause-effect relation. Therefore, if we are only looking to describe the world in terms of cause-effects, our descriptions will remain incomplete because the cause-effect relation ends after each interaction. To create yet another cause-effect, a cause-consequence relation must be summoned, which in turn requires the postulate of an observer, a conscious choice, and the necessity of moral responsibility for those choices.

Modern science is, and will remain, incomplete as long as it models all experiences as cause-effect relationships. It will repeatedly find that we can form theories about *individual* events but we cannot predict the *succession* of events for any individual observer because that succession is predicated not on an effect becoming a cause and creating yet another effect, but on the *consequences* of the previous choices (which are not the same as the *effects* and therefore not governed by the same kind of natural laws). In short, your mixing sugar into water is incapable of predicting what happens next—do you drink it, give it to someone else to drink it, or boil it with something else? That prediction can only be done by postulating that there are consequences being created from our actions, which then enforce the creation of new actions and then new effects.

The Theory of Karma

The consequences are called *karma* in *Sāñkhya* and the "law" of *karma* is that all choices have consequences if those choices are mistaken (i.e., based on an incorrect understanding of reality). There are, however, several nuances in the determination of the nature of mistakes, which must be noted. The *Śrīmad Bhāgavatam* states that if a person performs a wrong deed under madness then there is punishment, but it is not very severe. If, however, a person performs a wrong deed but is aware that his deeds are indeed wrong, then the punishment is more severe than the person acting under madness. If, however, one is willingly an atheist and disobeys the injunctions of God, then the punishment is most severe.

> *If one acts in the mode of ignorance because of madness, his resulting misery is the least severe. One who acts impiously but knows the distinction between pious and impious activities is placed in a hell of intermediate severity. And for one who acts impiously and ignorantly because of atheism, the resultant hellish life is the worst. [SB 5.26.3]*

This is similar to how we view morality today: a person who knowingly does something wrong is more punishable as compared to one who just did not know that he was doing something wrong. A useful point of comparison in this regard is the following verse from the Bible:

> *Jesus said, "Father, forgive them, for they don't know what they are doing". And the soldiers gambled for his clothes by throwing dice. [Luke 23:34]*

In both conceptions, ignorance that your deeds are wrong is pardonable, but knowingly doing something wrong is not excusable. But one who does misdeeds out of compulsion of habits although he knows that he is doing something wrong, the punishment is less severe. The main issue is our distance from correct action. One who performs misdeeds without awareness could stop those actions if he were aware. Therefore, wrong action under madness is not considered as sinful, although there are consequences. Those who aware that they are doing sins but unable to control their habits or nature, must be punished more because they are acting despite their awareness, although there is guilt involved in it, which means that their correction involves a change in habit, not a change in understanding. However, those who are explicitly atheistic and reject the moral path are willfully sinful and their punishment is most severe.

The atheistic rejection of God in science followed by speculation about the truth (and therefore not knowing the truth) is most sinful, evan as it is celebrated. This results in a sense of complacency in our quest for knowledge, and we believe that delayed knowledge is not a crime, and rejection of God in the quest is okay. In fact, most atheists take refuge in the fact that they are following the scientific method of knowledge, and even if that method seems to take more time, the scientists could not be held responsible for the actions that are performed under ignorance.

A moral law can be formulated in science only if ignorance is a crime, because every crime is committed under some ignorance. Every legal system recognizes that crime is reduced by teaching the nature of good and bad, and the repentant (even if sentenced to long years in jail) are freed faster than the unrepentant. This means that realizing your crime makes you less of a criminal than if you don't realize your crime. This principle of reducing the sentence, however, doesn't apply to the unrepentant. The Vedic recipe similarly is to punish the willfully sinful more. The ignorant are punished much lesser; while the punishment for those who are knowledgeable but unable to control their habits is intermediate.

The point is that the aim of punishment is education, and the greater the education required the greater must be the punishment. The law of *karma* is based on the *gap* between the truth and our perception of it. The greater the gap, the more severe is the punishment. Thus, those who are willfully rejecting the truth need a much bigger punishment to educate them. Those, on the other hand, who are aware of their mistakes, but happened to commit a wrong due to force of habit, or simply temptation, are less punishable. Finally, a mad man who doesn't know what he is doing is least punishable. The punishment only plugs the smaller gap until the knowledge is enhanced. This also means that no crime can warrant eternal damnation, because the gap between the truth and our perception of it is never infinite. In every falsity, there is always an element of truth, and in a sense, all these falsities are different degrees of truth[4].

The law of *karma* is that the gap between perception and reality becomes a new kind of experience in which the criminal can be educated. If the person learns faster, then the punishment is reduced, and therefore the devotees of the Lord can reduce the burden of their *karma* quickly by learning about the Lord. *Karma* is therefore just like school: if you learn faster you quickly jump classes. When perfect knowledge is attained, you "graduate" from the world of material experiences. Conversely, if you don't learn fast enough, you pass through the same classes again and again, and this repetition is called the *transmigration* of the soul.

Freedom from the Material Law

The Absolute Truth is more abstract than our own existence and cannot be rationally or logically "understood" because the abstract is bigger than the contingent. The fact that the complete reality is bigger than us means that this reality will never "fit" in our consciousness and we cannot know the entire world at once. By the knowledge of reality, therefore, we don't mean everything that exists in all its details. What we mean is the knowledge of the source of all truths, and the realization that we are also truth although a much smaller part of whole truth would be enough.

God, however, knows everything. The knowledge of the entire universe is merely self-knowledge for God because the world is expanded from the person of God. When the biggest reality divides Himself, the individual conscious soul is created. Similarly, when God divides His material representation into parts, the material universe is produced. Whether as part of the material universe, or originally as parts of God, the souls are part of the whole truth and while they can never completely understand that truth, they can understand that they are parts of it. The goal of life is to acquire this understanding and subordinate our actions in a way that we act as parts of the whole. Like hands and legs act in the benefit of the body, the living being must also act in benefit of God.

Since the entire creation is a representation of God, studying this creation is tantamount to studying the nature of God, provided the study produces the correct understanding of reality. If through this study the living being learns the truth, he too is freed from the laws of *karma*. The purpose of knowledge acquisition is thus freedom from the laws of nature. Scientists presume that if we knew nature's laws perfectly, then we would control the world perfectly. The spiritualist instead knows that if we understood the laws perfectly, we would be freed of the laws.

4

Problems in Modern Cosmology

Those who are seers of the truth have concluded that of the nonexistent there is no endurance, and of the existent there is no cessation. This, seers have concluded by studying the nature of both.

— *Bhagavad Gita* 2.16

A Brief History of Big Bang Theory

Big Bang is the theory that the universe came into existence through a massive explosion about 14 billion years ago. As atoms and molecules were formed, matter condensed due to the gravitational force, and nuclear reactions resulted in the formation of stars and galaxies. Some of this condensed matter emitted enough light to cool down and form planets, and the Earth is one of the places on which life evolved through random mutations and natural selection, according to evolutionary theory. The main idea in Big Bang is that everything is created from almost 'nothing', or at least something unlike the form in which we see the universe presently. The nature of this 'nothing' and why it exploded in the first place, remains the subject of much debate and research to this day.

Modern cosmology is based on the idea that gravity is the key force responsible for the formation of galaxies, and when matter condenses due to gravity, at some point quantum effects trigger thermonuclear reactions, thus producing stars and other visible objects. Therefore, it is supposed that the large-scale structure of the universe is governed by gravity alone, although the atomic structure of matter and the other three natural forces—electromagnetism, weak and strong forces—play a part in the creation of atoms, molecules, and other complex structures. Therefore, in the early days of cosmology, gravity was the only theory considered important for describing the large-scale structure of the universe. In 1915, Einstein rewrote the laws of gravity in a general relativistic form, by imbibing the idea that all causal forces must take a finite time to produce an effect, modifying Newton's laws of gravitation in which the gravitational force indeed acted instantaneously. Since then, Einstein's generalized formation of gravity has become the mainstay in cosmology.

When Einstein formulated the generalized theory of gravity, he did not know if the universe was contracting, expanding, or static. All the observations until that time seemed to suggest that the universe was static. Since the Big Bang causes the universe to expand, to counter-balance this expansion (and produce a static universe) there must be something that controls the expansion. Of course, gravity is an attractive force, and therefore if there is enough matter in the universe, then gravity can itself control the expansion. However, it wasn't obvious whether there was indeed enough matter to control the universe's expansion just from gravity. The idea is like that of *escape velocity* used in the launch of satellites. If the rocket that launches the satellite has a low energy, then it will move upwards until all the kinetic energy in the rocket is converted into gravitational potential energy, and then it will fall back to Earth. If the rocket has very high energy, it will continue rising until it escapes the gravitational pull of the Earth. The Big Bang is the kinetic energy while mass is the gravitational force. If the initial expansion has a lot of energy, then it will cause the universe to expand for a long period of time. If the matter in the universe is high, the rate of expansion and the time the universe will expand would be curtailed by the gravitational attraction.

To describe the various scenarios, cosmologists postulate a property called the *critical density* that will decide the fate of the universe. If the critical density of matter is larger than this number, then there is enough gravitational attraction to halt the expansion and turn it around (like a rocket falling back to Earth). If, however, the matter density of the universe is lower than the critical density, then the mass of the universe does not exert enough gravitational attraction to stop the expansion (like the rocket escaping the gravitational pull of the Earth). Different values of the critical density entail different Big Bang scenarios. These values and the resulting fates of the universe are shown in Figure-12.

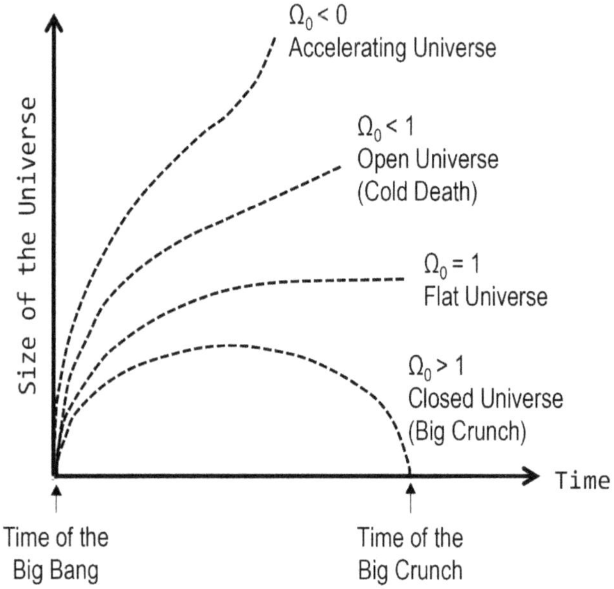

Figure-12 Big-Bang Scenarios in Modern Cosmology

- Big Crunch model: The universe expands initially but the gravitational pull overcomes the expansion and the universe collapses,
- Flat Expansion model: The universe expands for a while, but the expansion rate decreases with time, and eventually becomes zero,
- Open Expansion model: The universe continues to expand forever, although the rate of expansion eventually becomes a constant,
- Accelerating Expansion model: The universe expands forever, and the expansion rate continues to accelerate over time.

To estimate the fate of the universe, scientists estimated the total mass in the universe. The result of the estimation was that if we only consider the visible matter, then the value of Ω_0 is about 0.04 (much less than 1, but positive) which indicates an Open Expansion model. This idea was confirmed in 1929 when Hubble showed that light from certain galaxies is redshifted, suggesting that these galaxies were moving away. For nearly 70 years after this, the universe was regarded as continually expanding, although the rate of expansion was expected to slow down, since the energy of the Big Bang would be converted into the gravitational potential energy, which would then mean that there is lesser force pushing the universe apart. However, by the time the inflationary force reduces, the gravitational force has reduced further, and the universe thus continues to expand forever, although the rate slows with passing time.

All this changed in 1998 when the redshift measurements on some galaxies revealed that rather than slowing down, the galaxies were accelerating, implying that Ω_0 is negative. To explain the acceleration physicists postulate something called "dark energy" which is like anti-gravity: i.e., it pushes matter apart. Therefore, as the distance grows, the inflationary force increases, and not only will the universe continually expand, but expand at faster rates. This might result in what is now called the Big Rip, which eventually tears the universe apart into many small parts. Dark energy, therefore, is the opposite of the gravitational pull and requires a new kind of force that acts with the Big Bang rather than against it. There is no terrestrial evidence for dark energy, and therefore no way to actually perform measurements to confirm its existence. And yet, to explain the observed rate of acceleration, scientists estimate that dark energy is about 68.3% of all the matter-energy in the universe. The theory of this dark energy is the biggest open problem in cosmology today.

Cracks in the Gravitational Model

An equally problematic issue arises in the measurement of speeds for distant galaxies, when the gravitational theory is applied to explain this motion. According to gravity, the closer masses must rotate faster relative to the farther masses. For instance, in the solar system, the inner planets are supposed to move faster than the outer planets, and since the same theory applies to the galaxies, the outer parts of the galaxy are also expected to move slower as compared to the inner parts. Observations, however, indicate the opposite. It has been observed that the outer edges of our galaxy are moving much faster than they should be if all the matter in the galaxy was of the "visible" variety governed by the laws of gravity.

The problem with this observation is that if gravity is the only force that holds all parts of the galaxy together, and these parts are moving much faster, then, the outer edges of the galaxy must "fly off"—i.e., detach from the galaxy—but it doesn't happen. If, therefore, they are not flying off, then there must be something that holds them within the galaxy. This problem is now known as the Galaxy Rotation Problem[1], and the evidence suggests that most stars in a spiral galaxy (barring those at the very center) rotate at roughly the same speed. That is, the speed of rotation grows near the center of the galaxy, but then become relatively constant

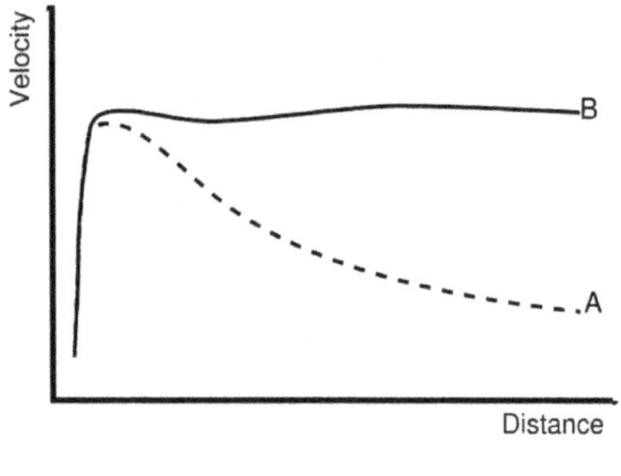

Figure-13 Rotation in a Spiral Galaxy

If the galaxy contains only matter governed by the laws of gravity then the observed speeds must follow curve A (i.e., decline as we go outward from the center of the galaxy). The observed speeds, however, follow the curve B—they remain roughly constant with distance. To explain this anomaly, cosmologists postulate that there is more mass in the galaxy than we see, and the invisible mass exerts a greater gravitational pull, which then causes the outer parts of the galaxy to move faster. This invisible mass is called "dark matter", and it is supposed to exist in a halo concentrated at the center of the galaxy. Obviously, it is difficult to estimate the *shape* of this halo (its distribution in the galaxy) unless the properties of dark matter are better understood. If this dark matter were just like visible matter, the halo would be roughly spherically symmetrical, but we don't know if dark matter is just like visible matter. Hence, the shape of the halo cannot yet be predicted, although many scientists, assuming that dark matter is just like visible matter, postulate a spherically symmetric halo. To correctly explain the rotational speeds, dark matter is estimated to be 26.8% of all the matter in the universe, which is in addition to the 68.3% matter which is estimated as dark energy to address the expansion issue. The laws of physics, as we know them today, therefore, only cover 4.9% of the universe; the other 95.1% is "dark". This is one of the biggest outstanding issues in current cosmological theories.

The Inverse Square Law

Distances to far away galaxies are measured in modern cosmology using the Inverse Square Law, which states that the luminosity of light decreases inversely with the square of the distance. Thus, if the galaxy is twice as far away as compared to an equally big galaxy, then the luminosity of the farther galaxy must be $1/4^{th}$ of the luminosity of the nearer galaxy. But to measure distance using this method, one must *a priori* know what the luminosity of the star is. For instance, if you know that you are measuring the light intensity of two 60W bulbs, and you knew the distance to one bulb, then you could measure the distance to the other too. But how do we know that both bulbs are 60W? Isn't it possible that one bulb is 40W while the other one is 100W? If the star is dimmer, but we compare its luminosity to that of a brighter star, and thereby interpret the smaller luminosity as a larger distance, then distances would be misinterpreted. To address this issue, we must find a way to estimate the luminosity of the star, before using it for distance measurement.

The primary method in this luminosity measurement is finding a star whose luminosity periodically oscillates in time. Such stars are called Cepheid stars and their luminosity oscillates (the periods could range from a few days to a couple of months). It is supposed that these stars oscillate due to an outward thermal pressure and an inward gravitational force being out of sync. As the star becomes bigger due to thermal pressure pushing it outward, more light is emitted thereby resulting in higher luminosity. As the star becomes smaller, the luminosity decreases. In 1912 Henrietta Leavitt published a relationship between the pulsating frequency and the observed luminosity across a number of stars. While we may not accurately measure luminosity, we can accurately measure the luminosity increase and decrease with time. This relationship is therefore expected to measure the period of the star, then use it to calculate the luminosity, and then use the luminosity to find distance using the Inverse Square Law. That is, periodicity → luminosity → distance. This is the method currently used to measure the distance to stars. In the above inference the relationship between luminosity and periods is the *observed* and not the *actual* luminosity, which implies that the Cepheid star may be more luminous but much farther away, or vice versa.

The relationship between luminosity and periodicity is quite like the relationship between the pitch and the tone of a vibrating string (e.g., in a musical instrument). If you pluck the string hard, it will create a louder sound (the analogue of luminosity) but still vibrate at the same frequency (the analogue of periodicity). Therefore, it is very hard to establish a relationship between the frequency of the string and how hard that string must be pulled. If you double the size of the string, then there is obviously more energy released which makes the pitch higher, although the frequency can remain the same. And if you move this higher pitch string farther away from yourself, then the sound can be simply dissipated in the distance and result in low pitch measurement. The point is that a string can be pulled harder and be farther away or be pulled softly and be close by. In both cases, it will vibrate with the same frequency. So, the frequency-luminosity relationship actually doesn't constitute a law.

The problem lies not in the observed relationship between luminosity and periodicity, but in the subsequent use of the Inverse Square Law to derive the distance from the luminosity. There is no reason to suppose that just because a star is less luminous it must necessarily be farther away, although we can say that if the luminosity of the star is known, then a higher distance would entail a lower luminosity. A loudly vibrating sting far away and a softly vibrating string nearby can produce the same luminosity and the same frequency. The Inverse Square Law works forwards (i.e., from known intensity and known distance to perceived intensity) but does not work backwards (from observed luminosity to actual luminosity and distance). The Cepheid star luminosity is observed luminosity, not the actual one. When this observed luminosity is used to compute distance, the observation is converted into a claim about reality.

Distances from Doppler Shifts

Another key problem in distance measurement lies in the use of Doppler shifts to infer distance. The Doppler Effect is the everyday phenomenon that sound emitting objects (e.g., an ambulance) moving farther away from us produce a lower frequency sound (i.e., the tone of the ambulance's siren lower as it moves away from us). In the case of cosmic distances, it is supposed that the universe is expanding due to the Big Bang, so if we observe the Doppler shift in light, we must infer that the stars must be moving away. Hubble's Law provides this relationship between the Doppler shift of light and the distance. In the case of the Doppler effect (for sound), the shift depends upon the speed of the moving object. So, the shift itself cannot be used to infer the distance. For instance, you can have a toy ambulance in your living room produce the same effect of fading sound as the real ambulance far away on a distant street. This fact is possible because the speed of sound is supposed to be relative to the motion of the source and the destination (i.e., if the source or the destination are moving, then sound will take a longer time to reach its destination).

However, the speed of light has been measured to be independent of the motion of the source and destination, and this fact forms the basis of the modern theory of relativity where the speed of light is treated as a *law* of nature which remains invariant for all observers. Therefore, the Doppler shift (in the case of light) is explained as arising from the expansion of space itself between the source and the destination:

if we observe the Doppler shift, it must be because the intervening space must have expanded *after* light left the source and just *before* it reaches its destination. The greater the distance, the greater must be the expansion, and by measuring the shift, therefore, we should be able to estimate the distance.

Thus, in the case of a Doppler Effect in sound, the shift is due to the relative speeds of the source and the destination, and there is no dependence on the distance between them. However, in the case of a Doppler shift in light, the shift is due to the expansion of space, and a greater distance implies a greater time available for space to expand even more, and therefore the shift becomes a function of the distance between objects.

This is a classic case of postulating a theory (the Big Bang), using it to interpret the observation, and then finding that the interpretation confirms the theory. For instance, this interpretation would be false if the stars were transmitting a Doppler-shifted spectrum and the universe was not actually expanding. The problem of interpretation therefore hinges upon asking: Is the universe expanding and the Doppler shift is an *effect* of that expansion? Or, are the stars transmitting a Doppler shifted spectrum, which is then used to *infer* that the universe is expanding? In the former case, we formulate a theory of expansion, and use Doppler shift as evidence for that theory. In the latter case, we formulate a theory of Doppler shift in the stars, and don't need the notion of universal expansion. Which of these approaches must be preferred and adopted remains a theoretical question, but one that is seldom asked in modern physics.

One of the dogmas in modern science is that the universe is *uniform* everywhere. That is, the same laws of nature apply everywhere, and the same kind of matter exists everywhere. This dogma precludes the idea that the stars could themselves be transmitting a Doppler-shifted spectrum, as it would entail that the stars are different from us. So, we begin by assuming that the stars are just like us, and the Doppler shift must therefore be attributed to expansion. If you dropped this dogma, the entire Big Bang hypothesis would become unnecessary, although it would require us to form a new theory that explains Doppler-shifted stars.

Philosophers of science recognize that data underdetermines the theory. You can interpret the data in different ways, and before you can start interpreting, you must have a theory. If the theory is wrong, then you arrive at a wrong interpretation, although it appears to be internally consistent. You can also find another theory that, too, is internally consistent, although it interprets data in a completely different manner. Over time, however, this equivalence between theories begins to fail as we find more and more phenomena that don't fit the essential dogmas underlying some theory, although they fit the other theory quite well. Practically, therefore, science should simultaneously evaluate multiple hypotheses in parallel and continue evaluating which of them fit better with the observations. However, this generally does not happen in science. When the observations don't fit the premises in the theory, there is a tendency to add a different set of assumptions to upgrade the theory. For instance, the observed Doppler shifts now indicate not just expansion, but accelerating expansion, which doesn't fit the gravitational theory, and to explain it, we must postulate "dark energy", which needs a new theory.

The Constant Speed of Light

When Newton formulated the gravitational law, he presumed instantaneous action at a distance. Since the planets were pulling each other, there was action at a distance, but this action was supposed to occur instantaneously through the action of a 'field' between them. Over time, it was discovered that there is action, but it is not instantaneous. That is, it takes some time for the cause to become an effect. The simplest scheme at that time to explain this idea was to suppose that the cause is also a *particle* and it *travels* in space to its destination before it becomes an effect, and since this travel must take a finite amount of time, the action cannot be instantaneous. In modern science, these traveling messengers of cause are called *bosons* (photons, gravitons, etc.). A problem, however, quickly arose that if a boson is traveling in space, and an observer travels towards it, then it should meet the boson faster than if the observer was static. This was contrary to observations on the speed of light, where it was shown that even if the observer travels towards the light, he will not 'meet' light sooner than if he was just stationary. This then led to the postulate that the cause moves, and therefore it must have a speed of motion, but that speed is constant for all observers. This speed now came to be understood as the speed at which all forces travel, including gravity.

The problem in this view arises from quantum physics where space and time are discrete (not continuous). If there are a finite number of hops between a source and a destination, and light hops from one place to another, and you happen to hop towards the light, then you have already covered some number of hops, and you should therefore meet light sooner. How can the light 'know' that you are hopping towards it, and therefore slow down its rate of hopping so that you and the light meet at the same time as if you were never hopping? This fact is never understood or explained in modern science; we just assume that the speed of light is a constant, and scientific theories take this to be a law of nature. Indeed, all distances to stars and galaxies are measured in light-years.

There is, however, another way of interpreting the constant time taken for a cause to manifest into an effect: we can suppose that the light takes zero time to reach the destination, but it takes a finite amount of time to be 'absorbed' into the destination to produce an effect. That premise would explain the constant delay from source to destination (regardless of the observer's motion) much better because now the time spent in travel is immaterial (it always takes zero time), and only the time taken to absorb light would contribute to the delay in the effect being manifest. If the light is indeed a discrete particle, then it can only be absorbed in chunks, so we cannot say that the light is 'slowly' being absorbed. Therefore, the effect is only manifest after the particle has been completely absorbed, although a finite amount of time is necessary to absorb it.

Think of light as a message being sent from a teacher to a student. If the student is already familiar with all the things that the teacher has been teaching, and the new message only adds little incrementally to the previously existing knowledge, then the message is quickly grasped. If, however, the student lacks the necessary concepts, then a far greater change to the receiver must occur to incorporate this new meaning, since the previously missing concepts must also be incorporated. The time taken for a message to reach a knowledgeable and an ignorant student is the same. However, the time taken to absorb the knowledge is different. If light were a message, and it causes changes to configurations of the receiver's brain (or a measuring instrument), the difference would be attributed to the state of the receiver, not to the distance to the receiver.

This interpretation of light not only explains the constant speed of light much better, but it also alters the current interpretations of distances to celestial bodies. We can now say that the distance to the celestial body isn't necessarily very high (just like the distance between the student and the teacher need not be very great), although there is a state transition involved in the measuring instrument that takes time. This time must be described in terms of a quantum process causing a reconfiguration of matter, rather than a long time in receiving a photon.

In current science, we presume that light takes a long time to travel in space, but it is absorbed instantaneously. However, we can also say that light travels instantaneously, and absorption takes a longer time. In the latter case, a reformulation of the laws of classical physics resulting in a relativistic theory of gravity would be unnecessary, and all subsequent consequences of this theory in terms of cosmological views—such as a Big Bang—would be unfounded. We would now say that objects cause action at a distance, and that action is transferred instantaneously (like in Newton's physics) but the conversion of that action into an effect takes time. This delay in action would now arise from state transitions of atomic objects, rather than from the delay in light propagation.

The key point is that we have assumed so much based on the constant speed of light, without understanding why that speed is constant, and whether our explanations represent a good understanding of nature or they are merely trying to retrofit the observed phenomena into a classical physical picture of nature. Ideas such as the constant speed of light take a purely classical phenomena—i.e., motion—and try to foist it upon quantum reality when that reality doesn't support the premises underlying motion (such as continuity of space and time) themselves. Lots of other things, including our cosmological theories, are then derived from these theories, when the essential foundations are themselves not sound. If the foundation collapses, so does the entire superstructure.

Remnants of Wave Theory

Prior to the advent of quantum physics, light was modeled as a wave, which spread equally in all directions. This was necessary to explain the interference of light. Subsequently, this wave was replaced by a probability function in quantum physics, and it is now empirically confirmed that light particles don't arrive at all equidistant points in space simultaneously as they were supposed to arrive earlier when light was modeled as a wave. Rather, there is an order in the arrival of photons, which current quantum theory does not predict. At some locations, the light particles may arrive frequently, while at others they may never arrive, or arrive much less frequently than at other locations. If these photons are passed through a certain number of slits in front of a photographic plate (in what is called the slit experiment[2]), bands of light and dark are formed on the plate, which correspond to the measured *intensity* of light at that point on the plate. The number of slits corresponds to our measurement procedure, and the observations on the photographic plate represent the *outcome* of that procedure. Different numbers of slits produce different patterns of light and dark, which entails that by doing different measurements on the same system, we would get different outcomes[3].

There is much debate currently about the real meaning of these quantum experiments, and it arises primarily because we don't have a well-agreed upon understanding of the nature of the slits. Are these slits part of the measuring instrument, or part of the measured system? I have discussed this problem at length previously[4], and will not delve deep into this topic here. However, a few things can briefly be said about this problem. If we treat the slits as analogues of our senses, then we can interpret the quantum problem as producing a different *view* of the same reality. Like $100 can be divided in many ways into different denominations ($1, $5, $10, etc.), similarly, the same reality can be partitioned in many ways. The order in which quanta are detected subsequently, is a function of two things: (1) our method of dividing reality, and (2) the nature of reality.

The number of slits we choose to divide reality represents the property being measured, and it interacts with reality to produce a representation of that property. However, this division is not physical, but semantic. That is, we are dividing meaning into symbols of that meaning, and these symbols appear in different orders depending on the vocabulary we choose to express that meaning. The slits in the quantum experiment are analogues of the choice of a language in which physical objects become symbols of meaning. A common example of this fact is that we can represent a number in binary, ternary, quaternary, octal, decimal, or hexadecimal representations. The number being represented is the same, but the *scheme* of expression is different. Accordingly, the meaning symbolized by a quantum object (e.g., a photon) also changes. Thus, for instance, in a numerical representation of a number, the digit denoted by the different quanta would never be identical but would depend on the chosen of scheme of representation. Similarly, the order of digit arrival depends on the scheme and the number being represented. If we can interpret the slits as a method of representation, then the order of quantum arrival becomes a sequence of digits, which can then be converted into a number, producing a *description* of the reality being measured.

The quantum phenomena represent the act of reading a book. The whole book is a single number, but it is divided into parts through a representation in terms of symbols, which depend on a chosen vocabulary and language. If we change the language, the symbols will change, and so will the observation. Similarly, if we change the book, the symbols will again change. The key point is that all possible words will never be observed, because there is a fixed reality, and a chosen vocabulary.

This fact is incredibly important for cosmology because it implies that depending on our chosen method of perception, light is not uniformly distributed across space, like we would have presumed in the earlier days of wave theory. Rather, there are bands of light and dark, which depend on the object being measured and on our method of measurement. The bands of light and dark represent the relative probability with which a particular word or symbol recurs in a description. This probability then becomes the luminosity of the light we observe, and it has nothing to do with the *distance* to the luminary from the observer.

In modern cosmology, we interpret these bands of light and dark as the luminosity of the stars, and then convert this luminosity into distance! If the cosmos was actually treated quantum mechanically, we would see that there is zero correlation between the luminosity and the distance, and all the correlation between the object being observed, and our method of perception. For instance, if you are reading a romantic novel, and the words 'passion' and 'love' appear frequently, this recurrence doesn't imply that these words are closer relative to the other words that appear less frequently. All the words are equally distant in this case, although their relative frequencies depend on the meaning encoded in the book, and the language in which the author has written the book.

When astronomers observe the distant stars, the pictures are built over time through the reception of thousands if not millions of photons. The exact time delay between these receptions, or the order in which different locations on the photographic plate receive the photons, is simply not considered in the interpretation of data. What we eventually obtain is just light and dark patches on a picture, and then we go about interpreting these patches using the classical *wave theory of light* rather than a quantum mechanical picture of reality. According to wave theory, light is going equally in all directions, and if we got less light, it means that the star is either small or very distant. According to quantum theory, light is *not* going equally to all detectors, and if we got less light, it just means that the location had a low probability of receiving the photons.

Just like we don't interpret light and dark patches in a two-slit experiment into distances to the light source, similarly, we need not interpret the observed luminosity of the stars into their distance. It may just be that we are not receiving the light either because the star is not transmitting enough in the direction in which we are situated, or because our method of perception divides the light in a way that the probability with which we can perceive light is far smaller as compared to other locations in the universe. In other words, if the same phenomenon is interpreted according to quantum theory, all notions about distance based on luminosity of light are simply vacuous. The problem today is that science doesn't understand quantum phenomena, and therefore restricts it to atomic reality. If the entire universe were described as a quantum system, rather than as a classical system, a radical new interpretation of the same phenomena would be constructed. As we have seen, data underdetermine the theory; the same data under a new theory produces a different model of reality. In this case, the model of the universe would be quite different under quantum physics, rather than relativistic physics.

The Problem of Unification

One of the key problems in modern physics is its fragmented nature. As we have seen earlier, there are three broad theories that apply to different scales: (1) quantum theory to atomic objects, (2) thermodynamics to macroscopic objects, and (3) general relativity to cosmic objects. Quantum theory is linear but non-deterministic. Thermodynamics is non-linear and non-deterministic. General relativity is deterministic and non-linear. Each of them emerged from classical physics, which was linear and deterministic, because some phenomena did not fit the theory. Finding the theory that fits all the *known* phenomena in physics is an unsolved problem today. Extending this understanding to even harder problems such as perception, meaning, and the nature of life, is even tougher.

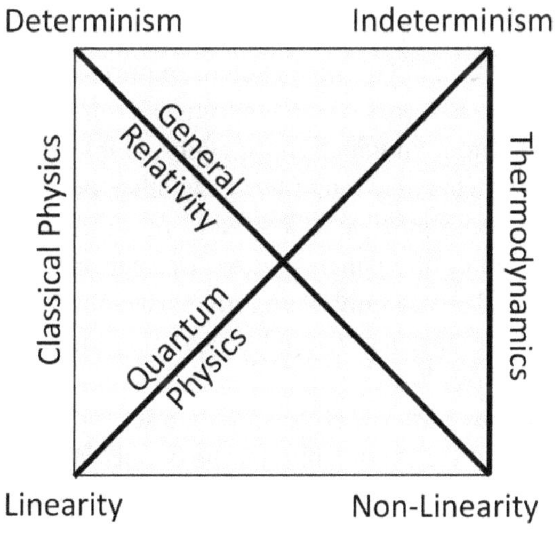

Figure-14 The Quadrant of Incompatible Theories

We have seen above how the induction of quantum theoretic ideas into relativity changes our understanding of basic ideas such as the speed of light and the uniform distribution of light in the universe. In this section I will describe how even more profound revisions to quantum theory would be entailed by the introduction of thermodynamic principles.

But, first, let's understand how thermodynamics is different from classical physics. In classical physics, when two objects collide, one object can transfer all its energy to the second object. In thermodynamics, this can never happen. When a hot and a cold body are in contact with each other, the hot body will transfer energy until it acquires the same 'temperature', and the transfer must then stop. Only if you put the cold body in touch with an even colder body, can the transfer of energy occur. However, the reverse transfers never happen. For instance, after transferring energy from a hot to a cold body, the cold body will never transfer the energy back to the hot body. This idea is very counterintuitive if we think of it in terms of particles, although it is so pervasive that we seldom stop to think about it. If there are particles, there should be no reason to transfer energy in one direction and not in the opposite direction. What prevents the opposite transfer, and if this prevention was included in a theory of heat transfers, how will it change physical theories?

A good understanding of this problem requires us to see that matter is constructed as layers of information. That is, there is a layer of abstract information, on which more concrete information is added. Thus, all the particles may look physically alike, but they are semantically different: one particle is a symbol of an abstract idea, while another is a symbol of a concrete idea. The concrete symbol cannot exist unless the abstract symbol already exists, and therefore we can never remove the abstract symbol unless the concrete symbol has already been removed.

A hot object has both concrete and abstract symbols, but the cold object only has the abstraction but not the details. When the hot object transfers heat to a cold object, some of the details are transferred, until both objects are equal in information. Thereafter, information transfer cannot occur, because both objects have the same information, so what are they going to exchange? In a physical theory, we can send information regardless of whether the receiver needs it or not. In other words, you can spam a system with useless information. In a semantic theory, we can only send information if it is missing, and needs to be added. Two considerations are important therefore: (1) the information is missing, and (2) the information is required. All missing things are not required, but something must be missing before it is even required. In that sense, whether information is missing is logically prior to whether it is required. In the case of two objects that have exchanged information and have arrived at the same temperature, there is no information they can exchange because there is nothing missing in them relative to each other. If this information is required, another hotter (or colder) object must be brought into contact, to produce a new information transaction.

These ideas are important for quantum theory because they indicate that quantum state transitions too cannot happen unless one object is causally entangled with another that needs information. Present quantum theory cannot predict when energy would be emitted or absorbed. And when this energy is emitted or absorbed, which quantum system will actually emit or absorb it. Furthermore, these two questions of when and which are considered separate due to the wave theory of light: whenever a system emits, whichever system lies in the path will absorb it. The implication of thermodynamics is that these two questions are actually a single question: the interaction of two systems must be fixed, which automatically fixes the time and the type of information exchange. The apparent randomness in quantum theory is therefore because we don't know how two systems are being causally entangled, and therefore we cannot predict when a quantum will be emitted, and where it will go. This indeterminism then leads to probability and we can only predict light and dark patches, not which quantum object will actually go where.

If there is a source S and a destination D, then no physical theory can actually predict when S will emit and D will absorb. Informationally, however, this is because there is another cause C, which entangles S and D, which then automatically creates a 'thermal gradient' of information flow between them. Unless C exists, S potentially has a thermal gradient with innumerable destinations, and no specific destination can be chosen, so the state transition is unpredictable. Similarly, D can receive information from innumerable sources, and unless a particular source is decided, no information is received. The cause C, therefore, is *different* from both the source S and the destination D, and we cannot explain the state transitions if we keep measuring only the material properties of S and D.

When heat is transferred from a hot to a cold object, the transfer hinges upon the *choice* of putting the hot and the cold in physical contact. The same process must occur in quantum phenomena as well, although now, the source and the destination are not necessarily in physical proximity. Rather, a new cause must be envisioned that establishes the channel of communication between the source and the destination. When this channel appears, the information is automatically transferred. If the channel disappears, the information flow is naturally halted. The new kind of causality in nature is therefore the creation and destruction of channels. These channels are the roads on which information can flow, but they don't always exist, and when they exist, they are not necessarily *allocated* to a particular pair of source and destination. Thus, innumerable objects can exist in the universe, but they are not always connected to each other. Rather, this connection must be dynamically established by a new kind of cause that science doesn't presently understand, due to which information flow from one source to a destination cannot be predicted.

This idea has an important implication for cosmology, namely, that the light from the distant stars was not emitted billions of years ago and is just arriving here right now, and we just happen to be in the path of the light. Rather, that light is emitted when the channel between the source and the destination is established, so there is no transmission of light until that channel is created. The stars are not spamming the world with light. Rather, there are messages *intended* for some receivers. The messages are transmitted, received, and absorbed. The transmission doesn't take time, although absorption takes time. But this time isn't longer than our lifetimes. Rather, the transmission is started at the beginning of our life, and it takes time to manifest in our life as experiences. When the information manifests, we imagine that the light is received just now, when the light has been received earlier and has taken time to produce an effect. This is like a person reading a book: he has the book in his hand, but he is reading it slowly, digesting, and assimilating information.

Current cosmology is based on the wave theory of light—i.e., light goes equally in all directions. When this theory is updated with quantum physics, light cannot go in all directions, but must go in some specific directions, and the luminosity of light received is not an indication of its distance, but simply an indication of the fact that it was transmitted to a specific location. Furthermore, when the quantum theory is enhanced with the thermodynamic notion that information only travels through some channels, which must be established before the information transfer can occur, the indeterminism in quantum theory is overcome, and we can see that the real cause of our experiences is the channel, and the part of our experience it impacts depends on which part of our body the channel is communicating with. The same light can therefore cause a different effect in us, which we cannot presently explain because we don't have a theory of channel establishment and how these are created.

Cosmic Microwave Background

Central to the empirical confirmation of the Big Bang theory is the detection of the Cosmic Microwave Background (CMB), which is supposed to be a relic of the Big Bang. It is hypothesized that early in the Big Bang the universe was so hot and dense that light could not 'freely' travel in the universe, as it would quickly hit an electron or proton. This interaction would prevent the formation of atoms such as Hydrogen. However, as the universe expands, it also cools down, and the photons are not preventing the formation of Hydrogen atoms anymore, and since matter only occupies a small percentage of the total space (which is expanding), light can now begin to travel freely. As the universe expands more and more, light can travel even more freely as it would not be absorbed by an object. Over millions of years, the universe has expanded so much that two things can be said: (1) the wavelength of the radiation that originally existed during the Big Bang must have also expanded, resulting in a large redshift, and (2) all the objects from which we could suppose this radiation to be originating must have already moved out due to expansion, such that we can no longer associate this radiation as an emission of a known star.

The time from which the light moved freely is called the recombination period, and Big Bang calculations predict the temperature of that period to be 3000 K. The CMB is currently detected to be 2.7 K, which means that the universe expanded 3000 / 2.7 = 1100 times since then.

CMB made a lot of sense when dark matter and dark energy had not been postulated, because the fact that we cannot attribute this radiation to any luminous object could be explained by the fact that this radiation is a relic of the past. Today, when we postulate dark matter and energy, there is no necessity to suppose that this radiation is indeed from the Big Bang. Why could we not suppose, for instance, that this radiation is an effect of dark energy or dark matter which we cannot see anyway? The problem in such an interpretation would be that if we take CMB as a fact about dark matter or energy, then the Big Bang itself would not have an empirical confirmation, which means that the subsequent problems that necessitate the hypothesis of dark energy or matter would itself not exist, which would then undermine the idea that CMB is due to them.

Unless the problem of dark energy and matter is solved, therefore, CMB cannot be viewed as a confirmation of the Big Bang, because CMB can also be explained due to other reasons, which exist in current cosmology, and which are in no way better or worse than the Big Bang itself.

In the semantic view described earlier, a longer wavelength (smaller frequency) radiation can be understood as abstract information while shorter wavelengths (higher frequency) radiation can be understood as detailed information. In quantum physics, the frequency of the radiation is proportional to the energy carried by the quantum (Planck's law), therefore, when an object is hot, it must emit shorter frequency radiation (on average) to quickly dissipate the heat, and as an object cools down, the object must emit lower frequency radiation (on average). We have seen above that the confusions in thermodynamics are resolved when we treat a hot object as rich in detailed information, and a cold object as possessing only abstract information. Therefore, the higher frequency radiation emitted by a hot object should be considered detailed information, while the lower frequency radiation should be treated as abstract information. When an object cools down, only abstractions are left, and therefore, the energy emitted from the cool object gets redshifted (i.e., becomes abstract), and this redshift therefore denotes abstractions.

The correlation between a hot and a cold object to the frequency of radiation observed, therefore, has a completely different understanding in the semantic view. The result of this understanding is that the CMB is abstract information and the reason that we cannot correlate it to cosmic objects is because they are more abstract than the observation of the senses, and cannot therefore be seen, although their *effects* can be seen. The CMB is an effect, whose cause is a much more abstract object. This cause will act upon an atomic object that is a symbol of an abstraction, rather than on atomic objects that are symbols of the details. Such abstract symbols are far fewer as compared to the details. When the radiation acts upon an abstraction, it simultaneously causes a number of changes to the details of the system, reorienting the system as a whole in a way that we cannot pinpoint which particular part is being changed. This is because all the parts are being changed simultaneously, which is quite counterintuitive if we think of radiation as changing only one atom. The result of this coordinated change is that we cannot say which direction the radiation is coming from, and we must therefore conclude that it is coming from 'everywhere'. This conclusion is not a fact, although it arises when we cannot pinpoint how the cause creates an effect.

To know the source of abstract information, we would need to describe the measuring instrument quantum mechanically; i.e., as a conceptual rather than a physical object. Then we can say that a specific type of information was received, and because it was abstract information, it reorganized the entire system. We measure that reorganized system and infer that information must have been received from many directions, considering the fact that the system is undergoing bigger changes.

The fact is that when abstract information is received, many small changes will occur to the entire system, rather than a big change to a single part. In other words, the energy received through a low energy radiation would be quickly distributed in the entire system, which would not happen when the information is detailed. Detailed information would only change a specific part of the measuring instrument, but abstract information will change many parts simultaneously. This is commonly called 'conduction' in a thermal system where the heat in the system is quickly redistributed. The redistribution is however much faster in the case of abstract information than in the case of detailed information. This fact, therefore, presents a new kind of empirical phenomenon, which cannot be explained in current quantum physics, and necessitates a semantic view. The key point is that the semantic view isn't merely a reinterpretation of the current data but enables additional predictions as well.

The above understanding of redshift can now help us go back to the question of Doppler redshifts, which are currently interpreted as implying an expansion. In the semantic view, they can be interpreted as transmitting abstract information, relative to the information we are accustomed to. This would mean that the source of this light isn't the atoms and molecules (such as Hydrogen and Helium) that we observe on the present planet. Rather, these atoms are in themselves constructions that we have made by interpreting our observations, and then extending these interpretations to the rest of the universe. If we drop the Cosmological Hypothesis that the universe is uniform throughout, then the semantic view allows us to reinterpret Doppler shifts as arising from a different *kind* of source than the energy sources we observe on Earth.

The semantic view therefore takes out the two most important reasons we believe in the Big Bang today: (1) CMB, and (2) Doppler shifts. The result of this interpretation is that the universe need not be *expanding*. Rather, the universe has a static structure, although that structure is based on semantic information rather than physical objects. If the universe is not expanding and has a static structure, then its explanation requires a different process than which is postulated in current science.

Gravitational Waves

While writing this book, the scientific community became enthralled by the discovery of gravitational waves. While this discovery confirmed one of the last predictions of Einstein's gravitational theory, the discovery itself brings in no new theoretical principles, such as the pending unification of scientific theories. The essence of the discovery of gravitational waves involves the detection of a periodic expansion and contraction of space. If, within a tunnel, radiation is sent in both directions the expansion and contraction of space would change the *phase* of the wave and cause constructive and destructive interferences at different times.

Figure-15 Experiment for Gravitational Waves

This interference can be detected through electronics, and if this change is periodic, then the measurement can be inferred as the confirmation of gravitational waves. The question is whether this detection represents the confirmation of gravity, or whether it could also be interpreted differently. Figure-15 illustrates the experimental setup used for the measurement of gravitational waves. In this setup, there are two legs of a long tunnel at right angles to each other. As electromagnetic waves propagate in both directions, they interfere with each other and the interference produces a combined wave. If the lengths of the tunnels remain invariant, then there is a standard interference pattern. If, however, the lengths change, then the interference pattern would also change.

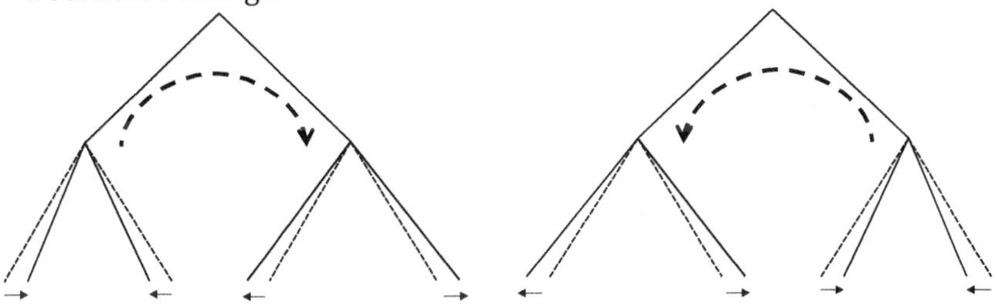

Figure-16 Contraction and Dilation by Information Flow

The essence of the Gravitational Wave detection lies in the question of length contraction and dilation. If gravity were indeed the correct way to explain the universe (which would mean that the observational anomalies that give rise to the need for dark energy and dark matter would not exist), then this wave would arise through the rotation of heavy objects in space. This rotation requires another heavy object, and the detection is therefore supposed to be caused by a pair of black holes, which is another kind of 'darkness' since light cannot escape a black hole. The same phenomenon can however be explained differently in the informational view as shown in Figure-16 in which physical distances increase and reduce when information flows from one node on the tree to another. The node that is losing information will contract because the loss of information reduces the distinction between the nodes. Similarly, the node that is gaining information will expand because gaining information increases the distinction between the nodes. Any information transfer would therefore result in the expansion and contraction of space.

Generally, however, information transfers are so small that it is very difficult to measure these changes using macroscopic instruments. If, therefore, the information transfer is substantial, then the changes can be detected macroscopically. This information transfer need not be caused by a black hole binary; it can also be created by massive amounts of detailed information transfer between two objects, which will cause one object to shrink in size, and the other one to expand, or, by a symbol that represents abstract information. An abstract symbol transfer can quickly and dramatically change the size of objects, while the detailed symbol transfer will require a large number of symbols. They key point is that the physical size of the symbol itself doesn't entail the resulting size of the object. It is rather the *type* of information denoted by that symbol which can alter the size of objects. The transfer of abstract information resulting in a change in size would, however, require a theory of types.

In the gravitational theory, changes occur due to the expansion and contraction of space. This assumes that there is a space comprised of physical points, the *metric* of which changes due to gravity. In the semantic theory, there isn't an *a priori* real space unless information is used to construct that point. The physical distance to a point doesn't entail that all the intervening points are real. We know that any theory that supposes that all possible points in space between any two points exist, would be inconsistent with quantum physics. Therefore, the explanation of space expansion and contraction in the gravitational theory (which assumes continuity of space and time) is inconsistent with quantum physics and presents the same problem of theory unification in science.

In the semantic approach, space does not expand or contract, although the *physical distance* (which represents the semantic difference) can change. The cause of this change is informational content change either to a node in space which represents abstract information, or to many nodes that represent detailed information. The number of quanta exchanged in this process may therefore be high or low. The former change would also result in minor changes to the details of many other objects, while the latter change would require only a change to the abstract conceptual representation of the macroscopic object itself. The observation that currently appears to confirm the existence of gravitational waves can therefore have a radically different interpretation as well, which would not require gravity, although it would require a new theory of atomic phenomena. That shift would also get rid of the conflicting conceptual approaches in quantum and relativity theories. Indeed, they would explain atomic, macroscopic, and cosmic phenomena by the same theory.

The Relation to Vedic Philosophy

In Vedic philosophy, the channels of communication are called *karma* and the material objects to which these are established are called *guna*. The light from the luminaries is therefore not traveling arbitrarily all over the universe. Rather, a specific type of information is transmitted to a specific part of our existence, to produce an effect. This transmission is fixed at the beginning of our lives, and it manifests gradually, as the information is gradually absorbed, thereby producing various kinds of effects. There is an intricate connection between the *karma* and the *guna*—the *guna* represent our biases of perception, and the *karma* represents the *consequences* of seeing the world in a particular biased way, which is not currently modeled in modern science. The *karma* lies dormant, like a book that is in our hands, although we haven't read it yet. As we read the book, this *karma* manifests, bringing new experiences in our life.

The *karma* and *guna* are the "dark" parts of reality because we cannot see them *before* they manifest. And yet, their existence is a theoretical necessity to explain our observations. From this "dark" reality, many more levels of dark reality are produced—namely, senses, mind, intellect, ego, and morality—which too we cannot perceive. However, the *effects* of all these realities can be perceived, either immediately when the experiences manifest, or later, when the consequence of the *guna* produces a *karma* which lies dormant but is eventually manifest as experience.

Even if we don't understand or accept all these aspects of Vedic philosophy, but simply follow the path of scientific theory unification as outlined above, it would be possible to understand why Vedic cosmology is so different than modern cosmology: the difference is not due to the ignorance in Vedic seers preventing them to see some parts of the universe, but lies within science due to which it is unable to unify its own theories, and when experimental data is interpreted according to the false theories, a misrepresentation of the universe is naturally produced. Since all models come from theories, the discrepancy in the models isn't of primary importance, as most people tend to think. Rather, this discrepancy must be traced to the theory of nature, and why the current scientific theories are inadequate, even by the present scientific standards. It is not necessary to rely on Vedic theories to arrive at an understanding of why science is inadequate, because, as described earlier, there are well-known problems in science that necessitate a change. The understanding of Vedic theories only accelerates the process of their correction.

Science begins by assuming that the universe was produced from a Big Bang, and this dogma is then used to interpret the observations. Sometimes, we find confirmations—e.g., when we see Doppler shifts of galaxies moving away. At other times, the same dogmas produce new problems—e.g., when we see that the Doppler shift indicates that the galaxies are accelerating away—which then create new ideas such as dark energy and dark matter that need to be reconciled within current theories, when these theories themselves are mutually inconsistent.

The mystery of dark energy and dark matter is puzzling because dark matter is that which pulls the universe inward while dark energy pushes it outward. We would typically imagine that if our current understanding of the universe is inadequate, it must be inadequate in either the inward pull or the outward push, not both. The fact that both forces are required to explain different observations makes the problem that much harder. The observed speeds of rotation (under the gravitational model of the universe) suggest that there must be much more hidden matter—which is of the same kind as visible matter. The observed expansion of the different galaxies from each other suggests that there is more hidden energy—which is of the opposite kind than the visible matter (dark matter is attractive while dark energy is repulsive). How can there be more of both attractive and repulsive stuff in the same universe?

Most parts of the universe are dark for our sense perceptions, in the same way that we can see a car's body, but we cannot see the idea of a vehicle. The idea of a vehicle is more abstract than the idea of a car, which is more abstract relative to an actual car. In the semantic view, a car is also a concept, although more detailed. That is, a real car is produced by detailing the idea of a car. These abstract and contingent concepts are organized in an inverted semantic tree: the root of the tree is the most abstract idea, and the leaves of the tree are the most contingent ideas.

Far from the root, and closer to the leaves, are our *senses:* they are more abstract than the objects they observe, but less abstract than the mind which sees meanings, the intellect which judges, the ego which creates intentions, and the moral sense which generates moral values. The senses represent the ideas of color, form, tone, taste, smell, touch, etc. We can see a shade of color—e.g., redness—but we cannot see color itself. Similarly, we can hear a tone—e.g., the note "C"—but we cannot hear tone itself. Our senses are more abstract than the objects they perceive, but this is only the beginning of abstractions. There are many other tiers of abstractions beyond the senses—meanings in the mind, judgments in the intellect, intentions in the ego, and moral values in the moral sense.

All these tiers of abstractions—beginning with the senses of observation—are "dark" from the standpoint of our sensual observations (sight, sound, touch, taste, and smell) because we cannot perceive them. The inability to perceive these properties, however, does not make them causally inactive: the abstract entities have effects on the visible entities, although we cannot *model* these causal effects in the same way that science has so far modeled causes—i.e., using *physical properties*.

For instance, if you say that you have some intentions, and someone asks you to "demonstrate" their existence, you would not be able to point to a specific physical object that corresponds to the intentions. However, you can still demonstrate your intentions by acting in accordance with them. The intention itself, therefore, cannot be shown, although its effects can be demonstrated. If, however, you eliminate the intention from the picture, and try to explain the behavior simply based on physical properties, then the explanation would only be statistically accurate. For instance, you will find that the same physical state can lead to different behaviors, making the predictive process only a correlation, not a cause. Intentions therefore have effects on behavior, and they must be used to explain behavior, but we cannot perceive the intentions themselves. This is unlike physical causality where you can perceive the object and postulate that it causes some effects—e.g., gravity. The correct way to understand intentions is that they are "dark" from the standpoint of our senses—i.e., they cannot be perceived by the senses—although they exist because they have effects on the material objects which can be perceived.

The mystery of dark energy and dark matter is that there appears to be something which is pushing and pulling the matter in the universe both inwards and outwards, and while we cannot perceive the existence of this matter or energy by the senses, we can perceive its *effects*.

It is possible to understand why something cannot be perceived although its effects can be perceived: these entities are conceptually more abstract than the senses themselves. The senses can see the objects, because they are more abstract than the objects. Therefore, for us to perceive the subtle material entities, we must employ a method that is even more subtle than the property we are measuring. The matter that we can see via our senses is a fraction of the matter that exists in the universe, and this fact is evidenced by the discovery that over 95% of matter in the universe is "dark". To understand this dark energy and dark matter, we need to redefine the nature of matter from being things to being ideas. If all matter is just things, then all things must be perceivable. If, however, matter is ideas, then some ideas can be perceived, while other ideas can only be thought, judged, intended, and valued, although not perceived. To even understand the existence of such ideas, we must refine our notions about perception to include deeper forms of perceptual abilities.

Dark energy and dark matter are therefore "dark" because they are more abstract than objects and cannot be modeled as *physical properties*. Their existence and effects need a shift in our view of matter. If all matter is physical, then it must also always be perceivable. It must also cause changes via forces. If some matter is ideas, then how could it interact with things? For ideas to interact with things, things themselves must be redefined as ideas—although more contingent than the ideas in the mind.

I previously described how abstract and contingent entities can be seen as nodes of a space-time tree structure. The universe—under this structure—is governed not by mass or gravity, but by the structure of space-time itself. The forms in this space-time represent not just mass (as in the case of Gravitational Theory) but any kind of semantic information. Some forms are abstract ideas while other forms are contingent ideas. Our bodies and minds are, in a sense, simply modifications of space and time, but these modifications are treated semantically as ideas rather than physically as metric, curvature, energy-mass density, etc.

Interpreting the Dark Matter Anomaly

As explained above, the Dark Matter anomaly arises if we use gravitation theory to explain all moving parts in the universe, because we find that the outer parts of the galaxy are moving at much faster speeds than gravity would permit. This clearly seems to be at odds with the theory of the solar system where the planets are supposed to go around the Sun at different speeds. In Vedic cosmology, this problem never arises because all planets move at a constant speed of their own, although the *apparent* speeds are different due to dragging by the Sun and the zodiac. The zodiac similarly also travels at a constant speed and takes with it all the stars. The distant parts of the galaxy are parts of the zodiac, and they are moving with the zodiac. The fact that they are farther away doesn't mean that they should be going slower, as slowness is entailed only by gravity, not if the zodiac is considered to be moving as a single very large 'disk'. These aspects of the Vedic cosmology will be described in later chapters.

Since gravitation is rejected in Vedic cosmology, the distances to the planets are also described differently. As we will see later, there is enormous agreement between the rotational periods of the planets in the Vedic and the modern estimation, and a complete disagreement in the distances. This is because rotations are what we observe empirically, based on when the planets return to the part of the sky where they were previously seen. However, distances are always inferred based on methods such as Parallax, Inverse Square Law, or Doppler Shift. These interpretations are in turn based on the theories, such as the idea that light travels in straight lines (Parallax Method), that light is equally distributed in all directions (Inverse Square Law), or that all parts of the universe are uniform in the type of matter (Doppler Shift). When these theoretical assumptions are dropped, and new ones incorporated, a completely different model of the universe is constructed. In this model, we can see that the planetary distances are not the same. For instance, the distances from Earth to the Sun and the Moon are not as they are in modern astronomy.

Seeing the Universe Semantically

The key takeaway is that cosmological theories present formidable challenges not just because we haven't yet been able to reconcile quantum theory, general relativity, and thermodynamics, but also because we don't understand what that reconciliation looks like. Physicists postulate dark energy and dark matter, believing that what we cannot see is just like what we can see. Clearly, this path is fraught with challenges, if what we cannot see is quite different from what we can. But I will argue that the problem stems not from cosmology, general relativity, quantum theory, or other such intractable theories today, but from our inability to incorporate what we see every day—i.e., meanings—into science.

There is an alternative view of the world that incorporates meanings into the nature of material reality, which can be used to resolve these difficulties. However, that approach to the description of matter fundamentally alters our theories about matter, space, and time: rather than viewing space and time as linear and flat, and matter as physical objects, we must understand the nature of concepts, and the type of space and time in which these concepts exist. This space and time is hierarchical and closed (closed time becomes cyclic). This revised view of space and time also clearly alters our interpretation of the observations. In this new interpretation, dark matter and dark energy are not needed because the problem of something being dark (i.e., not perceivable by the senses) does not create a conceptual or theoretical difficulty. We just treat this darkness as a type of reality, which is more abstract than our senses.

When the world is physical, space-time too is physical—i.e., linear and open. When the world is semantic, then space-time too is semantic—i.e., closed and cyclic. This shift in the structure of space-time alters our theories and models about the universe. Now, there are many kinds of space-times, each conceptually more abstract than the other, although all these space-times *appear* to exist in the same space-time in the physical view. Like the country, state, city, and street, are all present in the physical space, and yet they aren't the same *type* of location, similarly, there is a structure in space and time that current science ignores due to the current physicalist dogmas. When these dogmas are removed, a new picture of the cosmos emerges, in which many ideas currently held true in modern science either become irrelevant, or outright false, or both.

5

Fundamental Principles of Vedic Cosmology

He whose heart is purified can see that the whole cosmic manifestation is but the Supreme Personality of Godhead, but he whose heart is contaminated sees things differently.
— *Chaitanya Charitāmṛta, Madhya,* 22.54

The Definition of a Universe

A central problem in trying to define the idea of a universe concerns the question of whether there is only one universe or many of them. If there are many universes, then how these universes differ amongst each other becomes the basis of defining each universe. If, however, there is only one universe, then defining it becomes harder. If there are many universes, then a different problem of how these universes can be known arises. Can these universes be known from within the present universe, or will they always be unknowable? This question is worth pondering because if the other universes are indeed unknowable, then how do we know that they exist? Whether or not there are multiple universes therefore presents different problems, depending on whether we are looking at the issue of defining a universe or trying to empirically validate its existence.

The question of multiple universes in modern cosmology stems from issues about theoretical *completeness*: we know that the present universe has a structure, but it could have had a different structure. These structures are matter distributions. We know that current scientific theories permit an infinite number of possible matter distributions, so we have no way of explaining why the present universe is a particular matter distribution. The theoretician surmises: Would it not be nice if we allowed all possible matter distributions to exist as "parallel" universes? The reason this kind of proposal becomes attractive is because it helps us achieve completeness in a theoretical and mathematical sense: the world is all that can *possibly* exist, not just what exists within our universe. It allows us to say that the present universe is one of the many possibilities, which alleviates the problem of having to explain a specific possibility.

In the early days of science, a divide between experience and reason was drawn, suggesting that rational sciences such as mathematics describe all that is possible while experience tells us what is real. The world of possibility is greater than the observed reality, and we can, through empirical discovery, find which of the possibilities are real. As it turns out, this gap has not been bridged, because all theories permit an infinite number of possibilities, although not all possibilities. For instance, if we postulate the conservation of energy as a law of nature, many physical interactions that violate this law would be precluded by the law, but an infinite number of interactions would still be permitted. All physical laws of science suffer from this problem: you can fix the state of the universe if your theory is deterministic, provided you supply the initial state. However, we just don't know how that initial information would be supplied. Furthermore, the theories are always indeterministic; even the deterministic theories become indeterministic under inelastic dynamics[1].

This failure to bridge the gap between possibility and reality leads to the need to hypothesize many possible universes, which exist simultaneously, although as matter distributions different from our universe. For example, we can now postulate a mathematical space vast enough to accommodate all universe possibilities, of which a specific universe is a proper subset. This postulate then frees us from the need to explain why a given universe has a specific *structure* because that structure would be automatically explained as a specific 'location' in the space of all possibilities. This hypothesis, however, still doesn't overcome the indeterminism in modern science because all theories are indeterministic (under inelastic dynamics) even if their initial distributions are fixed. Nevertheless, if the problem of inelastic dynamics were to be overcome, then the idea of multiple universes is theoretically very convenient because it helps us avoid the issue of fixing the initial state (or structure) of matter distribution, without precluding a number of other possible structures.

In Vedic cosmology, there are multiple universes, each of which enables a different set of possibilities. The structure of a universe, as opposed to all the possible structures, is defined as a specific location of a universe in the space of all possible universes. In the semantic view, this location is a node in the semantic tree, upon which the universe grows like a leaf or fruit on a tree. The problem of inelastic dynamics does not arise in the semantic view due to meanings: all possible distributions of matter are not permitted in the semantic view; rather, only those distributions which represent something meaningful are possible. Furthermore, the structure of time defines which of these meanings would be manifest when, and the law of nature prescribes which observers will participate in which subset of events at any time. The changes to matter distributions are therefore changes to meanings and caused by meanings. Each semantic transaction has two outcomes: an *effect* which is described collectively as the interaction of meanings, and a *consequence* which pertains to the individual observer. Each universe thus evolves due to the causality in meanings, in a hierarchical and closed space-time.

A new kind of problem, however, arises in this scheme too, when we identify a branch of the semantic tree with a universe: at which node in the tree should we consider the space-time of a universe to begin? Can we not go a little deeper and expand the definition of a universe? In fact, why would we not consider all the branches of the tree, along with the root, to be a single universe, instead of many different universes?

This issue is addressed in Vedic cosmology by separating the material tree into four different parts called *parā*, *paśyanti*, *madhyamā*, and *vaikharī*. The root of the tree is God and represents *parā*; from Him originate both the material energy as well as the marginal energy or the soul who enjoys or suffers in the material energy. Both the soul and God are considered *parā* because they are transcendent to the material energy. They are therefore considered to be outside all the universes.

The material domain begins in a form of unmanifest matter called the *causal ocean* and is called *paśyanti*, which represents a subtle form of meaning that we can call *justifications*. It comprises of three parts. First, it includes *karma*, which is the justice meted out to each person based on the consequences of their past actions. Second, it includes the *guna* or specific desires of pleasure in each person which drive them toward different kinds of activities. Third, it includes *chitta* or subtle beliefs about the nature of truth and reality from which other ideas are constructed. The realm of *paśyanti* is unconscious reality; it manifests the conscious reality, but we are unable to perceive its existence. It is deeper than material objects, senses, mind, intellect, ego, and the moral sense.

From this subtle reality of *paśyanti* two other forms of reality are created, which are called *madhyamā* and *vaikharī*. *Madhyamā* constitutes our conscious experience (sensations, meanings, judgments, intentions, and morals). Each of these involves a different kind of instrument; for instance, sensations require the senses, meanings require the mind, judgments of truth require the intellect, intentions require the ego, and the moral judgment involves the moral sense. The collection of all these instruments and the experiences produced from them are called *madhyamā*. It lies intermediate *paśyanti* and *vaikharī*. Finally, *vaikharī* constitutes the gross body and things that we can perceive by our senses.

Paśyanti is sometimes called the causal body, *madhyamā* is called the subtle body, and *vaikharī* is called the gross body. These three kinds of bodies cover the *parā* or the soul which is transcendent to matter.

The material creation begins from *paśyanti* when the causal body of the soul is created, in a realm called the causal ocean. This causal ocean is the origin of innumerable universes. A material universe is everything that begins from *madhyamā*, and *paśyanti* is the space-time in which all these universes are situated as individual objects. The division of the entire creation into individual universes is based upon the nature of *paśyanti*: each universe affords the fulfillment of certain kinds of pleasure, the enduring of certain kind of *karma*, and the possibility of a certain kind of reality based on an unconscious belief system. Thus, there is a similarity between all living entities within a given universe, based on the nature of their causal body. They, however, have different subtle and gross bodies. Each universe is thus defined as a domain of *madhyamā*, and *vaikharī*, which resides in a deeper unmanifest space-time, called *paśyanti*, which is in turn a small fraction of the space called *parā*.

The Nature of a Brahmanda

The technical term for a universe in Vedic cosmology is *brahmanda*, which is the domain of a single *Brahma*, whose method of producing the cosmos is represented by a different number of heads. Each *brahmanda* has a *Brahma* with a unique number of heads; the smallest universe has a *Brahma* with 4 heads, but there are universes that have a *Brahma* with 8, 16, 32, or more heads. In each universe, *Brahma* is the embodiment of *mahattattva* or moral principles, which is the highest of the material elements within the conscious realm. *Brahma* establishes the moral principles through his different heads. For instance, in the present universe, *Brahma* has 4 heads, and he speaks 4 Vedas through each of these heads: *Rig, Yajur, Sāma* and *Atharva.* These 4 Vedas constitute the four aspects of *yajña* or sacrifice, which is the basis of the universe as everything in the universe involves a certain kind of sacrifice or tradeoff. Unlike the transcendent world, which is devoid of duality or oppositions, and you can therefore choose opposites simultaneously, in the material universe, the opposites cannot be chosen simultaneously. Therefore, to make a choice, you must sacrifice something to get another thing. *Brahma* establishes the ideal form of sacrifice in which our desires are subordinated to morality, and the truth is subordinated to the fulfillment of desire.

Each universe is modeled as a *yajña* or sacrifice, and the basic structure of subordinating our desire to morality, and truth to desire, exists. However, in each universe, the number of moral principles, the divisions of types of desires, and the definition of how we attain truth can vary. For example, in the present universe, there are 4 principles of morality called truthfulness, kindness, austerity, and cleanliness. There are 4 basic kinds of pleasures, namely, eating, sleeping, mating, and defending. There are four basic principles of knowledge, namely, consistency, contradiction, complementarity and completeness. A detailed description of these 4-fold divisions will take us beyond our current focus, so I will not delve further into it. But the main point is that the 4 heads of *Brahma* denote a fundamental property of this universe used for organization. In other universes, *Brahma* has a different number of heads, and accordingly, the *yajña* system is different; the number of Vedas will be different; and the method of organizing the universe will involve more divisions.

Once the ritual structure has been defined, the divisions of the ritual become the *directions* in space; for instance, each ritual structure involves 4 priests called *hota, adhvaryu, udgata,* and *brahma.* They sit along 4 cardinal directions and the central space in the ritual (the *vedi*, which represents the living entity who is worshipped by the ritual) is constructed as a square. All offerings of the ritual are made into the *vedi*, where a fire is burnt, and offerings are made into that fire to worship a deity. The aspect of this construction relevant to cosmology is that the ritual structure begins to define the structure of space: the horizontal dimension is divided into four parts. As different universes have a different ritual construction, the nature of space in these universes will also differ; they will have a different numbers of directional space divisions.

It is amazing how a simple notion is used to construct an enormous amount of complexity, and the *Sāñkhya* theory describes how matter develops from morals into intents, judgments, meanings, senses, sensations, and sense objects, each time detailing the previous abstract notion.

Vedic literature describes many universes, much larger than the present one, each governed by a *Brahma* with a greater number of heads. For instance, when *Brahma* steals all of Lord *Kṛṣṇa*'s friends and cows for a year, Lord *Kṛṣṇa* recreates the friends and cows just as they were previously. Bewildered by this prowess, *Brahma* asks Lord *Kṛṣṇa* about the "creator" of these friends and cows, assuming himself to be the creator of the entire universe. In response Lord *Kṛṣṇa* summons many *Brahmas* from other "universes" to appear before the present universe's *Brahma*. Lord *Kṛṣṇa* demonstrates how He is a far superior creator and there are even bigger creators of bigger universes. Unlike the four-headed *Brahma* in the present "universe", the other *Brahma* have many more heads, with a correlation between their number of heads and the sizes of the universes that they govern. Thus, the universe with a *Brahma* with 8 heads is twice the size of the universe whose *Brahma* has only 4 heads. I will describe the significance of these ideas later in the book and show how the space and time in different universes differ based on this principle. While we cannot *experience* those universes, we can *know* about them.

Inter-Universe Communication

The existence of multiple universes presents the question of whether these are only theoretical necessities (arising from the need to explain why a universe has a specific structure among all the possible universal structures, which is resolved by many universes) or they can also be empirically experienced. We have already noted how the problem of theoretical necessity for multiple universes is addressed, but the issue of empirical confirmation of their existence isn't as straightforward. For instance, the incident of the present *Brahma* becoming aware of the other universe *Brahma* itself suggests that this knowledge did not earlier exist in the present *Brahma*. Should we then suppose that the other universes cannot be known through observation, although they are theoretical necessities used to solve the problem of selecting a specific structure?

This stance is by far the most dominant in both modern and Vedic cosmology: we accept that the other universes cannot be accessed from the present "universe", although their existence arises from theoretical problems in trying to describe them, and therefore everything we can observe must exist in the present universe. The notion of multiple universes can therefore only be justified theoretically, and not empirically.

This stance, however, presents some important questions. For instance, if it were impossible to experience the other universes from the present universe, then how were the various *Brahma* seen in this universe? What path did they take in going from one universe to another?

If the universe is constructed as an inverted tree, then going from one universe to another requires traveling up and down the tree; the upward travel necessitates passing the coverings of each "universe" and traversing the causal ocean. If the *Brahma* in one universe can see the *Brahma* in other universes, then information exchange between the universes must be possible. However, this information must pass via the root of the universes (the material root is a form of God called *Kāraṇodakaśāyī Viṣṇu* who produces the unmanifest matter), but this is no different than any other transaction, where information goes through up and down a tree. We can see why the *Brahma* appear on being summoned by Lord *Kṛṣṇa*: that approval has been obtained, since *Kṛṣṇa* is the origin.

Empirical acquaintance with another universe is possible, and the process is no different than any other type of experience. But as all other experiences must be causally explained, the experience of other universes also needs an explanation. In modern science, we suppose that if something exists, we must be able to see it, although there are things which we can never see. The vision of something must be explained, although the absence of that vision requires no explanation. Similarly, the observation of the other universes needs an explanation (because it involves information transfer from one universe to another) although not observing the other universe would not require any explanation.

All material information exchanges in Vedic philosophy are caused by *karma* (there are also experiences caused by the grace of God, but we can sidestep this possibility for now). For information to pass from one universe to another, the universes must exchange *karma*. That is, some information from one living being in one universe must leave the universe and enter another living being's experience in another universe. This exchange requires a source and a destination of information to be 'entangled' before the exchange begins. If the *karma* in the different universes cannot be 'entangled' then living beings also cannot communicate. The passing of *karma* between two entities requires the 'approval' of a higher entity, because the communication occurs *through* that entity. In this case, to communicate between two universes, one would require the approval from *Kāraṇodakaśāyī Viṣṇu*. Apart from this approval, we must also recognize that due to the differences in the division of space, each universe has a different *natural language*. For instance, in a larger universe, everything can be divided into much finer details than in the present universe. We can imagine that a larger universe is one in which language has many more words that describe subtle nuances of ideas, judgments, intentions, morals, pleasures, the notions of right and wrong, etc. To communicate with such a universe, we will need to employ a similar language, and linguistic incompatibility will make the communication incomprehensible even if it were possible. Therefore, aside from the approval of *Kāraṇodakaśāyī Viṣṇu*, a linguistic compatibility is also needed to establish communication between the diverse universes.

Given the problems in such inter-universe communication, the vision of the different *Brahma* in the example above should be viewed as the grace of *Kāraṇodakaśāyī Viṣṇu* rather than something that would happen ordinarily. The consequence of the causal model underlying any material experience is that the individual universes must be causally complete since they cannot exchange information with each other, except in very rare scenarios, facilitated by the will of God. In general, this interaction is not possible, therefore, each universe is *causally* complete, although not *theoretically* complete. Note that theoretical completeness requires the explanation of why a universe has a particular structure, but causal completeness only needs to isolate a universe from the other universes. In this case, causal completeness entails that *karma* doesn't 'escape' a universe, and before a living entity exits a particular universe, the *karma* produced in that universe must been completely exhausted.

The Inter-Universe Space-Time

One way to understand the difference between *parā, madhyamā,* and *vaikharī* is to think of three ways in which we offer explanations—causes, reasons, and justifications. The realm of causes is the grossest. For example, if you pull the trigger of a gun, the cause is the pressing of the finger. But if you were asked about why you pulled the trigger, you could explain it based on your mental state, such as it was my duty to pull the trigger, or I was angry at the person I was shooting, or I believed that he had done something wrong. This lies in the realm of conscious experiences. But even more subtle than this realm of experience lies the unconscious. It constitutes the justifications, which manifest in three main forms. The first important type of justification is *justice* and it manifests as *karma*. For instance, the justification for why someone is rich can be provided in the gross sense, namely, that they were able work in a high-paying job or were born in a rich family, which afforded them the riches. More subtle than this explanation is that of mental states, namely, that they had the intellect, mind, and sensual abilities by which they were able to do things that others could not do, and hence they are richer than others. But you can still ask: Why is someone born in a rich family or why do they have better intellectual, mental, or sensual capabilities? In asking these questions, you are not seeking the causes or the reasons, but the justifications. In Vedic philosophy, this justification is provided by *karma*—it is due to deeds done in the past that someone is entitled to a rich life.

The second type of justification involves a subtle personality of desires and what we like or dislike. We are innately born with certain preferences. For instance, some people are naturally attracted to music and art, while others are naturally inclined toward sports or outdoor activities. Their natural proclivities for enjoyment can be partially explained by the gross body (e.g., that they have the physical strength, height, or stamina to play sports), or the subtle body (e.g., they have the sensual, mental, and intellectual ability to play music or do art). But by these explanations you cannot justify whey they enjoy these things. Is enjoyment merely enabled by our bodily capacity and the sensual, mental, and intellectual acuity? Or, is there a deeper explanation to this?

Our likes and dislikes are innate justifications produced due to a personality made of *guna*. By these *guna* we are naturally attracted to certain types of things, even before we develop the bodily, sensual, mental or intellectual capacity. For instance, someone is naturally attracted to music even when they may not have the capacity to play instruments. By that attraction, they practice and learn and acquire the mental and bodily capabilities to become experts in the fields. That attraction precedes their efforts, and that effort precedes the abilities which follow. The justification for why someone is attracted to certain things is their unconscious personality of likes and dislikes which gives them pleasure. Thus, the same thing can be enjoyed or suffered by different people because they have different innate personalities, or the sense of like and dislike.

The third kind of justification constitutes our subtle belief system, which is produced through many lifetimes of impressions. For instance, if you are constantly told that people of black skin are inferior to the people with white skin, you will develop an unconscious racial bias. You will not even realize that you are being biased due to repeated exposure to a certain type of belief system. Similarly, in modern science, people repeatedly hear that the world is constituted of material particles, and everything reduces to these particles, due to which anything that is not measurable by the senses is unconsciously avoided or judged to be false. If you have grown up in a conservative environment, you will have an unconscious revulsion toward libertarian ideas. You would not even like to listen to the reasons that they hold certain beliefs because you are convinced innately that their viewpoint is fundamentally wrong.

When we speak about justifications, therefore, we mean one of these three varieties—the justification of why someone is compelled to face good or bad situations, the justification for why someone innately likes or dislikes something, or the justification for why they believe in something. When we speak about causes, we look for empirical evidence. When we speak about reasons, we look for rational arguments. But when we speak about justifications, we discard empirical and rational evidence. A classic example in case of *karma* is that someone may be born with a deadly disease right from birth; you cannot explain it by observation and reasoning in the ordinary sense of current conscious experience. Similarly, why we like or dislike something or someone has to do with our innate preferences rather that empirical evidence or rational argument for what that thing or person is. Likewise, we can stick on to our beliefs despite rational and empirical evidence to the contrary, because it has become our belief system over lifetimes of sustained impressions.

The *vaikharī* reality constitutes the realm of causes, the *madhyamā* reality constitutes the realm of reasons, and the *paśyanti* reality constitutes the realm of justifications. The *vaikharī* and *madhyamā* exist within a specific universe, affording a different kind of experience. But the basis of entering a specific universe is based on the *paśyanti* reality. We have an innate personality of likes and dislikes, an innate belief system of truth and false, and an innate *karma* produced from previous lifetimes. To enjoy a certain kind of personality, using a certain belief system, under the control of a certain type of *karma*, we enter a specific universe.

The space outside the universes constitutes the varieties of *paśyanti* realities, which constitute the realm of unconscious desires, beliefs, and consequences. In Vedic philosophy, this is the real cause of all conscious experience, because from it springs the conscious experience. Therefore, it is called the *kārana* or 'cause' of our entry into a given universe. It is not the cause in the sense of push and pull of gross material objects. It is also not a cause in the sense of sensual, mental, or intellectual reasons. It is an even deeper type of explanation which constitutes justifications.

The space-time between the universes is the domain of the undifferentiated unconscious, formed over previous lifetimes. Each type of unconscious selects a different universe. The unconscious is also comprised of many layers, which constitute the 'coverings' of a universe, and there are seven types of coverings, which we will discuss in a later chapter, until we arrive at the innermost part of the universe called the *brahmanda*, or the realm of *Brahma* who creates conscious experience, namely different kinds of bodies and minds. The reality beyond the universe therefore represents the unconscious of Western psychology.

The coverings of the universes are the *filters of perception* through which we incompletely perceive reality and even things in plain sight may not be seen. The term *paśyanti* means "seeing" and it is the goggles through which we see. *Paśyanti* is not consciousness and it is not "seeing" in the sense of experiencing. As a deeper level of reality, it represents the perspective through which we perceive reality. While the entire conscious perception is about seeing what exists in the world, becoming conscious of *paśyanti* is about seeing the goggles through which we see.

These goggles are also material, but they are produced as a consequence of our actions. Due to repeated exposure to a certain type of reality we form biases of perception that dictate what we consider true. Due to these imperfect actions, we create the consequences of actions called *karma*. And due to our innate personality of likes and dislikes, we enjoy or suffer the effects of *karma*. The covering of the universe is thus the goggles that cover consciousness. When a living being is liberated from a universe, he may not be free of all the goggles. He may live inside one of the coverings of the universe, or even outside all the universes. Here, the living being does not have the experiences of the senses but experiences his goggles. Voidists may enter this realm on exiting the sensual experience of a universe. This exit is liberation from a gross and subtle body, but not from the material covering. From this position, they may again enter a specific type of universe based on their unconscious bodies.

The different universes comprising various types of conscious experiences are "objects" in a deeper space-time in which these universes are distinguished. The deeper space-time is in effect the space-time between the universes by which they are demarcated as different zones of desires, impressions, and *karma*. Just as objects in a universe are identified by their knowable properties, similarly, the universes in the deeper space-time are identified by a deeper kind of unconscious existence. In a simple sense, each universe is meant to fulfill a particular type of desire, impression, and *karma*. The universes are thus distinguished in a space-time in which locations themselves denote various kinds of unconscious.

Current science models all space in the same way, which means that the space in between the universes would be treated similarly to the space within a universe. In the semantic view, there are two kinds of space—within and between universes—and both are semantic, although they represent different kinds of meanings. To understand the space outside and in between the universes we need to dive deeper into the recesses of our existence and see beyond bodies and minds: we must understand how the mind and the body are products of an unconscious.

The Material Creation

The material creation is the space of all material experiences, which are chosen by the goggles of perception. To be free of the material creation, the soul must not only get out of a universe, but also discard the habits of perception and action—i.e., the filters that discard parts of reality.

Once these filters are discarded, the living being can perceive reality completely. By seeing the complete truth, the living being is freed of all consequences, and is called "liberated". Getting out of a specific universe alone is therefore not liberation; rather, liberation is freeing oneself from the unconscious materialistic coverings of the soul, which exist even outside each of the universes. The freedom from such material ideas is also called freedom from *māyā* and once the goggles of subtle material ideas are removed, the living being loses the distinction between itself and others. This state is called *Brahman* or the undivided oneness.

In this undivided oneness, the living being *exists* but has no perception of its individuality or distinction from others. The living being cannot select or reject, and without choice there is no experience. While freed from the illusory experiences of the material world, the elimination of all experiences is not considered the perfect state of a soul. A soul, in Vedic philosophy, has three aspects—*sat* or consciousness, *chit* or cognition, and *ānanda* or pleasure. In the *Brahman* stage, the soul has *sat* or consciousness—i.e., the awareness of itself, cognition of itself, and pleasure from the self—but no cognition or pleasure from others. This stage is not perfect, although it is better than the material illusion. Under the illusion, the soul has a faulty perception of reality, and in *Brahman* there is no external perception. In some ways, lack of perception is better than a faulty perception. In other ways, lack of experience is unnatural, and the soul can fall back into matter to regain its natural state of experiencing.

Each universe begins in a type of illusion, which is then magnified by adding more illusory ideas. Each universe is thus a succession of ever more complex illusions. The bigger universes—produced from more morals—are more illusory because the amount of diversity increases. With growing diversity comes increased contradictions. For instance, the contradictions between different values in a larger universe is much higher than if the universe is built from fewer morals. Deciding your real *dharma* becomes harder when there are numerous values that you can choose from and these values contradict the other values.

For instance, you may value honesty, but being honest with dishonest people contradicts being honest to yourself. At that point, you are not sure whether you should be dishonest to other people or dishonest to yourself. The greater the number of values, the more numerous are the possible contradictions amongst the values. As you vacillate between them, the confusion is never resolved, and the living being is unable to recognize that neither of these moral values can be individually or collectively consistent and complete; one chooses among the possible values, making imperfect choices.

At the end of the duration of a *Brahma's* lifetime, the material creation is destroyed and the *Kārana* ocean is annihilated. This state without illusion is not enlightenment. It is one in which the domain of material pleasure has been temporarily suspended. Since the universes are dissolved, the living beings are said to be "liberated" from illusion. However, this liberation is not permanent; in the creation following this destruction, such "liberated" beings are reinjected into the material illusion.

Universe as Conscious Experience

Each universe begins in *mahattattva*, which is also called *ṛta* or moral principles, and it represents the values of a universe. We might call it the 'laws of the universe' but these are not mathematical formulae; they are a form of subtle matter in the universe. In the strictest sense, these are not laws that govern matter; these are principles that govern our choices and their consequences. Different living beings choose different values, creating their own notions of right and wrong. For instance, some people might consider hard work as an important value, while others think that relaxation is a value. Accordingly, what is good or bad changes: If you are relaxing when the value is hard work, then you are doing something wrong. *Mahattattva* is moral values, which decide our definition of right and wrong, and each soul is covered by a specific type of moral sense or a moral compass. Each universe represents a combination of values—i.e., *dharma*—which constitute what is considered good or bad in that universe and defines the moral values of that universe. These values are not absolute and are not shared across the other universes; they are things that beings in a particular universe consider to be morally good.

From these morals two things emerge—the *subtle body* (called the *sūkshma sarīra*) and the *gross body* (called the *sthūla sarīra*). Loosely they correspond to the mind and the body of Western philosophy. The subtle body is what we might call the *conscious experience* of a living being—it comprises sensations in the senses, thoughts in the mind, judgments in the intelligence, intentions in the ego, and morals in *mahattattva*. This conscious experience is not *consciousness* per se, which is transcendent to this experience and exists even when the experience doesn't.

The entire subtle body is also sometimes called *madhyamā* or "middle" or "mediating" matter, as it mediates between the material objects and consciousness to create conscious experience. Thus, unlike the "mind" of Western philosophy which is equated with consciousness or the soul, the subtle body in Vedic philosophy is a material reality that encompasses the *content* of experience, although not the conscious observer per se. From this subtle body, the gross body is developed.

The sensations—form, color, flavor, tone, intensity, etc.—are considered parts of the subtle body, and they correspond to the *qualia* in Western philosophy. Grosser than the sensations are the *material properties* objectified from the sensations. For instance, color has values like red, green, and blue; form can be square, circle, and triangle; flavor is sweet, bitter, and sour; etc. These are the "values" for the properties of color, form, flavor, etc. Both the property and the value are *types*, and the properties don't depend on the values, as they are logically prior to the values. Thus, the idea of "color" exists even when individual colors like green, blue, and red don't exist. Before red, green, and blue can be defined, color must be defined; but color doesn't depend on red, green, and blue.

The values of material properties are *vaikharī* or gross matter. It is objectivized and can be measured in relation to other objects, but all these objects or the measuring instruments must be defined through sensations, which must be defined through the senses, and so forth.

The gross and subtle matter comprise two space-times—*vaikharī* and *madhyamā*—and are called the "waking" and "dreaming" stages of our experience. The waking stage is experience when our sensations, thoughts, judgments, and intentions, and morals are *about* an objectively existing external world of material values, while the dreaming stage is when we have sensations, thoughts, judgments, and intentions, but there is no correspondence to the external world. The dreaming stage is considered "higher" than the "waking" stage, not because sleeping is better, but because the *madhyamā* space is logically prior to *vaikharī*.

Behind all experiences lies the unconscious—which makes our experiences *valuable* and *significant*—and thus worthy of being attended to by consciousness. We seek some value in every experience, and if an experience has nothing to offer that we personally value, then consciousness withdraws from the content, and the experience disappears. As we saw previously, the unconscious become the basis of our experiences.

Demigods and Demons

The cosmos in Vedic cosmology is a collection of places that afford different kinds of experiences, unlike modern science, where the cosmos is largely devoid of life. The different places in the cosmos are divided into many planetary systems, which differ in the type of experience they offer. In the higher planetary systems, the living beings perceive abstract forms of reality. In the middle planetary system (where our planet is said to reside), there are gross material objects along with the subtle material realities, but if our perception is dominated by sensual experience, then we cannot understand these deeper kinds of material realities. In the lower planetary systems, experience is dominated by gross reality, but it is even more detailed and refined than in the middle planetary system.

The living beings in the higher planetary systems thus enjoy subtle matter through mind, intelligence, ego, and the moral sense; in the middle planetary systems the living beings enjoy the sensation of macroscopic objects through their senses of knowledge and action; in the lower planetary system there are life forms whose senses are far more developed to perceive the details in matter that our senses just cannot perceive.

The atomic world is therefore experienced in the lower planetary systems; macroscopic objects are experienced in the middle planetary system; ideas are experienced in the higher planetary systems.

To know the atomic world, living beings in the middle need to add a lot of information to 'magnify' atomic reality to the level of macroscopic sense perception. Thus, our knowledge of the atomic reality involves the use of particle accelerators which add an enormous amount of energy to produce detectable effects. However, the 'demons' who reside in the lower planetary systems don't need to add this energy, because their senses themselves can perceive the atoms, which our senses cannot. Even on the present planet, there are species of life which have a superior sense of smell (e.g., dogs), or sight (e.g., eagles), or sound (e.g., bats). The things that we cannot sensually perceive, can be perceived by these species. The ability to see atomic objects is therefore an advancement of sense perception due to which the things that our senses cannot see, the living beings with advanced sensual capabilities are able to perceive.

The beings in the upper planetary systems use their senses to perceive subtle reality. What is abstract for us becomes sense perceivable for them. For example, mathematical structures are abstract for us, but they become sense perceivable for them. Similarly, the forms in music are abstract for us, even though we can listen to the sounds; but these forms of music become sense perceivable. In short, even sense perception for the higher beings is different from our sense perception because they can see, taste, touch, smell, and hear what we can only imagine or think.

The beings in the middle planetary system use their senses for relatively grosser forms, but they cannot perceive the extremely finer details. For example, when the wind blows and touches our skin, we feel a good sensation, but we cannot perceive the sensation caused into each pore of our skin. Similarly, when we go to a garden of flowers, we can see forms and colors, but we cannot enjoy the subtle refinements of shade and shape in each individual thing. We generally call these things 'microscopic' because they are not normally accessible to our senses.

Finally, the beings in the lower planetary system have such advanced senses that they can perceive things that we would need to spend a lot of energy to magnify for our sense perception. Of course, when you are enjoying the minute details in matter, you must process a lot more information than if you are enjoying the abstractions. This ability to process enormous amounts of information is what makes the demons extremely powerful as compared to the beings in the middle of the cosmos. In fact, the demons, by the sophistication of their information processing power can sometimes overpower the demigods in the higher planets who only perceive the abstractions. The power in the demigods is their ability to understand highly abstract ideas, while the power in the demons is their ability to comprehend enormous amounts of details. The living beings in the middle see neither the abstractions, nor the intricate details.

The experiences of demons are high-definition, and their planets are more pleasurable. The greater pleasure arises from receiving a greater amount of information from the same world. In this form of life, you can smell every minor scent in a garden, feel the touch of air at every pore in your skin, see the infinite variations in color in a garden, and hear every minor variation in tone. Their craftsmanship, sex, and speech are also similarly more elaborate, intricate, and detailed. These high-definition experiences then facilitate a more refined understanding of the mind or meaning—e.g., the ability to understand every thought simply based on minor variations in tone, body language, or eye movement. The intelligence of such beings then is like a lie-detector, which can judge the truth of meanings based on minor changes to blood pressure and heart rate. They have a more refined sense of morality and are able to judge right and wrong better than humans on the "earthly" planetary system.

In these ways, therefore, the demons are far more advanced than the modern 'advanced' civilization, but due to their heightened sense of pleasure derived from the senses, they cannot relinquish this pleasure. It is therefore noteworthy that the 'demons' in Vedic descriptions are quite a different use of the same word in Christianity or other religions where they are identified with the devil, which has no real existence in Vedic philosophy. The living beings in the material creation are influenced by the three modes of nature and they have different qualities based on the three modes. The demons (and demigods) are influenced by these modes, and therefore their 'superior' and 'inferior' status is only a reflection of the relative proportion of the modes and material advancement, not truly an indication of their spiritual standing in the material world.

The demigods too are more advanced than the humans because they have a more direct understanding of mind, intelligence, ego and *mahattattva*. They don't have to write music on paper, they don't have to publish their knowledge in academic journals, they don't need a TV and telephone to talk at great distances, and they don't need museums to record their history. When the mind is more advanced, it can perceive meanings across greater distances and times, it sees abstract objects like we see things, and it is able to find truths because it perceives abstractions like we see objects. The modern civilization is trying to emulate the demigods by using telescopes that can see at greater distances, and the demons by creating microscopes that can see the details. When you depend on such implements, you must translate everything into the perception of your senses, and the *pleasure* from this perception is limited to that achievable from coarse-grained senses, although we gather information about the universe, or measure the properties of the atomic objects.

Though sometimes we claim to have become advanced by creating technology, the fact is that we still see macroscopic objects, as we did before. The pleasure from the objects remains unchanged. Relative to the abstract enjoyments of the demigods, and the detailed pleasure of the demons, we are stuck with the pleasure of macroscopic objects. That pleasure itself isn't great, no matter how we refine it. The "advancement" of human society is trying to stretch the limits of our experience by going above and below the normal "earthly" experiences. But since this advancement is not accompanied by a corresponding development of the mind, intellect, ego, morality, or even the five senses of perception, it delivers only the pleasures that would be obtained even without such advancements. With all this materialistic advancement, we barely scratch the surface of the pleasure that demons and demigods have, but that is enough to dramatically intensify our attachment to matter.

The "earthly" planetary system is the best place in this universe because the pleasures are so ordinary that we can easily renounce them and develop a true understanding of the reality that lies beyond these phenomena. Modern civilization, on the other hand, is trying to stretch the limits of the phenomena themselves. The great purpose of self and God realization that can be attained in the human life is thus being squandered in activities which will never attain the levels of pleasures easily obtainable in other planetary systems although it will take away the precious human opportunities to end the cycle of material birth and death, suffering and pleasure. The pleasure of the senses is not the happiness of the soul. The sensual pleasure is created when the stress created by *māyā* is relieved by uniting with objects created by *karma*. When *karma* is finished, the stress returns. The real happiness is the result of innate properties of the soul which are manifest when the soul comes out of the material universe and becomes part of God's conscious experience.

The System of Diminishing Returns

It is notable that abstract and contingent are ideas and they can be represented as symbols. The symbol that denotes an abstract idea (e.g., a car), however, requires fewer symbols than a contingent idea (e.g., a real car). Accordingly, the amount of information exchanged in abstract communication is far lesser *if* the sender the and receiver are able to actually exchange abstractions. If the abstractions are constructed from the details, then both abstract and contingent communication will require equal amount of information transfer. However, if the living beings are capable of abstract communication, and if they can enjoy these abstractions, then the *effort* involved in sending abstract information is considerably less than the effort consumed in exchanging detailed information.

Accordingly, the pleasure of demigods needs less effort, the pleasure of the earthly beings comes with more effort, and the pleasure of the demons requires even more effort. Depending on the kind of perception and pleasure a living being enjoys, he must expend different levels of effort. Ultimately, demigods, earthly beings, and demons are all enjoying, but the effort they are investing in that enjoyment is starkly different. If the goal of life is pleasure, then the pleasure achieved with minimal effort can be considered the best. From that perspective, the pleasure of demigods is higher, not because they enjoy the same kind of experiences as we do, but because they can enjoy with minimal effort. Conversely, the pleasure of demons is lower because they invest a lot of effort to enjoy details.

From top to bottom, the universe follows the *law of diminishing returns*. As you go downwards, you have to work harder and harder to find the pleasure you desire. Of course, if you want to enjoy a certain type of pleasure, you would not mind expending more and more effort and energy to obtain it. But the question is what one gets in return for the effort one invests. If you are investing a lot of effort to just obtain something very small, you are squandering away your good *karma*, which was previously obtained through great effort. The living beings in the lower planetary systems are therefore considered less intelligent because they *desire* to enjoy a kind of pleasure which requires a tremendous amount of sensual, mental, intellectual effort, which in turn needs a lot of *karma*.

Each symbol we transact corresponds to one instance of *karma* in the sender and the receiver. The pleasure of abstractions has a longer *life* because it corresponds to a more abstract location in space and time (the abstractions are bigger domains and durations). The time of the demigods therefore flows slowly because they enjoy the abstractions, which live longer. Their life, however, is still said to be 100 years, just like ours, which means that the *karma* they are enjoying has only as many instances to last 100 years, even though those instances of *karma* live longer by our standards. The measurement of life as 100 years is like currency: you can buy one token with each unit of currency, but that token can denote something abstract or contingent, depending on your choice. Each unit of *karma* produces one symbol, but you can choose if the symbol to enjoy is detailed or abstract. Accordingly, you spend your currency slowly or quickly. When *karma* is spent on abstract objects, the pleasure is longer lived, because the ideas are bigger and longer lived. Conversely, when *karma* is spent on a lot of minute things, then the pleasure is shorter.

Even on Earth, rapid engagement in sensual pleasure finishes a person's life quickly than if he lives on just the essentials. By leading a simple life, one can elongate their lifespan. One hundred units of abstract *karma* will produce a longer life for demigods, the same number of units of contingent *karma* will produce a shorter life for demons. The difference between upper and lower planetary enjoyment can be understood through an example. All of us can, for instance, distinguish between colors such as red, blue, green, etc. The ability to individuate these colors is not a great sense pleasure, relative to the ability to divide red itself into many types of subtle shades of redness such as crimson, scarlet, currant, merlot, garnet, carmine, auburn, burgundy, etc. To enjoy such minor hues, we must invest the effort in dividing redness into more subtle hues, by adding information to redness to subdivide it into numerous subtle shades of red. The physicists who perform particle physics experiments similarly add energy to macroscopic objects to produce many sub-atomic objects (the macroscopic objects are bombarded with energy to produce sub-atomic particles). You might say that burgundy or auburn is more pleasurable than red, and that may be true, but it needs more effort in modifying the object in a way that can actually display those subtle distinctions.

The effort in creating *karma* is proportional to the instances of *karma*. However, this *karma* may be created in different ways. If you are producing *karma* with a subtle sense, you need longer periods of activity. The same *karma* can be quickly produced by a gross sense. Similarly, *karma* is also slowly enjoyed by the subtle sense, and quickly enjoyed by the gross sense. A person desiring a long life of sensual pleasure must engage in long periods of high intensity effort, but a person desiring a long life of subtle pleasure needs to engage in long periods of low intensity effort. For the same duration of life, therefore, the effort in creating sensual pleasure is greater than in creating abstract pleasure. The austerities by demigods and demons are thus different: when demons perform austerities, they undertake severe pain, while the demigods perform meditation that controls the mind and senses, without inflicting physical pain.

For instance, when the demon *Rāvana* performed austerities, he cut off his body parts and offered them to Lord *Śiva* in a fire sacrifice. Similarly, when *Hiraṇyakaśipu* performed austerities, he sat in the same place for so long that his body was eaten up by termites. But as a result of such austerities, they were able to obtain a long life of material control.

Vedic cosmology describes that the bottom of the universe has "hellish planets" where living beings are tortured. Every living being has some *guna*, which define the pain and pleasure for them. Studying books may be pleasurable for one person, and very boring for another. Therefore, pain and pleasure are subjective, but, nevertheless, the opposite of whatever you enjoy is painful. The hellish planets have as much variety as the other places in the universe, where the living beings undergo painful experiences depending on their very definitions of pleasure. Of course, the living being can consider this suffering as "pleasure" if this can alleviate their future pain. The living beings in this state thus survive their miserable existence by hoping for a better life in the future, quite like we might work very hard sometimes hoping that we will one day lead a happy life. That hope of relief from suffering allows them to endure the pain.

Examples of such "pleasure" are seen in the practices of sadism and masochism. The agents of *Yamarāja*—who is said to rule the hellish planets—are the quintessential sadists who enjoy torturing other living beings and the living beings who suffer at their hands are the quintessential masochists. If living beings with a sadistic mentality have performed good *karma*, they are given the opportunity to enjoy their mentality by punishing other beings. Similarly, the living beings who have accumulated bad *karma* are punished by these sadists. The beings who suffer must convert their suffering into pleasure to survive this kind of life. The pain-to-pleasure reversal arises when the suffering individual considers the inflicted pain as justified price for the eventual relief from this suffering. Such rationalization is similar to the Stockholm syndrome[2] in which hostages begin to defend and justify the actions of those who inflict suffering on them, because the captors may eventually free them.

Universe Divisions and Modes of Nature

The universe of planetary systems is therefore divided into three parts:

- The top part dominating in *sattva-guna,* inhabited by *demigods,*
- The lower part dominating in *rajo-guna,* inhabited by *demons,*
- The bottom part dominating in *tamo-guna,* called *hellish planets.*

The *bhūloka* or the "earthly" planetary system, is the lowest in the top half of the universe. It is thus described as lying in "between" the upper and lower parts of the universe. Due to the emergence of work by the five working senses in this planetary system (in order to manipulate macroscopic objects), it is the beginning of the mode of passion and it is a domain in which "work" begins to manifest. However, in the Vedic system, the human beings are not expected to work too hard; only the *śūdra* or the laborers are expected to perform manual labor, while the other three classes perform relatively more mental tasks such as teaching (*Brahmana*), administration (*Kshatriya*), and business (*Vaiśya*). It is worth noting that these classes are not organized by heredity but by intrinsic qualities (called *guna*), abilities, and the accumulated *karma*.

In modern democratic society where we believe in the equality of all humans, the class divides are viewed as oppressive. However, the fact is that these class divides exist even in current times, and are gradually increasing, counter to what democracy is supposed to achieve: the rich and powerful continue to become even richer and even more powerful. Indeed, it is now well-known that even nations and governments are merely puppets in the hands of multinational corporations who manipulate people and laws to ensure the success of their enterprises. So, the idea that society must be divided into classes is not archaic. It exists even in current times, although in a distorted and abusive manner. Its proper realization involves division of workforce into different duties.

Human society is supposed to live by what nature easily provides without much effort. This includes grains, milk, flowers, fruits, precious and other metals, gems, etc. which can be effortlessly molded into consumables. This trend has now been reversed and a lot of effort is being invested to produce technologically modified food, clothes, big buildings and cities, advanced military and defense, gadgetry for communication and entertainment, etc. Everything that is naturally available is processed, packed, transported, stocked, and distributed by technology, and numerous people are involved in bringing a simple thing for our consumption. To consume such products, one must work hard—in professions where one endures long hours of physical and mental stress—only to fulfill eating, sleeping, sex, and security needs, which could have been satisfied even without this effort, if one lived a very simple life.

Modern society is drifting towards a demoniac life in which more energy is invested into enjoying minor variations in matter. Burgundy vs. auburn may seem better than red, but the effort in obtaining this pleasure outstrips the benefits. As people complain about a busy and complicated life, some materialist invents something that is supposed to "simplify" your life, and then you have to work for that too. This hurly-burly life of incremental sense-gratification is the beginning of the law of diminishing returns in which enormous time is invested not in advancing to higher forms of existence but in satisfying the senses. The leaders of society propagate this as "advancement", propelling the human species towards a demoniac life that trades huge amounts of effort for little pleasure.

As this trend continues, life becomes hellish, and the powerful enjoy by laboring the weaker segments of society. Instead of realizing that they are working for the benefit of the powerful, the weak begin to adulate their masters and seek to take their position of power and opulence.

Capitalistic societies have magnified this trend in which the rich continue to get richer, leaving the poor ever more at the mercy of their whims. Meanwhile, rather than realizing their oppression, the weak continue to think that they would—through their hard work—also one day become rich and powerful and exploit the others. Society makes examples out of the lives of the few who have climbed the social ladder, telling others to follow them, even as the weak continue struggling under the illusion that they would one day attain the social status of the masters they currently serve. This ignorance is also called "the rat-race".

The Existence of Galaxies

A notable aspect of Vedic cosmology is that it does not distinguish between what modern cosmology calls galaxies, galactic clusters, supernovae, etc. While each universe is divided into many planetary systems, the modern division based on galaxies etc. does not exist in

Vedic cosmology. In fact, given that a universe is all that can be perceived from inside that universe (each universe is causally complete), and these galaxies can be perceived, they belong to a single universe. The galactic divisions in modern science should be understood as parts of the star constellations. We perceive these star constellations to a stronger or weaker extent. When the strength of the light received from a star is strong, we claim that the star is closer. If the strength of light received from a star is weak, we claim that the star is far. Accordingly, from the same constellation a variety of galaxies are constructed by modern science. Since all the members of each star constellation are not described in Vedic cosmology (only the principal stars of each constellation are described in the *Surya Siddhānta*), we cannot discuss the membership of constellations here. However, we can discuss the conceptual basis of the separation of galaxies in modern science and why it is rejected in Vedic cosmology.

Of course, even modern astronomy describes the galaxies in relation to the constellation in which they are found[3]. For instance, the Andromeda galaxy is seen in the Andromeda constellation and other galaxies are described in relation to the constellations in which they are seen. However, in modern astronomy, the galaxies are not considered to be parts of the constellations in which they are seen due to measurements of light strength which seem to indicate that these galaxies are much farther or closer than the star constellations. Therefore, to understand whether or not the galaxies are parts of star constellations, we must comprehend how these measurements are interpreted. As we have seen, all models are interpretations of observations, and these interpretations are based on the theory of nature. If, therefore, the theory of nature changes, the manner of interpreting data also changes, which alters the models.

One key method of interpreting the distances to galaxies is comparing their luminosity in relation to the luminosity of well-known stars: e.g., those that belong to a particular star constellation. To perform this comparison, we must place the measured body in the same class as the measuring standard[4]. This is analogous to the use of a bigger standard weight in order to measure heavier objects, while using a smaller standard weight to measure lighter objects. The use of a particular measuring standard itself therefore assumes a ballpark estimate of the distance and size of a galaxy, which may not be correct. In the case of distance measurement based on luminosity, the object with lesser luminosity is considered farther in relation to the star with the stronger luminosity, the distance defined by the Inverse Square Law[5]. Based on the comparison of intensities, therefore, modern science derives the distance to stars.

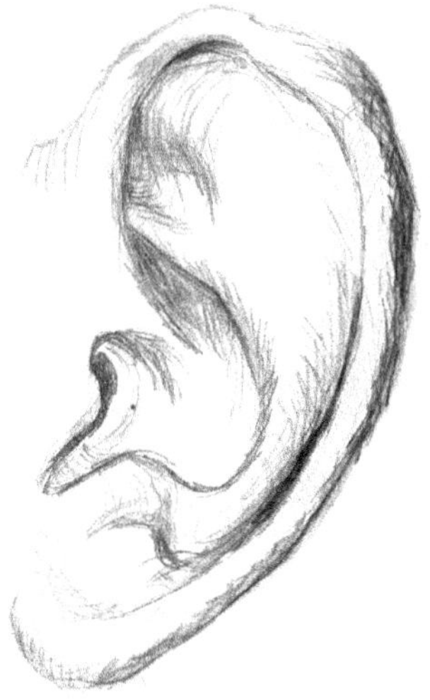

Figure-17 Depth Perception Created Through Shades

The key problem in this measurement is that differences in luminosity don't necessarily imply a *real* depth, although we might *perceive* depth. An example of this fact exists in all drawings: the pixels in a drawing (as shown in Figure-17) are at fixed distance from the viewer, and yet, a sense of far and near is created due to the color contrasts amongst the pixels. In a picture, we don't measure absolute luminosity of the parts in the picture; we measure the relationships in luminosity between the adjacent parts of the picture. With shade gradation it is possible to create the illusion of depth when no such depth exists. For instance, the darker parts of the picture would seem to be farther as compared to the lighter parts. An artist or painter utilizes this principle to create depth perception in a flat drawing or painting. He or she will create darkness to denote greater distance, and lightness to represent proximity to the observer. A similar kind of effect can exist in all distance measurements that rely on light intensity from the distant stars: through measurements we can conclude the existence of real depth when it is only pictorial depth.

The key point is that depth perception can be created in two ways: (1) when there is really depth, and (2) when differing light intensities between adjacent measurements produce the illusion of depth. How do we distinguish between these two cases? In other words, how do we know that we are seeing the picture of an ear versus a real ear? It is notable that star constellations have conventionally been given pictorial interpretations, and most star constellations are still called by such names today; their forms are often compared to animals, or other types of entities. In modern science, these pictures are treated metaphorically rather than realistically. If, however, these pictures were real, and our physical interpretation of them false, then we would be mistaken in inferring real depth, when the depth is created by grades of lightness in a picture.

The semantic view helps us see why pictures may be more real than the physical objects: the bigger picture is more important and star formations are symbols rather than things. The causality in these objects is not in their *individual* positions (as gravity infers) but in their *collective* formation which denotes a picture. The fact is that we cannot measure the star distances individually, and when we measure them in relation to other luminous objects, they can be treated both physically and semantically. This is a classic example of scientific underdetermination where the same phenomena can be interpreted in two different ways—as things and as symbols—and the result of these interpretations produces radically different conclusions about the distances to the stars. If some stars appear to be farther away, because they are darker parts of a picture, a physical interpretation of the observation would produce a greater distance, when the semantic interpretation would produce a picture.

The differences between modern and Vedic cosmologies regarding star distances, therefore, don't necessarily entail that Vedic cosmology is missing in the description of numerous galaxies which modern science has recently discovered. It can also mean that star observations have been interpreted in two different ways to create two different descriptions of nature. The choice between these two interpretations then depends on which constitutes a more complete and consistent theory; clearly as we have seen, the semantic view presents a more consistent and complete theory. In this theory, there is indeed distance, but that distance represents a semantic difference from the observer.

We can construct many pictures in the sky, depending on how we divide the sky into parts. As children, many of us have spent many hours gazing at the sky, creating patterns by joining and dividing different stars. In a physical theory, all such patterns of joining and dividing are illusions, because a physical space has no real boundaries. Regardless of how you divide space into parts in your imagination, no such division could have any implications for reality itself. However, in a semantic theory, the boundaries in space are real; while we cannot sensually perceive the boundaries, their *effects* can be sensually measured. The fact that we can draw boundaries in space, therefore, results in different pictures, which alters our distance measurements (because this distance is produced out of a contrast between star luminosities, and depending on which parts you contrast with, you can interpret greater or lesser depth). It is thus obvious that we cannot arrive at a correct description of distance until we have an accurate understanding of the spatial divisions.

If distance inferences can be illusions produced by pictures, and pictures are byproducts of spatial divisions, then without an absolute sense of how space is divvied into parts, we could not measure distance accurately. All physical measurements that compare the luminosity of one star with another, can be mistaken because they are unable to distinguish between real and pictorial distance. The pictures themselves are imaginary unless the spatial divisions are performed, and hence there can be infinitely many versions of distances in space, depending on how we divide space, and then what we consider real versus pictorial.

The hierarchical space-time is important because it tells us that there is a real sense in which space is divided into parts, although we cannot perceive these divisions by our senses. As a result of this division, we create pictures, and from these pictures we infer distances. Only by fixing spatial divisions, can we actually measure distances. But when space is divided in this way, then distances themselves are semantic; i.e., they denote difference in meanings, rather than the length between objects. The conclusion is that no physical distance measurement can be trusted, even if we have verified it through observation many times over. Correspondingly, the notion that all depth perceptions entail the existence of faraway celestial objects is also mistaken. These ideas are outcomes of presuming a flat, linear, and physical space-time in which there can be objects but no pictures. If science allows pictures to exist in nature and requires their existence to be considered in all measurements, then the modern depiction of many galaxies will have to be reviewed.

How Many Stars in the Universe?

The problem of many galaxies arises from the discovery of many luminaries. Even if we accept that these objects aren't necessarily very far, we are still left with the perplexing question: Why are there so many stars? What purpose do they serve in the universe? In the physical view of nature, the universe has no purpose, and the different parts of the universe don't have to represent any meaning. In a semantic view, all parts of the universe have some meaning and therefore purpose (the meaning is the concept understood by the mind, and the purpose is the intent grasped by the ego; the intent is in turn based upon a deeper moral necessity grasped by the moral sense called *mahattattva*). When the universe has billions of stars, then we must consider the meanings of these billions of places. How do we understand this large variety?

The variety in the universe, which appears as the numerous stars must be understood in the same way as the other variety that arises from dividing the symbol of abstraction into many parts. The symbol of abstraction is the principal star in a constellation, and its details are the many stars that appear around it. The boundary of the constellation represents the collection of all the ways in which the abstraction is detailed. In one sense, there is a lot of variety, because the abstraction is detailed in many ways. In another sense, there isn't variety because all these details are parts of, and expansions from, the symbol of abstraction.

The problem therefore isn't that there are many stars; it is rather that we don't see them as parts of a whole, since we perceive these stars as individual objects, rather than parts of a singular connected whole. This connection isn't necessarily physical proximity, but semantic similarity. We suppose that if two things are separated in space, then they must be distinct objects. The semantic view allows a disparate set of objects to be treated as parts of a single object, quite like there are many cars of a type produced from the abstract type. The stars in the zodiac are like different types of cars, and the stars are thus symbols of the type. In Western astronomy, the constellations are generally described as a few stars (generally not more than a dozen) organized in a specific shape. In Vedic astronomy, the constellation is described as a region of space with a principal star. The principal star is the perfect embodiment of the idea, while the other stars are imperfect symbols of the same idea.

Each of these symbols can become the perfect symbol of another symbol set and produce yet another large set of stars. The fact that we see them means that they are having an influence on Earth. This influence, however, is subject to time, and these stars will, over longer periods of time, become invisible. The fact that stars are constantly being 'born' and 'dying' is avidly studied in modern astronomy to give us insight into the origin of these stars. In Vedic astronomy, none of the stars are being born or dying; they are simply becoming visible and invisible from our perspective. Therefore, the vast regions of empty space in a constellation are not empty; we just don't see those symbols because of the change in time due to which the stars begin or start interacting with us.

The current interpretation of galaxies rests on different observations: (1) the stars are physically separate from each other, and (2) some stars are brighter or darker, (3) we see a Doppler shifted spectrum. All these observations can be interpreted differently, and they are described differently in Vedic astronomy. Today those ideas seem distant to us because we aren't familiar with the Vedic *theory* of space and time.

Aside from the above facts in which a semantic unity underlies a physical diversity, in some cases, there can also be a physical unity underlying an observed diversity. This arises when there is a single physical object, but many paths to that object, which produce the impression of many objects, although this diversity exists only in our perception.

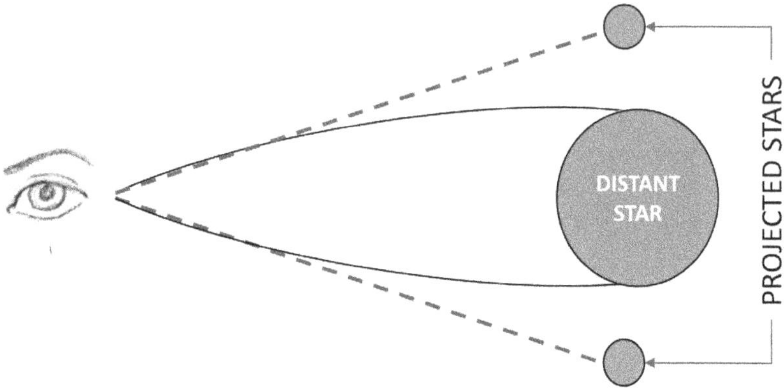

Figure-18 Multiple Paths Produce Multiple Images

Figure-18 illustrates how an object would be *physically* perceived as many objects if there are multiple paths of light to that object, because we extrapolate the perception to a point far away in *front* of the vision. In the physical picture, the objects are always in front of our eyes, if light falls perpendicular to our eyes. If there are many paths to an object, each path will produce a distinct image, which would then be interpreted as a distinct object. In the semantic picture, we determine the objects based on their source and destination. However, in the physical picture, we cannot interpret the properties of the object in this way, and therefore the source of the object is decided simply based on the *path* the light *appears* to take. If a user sent two parcels to a destination, employing two different couriers, in the semantic picture, we will know that the source is the same, but the couriers were different. In the physical picture, we would conflate the courier to be the source of the message, and thus a different courier would imply a different source. Thus, the number of objects we perceive equals the number of objects times the number of paths to each object. If there were only N objects, but there were M paths to each object, then we would perceive N x M objects in the physical picture.

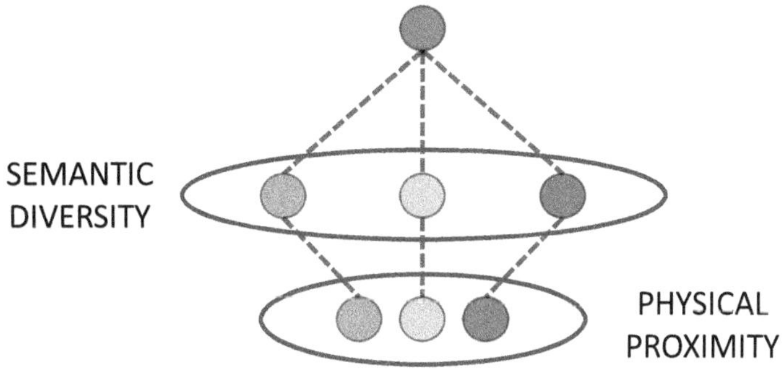

Figure-19 Multiple Paths Produced from Type Differences

One might wonder how path diversity can arise in a semantic tree, as a tree only supports one path to a root. The answer is that we are simultaneously on many branches. The types are semantically different, but the parts are in physical proximity. Just like in our body, the hands and legs are semantically different, but they are in proximity. What we receive from the luminaries can come to us from many paths, because our bodies themselves are passing through many paths. The physical proximity and semantic diversity are not contradictory ideas; the real structure is still a tree, but appears to us as a physical body, although the body parts are only physically close to each other and not semantically similar. As seen in Figure-19, the light from three different paths in the body would be projected in three different directions, resulting in physical diversity. The greater the number of paths crossing a physical object, the greater is the number of paths on which information can be received, and each path now results in the production of many projected object pictures.

The variety in stars therefore is two-fold: (1) there is real variety produced from an abstraction, and (2) there is illusory variety produced from many paths to a single luminary. Through a semantic view of space and time, we can distinguish between these two varieties, although in a physical view they will result in misrepresentations such as the idea that there are many galaxies which are moving away from this galaxy.

Fixing the Cosmic Model

Recall that relativity permits infinitely many models of the universe, because we cannot pinpoint the cause underlying an effect, since there can be infinite different causes that produce the same effect. Effectively, when we receive a message, we don't know the source of that message, or its meaning. We reduce the meaning to a physical change, and we lose the source of the message. Since we lose the source of the message, potentially we could have received the message from any number of different sources. Each of these sources then presents a different model of the universe—i.e., a particular distribution of matter in the universe.

This problem can only be addressed if the message we receive carries the *address* of the source. Since the same message can potentially be received from many sources, if we know the source from the message itself, we can eliminate all the possible sources, except the source indicated in the message. Thus, every observation now has only one interpretation, because the various interpretations arise from the inability to determine the source. Consequently, when we observe the universe semantically, and decode the message sources, the universe has only one model. By knowing the model of the universe, we can know the locations at which material objects exist, but we still don't know their properties.

These properties can again be treated physically and semantically. If we treat the universe physically, the objects have some physical properties {P} which cause some effects {E} according to some laws {L}. The mappings between these three entities are again indeterministic, and a different set of laws would produce the same effect with a different set of properties. The exact nature of the objects in the universe cannot be known simply from the measurements, unless we presume some laws, and whatever laws we presume, other laws are possible. This issue never arises in the Vedic approach because there isn't a "law" that converts properties into effects. There are three modes of nature that interact, not according to a law, but according to a dominant-subordinate relation. Whichever mode dominates becomes the abstraction, and whichever mode is subordinate, becomes the detail to that abstraction. There is hence no "law", other than the notion of a semantic hierarchical tree. The "law" only concerns the *consequences* of actions, also called *karma.*

If therefore a semantic view of nature is accepted, then we can derive two things: (1) the source of the messages, and (2) the meanings of the messages. By knowing the sources, we can determine the object locations, and by knowing the meanings, we can fix their semantic states, thereby resulting in a complete understanding of the universe. The underdetermination of models from observations is therefore solved in the semantic view, because we can know completely about the *cause* from the *effect*, which we could not have known in the physical theory.

However, if we don't have a perfect understanding of nature, our perceptions themselves would be impacted by the false notions. This impact would appear in two forms: (1) we mistake the source of the message, and (2) we mistake the meanings in the message. The extent to which our understanding is mistaken, the object locations would be misrepresented in our theories, and their properties misunderstood. For instance, a single object can be split into many sources, as the message arrives through different paths. Or, many objects can be joined into a single source, because the message arrives through a single path.

6

The Structure of a Universe

When the mind is fixed upon the Supreme Personality of Godhead in His external feature made of the material modes of nature—the gross universal form—it is brought to the platform of pure goodness.

— *Śrimad Bhāgavatam* 5.16.3

The Horizontal Dimension

We have discussed how an inverted tree goes from abstract to contingent, and this "layering" of material elements from top to bottom represents the detailing of material ideas. The conversion of abstract to contingent is, therefore, the "vertical" dimension in a universe. At each level of abstraction there are several ways in which an idea is elaborated thereby forming a *system*: these systems are called *planetary systems* in Vedic cosmology. A system in science is an aggregation of parts which exist independently of the other parts. A system in the Vedic view, however, is one that is *defined* by elaborating an abstract idea into *functional* divisions.

For instance, the human body is a contingent description of the senses, which are a contingent description of the mind. The body is also divided into functions that perform different tasks and are described by functionally different names such as digestive system, circulatory system, nervous system, immune system, etc. It is noteworthy that these divisions of the body are in themselves "systems", which means they are further divided into parts. While the levels of abstraction represent the "vertical" dimension, the further functional divisions of a system within a particular level of abstraction represent its "horizontal" dimension.

The horizontal dimension is not a straight line; it is divided into four "directions": East, West, North, and South. The use of these four directions represents the idea that the horizontal dimension is four distinct types, which together form a square. The square geometry of the horizontal dimension, however, need not be the only way to express the functional divisions; there could be, for instance, a pentagonal, hexagonal, or heptagonal geometry, in which a system is described as comprising a different number of parts. There would be, in such a geometry, more functional parts within a system than seen in a square geometry.

Understanding the horizontal dimension is important because Vedic cosmology describes the planetary systems as being "flat" structures. The *bhū-mandala* system, for instance, is flat, and when this system is identified with Earth, a straightforward contradiction with the idea that the Earth is round is produced, which appears to hark back to medieval flat Earth theories. However, the flatness in this case refers to the idea that the objects in a system are roughly at the same level of abstraction. For example, the experience in the *bhū-mandala* is dominated by macroscopic objects, and all living beings here can perceive matter at a certain level of abstraction. In that sense, the vertical dimension is the extent to which a living being's senses, mind, intellect, ego, and moral sense are advanced to perceive more abstract or more detailed ideas. The horizontal dimension denotes the functional division of these layers into parts.

There is hence a difference between the three-dimensional space that science uses, and the two-dimensional space used in Vedic cosmology. The difference is that our bodies (and by implication all gross material objects) are two dimensional entities because the third dimension represents more *abstract* objects. Since modern science describes our material bodies in terms of three dimensions, there is a need to understand the difference between these two kinds of descriptions.

Objects and Changes

The vertical dimension represents the mode of *sattva* while the horizontal dimension represents the modes of *rajas* and *tamas*. *Tamas* denotes the material objects, and *rajas* represents the change to these objects. To describe the world, we need two dimensions—what an object *is* and what it can *do*. So long as the abstractions—e.g., the concepts or theories by which the world is described—are fixed, material objects and their motion can be described using only two modes. In the first *dimension*, we would *order* or sequence all the objects, and in the second mode or dimension we would order or sequence all the different kinds of changes.

In physical theories, spatial locations can be ordered regardless of how many numbers (e.g., x, y, z) are used to express these locations—*if* these locations are *discrete*. For instance, we can first order the objects by their x coordinate, then by their y coordinate and finally by their z coordinate. After the locations have been ordered, they can be labelled by numbers—1, 2, 3, 4, 5, etc. The result of ordering is that all these objects can be placed on a single dimension. To be countable, the locations must be discrete; i.e., we cannot use irrational numbers (such π or $\sqrt{2}$) to denote the locations. Similarly, all changes can be associated with integers, which can then be sequenced on a single dimension. The point is that the result of such ordering entails that all objects, and all their changes only require two dimensions, *if* these changes and objects are *discrete*.

Current scientific theories treat the world physically and its type differences (abstract and contingent) are thus lost. The three dimensions in space are labeled by three numbers—x, y, and z—and objects at these locations are denoted by three coordinates. Similarly, the motions of objects are denoted by three dimensions of a property called "momentum", which are labelled as p_x, p_y, and p_z. All physical theories require only two properties—position and momentum—but these properties are expressed in three dimensions, because spatial locations and changes are not discrete. This treatment is necessary in classical physics wherein space and time are viewed as *continuous* because the three sets of numbers (x, y, and z) cannot be reduced to a single dimension if these locations are denoted by *irrational numbers* because we fundamentally cannot finish enumerating all irrational numbers in any interval (e.g., between 0 and 1) to even begin counting numbers on another dimension. Similarly, even when objects are counted by natural numbers (1, 2, 3, 4, 5, etc.) we cannot finish counting the objects if the space is infinitely extended on any dimension. To count the objects, therefore, two conditions are necessary: (1) the space is discrete and not continuous, and (2) space is finite and not infinite. If either of these conditions are not fulfilled, a tuple of three numbers cannot be reduced to a single number.

The above two conditions are satisfied in a universe if space and time are treated hierarchically. Essentially, each higher concept represents a larger but finitely extended domain of objects, and objects within that domain don't have to be counted from $-\infty$ to $+\infty$. Similarly, the objects in the material world are discrete and not continuous; this is now known through atomic theory. These conditions were not true in classical physics, because space and time were infinite, and matter was infinitely divisible. When space and time are finite and matter is discrete, the three dimensions reduce to one. Then, all locations and changes—which represent the classical physical properties of x and p—can be reduced to two numbers, without breaking them into three distinct coordinates.

When Vedic cosmology speaks about a flat *bhūloka*, it is not talking about two *spatial* dimensions such as x and y. It is rather speaking about a 'space' comprising two dimensions x and p, which were classically called position and momentum and comprise the *phase space* of classical physics[1]. The classical physical phase space has 6 dimensions (3 dimensions each for x and p) but the semantic phase space needs only two dimensions of *tamo-guna* and *rajo-guna*, which respectively represent material objects and their changes. The flat Earth topologies being described in Vedic cosmology are thus not referring to the flatness of Earth in the ordinary space of three dimensions but in the *semantic phase space* which only needs two dimensions to denote objects and their changes.

The cardinal direction north-south denotes less *rajas* in the north and more *rajas* in the south. The cardinal direction east-west denotes more *tamas* in the west and less *tamas* in the east. This principle is used in the construction of a house based on Vedic principles even today. For instance, north-east which is less *rajas* and less *tamas* is used for spirituality and worship of God. Conversely, the south-west which is high in both *rajas* and *tamas* is used as the bedroom of the householder and employed for sexual enjoyment (high in *rajas*) and sleep (high in *tamas*).

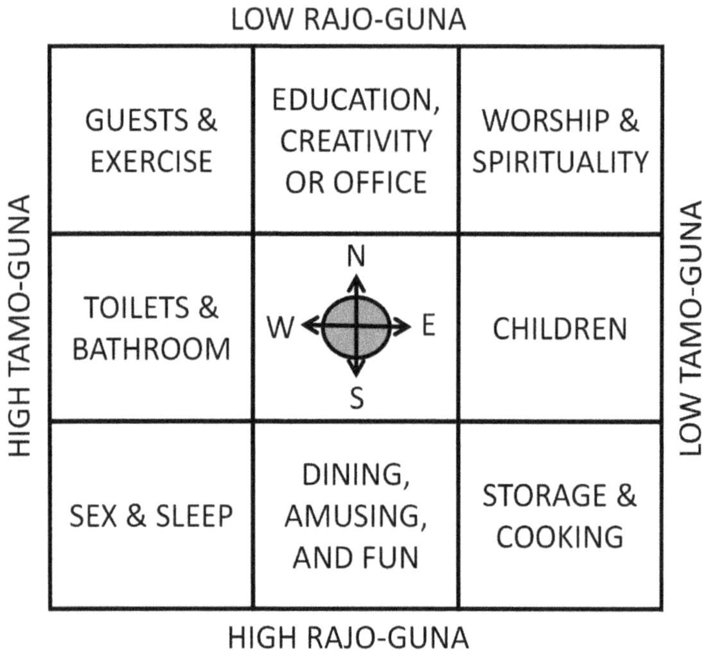

Figure-20 The Cardinal Directions in Flat Space

Other parts of the house are similarly used for different functions based on the relative proportion of the two material modes. The center of the house, which is balanced in both the modes is kept empty as a courtyard and it is the place where the three modes are "balanced". The emptiness of the central part represents the fact that the universe prior to the creation of imbalance in the modes is empty and is called *pradhāna*. Conversely, when the distinction between the three modes of nature begins to appear, the universe is called *prakriti*. The center denotes the perfection of balance from which the directions denoting a mode are created.

Thus, when we speak about 'space' in Vedic cosmology we must understand it as the domain in which we scientifically describe matter. It is not the space in which we perceive the objects. The phase space in modern science is a conceptual or theoretical space, while the space we perceive is the physical space. The two dimensions of space (x and p in modern science) constitute a complete description of matter and its changes. Additionally, in Vedic cosmology, space is hierarchical and closed rather than linear and flat. This hierarchy constructs the 3rd dimension.

Thus, when we speak about east being low in *rajo-guna* we don't mean in the sense of a flat space where you must go to the eastern most point in the universe to reduce *tamas*. Rather, since space is hierarchical, even within a house constructed according to the Vedic principles, the eastern part of the house is lesser in *tamas*. The eastern point in the universe is certainly lesser in *tamas* but the western side of the house on the eastern point would be higher in *tamas*. Similarly, for a house adjoining the first on its eastern side, the western side of the adjoining house is high in *tamas* although it is more to the east than the first house.

The relative proportions of the material modes should not be associated with an open space-time where an incremental shift to the left or right would proportionately change the qualities. Rather, they must be viewed hierarchically. The idea of a "house" is more abstract than the idea of a "bedroom". Therefore, the location of the bedroom is defined in relation to the house, and not in relation to the absolute east, west, north or south. Another house westward from the first one, but with a bedroom towards the east will disturb the marital life of the married inhabitant, even though it is more towards the west (in an absolute sense of the east and west cardinal directions) than the bedroom in the first house.

The two-dimensional geometry of the planetary systems in Vedic cosmology is indeed flat Earth geometry, but this flatness is rather deceptive because the flat geometry is not ordinary space but phase space, and this space is hierarchical rather than flat or open. There are then three key differences between the modern and the Vedic notions of space: (1) the space is a phase space rather than a location space, (2) the space is closed and not infinitely extended, and (3) the vertical dimension denotes conceptual abstractness. All three dimensions represent different things, and the directions are types. Unless these differences are grasped, comparisons between Vedic and modern cosmology will only baffle us.

Disconnected Surfaces in Phase Space

An important aspect of Vedic cosmology is that it divides the horizontal plane into circular domains called *dvīpa* and *samudra*—loosely translated as an "island" and an "ocean". The *bhū-mandala*, for instance, is divided into seven alternating concentric and circular regions of islands and oceans, not merely by the four cardinal directions north, south, east, and west. An understanding of these divisions requires a deeper grasp of the relationship between an object and its changes than discussed so far. This relationship, in turn, requires a discussion of atomic theory, rather than classical physics, and I will therefore turn to this discussion[2].

In classical physics, any object can have any position and momentum, and objects are decoupled from their physical states (described by their position and momentum). Later developments in physics—such as the Theory of General Relativity, however, discarded this separation between objects and phase space, preferring to describe material objects simply as events in phase space such that the object is identical to the event. The semantic view also requires the same approach, although the location in phase space is treated semantically rather than physically. Quantum theory adds a twist to this description in which position and momentum are not independent properties; rather, they are related by a complementarity relationship wherein fixing the position of an object does not completely fix the momentum, although it limits the possible momenta for that state. This complementary relation between momentum and position has been a source of many interpretations about its real meaning, and the debate on this relation continues to this day.

In the semantic view, the spatial dimension of the phase space represents *object concepts* while the change dimension represents *action concepts.* Every object can be described as a collection of object properties, such as taste, touch, smell, sound, and sight. Similarly, every object can be described in terms of the actions it can be used for. For example, a hammer can be used as a tool or as a weapon, and the objective properties of the hammer do not fix its possible uses. Similarly, tools and weapons are not limited to hammers; a screwdriver is also a tool, and an axe is also a weapon. However, a hammer cannot be used as a car, or a shirt. There is a diverse set of things that a hammer can do, but this diversity cannot be extended to every possible action. To perform other actions, the objective properties of that object would also have to be altered. In short, the objective properties of any object *limit* the possible use cases for that object, although every object can potentially be used for many different kinds of activities. It is also possible to envision some objects which can only be used for one type of action, and there is hence a one-to-one mapping between the objects and their possible actions.

This relationship between everyday objects and their possible actions helps us see why position and momentum are complementary properties in quantum theory when quantum objects are interpreted semantically. The complementarity represents the fact that fixing the position (i.e., the objective properties) does not fix the momentum (i.e., the possible actions) although it limits the possible actions of that object. Based on the above, we can envision different kinds of objects:

- Those which have many use cases that lie on a continuum: i.e., we can find use cases "in between" two use cases. E.g., a hammer can be used as a tool or a weapon, and sometimes the tool is a weapon. The different use cases can thus be ordered in a semantic scheme by the "type" of action, if the space itself denoted the action types.
- Those which have many use cases but are not on a continuum: i.e., some use cases are similar and therefore proximate to each other, but there are also use cases that are disconnected. For instance, salt can be used for cooking and for taste, but salt can also be used to clean stains or scrub floors. The cooking and cleaning functions of salt are like a wide variety of cooking and cleaning, but it is harder to find a function that lies in between these alternatives.

- Those which have only one use case and the object cannot be used to perform many dissimilar types of functions or actions.

We can also envision uses that can be realized with only one object, with many similar objects, and with objects that are not like each other.

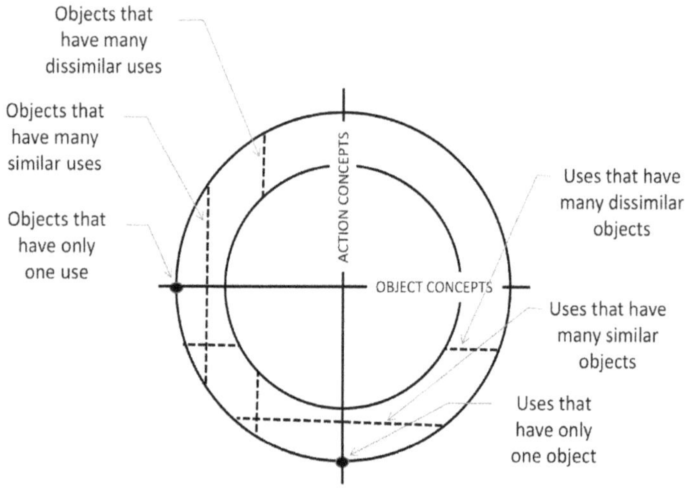

Figure-21 The Object-Use Relationship

The result of this complementary relationship between object and its use is illustrated in Figure-21; the result is that if we were to plot object and use relationships, we would have to use concentric circles to denote them. This is, of course, not a complete picture of the relationship, and gets more nuanced as we draw many successive concentric circles. The nuance is that unlike the scenario illustrated in Figure-21, which shows only two possible disconnected surfaces, there can be more than two disconnected surfaces in which an object can have many disconnected use cases, and a use case can have many disconnected objects. This more nuanced picture of the relationship between objects and use cases is illustrated in Figure-22 where an object has four disconnected types of use cases, and a use case has four disconnected types of objects. As more concentric circles are added into the picture, we would find a structure in the phase space in which the object-action relationship is even more nuanced by the discovery of even more disconnected surfaces. I will return to this topic in the next chapter when we discuss the nature of *bhū-mandala* and describe how Vedic cosmology suggests that in the flat horizontal plane of the present universe, there are seven disconnected surfaces, which opens the possibility for the exploration of the nature of the semantic phase space—i.e., why there are seven surfaces, and what those disconnections represent. The key point here is that when the world is described semantically, we can begin to see patterns in the phase space, which would otherwise be invisible in the physical space.

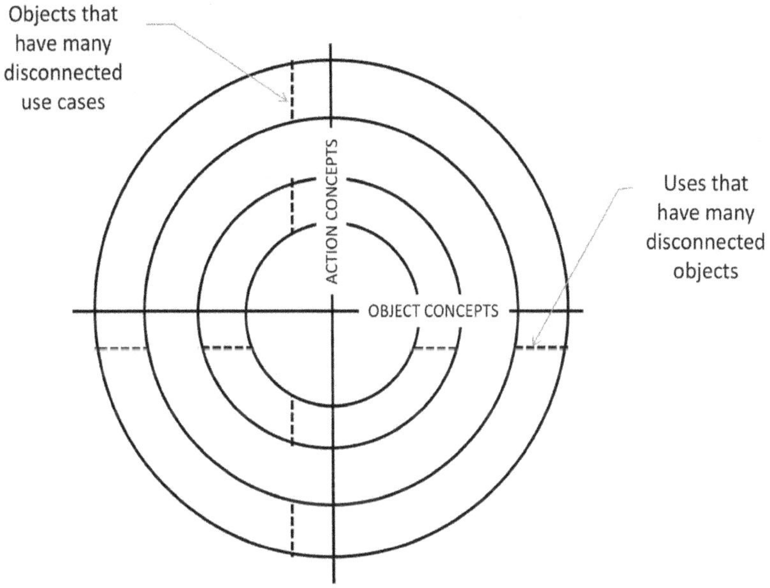

Figure-22 Multiple Disconnected Object-Use Surfaces

In Vedic cosmology, the disconnected surfaces don't have the same "size", and the successive disconnected surfaces are twice as large as the previous surface. These surfaces, as previously noted, are called *dvīpa* or "islands" separated by *samudra* or "oceans", and the successive islands and oceans grow double in size. This terminology has proved quite difficult in modern times because while we can intuitively understand that we have "deeper" or "higher" aspects such as mind, intelligence, or ego, it is much harder to understand why there is a flat Earth, and why it is then divided into many concentric oceans and islands which appear to have absolutely no counterpart in ordinary experience. The fact that we cannot see or observe these islands and oceans is simply because we are situated on a particular surface, and there is no way that we can *continuously* move from one surface to another using the same kind of object. For instance, we cannot keep walking to the end of one surface and hope to find another surface because that surface is disconnected in terms of activity from the original surface. To move to another surface, we would have to dramatically change the activities performed by our bodies.

The oceans separating the islands represent the extent to which an object must change its activity before a radically dissimilar activity or use case for that object would be found. Similarly, the oceans also represent the extent to which the object can be changed before another object that performs the same activity is found. The key point of this disconnection is that there are many objects which can perform the same activity, and many activities that an object can exhibit, but all these activities are not apparent in the same kind of "geography". Rather, to see that radically different activity or object, we must go to a different part of the phase space. The disconnection also means that many of the objects that we see in the present geography would be found even in other geographies and many of the activities that we see in the present geography would be visible even in other geographies. In particular, everything that exists in the central island would be seen in all outer islands, but many things found in the outer islands will not be present in the central island. The outer islands are therefore supersets of the successively inner islands and therefore they are naturally "bigger" in size than the inner islands.

The Lotus Geometry

The Vedic scriptures describe the various planetary systems in analogy to a lotus flower which is comprised of several larger and larger concentric circles of petals that enclose the smaller and smaller petals within them. Each disconnected surface or island therefore corresponds to one such circle. The *Śrīmad-Bhagavatam*, *Padma Purāna*, and other Vedic literatures, for instance, describe the *bhū-mandala* as a lotus flower. Similarly, Lord Brahma is said to be situated on a lotus flower, and the heavenly planetary system called *svarga* is also described as a lotus.

The key import of these descriptions is that each of the successively higher and lower planetary systems is divided into many disconnected surfaces of objects and actions, although at each such level of abstraction or detailing, the definition of the object and action would change.

For instance, in the highest planetary system of Lord Brahma, objects would be morals since Lord Brahma creates the *mahattattva*, which comprises different kinds of moralities found in the present universe, and the actions would be the kinds of activities that are consistent with the practice of that moral. It is noteworthy that morality is not merely a human trait, and even animals exhibit moral behavior and biologists have recorded altruistic behavior even amongst animals. Morality is therefore a property of living species, including humans and higher demigods.

In the next lower planetary system—called the *tapaloka*—the objects will be intentions, and actions would be those which are consistent with those intentions. The disconnected surface structure of any planetary system essentially means that every object can have many disconnected uses, and every use can be enacted by many disconnected objects, and this diversity is present at the various levels of material abstraction.

The lotus structure, however, also represents another finer structure in the phase space, if this space is divided radially as shown in Figure-23. In the radial division, some parts of the phase space are forbidden, and they cannot be accessed. This inaccessibility, however, is a temporary phenomenon and it entails that different kinds of objects and their activities become manifest at different times. At other times, either those objects or their activities cannot be manifest. For instance, at certain times, we might find a new use case for an object that always existed. And at other times we can create a new object for an existing use case. These objects and use cases, however, may disappear over time, or may be visible only in certain parts of the island.

For example, people until about a century back used to use chariots and horses for transportation, which has now been replaced by cars and trucks. The use case (transportation) has remained unchanged (relatively speaking) but the older objects enacting that use case have now disappeared. Similarly, paper books are being replaced by digital books, and newspapers by online news outlets.

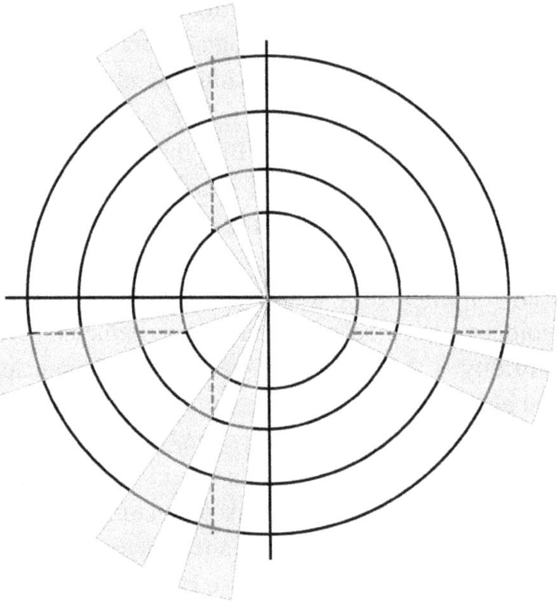

Figure-23 Radial Divisions in the Phase Space

This means that the radial division of the flat surface is not static at all times. Rather, this division evolves through the rotation of the radiating triangles. The triangles carve out a smaller region of the phase space in each disconnected island which is manifest when the triangle passes over it and is unmanifest at other times. All types of objects and activities are therefore not always visible and new kinds of phenomena are being created at different times. The "lotus" topology of the flat space is therefore not a fixed structure in the phase space. Rather, this surface should be viewed as changing with time. In a later section I will discuss how space in Vedic cosmology is said to rotate at a constant rate, and this constant rotation brings about changes in seasons. Different kinds of fruits and vegetables are visible in different seasons, different times of a year bring into focus different kinds of activities (e.g., work and vacation), and animals have breeding, migration and hibernation seasons. There are also bigger and smaller time cycles, which then further fragment the phase space into smaller and smaller parts, making different objects and activities visible and invisible at different times. All these objects and activities are always *possible,* but they become real by changing times.

The flat surface should not be seen as a fixed lotus. Rather, the lotus "revolves" with time, making different parts of the phase space visible. The rotation thus represents cyclic time such that the same kinds of objects and activities become visible and invisible with the passing of time. The entire phase space is therefore never visible at all times, and the description of the flat surface in terms of islands and oceans is only therefore an approximation of the rotating lotus structure. Since the rotating lotus sweeps a broad circular area, the description of the horizontal dimension as islands and oceans is a time agnostic description of the world. The static lotus picture of the world is a snapshot of the same world at any given instant in time. And the real time description of the same world is a rotating lotus. Through such successive refinements, it is possible to understand why the same universe is described in different ways.

Ultimately, a predictively accurate description of the world requires a theory of the hierarchical space-time which would predict the events and activities visible at any time. But even without such a predictively accurate theory, the general structure of the universe can be grasped if only some basic ideas about semantic space and time are understood.

The Vedic descriptions of cosmology are therefore not silly, unintelligible, or grandiose pictures of nature. They are rather based on a very simple theory—that the world is comprised of the three modes of nature which repeatedly subdivide the elementary axioms underlying a universe to produce different kinds of variety at different times. Since this simple picture of nature has been misunderstood in science, numerous incorrect theories of reality have been produced, which then appear to contradict the Vedic description, creating the impression that scientific descriptions are superior to the ancient Vedic revelations. Of course, the scientific theories are themselves either false or misunderstood in various ways as we have already noted. For instance, the physical treatment of space loses touch with the real world of types. The linear and open space-time is a construction from the physical view. Under this physical view scientific concepts such as quantum complementarity become intractable and are misunderstood as representing some sort of incompleteness in nature when the incompleteness really is a feature of the theory. A semantic view of nature will not only produce a better understanding of nature, bring it more in contact with the world of everyday experience, but also ratify the Vedic descriptions of the world as being far superior.

Universe as a Vibration

While all physical theories treat time linearly, the measurement of time requires a repeating pattern. Thus, ordinary clocks have rotating hands for hours, minutes, and seconds, more accurate measurements of time are performed with light bouncing back and forth in a silvered box, and clocks in electronics are constructed using the vibrations of atomic objects. Quantum theory itself describes the atomic world as a "wave" although under the physical interpretation of the world, this wave becomes a "complex" variable function and cannot be given a realistic interpretation. As a result, the "wave" in quantum theory is reduced to a probability function, which then gives the impression that nature is uncertain.

The semantic view frees us from these problems, and nature is again seen as a vibration, which Vedic philosophy calls "sound". This sound is big and small, which means that there are abstract ideas and detailed ideas. Everything in the universe is therefore vibrating like a string, and that periodic change represents cyclic time. This cyclic change, however, is not *in time* where we suppose that the time is linear, and the motion is cyclic. Rather, the cyclic change itself *is time* where we change the structure of time itself, since all changes are cyclic. Even what we see as linear motion or "progress" is actually a smaller part of a much bigger cycle and if we only see a very small segment of a very large circle, it appears to us as a line although this view cannot be extended limitlessly.

It is therefore incorrect to say that the world is changing *in* time. It is correct to say that the world *is* cyclic change. That is, we don't separate objects from the structure of space and time and assume that these objects are *in* space and time. The structure of space and time *is* the nature of objects. If we simply described the structure of space and time correctly, we would have also completely described the nature of matter.

Thus, the universe and its parts are changing periodically not caused by a "force" that originates in the properties of those objects. Rather, the cause of that change is time itself: time has a cyclic nature, which then causes everything in the universe to change cyclically (there are smaller cycles nested in larger and larger cycles). It is therefore said that the cause of all changes in the world is time, and the three modes of nature are simply working under the control of time. Their relative dominance, appearance, and disappearance is caused by time. This is different from the scientific view where the causality is in the three modes of nature (the material properties) and their interaction creates the "impression" of passing time according to some law that has no physical existence.

Thus, if we attribute causality to matter (rather than to space and time), then we have to postulate laws we can never "see". As I noted earlier, science postulates many ideas to describe matter, which are never given any reality beyond pragmatic utility. That approach, however, leads to the problem of explaining their origin—e.g., the origin of numbers. In the Vedic view, this problem does not arise because ideas (and numbers) are produced by time, and they are material entities as well. Their production and annihilation therefore must be explained by a theory of nature, and that is possible only if we attribute causality to space and time rather than to the objects that are being produced and destroyed.

All vibrations are, in Vedic philosophy, properties of the "ether" in the sense that they are not separated from the ether. This ether, however, is semantic space, in a vibration which denotes a meaning. If we discard these vibrations (and therefore the meanings) we arrive at a physical picture in which all locations are identical, and matter resides *in* space. Now, we have a problem in explaining why light always moves at a constant speed. When this problem is resolved in the physical view by replacing a universal space with that of an individual reference frame, new issues crop up: e.g., if everyone can describe the world in different ways, then many possible descriptions must be true, from a *given* standpoint. All these descriptions arise in the attempt to give *meaning* to our observation (e.g., that my force is due to my motion, rather than due to a massive object), and if all these descriptions are equivalent, there cannot be universal meanings. Once you discard meanings, then the theory becomes indeterministic: it is compatible with many possible matter distributions.

These issues don't arise in semantic ether because there is a universal space, in which locations denote meanings. The space is therefore not flat or linear or inert. Rather, each location in space is a type of vibration that denotes a type or meaning. Light takes a finite time in *modifying* this vibration, or in getting absorbed, which denotes the time taken to modify meanings. If meaning modification needs time, and meanings are denoted by locations in space, then science essentially becomes the study of meanings, which is no different than the study of the structure of space and time. This stance is similar to that in general relativity where matter is the curvature of space-time, although there are obvious differences such as the fact that this curvature is associated both with a universal space and with an observer's frame. In the universal space, the curvature denotes reality, and in the observer's frame, it denotes how that reality would be distorted in perception. The modern theory of curvature therefore only studies the properties of perceptual distortion but rejects the reality that is being distorted. The semantic theory allows both distortions and views the observer's distortion as the cause of illusion.

Core vs. Context in a System

Vedic cosmology does not end at descriptions of the large-scale structure of space and time, but also dwells on the social and economic organization in each universe. The structure of these divisions is that they are divided into four classes, which are called by different names in different parts of the universe, although the structure of four-fold division remains invariant. This four-fold division has been misunderstood in modern times as a "caste system" because the semantic structure of society and economics is itself not well-understood. Here, I will try to describe the basis of the Vedic social system using concepts of types and hierarchy as previously used in the context of space, time, and universal divisions.

To understand the nature of the Vedic social order, we must first grasp some everyday concepts in terms of which our social system is described. If these concepts are sufficiently generic, they can be extended to construct a model of the social system. Here, I will use the concept of dividing a system into core and context, which applies equally well to organizations, individuals, ecosystems, economies, and societies.

Every system is comprised of a core which is its purpose of existence. There are other things that are context to this core, although they support the core. For instance, a tool manufacturing company has tool design—that differentiates them from their competitors'—at its core. To track its employees' work hours and holidays, payroll, performance evaluation, etc. the tool company needs other "tools" which are context to the company. The things in the context are necessary to support the core practices of tool design because the company will not have employees who design tools if they weren't getting paid on time, or their performance was not being measured against the goals of the company. Nevertheless, the tooling company cannot afford to spend most or even large parts of its time in dealing with work hours, holidays, payroll, and performance evaluation if it must be successful in building the best tools.

In our daily lives too, there are things that are core to us, and other things that are contextualized from this core. For some people, their family life may be core, and their jobs may be the context which supports the core purpose of enjoying a happy family life. For others, their jobs may be the core purpose of their existence while their family life may be the context which gives their work life a semblance of social acceptability. Some people live to eat, while others eat to live. Some people exercise just enough to have a healthier work life, while others work so that they can pay for a physically active life. Every system therefore divides itself into a core and a context and focuses upon the core while giving the context only fringes of attention. The core therefore lies at the "center" of that system while the context lies at the "periphery" of the same system.

When we make something the context in a system, it should, in general, become the core activity of another system if that function is important. For instance, if a company needs to run payroll effectively, it must either buy a good payroll software, or outsource the payroll activity to some contracting company that ensures that employees get their salaries on time. The company that builds the payroll software, or renders payroll services, has payroll as the core of its work, while other things like managing the building in which its employees work, ensuring that the restrooms are clean and hygienic, or that the offices of the company are secure, become context. These contextualized activities would then become the core of someone else, while leaving other contexts out.

We normally suppose that everyone has some core and context, and the core-context relationships should therefore exist in a "network" of relationships where some individual or organization's core is another individual or organization's context. The context "serves" the core, making the focus upon the core practically possible. We generally suppose that everyone has some core and context, and these cores and contexts must be mirrored in the world. In fact, we suppose that no one should be only the context for other cores. Rather, everyone—depending on their functional capacity and expertise—must be both core and context.

This networked picture of core and context, however, presents us with the same difficulties that we saw in the definition of concepts by using objects. What becomes contextualized also become conceptualized or abstracted from the system that is contextualizing it. That is, in contextualizing, the system doesn't care about the internal details of how that function is organized or structured. One simply expects the outputs of that system to meet the needs of supporting its core purpose, because if the attention is diverted to understanding the details of how the context is structured and organized, then it naturally becomes the core, defeating the purpose of having a context. This doesn't necessarily mean that the abstracted function is actually abstract; it only means that we are not aware of the details, and therefore see the context abstractly. However, if this abstraction must be defined after the details have already been constructed, then the details themselves cannot emerge on their own.

As an example, if you need payroll services and want to contextualize your payroll activity but no one else has thought of a payroll service so far, you would not obtain that service. When you want a payroll service, there must be enough demand for this abstraction to be present in the marketplace for someone to come up with a company that provides payroll outsourcing. In other words, the mechanics of payroll outsourcing does not begin in some material parts automatically combining to become a mechanism which *you* perceive as a payroll outsourcing. Rather, the process begins in defining payroll outsourcing as a *concept,* which is then developed into the mechanics. The concept of payroll outsourcing is logically prior to the mechanics that implements that concept.

This leads us to the same conclusion as in the development of a hierarchical theory of concepts, that the division of a system into core and context must also follow the hierarchical pattern in which there is a core function which is not context for anything. This core, however, creates some contexts, which may then create more contexts, and so forth, until we arrive at some function that is only core and has no other context.

The original core (that is not anything else's context) is the root of that system, while the final core without a context is the leaf of the system. In other words, the real structure of society cannot be a network. It must rather be a tree structure that begins in some individuals or organizations that are the "core" of the society. To support this core, the core must contextualize other things, which then become the core of another organization or individual, and so forth, until there are individuals or organizations which simply have a core but no context. Note, however, that we are not speaking about the original core being more abstract than the eventual core. Tool manufacturing is not more abstract than conducting payroll functions. Both are equally contingent, but tool manufacturing just happens to be something that is certainly more core than payroll.

In the business world, the distinction between core and context is called the distinction between products and services. The organization that creates products also contextualizes some services for the other organizations, which may then contextualize even more services for other organizations. If nobody made any products, then no services would be needed to support the creation of such things. The ultimate core is therefore something that is just products, while the ultimate context is something that is a service whose functions are never contextualized.

In the Vedic model, this social system is represented by four classes—*Brahmana*, *Kshatriya*, *Vaiśya*, and *Śūdra*. The *Brahmana* are the core of the society as they produce the core "product" of society—knowledge. To support this knowledge-producing activity, the *Brahmana* are supported by kings, governments or administrators, who provide all the necessary ingredients to the *Brahmana* to assist their production of knowledge. The kings may provide *Brahmana* with money, food, and land, allowing them to focus on the core activity of knowledge creation, rather than earning a livelihood. Of course, for the kings to help the *Brahmana*, the *Vaiśya* or businessmen must support the kings by performing economic activity, part of which is given to the kings as taxes, which is used to administer society and fund the knowledge creation activity. The *Vaiśya* are in turn not the core workers, but those who connect to other businessmen and exchange goods, thereby creating "organizations" that employ workers. The workers work in the institutions created by the *Vaiśya* and the resulting business profits are funneled to them as salary or other compensations. In this social model, the *Kshatriyas* serve the *Brahmana*, the *Vaiśya* serve the *Kshatriyas* and the *śūdra* or workers serve the *Vaiśya*. Society thus works cooperatively to produce its core product of knowledge about the nature of reality. Society is therefore not a "network" of "equal" individuals, because this equality does not present a consistent or complete social model. Rather, society is organized in a hierarchy, and divided by various core and context divisions.

The four social divisions are described in the *Śrīmad Bhāgavatam* as the ideal social model for every island of the *bhū-mandala*; these social orders exist even in the higher and lower planetary systems. The fourfold division of society is not a man-made creation, let alone the social peculiarity of ancient Indians. It is rather a *theory* of social systems in which society is organized into a hierarchy constructed through core and context, with a specific kind of aim, which is to acquire knowledge. The *Brahmana* are therefore the core of society because the goal of society is knowledge, and not economic development, sense pleasure, or material advancement. When the focus of society changes, and other kinds of activities such as economic or material advancement become the core, then the *Brahmana* are either made to serve the purpose of economic development and material advancement, or they simply cease to exist.

A proper understanding of the Vedic social system depends upon an understanding of the purpose of society, which depends on realizing that without such an understanding, the living being is simply under the control of the law of *karma* produced from various illusions about reality.

The Theory of Modal Realism

The fantastic descriptions of Vedic cosmology are distant today because we don't seem to perceive most of what this cosmology describes. Why? One of the key reasons is that we suppose these descriptions to pertain to different *physical locations* that comprise of physically different material objects rather than different *observational perspectives* on the same reality. If you are looking at a cube from different sides, you can see different things, but the cube is the same. Similarly, the different planetary systems and their subdivisions have to be viewed not as physically different objects but as different "perspectives" on the same reality.

Vedic philosophy describes that demigods live in our body because parts of our body are *instances* of the abstract concepts they represent. Thus, for instance, *Indra* resides in the hands, *Surya* in the eyes, *Chandra* in the mind, and *Varuna* on the tongue. The parts of our body are therefore also parts of the bodies of the demigods since these demigods are controlling specific types of concepts. Similarly, the demons can control the minute details in our body over which we have no control, and these details can therefore also become part of their bodies. In fact, other living being can be 'invited' to share our bodies, and thereby control them, and Vedic *mantra* (both for demigods and for demons) are often used to facilitate this control for mutual interest. In the horizontal dimension, however, this kind of control is not possible, unless facilitated by the demigods or demons. When it has been facilitated, we can also share other living being's bodies within the horizontal dimension (e.g., *bhūloka* planets).

When this kind of sharing arrangement is understood, we can see that we are not this body, because the same body can be performing a different action in another world due to some actions that we perform here. Similarly, we are not our actions, because the same action can be performed by a different body in another world, and we are not aware of it. Our thoughts, intentions, and judgments are producing changes in the bodies of demigods, and the changes in the bodies of the demigods are producing changes in our thoughts, intentions, and judgments. The actions we perform with our body can please or displease the demons, because via these actions we cause changes to their bodies too. Likewise, the actions by the demons can give us pleasure or displeasure because through their actions, the demons can cause changes to our bodies.

In the physical view, we are our bodies and minds, and only causes that "travel" in space can affect us. In the semantic view, our bodies and minds are also parts of other bodies and minds, and other bodies and minds are parts of our body and mind. There is no such thing, therefore, as "me" as a body and mind. We are simply experiencing different "perspectives" or "parts" of the total cosmic experience. Things that we experience are not available to other living beings, and things that other living beings experience are not available to us, not because they are different things, but because they are different perspectives on the same thing. This fact can be illustrated through a simple everyday example.

Think of a movie reel with a sequence of pictures. If two people are shown alternate frames on the reel, they would see the same film and yet not have the same experience. Their mutually exclusive experiences are based on the same reality of the movie reel, but they only see parts of it, depending on which parts are available to their vision. We can say that they are having different "perspectives" about the same movie reel.

We earlier noted that *māyā* covers our vision and causes us to see only parts of reality. As a consequence of that misapprehension, *karma* is created which causes us to become exposed to the other parts of the reality, while the previously visible parts may be covered. *Māyā* and *karma* therefore produce different phenomena by hiding the different pictures on the same movie reel, which we interpret as the existence of many different movies. Our diverse visions of the world should be viewed as our constructions that hide parts of the real movie. In Vedic philosophy, only God has the complete experience and we only have parts of that experience; we are like the viewers who see a fraction of the frames on the complete movie reel, while the other frames are invisible to our vision.

This analogy is a useful way to understand why we don't see many parts of the Vedic cosmos: the reason is that the different parts of the cosmos are *defined* by the different types of frames of the movie reel that are visible. These parts are therefore not material entities in the physical sense, and the living beings are not those physical entities. Rather, their experiences are perspectives of limited vision on the complete movie reel. Being in a particular part of the cosmos is like experiencing a particular face of a cube. No part of the material world provides a complete comprehension of reality, because all these parts are defined by the manner in which the whole reality is *selected* to present a specific type of vision. The parts of the cosmos should therefore not be seen as giving us a complete understanding of a part of reality, but a partial understanding of the full reality. In the physical view of reality, we think that if I see an apple, I completely understand the apple as a physically distinct object, although I may not know the rest of the universe. In the semantic view, there aren't many distinct objects; there is only one object—God—but our vision of His existence is covered by *māyā*, thus creating different phenomena. God is the *object* and all these partial visions of God are the phenomena; we might say that the material world is a *property* of God, and these properties can be attributed to God, because they are parts of His personality although we don't see the entire personality due to *māyā.*

Like the movie reel is one, but can be presented partially to different observers, the semantic universe is also one object which is partially seen by different beings, and the *types* of things they see define their "location" by defining their "perspective" on reality. Normally, we all assume that we have different experiences because we are watching different movies, and while watching some movie we cannot watch another movie, but we have the choice to change the movie we are watching and therefore all the movies are potentially viewable by everyone. In the semantic view, the movie that you see is part of the whole movie, and we cannot arbitrarily decide which parts to see because the law of nature itself determines which parts would be made available to your experience.

If you see every 5th frame in a film, and I see every 4th frame of a film, we will both see the 20th frame. That frame will then be the shared experience, and it will represent our shared bodies and minds. The same experience may be shared by many living beings, and they too are then sharing our body and mind. The problem arises only if we think that we are our body and mind and therefore nobody can share our body and mind because that body and mind is our "identity". The fact is that we aren't bodies and minds. These are simply phenomena being presented to consciousness and there is no privacy in this presentation. Many living beings can share the same experience, and even when they are not sharing it, there is in fact a shared reality—God's experience. These bodies and minds are not actually "ours". They are rather God's body and mind, and we just happen to see parts of that universal body and mind and consider that to be ours. From a semantic standpoint, demigods and demons, or other living beings in the *bhū-mandala* could share our body and mind, which they may consider "their" body and mind under illusion.

This viewpoint is similar to the idea of *modal realism* proposed by David Kellogg Lewis who argued that there are many possible worlds, and all those worlds are actually real. The domains of phase space are different kinds of possibilities. Which possibility becomes *our* reality is determined by the laws of nature. The same reality may also be someone else's reality, and therefore many living beings can suffer and enjoy the "same" body. In fact, it is said that ghosts don't have their own body, but they try to share another living body and that body then becomes haunted because the body and the mind start doing things that are actually being done by the ghost. This sharing is like two people watching the same frames of the movie such that they have identical experiences.

Vedic cosmology describes a realm of ghosts which is likely a place where different living beings end up sharing the same experience and they are not able to enjoy their individuality because every ghost tries to control the world differently, like many drivers trying to drive a car at the same time, in the attempt to reach different destinations. Theirs is obviously a very frustrated existence because their bodies and minds are overlapped with others' bodies and minds. All of them have individualities but they cannot assert their individuality without overriding someone else's individuality. The "world" of ghosts is therefore a place where one gets the experience of loss of free will and self-determination.

The Virāta Purusa Form

It is therefore incorrect to suppose that we have full knowledge of a part of reality. It is rather correct to say that we have a partial knowledge of the complete reality. The fact underlying the idea of *modal realism* is simply that our vision of reality is covered by the modes of nature, which essentially create different "views" of the same reality. The Vedic description of the cosmos is not about different *parts* of reality, but about different *partial visions* of the same complete reality. When we turn to the skies and see some stars and planets, therefore, we are not seeing some parts of the reality. We are rather seeing a partial vision of the same reality that is being seen differently by other living beings because they happen to see different things in their partial vision. The "world" is not comprised of many parts. Rather, there are many partial views of a whole.

These partial views may overlap in different ways, and through this overlap the different observers may also see what we are seeing. When they manipulate these parts, our vision also seems to have been manipulated and scientists try to explain this manipulated vision through some "causal interactions" between the parts that they could previously observe. That approach to science is flawed because there are many things outside our vision, which exist in the vision of others, and the only way we can explain what is happening is if we had the complete vision.

Think of what happens when we work in an online collaboration tool such as a Google spreadsheet, comprised of many different tabs. Assume for the moment that Google allows different users access to the different tabs in the spreadsheet, such that no user can see all the tabs. Also assume that cells in these tabs have references to cells across the different tabs. A particular cell in one tab, may be, for instance, the sum of values in two cells present in two other tabs that a user cannot access. When a user modifies some values in the tab that she can access, it has an effect on the other tabs which the other users see. If a user simply sees what is happening in their tab, and a particular cell value changes, and the user tries to explain everything based on what he can see, then he has two options. First, he can try to attribute the cell value change to some other changes in that tab and try to construct a "law" that supposedly "explains" these changes. Second, if he is unable to explain such changes based on what he can see, he would be compelled to consider them "random".

Both approaches are flawed because there is a lot of reality that is simply hidden from the view of a particular user. Even if it appears that we can find "laws" that correctly explain the relationships between what we can see, and the laws of nature appear to work (i.e., causally explain the observations), the correlation between cause and effect established by such a law is simply an illusion. In the same way, when we are seeing only parts of reality, all our causal explanations are flawed, even when they appear to work. Their working is no guarantee that they are in anyway indicative of the real laws of nature. Therefore, when these laws fail to predict what we see, we are forced to postulate that there are some "dark" parts of the reality, similar to the tabs hidden from our vision.

The descriptions of the cosmos in Vedic texts therefore refer to a *Virāta Puruṣa*—a cosmic observer—whose bodily parts comprise the different perspectives. The different planetary systems are described as head, hands, chest, stomach, legs, feet, etc. of this cosmic form. This form is imaginary because there isn't a real observer who sees the cosmos simultaneously from all the perspectives; in fact, these perspectives are mutually orthogonal. The *Virāta Puruṣa* is therefore said to be a form of God, not in the sense that He simultaneously experiences the world from different perspectives, but as the *collection* of all possible perspectives. Each perspective is like the vision of the five blind men trying to know the universe: they can only see the trunk, tail, legs, stomach, or ears of the elephant, and therefore if we try to explain the elephant from a perspective, the explanation would always be incomplete. Any theory of nature based on a particular perspective will also be incomplete. A material scientist is therefore advised to think of the entire *Virāta Puruṣa* form, recognizing that there are many perspectives, even though we may not see them.

By meditating on the *Virāta Puruṣa* form, and recognizing that there are many perspectives, the material scientist can reach the mode of pure goodness, in which he is able to recognize the need to go beyond these perspectives and perceive reality as it exists beyond each perspective. The study of the cosmos is therefore fruitful only if we correlate the observations to the reference frame from which the cosmos is observed and go beyond the observations to study all the reference frame properties. These reference frames, as we have seen earlier, are produced from the three modes of nature, due to which they naturally *hide* some part of reality, while revealing the others. In essence, these modes construct the goggles through which we can see only some parts of the whole.

The fact that we cannot see all parts of the universe in Vedic cosmology is inherently related to the view that our vision is constructed by hiding some parts of reality, to produce a *partial* understanding of the whole. Again, we are not seeing a part fully; we are seeing the whole partially. In modern science, theories are created by separating the influence of 'distant' things to create 'isolated systems'. That is, we only consider a part of all that we can see in theory formation, which is a very small of everything that exists. These theories may approximately explain the observations, but they are never true, even if we expanded our observation to all that we can see, because it is still an observation from a *perspective.*

The description of the *Virāta Puruṣa* tells us about all the perspectives, and how different living beings can know the same reality differently from their perspective. All such perspectives are partial, although as one rises through the planetary systems, the perspectives become more and more complete: the higher planetary systems predominate in the mode of goodness or *sattva-guna* in which we can see the world from a highly abstract viewpoint, and thereby subsume more and more detailed pictures of reality within that viewpoint. All living beings are limited in their perception in a very specific sense: we cannot process more than one symbol at a time. That symbol can be the picture of an atom, or the picture of the cosmos. By knowing the atom, naturally, the bigger and more abstract picture is neglected, just as in knowing the bigger picture, the details are ignored. While both the abstract and the detailed can be known alternately, they cannot be known simultaneously by us.

The big picture is more important than the details because the laws of nature are based on the meanings, and the details are produced from the abstractions. By knowing the abstract or big picture, therefore, we have a more complete knowledge, given that all knowledge is a partial knowledge of the whole, not a complete knowledge of the part. The person studying the atom too therefore knows the same reality, although so much is neglected that the resulting picture appears material. The enlightened person realizes that there are many ways to know the world, each representing a different *method* of knowledge, and it is necessary to analyze the properties of the methods before we study the knowledge resulting from those methods. The *Virāta Puruṣa* form is the collection of all the methods of knowing. They produce different impressions of reality, which is an outcome of the properties of the method itself. The result of that realization is that the enlightened person seeks that method which can *in principle* produce a complete understanding of reality. Once that complete picture has been obtained, the details can also be explained much better. But without that complete picture, the details themselves cannot be correctly understood, and all theories remain incomplete.

Types of Invisibility

With this background, we can now describe the many ways in which the invisibility of different parts of the universe can be understood, depending on which perspective is becoming invisible to our vision:

- The vertical dimension is invisible to us because we don't see the world with our mind, intellect, ego, and consciousness.

Since our perception is limited to sensations, we can never perceive meanings, truths, intentions, and morals as real things in the world. They simply remain entities in our heads, but even this head is only seen by our senses, rather than by higher faculties of perception. The result of that method of perception is that we cannot see ideas, sensations, pleasures, intentions, or morals even in our heads. All that we can see with our naked eyes is a mass of muscle, cells and plasma with a light microscope, and atoms, with a high-energy microscope. If we cannot see meanings in our heads, there is no way we can see higher and lower planetary systems with the eyes.

- The lower parts of the universe are invisible because we don't understand how the gross material objects can be modified by adding information, thus giving us control of the atomic rather than just microscopic objects. Our pleasures are limited to viewing the world "coarsely" because our senses aggregate large amounts of material information without the details. We know that eagles can see very far, dogs can smell much better, and bats hear much higher frequencies. Therefore, even in this world, high-definition experience is available to limited extents. The inhabitants of the lower planetary systems possess even more sophisticated senses, which can see even the details, and correspondingly can perceive more detailed information in objects. We cannot see this information and even if we saw it, it would appear to be "noise" rather than "signal" to us[3].
- Different parts of the horizontal dimension are invisible to us because they lie on disconnected surfaces and to see the other parts, we need a discontinuous shift in objects and activities. Within our vision, a certain subset of objects and activities appear to form an ecosystem, which we consider as "parts" of reality, rather than "perspectives" on reality. The different *dvīpa* on the *bhū-mandala* are overlapped and only different in the vision of the inhabitants of those *dvīpa*. Just as demigods and demons can experience our bodies, similarly, living beings in other *dvīpa* are also experiencing the same body, although they also experience other bodies and consider that combination of bodies to be their body. We would be wrong

if we thought that our body is on this planet and therefore it could not be someone else's body in another planet, just as we would be wrong in thinking that we are this body. What we call our "body" is inhabited by bacteria who experience smaller parts of the world. Similarly, demigods experience more subtle parts of the world, and beings on other parts of the *bhū-mandala* are also experiencing parts of what we are experiencing. They share our body, just not fully.

- We cannot see other parts of the world because of who we are. To see those parts, the parts must communicate with us, which is possible if we have the necessary *guna* and *karma* to transform the causes into effects, and therefore we cannot see the other parts of the world because we don't have the necessary *guna* and *karma*.
- Many parts of the world become visible and invisible at different times due to the cyclic nature of time. When Vedic cosmology describes islands, for instance, the description is time agnostic. A more accurate picture is that of a lotus, which is segmented into "petals" which entail that only parts of that circular region would be visible at any time. As the lotus rotates in time, other parts of the phase space of possibilities become real. Similarly, the descriptions of rivers, mountains, and gardens are time dependent: they were true when the pictures were narrated, but their existence may have diminished or become unmanifest at present. Time, too, is therefore hiding and revealing things from *our vision* although they continue to exist. One of the cardinal principles of *Sāñkhya* is that when things disappear, they have just become *unmanifest*. They have not truly disappeared in reality, although we just cannot see them. The past and the future therefore exist even now, although we cannot see them. However, an advanced person, unconditioned by the modes of nature and their evolution in time, can see the past and the future.

Under the materialistic vision, Indologists speak about how Vedic scriptures were "written" by different "authors" at different times, and they are trying to historically date the scriptures, when the scriptures themselves are called *śruti* or information that has always existed and has been transmitted as sound from master to disciple. Its conversion to written form isn't the time when the scripture came into existence, neither were the scriptures written by many people. Indologists have a poor understanding of how gross information is produced from subtle information, or how ideas are embodied into symbols. The symbols of the scriptures were produced at a certain time, but the ideas underlying them had existed even before this formalization and were being transmitted orally. It is instructive therefore to understand that *Vyas* means 'division'. As we have seen earlier, the gross manifests from the subtle when the gross is divided into parts by adding details. What *Veda Vyas* did was expressing the abstract knowledge into details, considering the time in which the intellects and the minds of people have become incapable of understanding abstract things; to even retain the knowledge they have to see and to touch. Since we cannot grasp the abstract ideas directly, we require numerous demonstrations of these ideas through incidents, conversations, and perceptions. By writing the scripture, therefore, *Veda Vyas* converted sound into sight and touch. One only needs to be aware of the *Sāñkhya* philosophy to understand why this matters.

Our demands for seeing everything assumes that (1) the world is material objects, and therefore can be seen and touched, (2) communication to any part of the world is always possible because everything in the universe affects everything else through physical "forces", and (3) since the universe is uniform, the same kinds of phenomena must be visible at all times. If there are more kinds of matter than perceivable through the senses, if the causality in nature is not physical forces that act uniformly, and if time is not linear but cyclic, our current objections to the world not being visible to our senses would have a natural explanation. The demand for seeing everything stems from a particular kind of theory of nature in which everything is material objects, which are governed by forces created from the object properties, and space-time is open, flat, and linear. As you change these assumptions, the universe as a whole becomes richer, although your senses may not be able to perceive that richness unless you develop your perception, alter your activities and habits, and understand the nature of the place and time that we inhabit.

Modal Divisions in the Universe

All universes are built from the three modes of nature, which form the three dimensions of ordinary space: the up-down direction represents greater or lesser *sattva guna* (conceptual abstraction). The north-south direction represents lesser or greater *tamo-guna* (inertia and structure), while the east-west direction represents lesser or greater *rajo-guna* (activity and change). The three modes of nature therefore create the six cardinal directions, and the space on and in between these directions is incrementally divided by the three modes again and again thereby producing a hierarchical structure. In the horizontal dimension, for instance, the four directions of east, west, north, and south are subdivided by the three modes to create 12 subdivisions of the phase space, which represent different kinds of objects and activities enacted in these parts of space.

Thus, for instance, in the present universe there are 12 months, 12 tones in a musical scale, 12 colors in a palette, 12 signs and houses in a horoscope, 12 systems in a living body. These divisions of the material modes are not invariant across the universes and they change from one universe to another. The implication of this division is that *types* in the present universe are counted in multiples of twelve; we can say that the *base* of the counting system is duodecimal[4]. This is, of course, not the only possible counting system. Octal, binary, and hexadecimal counting systems are prominently used in computers, and nearly all counting in the everyday social world is done in the decimal system. Ideally, however, counting in this universe must be done in duodecimal, because it is the *natural* system of division in the present universe. In other universes, a "year" will not have 12 "months", musical instruments will not have 12 notes, and living beings will have a different number of functional systems. In terms of the semantic hierarchical space-time, each node in the hierarchical tree will sub-divide into a different number of branches.

As the numbering system of the universe changes, the number of demigods, planets, galactic divisions into "planetary systems", the number of planets in each such system, the structure of living bodies governed by the number of functional systems, etc. must all be changed. Indeed, the number of distinct words in the universe's language, the sizes of musical verses, the duration of a beat in a musical rhythm, the functional divisions of society and organizations which make for effective organization, will also change. In Indian classical music, there is a system of *ragas* which are aligned with time of the day, seasons of the year, life occasions, and emotional moods. If the sub-divisions of time and space are changed, musical systems will also undergo change. A different universe will therefore have a different system of notes, rhythms, verses, and *ragas*.

The basis of this change is that numbers and types must be treated identically in a semantic scheme. If the universe has 12 basic types, then everything else must be counted and described in terms of these types. If the universe had 16 basic types, then it would be described differently.

This fact has important implications for how a physical property—such as the frequency of light—is interpreted into meanings. If there are 12 colors, then the *meaning* of a color—e.g., red—is given through its distinction to the other 11 colors. If, instead, there are 15 colors, then the meaning of the same color would be different. This is analogous to the fact that the property of digits "10" denotes the number ten in a decimal system, twelve in a duodecimal system, three in a binary system, and sixteen in a hexadecimal system. What a given physical property represents, therefore, cannot be known unless the *basis* of counting is known.

Thus, the *meaning* of the light coming from a different universe cannot be understood unless the basis in which that universe counts is also understood. If we count in duodecimal and another universe counts in hexadecimal, then their meanings will be different. Similarly, the *direction* in which we count things also matters. For instance, if a palette of colors is arranged clockwise and we count them counterclockwise, then the meanings associating with those methods of counting would also differ. These universes are in effect using different *languages* in which the *same* physical property is mapped to meanings differently.

The observed redshift and blueshift in light from stars, and its interpretation as expansion and contraction of lengths, thus makes sense only if we know the counting basis, and the direction of counting, and if these bases and directions have been correlated to the specific kind of space-time in that particular universe. These values will naturally change with the passing of time and different locations in space. E.g., a redshift could denote a morning, and a blueshift could denote night, and these colors would be created depending on whether the universe is passing through its "morning" (phase of growth) or "night" (phase of decline).

The changes to space-time structure would change the number of fundamental particles in the universe. For instance, we would not have 12 quarks and 12 leptons[5] in another universe. We would rather observe a different number of quarks and leptons, which would break the structure of what we call the "Standard Model" of particle physics. Effectively, in a semantic scheme, each universe requires its own model of fundamental particles, because these particles denote fundamental meanings.

Measuring the Sizes of the Universes

Suppose you are trying to divide a circle into smaller arcs, by drawing lines from the center of the circle to the circumference, and you have picked a base-12 counting system to count the divisions. In a hierarchical scheme, you will first divide the circle into 12 parts, each of which can then further be divided into 12 parts, each of which can further be divided into 12 parts. As you go into smaller and smaller sub-division, you will ultimately end up with the smallest possible divisions, which represent the most "atomic" ideas possible in your system of division.

The number of steps it takes for you to divide the circle into the smallest parts depends on your numbering system. For instance, if your numbering system is base-12, you will need more steps than if your system is base-16. The successive levels of division therefore represent the levels of hierarchy you must traverse in going from the "biggest" to the "smallest". However, this divisional system holds true only if the size of the circle is fixed. If the circle grows in size, then to arrive from the biggest to smallest, a greater number of steps are needed. These steps, as we have seen, represent the hierarchical tiers in the universe, and these tiers are in turn defined by the layers of matter in *Sāñkhya* which transcend all the universes. Therefore, all the universes must have the same tiered structure: i.e., the same division of the 14 planetary systems.

The living beings in each of the universe are also identical in their fundamental capabilities, which include the smallest ideas they can potentially grasp. This means that the 'atom' of each universe is predefined by the capabilities of consciousness, and the *vertical* structure of the universe is fixed due to the categories enumerated in *Sāñkhya*. That leaves us with only one method of distinguishing between the universes, namely, the division of the horizontal dimension into different parts.

This also means that if we divide the horizontal dimension into more parts, and the smallest part that a living being can know is fixed by the basic abilities of consciousness, then the universe that is divided into more parts must naturally have a bigger circumference. Thus, for instance, if we divide the universe into 8 directions instead of 4, then the circumference must be divided into 8 parts instead of 4. If the smallest segment that we can perceive is fixed, then a greater number of divisions entails a bigger circumference as well. Similarly, in the vertical dimension, as the division is continued over the 14 planetary systems, we must arrive at the smallest segment that consciousness can perceive. Each tier must therefore be bigger to accommodate this variety, given that there is naturally more variety due to a greater number of divisions, although the smallest division we can perceive is fixed. The induction of a greater variety, with a fixed set of perceptual capabilities, entails a bigger universe. The size of the universe is directly correlated to the variety it presents, which is proportional to the number of horizontal divisions.

The present universe divides the horizontal dimension into 4 parts, and this is said to be smallest universe in the material creation. Bigger universes divide this same dimension into 8, 16, 32, or more parts. They are therefore, also, successively twice as big as the present universe. This division entails that generally there will be more rooms in a house, more digits on the clock, a greater number of months and seasons in a year, a greater number of body parts and functional divisions of the body, the society would be structured into many more classes, their languages will have a greater vocabulary, their songs and verses will be much longer, all the living beings will have bigger bodies, and will live longer years.

The size of the universe, in this case, depends upon the number of ideas that constitute its axioms. As the axioms increase, the propositions formed using these axioms would grow correspondingly. The Vedas state that the present universe is the smallest, and this can be correlated to the number of axioms in a semantic view. The size estimation of a universe comprising semantic propositions is given by the number of possible propositions in that universe, which depends on the number of axioms from which these propositions are constructed. The greater the number of unique axioms, the greater would be the number of unique propositions built from these axioms. In essence, we can think of these fundamental axioms as the vocabulary of a language in which the material objects are propositions created from the words in the language. A greater number of words imply a greater number of possible sentences.

On the one hand, a greater number of axioms will flatten the tree structure for a given set of meanings, since these meanings can be constructed through fewer idea subdivisions. Similarly, the tree structure would be stretched vertically if the number of axioms is reduced (provided the total set of meanings remains constant). On the other hand, a greater number of axioms would also greatly increase the number of possible meanings. In the circle analogy above, for instance, the circumference of the circle would be proportional to the number of axioms.

Thus, by increasing the number of axioms in a system, we grow its size, and when the universe is developed based on these axioms, it would also correspondingly increase the size of the universe. The increase in the number of axioms also flattens the tree structure for a given set of meanings as compared to when the axioms are fewer. The increase in the size of the universe, however, outsizes the flattening in the levels of the universe achieved by the greater number of subdivisions. Therefore, if you have more fundamental words in your language, you can say the same thing with a fewer total number of words. However, the total number of things that you can say in the more refined language is far greater.

The smallest universe is therefore considerably limited in the extent to which the details or refinements can be produced. There are many meanings that lie 'in between' the meanings denoted by our present words, which cannot be expressed in this universe. Correspondingly, the pleasures arising from such material exchanges cannot be enjoyed, because the meaning can only be approximated to the closest word expression, and the listeners of that word would naturally assume that the word actually denotes the literal meaning of the word. Naturally, as we can see, this can lead to much confusion over time about the real meaning. Of course, this problem doesn't arise for material meanings, because the meanings too are constrained by the divisional abilities in the universe. Therefore, it is wrong to suppose that we can *think* some refined ideas, but we cannot *express* them in words. It is correct to say that we cannot even think those refinements, and therefore we also cannot express those meanings. Thus, for instance, we may not be able to accurately describe the incidents of a bigger universe in a smaller universe, although we can narrate the incidents of a smaller universe in a bigger universe.

Since all the universes are submerged in the *kārana* domain, the locations in the *kārana* space-time must be viewed as defining the *basis* of counting and the order in which to count using this basis within the universe. The combination of a fundamental set of axioms, and the order amongst these axioms becomes the foundation of the space-time for that universe. All successive propositions produced from these axioms presuppose a well-defined set of axioms and their relative order. Vedic philosophy describes how objects are counted or distinguished, and these elements are produced one by one from the *kārana* domain.

The key point here is that before we can start counting, we must formulate a basis and order of counting. The *kārana* domain represents the many counting bases, and these bases represent the different kinds of pleasures. In other words, the manner in which we divide and count is ultimately produced from the desire for a particular kind of pleasure. Once this pleasure type is defined, then each universe is a set of numbers produced from a specific counting basis. The objects produced in any space-time are identical with the location at which they are produced; therefore, the location of a universe in the *kārana* domain is identical to the counting basis. Like other space-times, the *kārana* domain is also counting. However, it is counting a different kind of entity—the bases of counting, rather than the numbers produced from those bases. The basis of counting is effectively the basis of material existence: the quest for material pleasure, obtained by participating in many kinds of divisions.

One more clarification regarding the sizes of universes. Commonly, we suppose that the total "size" of the set of all numbers is constant regardless of whether we count them in decimal, hexadecimal, or duodecimal. This supposition is in turn based on the idea that numbers are infinite. However, the universes (or the total number of objects in them) are not infinite. The total number of *possible* and *actual* propositions is finite for both and governed by two bounds: (1) the total number of axioms, and (2) the smallest subdivisions of ideas that consciousness can understand. The former varies from universe to universe, and the latter is fixed across all the universes, and given by the fundamental observational capabilities of all conscious entities. Our key concern therefore is not forming a theory of numbers from zero to infinity. It is rather formulating a theory of space-time in the universe with a finite number of possibilities. The existence of a number that is bigger than the biggest number possible in the universe is only hypothetical; such a number (and therefore meaning) can never be semantically *represented* within the universe[6].

Understanding the Hierarchical Tiers

Once we begin to describe a universe in terms of the possible propositions that can potentially be created, it becomes easier to comprehend the idea of different hierarchical "planetary systems" within a universe. Beginning with the topmost planet of *Brahma*—which represents the division of the universe by the number of his heads (which represent the most fundamental axioms in the universe) —successively lower planetary systems produce more contingent ideas until the most detailed or "smallest" ideas have been created. The limits of the universe are the biggest and the smallest, and these become the "top" and "bottom" of the universe. Between these, the number of tiers can be determined by the number of successive divisions of the previous divisions.

Each universe constructs the categories defined by *Sāñkhya* philosophy—i.e., *mahattattva, ego, intelligence, mind, senses, sensations,* and *sense objects.* To the extent that the objectification of consciousness follows a step-by-step by process invariant to how consciousness is described (i.e., its happiness and morality) in a particular universe, the subdivisions of the universe into different planetary systems would also follow the same pattern and successive steps of objectification.

In the present universe, which is the smallest, the above mentioned seven steps of objectification constitute the "top-tier" *loka* called *bhūloka, bhuvarloka, svargaloka, maharloka, janaloka, tapaloka,* and *satyaloka*. The *bhūloka* is the realm for macroscopic objects. In the next higher planetary system called *bhuvarloka* there are sensations but no sense-objects, and it is the place where living beings can see, taste, touch, smell, and hear, but these sensations are not "derived" from objects; rather, the realm is only *developed* or *objectified* till the point of sensations, and no more. In higher realms, there are only thoughts, judgments, intentions and morals, without objectifying these ideas into more contingent things. The living beings in the higher planetary systems can create the details from the abstractions, but they are generally not interested in those details. The sustenance of the body is, therefore, not a concern in the higher planetary systems, because the focus of life is on ideas, judgments, intents, or morals. When the residents of a higher planetary system travel to the lower planetary system, they 'manifest' the details, which were previously missing, because they were not required on their planet.

Thus, for instance, when demigods such as *Surya* or *Indra* travel to the *bhūloka* they manifest their presence in a form of gross vision that was earlier unnecessary. Similarly, when Lord *Viṣṇu* is satisfied by the sacrifices in a *yajña*, He manifests His subtle form into a gross form, suitable for the perception of the living beings on that planet. When their work is accomplished, this gross form is withdrawn. The process of manifesting and withdrawing is described by the words *prakat* and *antardhyāna*. We must thus understand that the higher beings don't carry a body with them like we do, although they can manifest that body. When these living beings travel to a lower planet, they acquire the body, and then the bodily necessities also arise naturally. For instance, they must now worry about how to feed and protect the body, which did not exist previously. The life in the lower planets is therefore more burdensome, but some exalted living beings travel to this part of the universe only to enlighten the living beings about a higher purpose in life.

The apostles and messiahs in Abrahamic religions are residents of higher planetary systems, who appear in this world to bring the message of a higher purpose in life. They are not God, and they call themselves a "son" of God. They don't need to be born via sexual union, as one forced to appear according to their *karma*. They can appear in any form of their choosing; for instance, Jesus appeared as a child to Miriam without a sexual union. When his body was crucified, the subtle body was alive, and it could be detached from the gross body to manifest another gross body, which is called the 'resurrection' of Christ. These are not miracles, although they are based on a profound understanding of how gross matter is produced from subtle matter. An understanding of Vedic philosophy can thus help even other religions demystify many difficult ideas.

Each higher and lower *loka* therefore represents a different *kind* of experience that predominates in different levels of material reality. In the topmost planetary systems, the practice of our deepest principles of morality and happiness are the most dominant and other levels of reality aren't even manifest. In the lowermost planetary system, the material objects are manifest, and predominate in terms of our experience.

Mountains, Rivers, Gardens, and Trees

A peculiar aspect of Vedic cosmology is that it describes planetary systems in terms of trees, rivers, gardens, and mountains. The different islands for instance are described as comprising many mountains, forests, rivers, and trees. To any outsider, the inclusion of gardens and trees in the description of cosmology would seem preposterous: Why are animals, birds, fish or reptiles not included when trees are? What about nations and cities, which apparently seem bigger than gardens?

The Vedic description of the many land masses focuses on what we call "nature" in the everyday sense of "going back to nature", "living amidst nature", or "conservation of nature". Science creates an image of progress dominated by electronics, concrete, steel, glass, oil, plastics, and synthetic materials used for food, clothing, and shelter. There is a well-understood contrast between natural and synthetic, and the world we see today trends more towards the synthetic rather than the natural. Given the current abundance of synthetics, and the increasing decline of nature, the Vedic cosmic picture seems obscure today, although it was understandable even a few centuries ago. Today when we describe a land, we refer to cities, high rise buildings, urban infrastructure, and other man-made structures. In the Vedic description, each land is described in terms of mountains, rivers, gardens, and trees. The contrast is palpable, but the difference results from what we consider important for life.

If we replace the natural habitat such as mountains, rivers, and forests, with urban infrastructure, the urbanization would collapse. The urban centers of activity are possible because clean water, fresh air, and healthy food is provided by nature, which we take for granted, and try to replace nature with urbanization. While this book is not about the preservation of ecology, the way Vedic cosmology describes the lands points to how such preservation is possible: we must begin to describe the world in terms of rivers, mountains, and forests, rather than the urban infrastructure. Unless we change the description of the present world, the primacy that should be accorded to nature will never be achieved.

Ecologists recognize that the ecosystem of life is based upon mountains that trap the water, rivers that carry the minerals from the mountains to enrich the soil, trees that consume minerals and purify the air, thus creating an ecosystem of clean air, fresh water, and rich soil, in which other kinds of plants and animals can survive. Rather than a description of the cosmos in terms of particles and waves, as in science, the Vedas describe living ecosystems. The implication of these descriptions is that all the different lands are meant for different kinds of life forms, and they are organized and structured to sustain the various kinds of living beings. Cosmology, therefore, is not the study of how physical forces distribute matter after a Big Bang, but how planets are organized to be living habitats. The description of a habitat is the foundation for constructing the pyramid of life forms, and if every land is described in terms of this foundation, then we can imagine that every land must also be inhabited.

Even in modern times we understand that the different kinds of living beings in a land form depend on the type of natural habitat that surrounds them. If the type of soil, the kind of water, and the variety of air is changed, widespread changes to the other species must occur, as environmental studies have discovered. The environment is therefore the "ground" in which the "tree of life" bears fruit. However, this ground is semantic and therefore higher than the life that grows upon it. In other words, the "tree of life" that grows on this ground is also inverted.

The life forms that take birth in the different parts of the world should be viewed as forming the details of the *body* of the ecosystem in which they are born, like how bacteria are the details of our bodies, and our bodies are their ecosystems. The tree of life does not grow upon a lifeless environment. It develops in the body of a higher life form. For instance, all life on Earth is developed in the body of Earth, like bacteria replicate within our bodies. The ecosystem is therefore a bigger body, inhabited by a living being. Thus, Himalaya is not just a very big rock; he is also a person. Those familiar with Vedic literature know that mountains, rivers, and trees are treated as life forms in these literatures. Similarly, all the rivers such as Ganges, Yamuna, Brahmaputra, etc. are personalities. Likewise, even trees such as Peepal (Bodhi), and Banyan are personified. Finally, entire planets such as the Earth are living beings.

When we say that we are growing on Earth, the growth is just like a fruit growing on the branches of a tree. The Earth is the abstraction, and we are the detail. The detail thus doesn't define the abstraction; rather, the detail elaborates the abstraction. In that sense, our lives depend on Earth, in quite the same way that a leaf's survival depends on the branch of the tree on which it grows being healthy. The entire universe is thus a "tree of life" whose root is Lord *Brahma* and whose branches are the various species. These species include mountains, rivers, and planets. The environment, therefore, is also "living" in the sense that it is more powerful than us. Environmentalists talk about the havoc that humans have created on the environment, which has irreparably "damaged" it. This idea stems from a materialistic view in which we think we are alive whereas the environment in which we live is just dead matter. In the Vedic view, our lives are like those of bacteria inside our body: they may think that they are the only ones alive and that there isn't a "bigger" life form than them. These bacteria can cause damage to our body, but the bigger life form can actually destroy the bacteria and modify its behaviors to allow only the creation of certain types of life forms within it.

It is thus incorrect to suppose that we are unilaterally destroying the environment. We are rather sustained by the presence of the environment and produced by the environment, due to our *guna* and *karma* and type of time. As these things change, the environment will produce different kinds of living beings suitable to enact a different world.

Nature as a Life Form

When nature is treated as a life form, its abuse and exploitation constitute bad *karma* and the ancient Eastern cultures therefore had an in-built system of nature protection that has slowly eroded in modern times. Like other living beings have "rights" and "duties", our natural habitat is also a living entity with its rights and duties. It is therefore not true that living forms emerge from a non-living material environment. Rather, even that environment in which living forms are sustained is also living forms. We may not understand how the various living forms function because we tend to think of life in terms of cells with cytoplasm, protoplasm, etc. This isn't the only definition of life in the Vedic view because rivers, mountains, and planets would be naturally precluded from this definition.

Life is described more abstractly in Vedic philosophy, as consciousness which develops into morals, intentions, judgments, meanings, senses, sensations, and sense objects. The life forms are therefore described not in terms of the cellular structure but by the type of mind that precedes the body[7]. Even entire planets such as the Earth are viewed as living beings in Vedic philosophy; the *Śrīmad Bhāgavatam*, for instance, narrates the story of King Prithu chasing Earth who takes the form of a cow. Similarly, *dharma* or religion is depicted in the *Śrīmad Bhāgavatam* as a bull. The Earth is not actually a cow and *dharma* is not actually a bull. But the same way we can symbolize a country through a flag, similarly, these living beings symbolize their presence by taking on a form. This viewpoint is easily understood when life is not viewed as the body but as the type of mind or meaning that is symbolized through that body.

The key point is that even geologic structures such as mountains, rivers, lakes, forests, and deserts, are life forms, and the description of Vedic cosmology is contiguous with the description of geology and biological living ecosystems. As a particular land mass represents a particular region of phase space in which different kinds of life forms and their activities are enacted, their sustenance in turn requires the prior presence of ecosystems that are then subdivided to create the different life forms that play different "roles" or functions within the ecosystem. The descriptions of enormous trees, mountains, rivers, and forests, are the abstract descriptions of a living world, which are then subdivided into greater and greater details. The correct way to understand them is that their existence creates the preconditions for different kinds of life forms and their activities: their presence is the intermediate level of cosmic detailing between planetary systems and the moving life forms. To understand why there are mountains, rivers, or trees, we must first understand how our lives depend on the existence of clean air, fresh water, and enriched soil, which is produced by the presence of these natural forms.

The key scientific import of this fact is that locations in the phase space don't appear individually. Rather, a *collection* of these states must manifest at once, although different subsets of the entire phase space may be manifest at different times. Unlike modern science, which begins in describing individual objects states, and each object exists individually, in practical life, many things must exist simultaneously for something to exist at all. The subset of states in a phase space that manifests at any time is not randomly decided, because such random collections would not form an ecosystem. Why only those parts that constitute a coherent ecosystem manifest collectively, therefore, has no explanation in current science, because the necessity of the ecosystem itself cannot be expressed in a science that only considers the individual states necessary.

The Vedic explanation of this phenomenon is time, which

collectively manifests some *karma* due to which living beings can exchange information with each other. Time therefore selects parts of the phase space, the resulting events are then manifest as the *karma* of the participants. There is no conceptual construct in present science that *selects* a collection, because any selection entails choices, which then entail consciousness. The result of that viewpoint is that all eco-systems must become random assemblages, and then explaining this randomness becomes a new kind of project in science, which is impossible because randomness is the very opposite of a rationally defined lawfulness. That is, to even use randomness as a theoretical construct, we must acknowledge that parts of the world cannot be explained rationally. When the central goal of science is to find explanations, the failure to do so is commonly converted in modern science as the thesis that nature is random.

The Vedic description is superior because what science considers random can be explained. This explanation involves collections beyond their members. Clearly, collections are not physical, although they can be rational. To speak about collections in science, therefore, requires us to consider everything that can be thought (although it might not be physical), to be real. When ideas are inducted into science, then the interaction between things and ideas must be defined, which has only one consistent solution: namely, that the things are produced from ideas. The Vedic notion of space and time is therefore a very powerful scheme for explaining numerous phenomena that modern science is incapable of. It presents an ideology that is at once very simple to grasp, and yet overturns most of the ideas that exist in modern science. By this overturning, it explains not just what can be explained by science, but also those things which are inaccessible by science. Cosmology is only one aspect of this description, but the theory extends to many adjacent fields such as geology and biology, besides mathematics, physics, computing, and psychology.

7

The Present Universe

Just like I am in America. I am not adopting any ways of life as the Americans do. So I am not in America. Not only myself, all my disciples who are following me, they are also not Americans. They're different from American behavior, American ways of life. In that sense I'm not in America. I am in Vṛndāvana because wherever I go in my apartment or in my temple I live with Kṛṣṇa and Kṛṣṇa consciousness. I don't accept any consciousness of America. And I teach my disciples also to take to that consciousness. So one who takes to that consciousness, he is also not in America, not in this world.

— *His Divine Grace A.C. Bhaktivedānta Swāmi Prabhupāda, Lecture on Bhagavad-Gītā 2.46-62*

Dimensions vs. Directions

Space in every universe is three dimensional because there are only three modes of nature, which create all the universes. However, these three dimensions of space can in turn be divided in many ways creating many more "directions" in space. For instance, in the present universe, the horizontal plane is divided into 4 directions, which is also sometimes presented as an eight-fold division of space. This eight-fold division of the horizontal space, together with the 2 directions in the vertical dimension, is sometimes described as the 10 directions, owned by the 10 deities of directions called *dikpāla*, when the horizontal space is itself divided into 8 directions instead of 4 (north, south, east, west, north-east, north-west, south-east and south-west).

Similarly, it is not necessary to divide the vertical dimension only as two directions of up and down; rather, it is also possible to speak of directions such as up-west, up-east, up-north, up-south, or down-east, down-west, down-north, and down-south.

In these and other ways, the three dimensions can be divided into many more "directions" producing numerous types. The question, while studying the structure of the universe, is only whether these "directions" are *fundamental* and irreducible within the universe, or they can be reduced to more fundamental ideas from which these are constructed. For instance, should we treat the 8 directions in the horizontal plane as being fundamental, or just 4 of these 8 are fundamental, while the other 4 are constructed through the combination of the previous ones?

The number of directions that are fundamental represents the number of basic ideas in terms of which the experience in the universe will be constructed. If there are more basic axioms, the language in the universe has more alphabets, which then allows us to construct many more propositions. Conversely, if there are fewer axioms, then the universe's language has fewer axioms, which means there must be fewer propositions, and the size of the universe would accordingly be small. Each universe can therefore be described very abstractly by defining the number of axioms in terms of which it is elaborated. The location of the universe in the *kārana domain* represents the number of fundamental axioms that would be used to construct the meanings in that universe, and the present universe is said to be the smallest universe in the material domain.

This means that in the present universe, there are only 6 irreducible directions, and while other directions can be constructed from these 6, those are not to be considered *fundamental* or irreducible. If we develop a theory that describes this universe, we will find that we need only 6 fundamental ideas to describe the entire universe, and only 4 fundamental ideas to describe a particular tier of the universe. Thus, Lord Brahma, who creates the morality of the universe as the *mahattattva*, is said to have only 4 heads, which speak the 4 Vedas, which represent the 4 moral values in the universe. These moral values are called: (1) austerity, (2) kindness, (3) truthfulness, and (4) cleanliness, and the 4 Vedas expand on these 4 values through Brahma's 4 heads in 4 directions:

- *Rigveda* represents austerity and its goal is to attain detachment from the worldly things, by development of knowledge,
- *Yajurveda* represents kindness and its goal is various kinds of sacrifices; it represents the knowledge of ritualistic activities,
- *Sāmaveda* represents truthfulness as its songs are descriptions of the nature of absolute truth, which are meant to be sung,
- *Atharvaveda* represents cleanliness, as its purpose is to help a person lead a spotless life, by describing regulations.

These four values are the core principles of religiosity or *dharma* in this universe, but they are not *sanātana dharma* or eternal religion, because the values of truthfulness, austerity, cleanliness, and kindness are not mutually consistent and together complete unless seen in relation to God. For instance, while kindness is an important moral value, criminals cannot be shown kindness. While truthfulness is a cardinal principle to be generally upheld, telling a lie to save a life may be more kind than a truth that kills a person. While detachment is an important religious principle, performing your duties in the material world may be a deeper sign of detachment than their renunciation. These values are not mutually consistent in all situations, when they are seen as purposes in themselves rather than in relation to God's experience. Legal systems which begin in moral values such as liberty, equality, or fraternity, struggle to define the right action because these values are not always consistent. Law must be, in a contradiction, "interpreted" by a judge. Deciding what your real *dharma* is, thus, not always easy. Different religions fight over their religious edicts, espousing one value over another, and since the values themselves are not universal, no edict can be applied universally.

All worldly religions espouse the core principles of austerity, truthfulness, kindness, and cleanliness. If we see the similarities between these religions, we would find that these moral values can potentially unify them. However, since these moral values aren't themselves always consistent, and the fact that they are not the only possible values, any religion, even if it follows all these values would still be baffled in deciding the nature of right and wrong. Furthermore, since the contradictions between the values can only be resolved by a true understanding of God, the religions that only offer the different ideas without God also remain self-contradictory and mutually inconsistent. The definition of *dharma* or *religion* is thus always incomplete and inconsistent. Only when a true understanding of God is developed, the contradiction between the values is reconciled, and even more values are developed. However, if we observe a particular universe, some set of values will predominate in it.

The Vedas state that the present universe is the smallest in the entire material creation because it espouses the least number of values—Brahma in this universe has only four heads, and there are only four Vedas in this universe spoken by the four heads of Brahma. In other universes, there are, accordingly, Brahma with many more heads, which speak many more Vedas, thereby espousing more moral values.

Since the values expressed through the Vedas are themselves material (if disconnected from the nature of God), all these Vedas are considered *aparā vidyā* or inferior knowledge, because the morality is never complete and consistent: they can be mutually contradictory, and sometimes these values may be overridden by some other value because all these values are collectively incomplete. Only some scriptures such as the *Brahma Sutras* and *Śrīmad Bhāgavatam* are considered *parā vidyā*.

The 4-fold division in directions has different implications at the different tiers of the universe. At the level of Lord Brahma, whose body is said to be built of *mahattattva,* there are 4 moral values or principles of *dharma.* Similarly, in the space of intentions, there would be 4 kinds of intentions, in the space of judgments, there would be 4 basic kinds of judgments[1], in the space of meanings, there would be 4 basic kinds of meanings, etc. These 4 directions similarly create the 4 divisions of society (*Brahmana*, *Kshatriya*, *Vaiśya*, and *śūdra*), the 4 types of permissible activities (*dharma*, *artha*, *kāma* and *moksha*), 4 stages of social life (*Brahmacharya*, *Grihastha*, *Vānaprastha*, and *Sannyasa*), 4 kinds of pleasures (eating, sleeping, mating, and defending). Numerous other 4-fold divisions are found in Vedic philosophy and these divisions are, in turn, divided by the three modes of nature, creating additional variety.

The Bhū-Mandala Planetary System

As mentioned in the previous chapter, Vedic cosmology divides the "horizontal" plane into concentric regions of *dvīpa* and *samudra*, loosely translated as "island" and "ocean". I also discussed the significance of these divisions and why the two-dimensional flat geometry represents the two modes of *rajo-guna* and *tamo-guna*, which represent activities and objects, respectively, rather than the two physical dimensions of space that are employed in modern science. The horizontal plane, through these divisions and their subdivisions represents different conceptual domains that differ in the types of objects and activities. Following this, the two-dimensional space is segmented into concentric regions because the object-activity relation is discontinuous: all possible uses of an object are not continuous, and all objects that can enact an activity are not continuous. The "oceans" interleaving the "islands" represent the discontinuity in the relation between objects and their activities.

In Vedic cosmology, there are seven oceans and seven islands in the *bhū-mandala*, which means that there are seven disconnected surfaces of objects and activities. The successive islands and oceans are twice in size which would mean that the successive regions of the phase space would have larger continuous regions of object-activity relationships. That is, in each successive island, there are twice as many types of objects and activities found. Each of these islands follows the four-fold division of society. The names of the islands and oceans, with their respective sizes is mentioned in Table 1. It is notable that the oceans too grow in size along with the islands, which means that as the continuity of the object-activity relation grows, the discontinuity also doubles with each island.

Name	Width in Yojana	Total Distance	Diameter in Miles
Jambudvīpa	100,000	100,000	800,000
Salt Ocean	100,000	200,000	3,200,000
Plakshadvīpa	200,000	400,000	6,400,000
Sugarcane Ocean	200,000	600,000	9,600,000
Sālmalidvīpa	400,000	1,000,000	16,000,000

Name	Width in Yojana	Total Distance	Diameter in Miles
Liquor Ocean	400,000	1,400,000	22,400,000
Kushādvīpa	800,000	2,200,000	35,200,000
Ghee Ocean	800,000	3,000,000	48,000,000
Kārunchadvīpa	1,600,000	4,600,000	73,600,000
Milk Ocean	1,600,000	6,200,000	99,200,000
Sākadvīpa	3,200,000	9,400,000	150,400,000
Yoghurt Ocean	3,200,000	12,600,000	201,600,000
Pushkardvīpa	6,400,000	19,000,000	304,000,000
Sweet Ocean	6,400,000	25,400,000	406,400,000
Golden Land	15,750,000	41,150,000	658,400,000
Diamond Land	83,840,000	124,990,000	1,999,840,000
Lokāloka	10,000	125,000,000	2,000,000,000
Āloka Varṣa	125,000,000	250,000,000	4,000,000,000
Total	250,000,000	250,000,000	4,000,000,000

Table 1: Oceans and Islands in Bhū-Mandala

The Sun is said to rotate with a radius of 15,750,000 *yojana* which lies in the middle of *Pushkardvīpa* and the Sun is therefore said to rotate over the *bhū-mandala* directly above *Pushkardvīpa* (this *dvīpa* extends from 12,600,000 *yojana* to 19,000,000 *yojana*, so the radius of the Sun which is said to be 15,750,000 *yojana*, lies in the middle of this *dvīpa*).

The Lokāloka Mountain

The *bhū-mandala* is divided into two parts: "lighted" and "dark". The lighted part is called *loka varṣa* and the "dark" part is called *āloka varṣa* and these two are separated by the *Lokāloka Mountain*. The total diameter of the universe including both lighted and dark parts is 4,000,000,000 miles, half of which is *loka varṣa* and the other half is *āloka varṣa*.

The *āloka* region is said to be "dark" as it cannot be known, and it is important to understand that the regions of dark and light represent our ability to *know*. The *loka* region is where objects, sensations, senses, meanings, truths, intentions, and morals can be distinguished while the *āloka* world is one where these distinctions can't be made. Just before the *Lokāloka* Mountain is a region made of "gold" which reflects all light, implying that it is not possible to send light (or any material information) to the *āloka* region, and there is hence no way for the *loka* world to communicate with the *āloka* world. The deeper point, however, is that even if we could exchange information, there aren't distinct objects to be known.

To understand the *āloka* region we need to view it as the absence of all information. The absence of something cannot be known, unless put in contrast to that thing. For instance, we cannot measure the absence of an apple through our senses; we cannot think of this absence without thinking about the presence, or judge truths about this absence, without judging the truth of presence. In that sense, this absence cannot be known. In fact, unless we put this absence in contrast to the presence, we don't even know if the object is absent. The *āloka* region should therefore be viewed as the place from which all information has been sucked out to create the *loka* world. By this sucking, a "hole" is created, which represents missing information. The key import of the existence of *āloka* seems to be that information is conserved; we cannot magically create or destroy information, although we can remove information from one branch of a semantic tree to create the other branches. Just as to build a house we must dig dirt from someplace else and create a hole, similarly, to create variety in one part of the universe we must create darkness in another.

Another way to understand *loka* and *āloka* is to think of positive and negative numbers. The positive numbers represent observable properties and the negative numbers represent their absence. The *āloka* world is the negation of all properties and observables, and hence it cannot be known by our senses, mind, intellect, ego or moral sense, because these senses themselves are produced as information. The material entities that represent information cannot perceive the lack of information, and therefore, the lack of information can never be known[2]. Similarly, in the history of numbers, negative numbers used to be a heresy until the idea of zero was introduced, and a formal theory of numbers had to be formulated. Physically speaking, if zero represents nothingness, you cannot hope to take something out of nothingness (i.e., subtract a positive number from zero to create a negative number). But logically speaking, such an operation could be performed. To have a consistent theory of numbers, it was essential to allow the existence of negative numbers, although physically it made no sense. The *āloka* world is therefore the domain of negative numbers which make no sense from the standpoint of the measurable and knowable properties in the *loka* region. Nevertheless, they must exist for the system of numbers to be logically consistent and complete. Since each universe is a set of objects that denote some positive number, the negative numbers become logically necessary.

The *Lokāloka* Mountain can be viewed as the boundary between positive and negative numbers and can be envisioned as the idea of *zero.* In geometry we treat zero as a single point, but this geometry entails an infinite set of negative and positive numbers on the left and right of zero, which then entails an open space, and an infinite universe. When space has to be treated as a closed domain, then the number zero has to be treated as a closed boundary rather than as a point. It may therefore not be a coincidence that the numeral zero is represented as a circle, because the *form* of a semantic zero is a closed boundary. The *Lokāloka* Mountain represents such a boundary. Everything on one side of this boundary is objects or positive numbers, and everything on the other side is darkness, lack of objects, or negative numbers. This mountain thus creates a "wall" between the regions of experience and those of darkness.

With this understanding, we can derive clues about how semantic numbers must be defined geometrically. Essentially, the boundary of every closed space denotes the number zero, because the counting within that space restarts from one. The member objects inside that space can therefore be counted starting from 1. This "1" is the first object inside the collection of objects and becomes the concept from which all other ideas are instantiated. Thus, all positive numbers are instances of one, which is the first object, and therefore the symbol of the most abstract entity in the collection. This fact is well-recognized in modern definitions of numbers which begin by defining zero and adding "1" to zero to produce successive numbers. The difference is that all numbers are treated as quantities rather than types. Thus, every number is produced by repeating the same operation of adding 1 in the physical scheme, but in the semantic scheme, different ideas must be added to zero to create numbers.

Depending on the *basis* of counting, we must have a different number of ideas. In the present universe, for instance, there are 12 ideas that constitute the duodecimal system of counting, produced when the 4 directions are divided by the 3 modes of nature. So, we add 12 ideas to zero to produce the numbers 1...12. These 12 divisions can further be divided into 3, creating 36 sub-divisions. It is also possible that the 12 divisions are treated as the next order zero, which is then divided into 4 parts, which is then divided into 3, 9, 27, or 81 parts. There are hence two ways to construct details. First, we can view the zero as a space comprising of 4 directions that are subdivided into multiples of 3. Second, at some point this division is stopped, each subdivision is treated as the next order zero, divided into 4 directions, which are then successively subdivided into multiples of 3 as before. The successive divisions performed upon a "lower order" zero, produce a hierarchical numbering. The successive divisions within a particular order zero produce linear numbering.

Since the *āloka* domain has twice the diameter, it has 3 times more area than the *loka* domain. However, the cardinality of these two domains (the number of positive and negative numbers in them) must be the same because these represent the presence and absence of information. Since the total information in the two domains is the same, the negative numbers must have a geometrically "bigger" *form* to occupy a larger space. In fact, the negative numbers must have a 3-times-larger form.

Since all things are produced only from the 3 modes, the negative numbers must also be created from the 3 modes. However, the inversion requires 3 times more information. This is an involved topic, but to give a computer analogy, the number 48 is represented in binary as 110000 but -48 needs 1's complement which inverts all the 0s to 1s and 1s into 0s. In effect, 1's complement counts backwards from the maximum possible number in a particular representation, and therefore requires more digits. For instance, in a 32-bit representation, the number -48 is defined as 11111111111111111111111111010000. The key point is that the negative region is bigger because it counts backwards from the maximum number, which in the case of the universe, represents the edge of the universe itself. The objects in the negative region therefore contain the same amount of information, although this information requires a far greater amount of space, due to a different method of counting employed.

Like the positive numbers are counted from the boundary of the space (which denotes zero, and therefore the *smallest* positive number), similarly, the negative numbers must be counted from the boundary of that space (which, however, must now denote the *biggest* negative number). In other words, we define the material objects in the *loka* world in relation to the *Lokāloka* Mountain, but we define the *āloka* world in relation to the outer covering of the *āloka*, or the edge of the universe. This is instructive because negative numbers in present arithmetic are defined in relation to zero, since there isn't a largest negative number.

Both positive and negative numbers are limited in each universe, first by the method of subdivision, and second by the smallest possible object that can be perceived by consciousness. No universe is therefore infinite, and the numbers in each universe only denote the *name* of the object. Similarly, the antiparticles are also finite, although they are counted backwards till zero from the maximum negative number.

The Upper Planetary Systems

We discussed in the previous chapter the division of the universe into higher and lower planetary systems. The higher planetary systems represent more subtle and abstract realms beginning with *bhūloka*, which is the realm of macroscopic objects. In *Sāñkhya* philosophy, there are several subtle material elements beyond the objects of the senses; these are sensations, senses, mind, intelligence, ego, and *mahattattva* (also called contaminated consciousness, *dharma* or morality). The higher realms in the material universe represent the development of matter to different levels of abstractions. Above these levels is the realm of Lord *Viṣṇu* who represents the realm of *śuddha sattva* or goodness unadulterated by the modes of passion or ignorance. It is notable here that Lord *Brahma* (even though he represents morality) is conditioned by *rajo-guna* or the mode of passion, and moral goodness also therefore involves passion[3].

	Delta Yojana	Total Yojana	Total Miles
Viṣṇuloka	26,200,000	260,100,000	2,080,800,000
Satyaloka	120,000,000	233,900,000	1,871,200,000
Tapaloka	80,000,000	113,900,000	911,200,000
Janaloka	20,000,000	33,900,000	271,200,000
Maharloka	13,816,000	13,900,000	111,200,000
Svargaloka	83,900	84,000	672,000
Bhuvarloka	100	100	800
Bhūloka	0	0	0

Table 2: The Upper Planetary System

Śrīmad Bhāgavatam, Padma Purāna, and many other Vedic scriptures mention 7 higher planetary systems, and these are called *bhūloka, bhuvarloka, svargaloka, maharloka, janaloka, tapaloka,* and *satyaloka*. The *Sisumāra* planetary system (described in a later section) is sometimes included as part of *svargaloka*, and sometimes left out. The *Viṣṇu Purāna* states that the entire region from *Bhuvarloka* to the topmost point of the *Sisumāra* (the polestar) is considered the *svargaloka.* However, the *Śrīmad Bhāgavatam* states that the *svargaloka* is on top of the *Sumeru* Mountain. These are not conflicting views because the different planets are also considered demigods, and if *svarga* is viewed as the realm of demigods, then it is appropriate to include the *Sisumāra* as part of it. However, I have used the *Śrīmad Bhāgavatam* method here, which separates the demigods in the *svarga* on top of the *Sumeru* from the demigods residing on the *Sisumāra* planets. Since *svarga* is on top of the *Sumeru* which is 84,000 *yojana* high and 16,000 *yojana* deep (below the *bhūloka*), the *svargaloka* in Table 2 is shown to be 84,000 *yojana* high.

Similarly, the *bhuvarloka* planetary system is described to begin about 100 *yojana* above the *bhūloka* and extend to the height of the

Sun, which is 100,000 *yojana* above the *bhūloka*. Since the Sun is part of the *Sisumāra*, I have just illustrated the start of the *bhuvarloka* in Table 2. We will later see why the *Sisumāra* is the *prāna* of the universe that causes the working of the senses and produces sensations, and due to this overlap, the *Sisumāra* also overlays upon the *bhuvarloka* and *svargaloka*. These planetary systems are actually separate, but given their functional overlap, they are described in different ways in different places.

The Lower Planetary Systems

Below the *bhūloka* are the 7 lower planetary systems. These are called *atala*, *vitala*, *sutala*, *talātala*, *mahātala*, *rasātala* and *pātāla*. As previously discussed, the lower planetary systems are richer in material experiences and offer far greater material pleasure than the higher planetary systems. The "richness" of the material experience in these planetary systems arises from a far greater amount of information exchanged during sensation. The pleasure of the lower planetary systems is therefore different from that of the higher planetary systems where the material bodies themselves may not be developed like our bodies, and the living beings enjoy a subtle pleasure of the senses, mind, intelligence, ego, and morality, without the gross bodies. The lower planetary systems offer a better sensual life because the senses and the objects are capable of exchanging far more detailed information than the senses and objects in the *bhūloka* or the higher planetary systems such as the *svargaloka*. The material experience in the lower planetary system is "high-definition" as compared to the higher planets where the experiences are abstract and therefore subtle. While the higher planets are gradually more detached from the sense pleasures, the lower planets are far more engrossed in sense pleasure. Due to this entanglement with sense pleasure, the lower planetary systems are said to be inhabited by demons. They are far more advanced than the earthly beings in terms of their powers of observation and technology than humans, but they have correspondingly less ability to detach themselves from material enjoyment and become liberated.

Name	Delta Yojana	Total Yojana	Total Miles
Bhūloka	0	0	0
Atala	-10,000	-10,000	-80,000
Vitala	-10,000	-20,000	-160,000
Sutala	-10,000	-30,000	-240,000
Talātala	-10,000	-40,000	-320,000
Mahātala	-10,000	-50,000	-400,000
Rasātala	-10,000	-60,000	-480,000
Pātāla	-10,000	-70,000	-560,000
Lord Ananta	-30,000	-100,000	-800,000
Unknown	-2,000,000	-2,100,000	-16,800,000
Garbhodaka	-249,800,000	-251,900,000	-2,015,200,000

Table 3: The Lower Planetary System

Below these 7 planetary systems is the realm of Lord *Ananta* who represents time and controls the universe's evolution. Lord *Ananta* is said to be the serpent on whom *Garbhodakaśāyi Viṣṇu* sleeps. This description of the cosmos is quite mysterious, and it can be understood if *Garbhodakaśāyi Viṣṇu* is seen as the origin of space because from His navel sprouts a lotus inside which reside all the planetary systems (the lotus, as we have seen, denotes space in Vedic cosmology). He is said to sleep at the bottom of the universe because this space is static, and defines all the possibilities in the universe, and the universe neither expands nor contracts over time, because all the possibilities are already fixed. Similarly, Lord *Ananta* is the cause of all changes and He therefore represents the origin of time; He converts the possibilities into realities, and this change is called time. *Garbhodakaśāyi Viṣṇu* and *Ananta* are therefore the origins of space and time, respectively, and they create the manifest universe, which lies above them, from an unmanifest realm of matter called the *Garbhodaka* Ocean, which lies below them. The *Garbhodaka* Ocean fills up almost half of the lower part of the universe. Unlike the higher and lower planetary systems which are realms for different material differentiations, the ocean represents the undifferentiated. Like we cannot differentiate the parts of water, this "ocean" is all that cannot be known and experienced because it lies "below" all the experiences as the possibilities. The nature of this ocean will be described in detail shortly.

The Sisumāra Planetary System

The *Sisumāra* planetary system is not counted amongst the higher 7 planetary systems even though it is higher than *svargaloka*. It comprises nine planets, seven of which are part of the modern solar system: Sun, Moon, Venus, Mercury, Mars, Jupiter, and Saturn, and two of which (*Rāhu* and *Ketu*) which are unique to Vedic cosmology. It also comprises a system of stars: (a) 28 stars called the *Nakṣatra* which are used in Vedic astrology, (b) 7 stars called the *saptarishi,* and (c) the polestar. The 28 star constellations and the locations of their principal stars is listed in Table 4.

	Nakṣatra Name	Degrees	Minutes
1	Ashvinī	8	0
2	Bharanī	20	0
3	Kṛttika	37	30
4	Rohinī	49	30
5	Mrigashīra	63	0
6	Ārdrā	67	20
7	Punarvasu	93	0
8	Pushya	106	0
9	Ashlesha	109	0
10	Māgha	129	0
11	Pūrva Phālguni	144	0
12	Uttara Phālguni	155	0
13	Hasta	170	0
14	Chitrā	180	0
15	Svātī	199	0
16	Vishākhā	213	0
17	Anurādhā	224	0

18	Jyeshta	229	0
19	Mūla	241	0
20	Pūrva Ashādhā	254	0
21	Uttara Ashādhā	260	0
22	Abhijit	266	0
23	Srāvana	280	0
24	Dhaniśtha	290	0
25	Shatabhisha	320	0
26	Pūrva Bhādrapadā	326	0
27	Uttara Bhādrapadā	337	0
28	Revatī	359	50

Table 4: The 28 Naksatra and Principal Stars

Of the above 28 *Nakṣatra*, however, 27 cover the entire 360^0, while *Abhijit* overlaps with *Uttara Ashādhā* and *Srāvana*. The *Surya Siddhānta* gives the following information regarding the sizes of the *Nakṣatra*:

The Bhabhoga (or the space of a Nakṣatra) contains 800 minutes, and the Bhoga of a Tithi (or the space which the Moon describes from the Sun in a Tithi or Lunar day) contains 720 minutes. [Surya Siddhānta 2.64]

The place of a planet, reduced to minutes, divided by the Bhabhoga or 800, gives the number of those Nakṣatra (counted from Ashvinī which are passed by the planet, and the remainder is that portion of the present Nakṣatra which is passed by the planet). [Surya Siddhānta 2.65]

The principal star of Uttara Ashādhā is in the middle of the space of Pūrva Ashādhā. The principal star of Abhijit is at the end of the space of Pūrva Ashādhā. The principal star of Srāvana is situated at the end of the space of Uttara Ashādhā. [Surya Siddhānta 8.4]

With each *Nakṣatra* comprising 800', 27 *Nakṣatra* comprise 800 x 27 / 60 = 360^0, which means that the 28th *Nakṣatra* has no additional space left to be accommodated in the circle, and one of the *Nakṣatra* must therefore be left out of the list. When the positions of all the principal stars are overlaid with the durations of the *Nakṣatra*, we find that the principal stars of *Pūrva Ashādhā*, *Uttara Ashādhā*, and *Abhijit*, all fall into the *Pūrva Ashādhā Nakṣatra*. This means that *Pūrva Ashādhā Nakṣatra* cannot be excluded from this list. Furthermore, since the principal star of *Srāvana* is at the end of *Uttara Ashādhā Nakṣatra*, we are led to conclude that the *Uttara Ashādhā Nakṣatra* too cannot be excluded from this list. Now we are led to leave *Abhijit* out of 27 *Nakṣatra*. This leads to various Vedic statements that the *Nakṣatra* are 27 or 28. The correct understanding is that there are 27 *Nakṣatra* and *Abhijit* is a part of that. When planets are passing through the zodiac and they are situated in the region that overlaps with *Abhijit* they are said to be in *Abhijit*. I will return to this issue during the discussion on astrology, once we have developed a better understanding of flat vs. round spaces, and what these distinctions entail.

The above stars are considered to be "lunar mansions" or the places through which the Moon passes in its revolutions over the *bhūloka*. It is notable that the Moon is also considered a star in Vedic cosmology, as it is said to reflect the light of the Sun. All the stars in Vedic cosmology are therefore like the Moon rather than the Sun. This is a very involved topic in Vedic cosmology, and I will return to it in the last chapter after having established the meanings of all the planets, which is when we can understand the nature of the light from the Sun, and why it is reflected by the other planets. The key point to note here is that while the Sun originates all the light, the stars (and the Moon) reflect this light. Apart from these 27 lunar mansions, Vedic cosmology also describes 12 houses of the Sun, commonly known as the zodiac. Vedic astronomy considers both the lunar and the solar stars to be part of the system of stars, and they are both used in Vedic astronomy for solar and lunar month calculations.

	Vedic Name	English Name	Element	Quality
1	Meṣa	Aries	Fire	Movable
2	Vṛṣabha	Taurus	Earth	Fixed
3	Mithuna	Gemini	Air	Dual
4	Karka	Cancer	Water	Movable
5	Siṃha	Leo	Fire	Fixed
6	Kanyā	Virgo	Earth	Dual
7	Tulā	Libra	Air	Movable
8	Vṛścika	Scorpio	Water	Fixed
9	Dhanuṣa	Sagittarius	Fire	Dual
10	Makara	Capricorn	Earth	Movable
11	Kumbha	Aquarius	Air	Fixed
12	Mīna	Pisces	Water	Dual

Table 5: The 12 Signs of the Zodiac

The structure of the *Sisumāra* planetary system is shown in Table 6. It comprises various luminaries starting from *Rāhu* to the polestar. There are 28 *Nakṣatra*, 12 signs of the zodiac, 7 main stars, the pole-star, and together these constitute the 48 important stars in the Vedic astronomy. Together with the Sun and the Moon, there are 50 key luminaries which play a key role in deciding the movement of time both from a solar and a lunar calculation perspective. I will discuss the significance of these 50 luminaries, and their relation to Sanskrit in the next chapter.

	Delta Yojana	Total Yojana	Total Miles
Polestar	1,300,000	3,900,000	31,200,000
Seven Sages	1,100,000	2,600,000	20,800,000
Saturn	200,000	1,500,000	12,000,000
Jupiter	200,000	1,300,000	10,400,000
Mars	200,000	1,100,000	8,800,000
Venus	200,000	900,000	7,200,000
Mercury	200,000	700,000	5,600,000

28 Stars	200,000	500,000	4,000,000
Moon	200,000	300,000	2,400,000
Sun	10,000	100,000	800,000
Rāhu	24,000	90,000	720,000
Svargaloka	68,000	68,000	544,000
Bhūloka	0	0	0

Table 6: The Sisumāra Planetary System

The above description of the *Sisumāra* is based on the *Śrīmad Bhāgavatam* and if we undertake a broader study of cosmology across the other Vedic texts, we find differences in the order of the planets in the various descriptions. I will discuss these differences in the next chapter after a better knowledge of the various planets has been developed.

The Jambudvīpa Description

The *Jambudvīpa* is the center of the *bhūloka* and it is divided into 9 *varṣa* called *Kuru, Hiraṇmaya, Ramyaka, Ketumāla, Bhadrāśva, Hari, Kimpuruṣa*, and *Bhārata*. The locations of these *varṣa* are shown in Figure-24. The Vedic texts also describe numerous mountains, rivers, forests, and trees, often far bigger than anything we are aware of, which are used to create the natural habitat for living beings in that part of *Jambudvīpa*. Before we can discuss those details, we must understand how these parts are different from each other. Unless we see how life in those parts of the universe is different, it is not possible to understand the nature of these entities. The central issue in describing *Jambudvīpa* is that its structure looks quite different from the kinds of structure that we have discussed thus far. As seen in Figure-24, the region is divided neither in concentric circles, nor is it obviously like a lotus, which is how we have studied the regions thus far. To understand this structure, therefore, we must find similarities between this and previously discussed structures, to formulate a new method of describing this region of the universe.

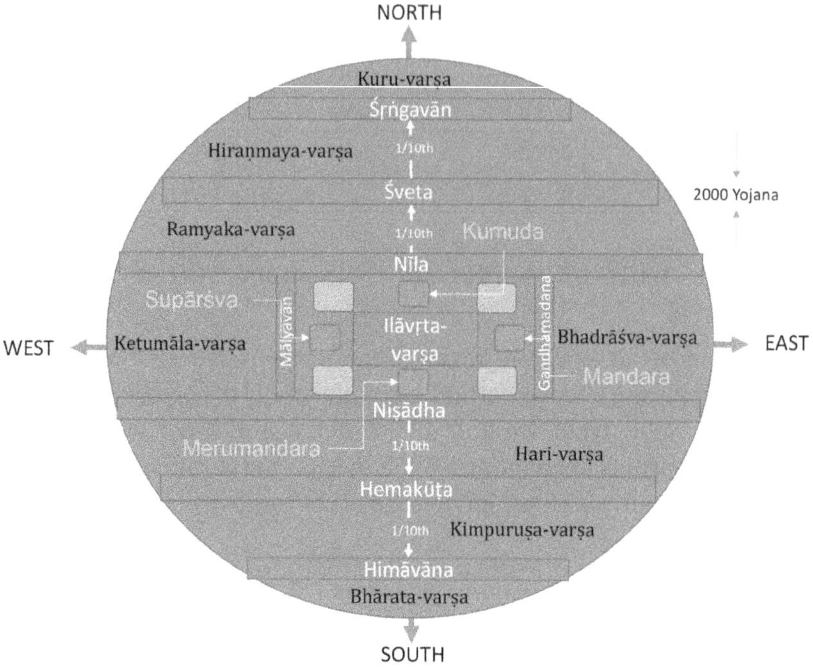

Figure-24 The Jambudvīpa Structure

As it turns out, all the concepts about space that we have discussed so far can be applied to *Jambudvīpa* as well, although this application requires a reinterpretation of the structure shown in Figure-24. These reinterpretations are valid only if we can find Vedic statements affirming the possibility of viewing *Jambudvīpa* in a different way. Fortunately, such reinterpretations are found in different Vedic texts. For instance, the *Mārkandeya Purāna* describes the *Jambudvīpa* as a four-petal lotus, in which the three *varṣa* on the north and south are subsumed into a single petal, the petals on the east and west are not divided in this manner, and the *Ilāvṛta varṣa* in the middle is viewed as the pericarp of the lotus. This description of the *Jambudvīpa* provides us with a familiar model for understanding, as the lotus geometry is found in many places in Vedic texts. If this description is incorporated into the above picture, we obtain a more complex, although a more complete picture of the *Jambudvīpa*. Figure-25 illustrates the combination of the lotus geometry and the previously described nine *varṣa*, key mountains, and water bodies.

> *Thus have I told thee of that four-leaved lotus-flower which is the Earth; its leaves are Bhadrāśva, Bhārata and the other countries on the four sides. The country named Bhārata, which I have told thee of on the south, is the land of action; nowhere else is merit and sin acquired; this must be known to be the chief country, wherein everything is fixedly established. And from it a man gains Svarga and final emancipation from existence, or the human world and hell, or yet again the brute-condition, O brahman. [Mārkandeya Purāna Canto LV, Text 9]*

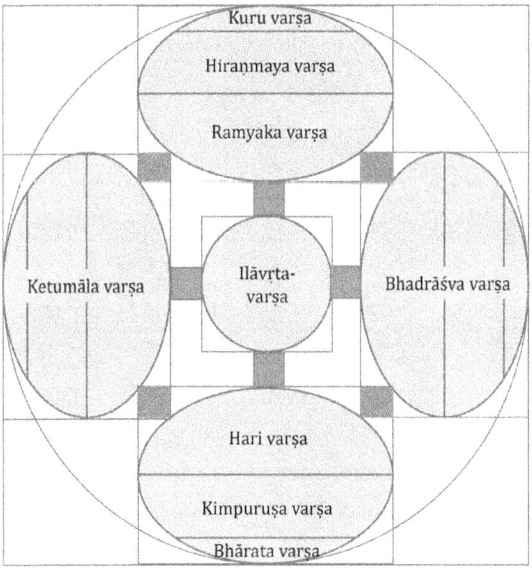

Figure-25 The Jambudvīpa Lotus Structure

If the picture shown in Figure-25 is considered the basis for our of understanding *Jambudvīpa*, then we can see that *Ketumāla varṣa* and *Bhadrāśva varṣa* on the west and east respectively should be subdivided into parts, but haven't been divided in most descriptions, quite similar to how the three *varṣa* on the south (*Hari varṣa, Kimpuruṣa varṣa*, and *Bhārata varṣa*) have been subsumed under *Bhārata varṣa* in the *Matsya Purāna* verse. From these descriptions, we can understand that there are different ways of subdividing and aggregating the subdivisions. When these descriptions are combined, we obtain a more complete picture.

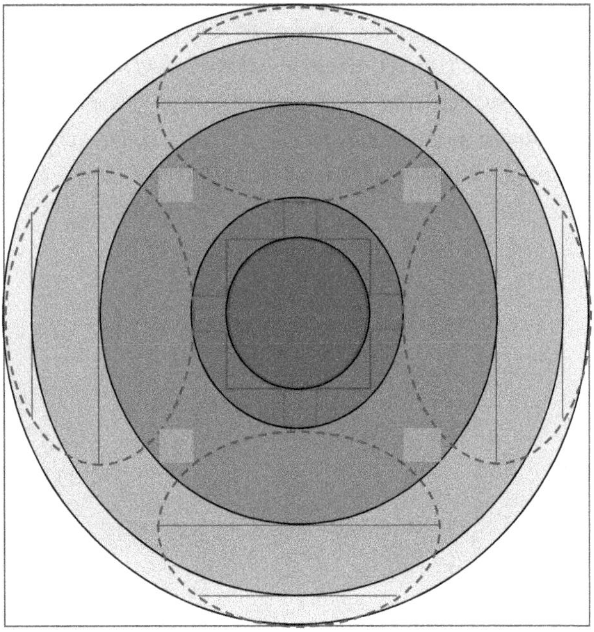

Figure-26 Jambudvīpa Concentric Circle Structure

Once we have understood the integration between the *varṣa* division and the lotus structure, we can also see how the same structure could also be described differently as concentric circles in which the four *varṣa* farthest from *Ilāvṛta-varṣa* are part of the outermost circular 'island', the next closest set of *varṣa* are parts of the next inner islands, and so forth. This structure is illustrated in Figure-26. In the *Surya Siddhānta, Jambudvīpa* is described as a stairway that leads to heaven in the middle. The islands beyond the *Jambudvīpa* can, therefore, be said to be successively lower, which means that the outermost *dvīpa* (*Pushkardvīpa*) represents the stairway's lowest rung and each successive inward *dvīpa* is a higher rung on the staircase, leading ultimately to the heaven in the center.

The division of each *dvīpa* into smaller steps represents the detailed description of the steps going from one *dvīpa* to another. The division of the *bhūloka* into successively higher *dvīpa*, and the division of *Jambudvīpa* into successively higher steps indicates that the stairway to the *Sumeru Mountain* in the center represents a general principle of describing the structure of the entire *bhūloka.* In the lotus petal model too, the successively inner layers of petals are slightly higher than the layers on the outside. This principle has also been depicted by many medieval Hindu pictures and diagrams, and it also constitutes an important principle in Buddhist cosmology, where it has been assimilated into the design of a *stūpa* in which the dome of the monastery represents the gradually increasing steps towards the center spire which represents the ultimate goal of going to the heavens. This similarity in models is not to affirm or deny the validity of the Vedic model, but only to note that this idea was pervasive and was incorporated in other cosmologies as well.

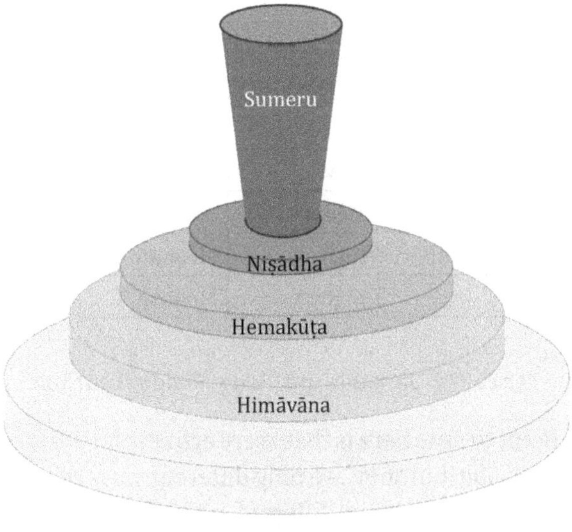

Figure-27 Jambudvīpa Stepped Circular Structure

The stepped structure of *Jambudvīpa* is depicted in Figure-27. The successive circular regions are higher than the previous one, indicating that they are conceptually more abstract than the previous regions. As we have earlier seen, the *varṣa* in the east, west, north, and south, will have greater or lesser modes of *rajo-guna* and *tamo-guna*. With four directions and three-fold division of each direction, there are 12 divisions of space of which 8 are counted as the *varṣa* excluding the central *Ilāvṛta varṣa*. These 12 divisions can be said to dominate in different modes of nature: the regions closer to the center have higher *sattva-guna* while the other modes of nature gradually reduce in their respective predomination.

	SATTVA	RAJAS	TAMAS
Bhārata-*varṣa*	Low	Highest	Medium
Kimpuruṣa-*varṣa*	Medium	Higher	Medium
Hari-*varṣa*	High	High	Medium
Ramyaka-*varṣa*	High	Low	Medium
Hiraṇmaya-*varṣa*	Medium	Lower	Medium
Kuru-*varṣa*	Low	Lowest	Medium
Ketumāla-*varṣa* - I	Low	Medium	Highest
Ketumāla-*varṣa* - II	Medium	Medium	Higher
Ketumāla-*varṣa* - III	High	Medium	High
Bhadrāśva-*varṣa* - I	Low	Medium	Low
Bhadrāśva-*varṣa* - II	Medium	Medium	Lower
Bhadrāśva-*varṣa* - III	High	Medium	Lowest
Ilāvṛta-*varṣa*	Highest	Medium	Medium

Table 7: Jambudvīpa Mode Predomination

The key point to note here is that there are several different descriptions of *Jambudvīpa,* but they are only different ways of describing the same structure, emphasizing different aspects, while subordinating others. In Figure-26, for example, the directional differences between east, west, north and south, are subordinated to the distance from the center of the *Jambudvīpa*, thus creating a concentric circle model. In

Figure-25, the directional differences are emphasized, while subordinating the distances from the center. And in Figure-24, directions and distances are emphasized, but some details in the east and west are subordinated. This is something typical of Vedic texts in general and *Purāna* specifically, which are based on narrations and conversations in which the speaker either emphasizes or narrates the previously received emphasis. By drawing different pictures, we can see how these descriptions actually pertain to a single part of the world, although presented variously.

The huge mountains described in the *Purāna* separate the different *varṣa.* In the *Purāna* we can find two kinds of descriptions of these mountains: (1) which describes the elevation of the mountain from the surface of a *varṣa* and the other which describes the mountain's total height. The below two verses from *Śrīmad Bhāgavatam* and *Matsya Purāna* describe these two approaches, and Figure-28 illustrates how these two accounts can be combined into a single composite picture of the mountains.

> *Hemakūṭa is shorter than Meru 12,000 yojana and Himavāna is shorter than Meru by 20,000 yojana. The great Hemakūṭa is 88,000 yojana. The mountain Himavāna is 80,000 yojana. It goes from east to west. [Matsya Purāna, Chapter 113, 24-25]*

> *Similarly, south of Ilāvṛta varṣa and extending from east to west are three great mountains named (from north to south) Niṣādha, Hemakūṭa and Himalaya (Himavāna). Each of them is 10,000 yojana [80,000 miles] high. They mark the boundaries of the three varṣa named Hari-varṣa, Kimpuruṣa-varṣa and Bharata-varṣa. [Śrīmad Bhāgavatam, 5.16.9]*

The description of the mountains should not be considered metaphorical, although many interpreters of Vedic cosmology have been befuddled by the enormous heights. For instance, the *Himavāna* is said to be 10,000 *yojana* high, although physical measurements suggest that it is only about 5.5 miles high. Many interpretive problems arise when we try to give Vedic cosmology a physical interpretation (e.g., when trying to compare the height of *Himavāna* to that of the *Himalaya* mountain in the northern part of India), and as we have seen earlier, all elements of this cosmology must be treated semantically. A certain part of this cosmology may be physically visible, but that vision and height is not directly related to the properties of the cosmological entities described in the *Purāna*. The mountains, for instance, should be viewed as representing eligibility barriers for living beings in one kind of domain to enter the other kind of domain, rather than simply some very large physical objects. The heights of these eligibility barriers must be understood semantically as changes in the qualities of a living being. For instance, if the height from the *bhūloka* to the Sun is 100,000 *yojana*, then 10,000 *yojana* represents 1/10th the qualification of going to the Sun. This barrier must be crossed in going from one *varṣa* to another. That means, if going to the Sun is hard, then going to another *varṣa* is only 1/10th the difficulty. This difficulty should be viewed in terms of the *guna* and *karma* of the living entity, not simply in terms of the physical distance. As we have seen earlier, the different *varṣa* predominate in different modes of nature. Therefore, going to those places requires changes in the constitution of our body and mind.

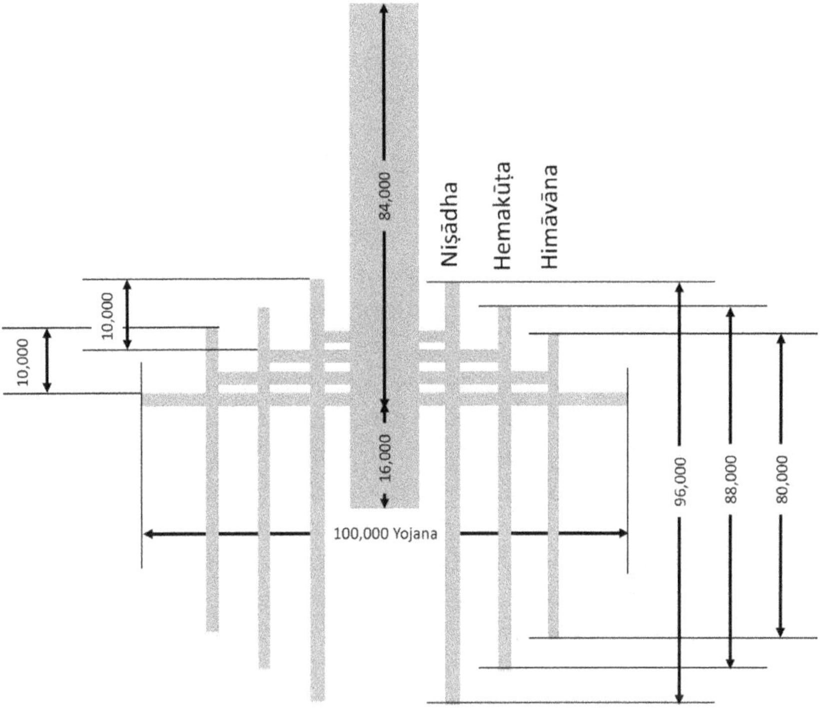

Figure-28 Jambudvīpa Mountain Heights

The barriers between *varṣa* are higher than the lowest point in the domain they protect, which means that one cannot enter the new domain simply by attaining the lowest minimum qualification needed to exist in that domain, although there are other living beings in that region of the universe who only have that qualification at the present moment. One can therefore enter a new domain with a far higher qualification than the qualification of the lowest type of living entity in that domain. Similarly, when the living entity has entered the domain, he could fall below the eligibility criterion with which he entered the domain, and therefore appear to be lower than the new living entities entering that domain.

Common examples of this kind of phenomenon exist in our everyday world. For instance, when a student enters a university, he must fulfill some minimum criterion, which is generally above the performance of the lowest performing student in the university at present. All students thus enter the university with good test scores, school grades, etc. which is frequently their best performance score. Thereafter, having entered the university, their scores often fall below the level of performance they had before they entered the university. Effectively, students tend to show a very good score at the time of entrance, and many of them fall below that promised performance after entering the university. Nevertheless, the university doesn't throw them out, although the performance may appear to be below par as compared to their entrance score promise, until, of course, the performance falls so low, that they have to be forced out. This phenomenon is generally called *hysteresis* where you have to clear a much higher bar to enter but require a much lower bar to exit.

The key point is that the mountains in the *Jambudvīpa* should not be seen physically as hurdles to physical movement, but semantically as eligibility barriers to entry. Like a physical object placed in a trough must acquire a greater amount of energy before it can jump out of the trough into the next higher trough, similarly, a living entity must acquire a better type of *karma* before he can escape the conditions of present life. Likewise, as water falling from the top can traverse through pots placed on different steps and falls to the pot below when the previous pot overflows, similarly, living beings will be pushed out by the new incoming beings who have better *karma* into a lower domain, which then pushes out beings who have an even smaller stockpile of good *karma*. In essence, the demigods can fall off the higher planets if someone more qualified appears to replace them. For this reason, demigods such as *Indra* are always insecure whenever someone performs austerities, for they fear that the new incumbent is likely to take away their position of power.

The universe therefore has a 'survival of the fittest' that applies, in which a more qualified person displaces a lesser qualified individual, and the less qualified can then come and enjoy their good *karma* in the earthly heavens, or they could even be displaced further into lower heavens. If a more qualified person does not appear, even a person who has fallen below the entry level qualification may continue to enjoy their current position, similar to how unqualified politicians can continue in their position until they are replaced by someone more powerful or qualified. This process continues until all the good *karma* is exhausted, or they have been displaced by some more qualified individual, and then, such living entities would be born in *Bharata-varṣa* in a prosperous, educated, aristocratic, or some well-off family, to again accumulate good *karma*.

The Field of Fruitive Activities

A notable feature of the above description is that *Bharata varṣa* is identified as the place where *karma* is created, which is therefore called *karma bhūmi*, and forms the gateway to the other parts of the universe, including liberation from material existence. The *Śrīmad Bhāgavatam* also confirms this distinction between *Bhārata varṣa* and the other eight *varṣa* in *Jambudvīpa*, by terming it *karma-kṣetram* or field of creating *karma*, while the other eight *varṣa* are called *upabhoga-sthānāni* or places for enjoying the *karma* leftover after life in the heavenly planets.

> *Among the nine varṣa, the tract of land known as Bhārata-varṣa is understood to be the field of fruitive activities. Learned scholars and saintly persons declare the other eight varṣa to be meant for very highly elevated pious persons. After returning from the heavenly planets, they enjoy the remaining results of their pious activities in these eight earthly varṣa. [Śrīmad Bhāgavatam 5.17.11].*

The *Matsya Purāna* also affirms the same view about *Bhārata varṣa* being a place for the creation of *karma*. It also states that this *varṣa* has nine divisions, of which the part called India (where the conversation is occurring, and which was previously the southern part of Asia, until it got divided into many parts during recent times) is one of them.

> *According to Nirukta, that place is Bhārata varṣa where human beings can obtain heaven, emancipation, and a middle course of the two. There is no field of action for man better than Bhārata varṣa, which has nine divisions—Indradvīpa, Kaśera, Tamraparni, Gabhastimāna, Nāgadvipa, Saumya, Gandharva, Varunā, and the ninth is this place surrounded on all sides by the ocean. The whole of this dvīpa is a thousand yojana in extent, from north to south. It is gradually broader from Kumāri (Cape Comorin, sometimes also called Kanyakumāri) to the mouth of the Ganges, whence it has risen to a height of ten thousand yojana in an oblique direction. [Matsya Purāna, Chapter 113, Text 6-10]*

Of all the *varṣa* in *Jambudvīpa*, *Bhārata-varṣa* has the highest dominance of mode of passion or *raja-guna*, as shown in Table 7, and this place therefore is expected to be used for performing fruitive activities. It is notable that *rajo-guna* does not mean indiscriminate enjoyment or engaging in hectic activity. Rather, *rajo-guna* means performing one's material duties diligently, philanthropy, education, satisfying the demigods by the performance of *yajña*, demonstrating compassion, generosity, and altruism, or undertaking penances for eventual material gratification. By this definition, the mode of passion is considerably elevated compared to how we normally define a 'passionate' person in modern times.

While *karma* is enjoyed (or suffered) in all parts of the cosmos, the creation of new *karma* is limited to *Bhārata-varṣa*. I will later discuss how *karma* presents opportunities to change our *guna* by updating our understanding of reality (God), and this opportunity is primarily available only in *Bharata-varṣa*. In the other parts of the universe, the *guna* of the person remain unchanged, and the living beings are engrossed in enjoying the results of their activities based on their *karma*. Of course, to rise to higher planets, one must have the appropriate *guna*, since these planets represent increasingly subtle material elements, which predominate in *sattva-guna*, and the *rajo-guna* and *tamo-guna* are subordinated. However, if the living being has risen to a higher planetary system, the pleasure is already high, and the soul remains satisfied with their current state and doesn't seek a change to their understanding or a change in their tastes of enjoyment. Only when a living being is frustrated in their life, and seeks relief from suffering (because the *karma* doesn't match the *guna*, and what we desire does not accord with what we are permitted), can one even think about rising above the modes of nature, or at least improving the quality of one's taste and perform meritorious deeds.

Even demigods therefore aspire to take birth in *Bharata-varṣa*, realizing the great opportunity for freedom from the laws of nature. However, by the time they enter *Bharata-varṣa*, either the enjoyment is so high that they forget about self-realization, or the suffering is so much that they are practically not able to overcome the quest for pleasure. The living beings, therefore, although going up the cosmic ladder, fall down again, and unless especially blessed by the grace of a self-realized soul, are unable to find the courage to renounce material pleasures.

Where is the Earth Planet?

A central point of contention in Vedic cosmology is the location of Earth. Unless we find our position in the universe, and then explain what we observe from our vantage, an understanding of cosmology remains distant. Most modern interpreters of Vedic cosmology equate *Jambudvīpa* with Earth, and *Bhārata-varṣa* with India. The mountain range called *Hemakūṭa* and *Himakūṭa* at the north of *Bhārata-varṣa* is then erroneously identified with the Himalayas at the north of India, which is incorrect because *Himakūṭa* and *Hemakūṭa* are not even close, aside from the fact that their heights are 10,000 *yojana* which is far bigger than the physical measurement of the Earth itself. Furthermore, *Himakūṭa* is described as a mountain of snow, while *Hemakūṭa* is a mountain of gold. Some similarities between the topography of South Asia and parts of the *Jambudvīpa* turn out to be quite misleading when several other statements from Vedic cosmology are considered. Consider the following statements from the *Śrīmad Bhāgavatam* regarding the structure of *Jambudvīpa*.

In these eight varṣa, or tracts of land, human beings live ten thousand years according to earthly calculations. All the inhabitants are almost like demigods. They have the bodily strength of ten thousand elephants. Indeed, their bodies are as sturdy as thunderbolts. The youthful duration of their lives is very pleasing, and both men and women enjoy sexual union with great pleasure for a long time. After years of sensual pleasure – when a balance of one year of life remains – the wife conceives a child. Thus the standard of pleasure for the residents of these heavenly regions is exactly like that of the human beings who lived during Tretā-yuga. [SB 5.17.12]

Śukadeva Gosvāmī said: In the tract of land known as Ilāvṛta-varṣa, the only male person is Lord Śiva, the most powerful demigod. Goddess Durgā, the wife of Lord Śiva, does not like any man to enter that land. If any foolish man dares to do so, she immediately turns him into a woman. I shall explain this later [in the Ninth Canto of Śrīmad-Bhāgavatam]. [SB 5.17.15]

From the above statements, it should be obvious that the Earth cannot be *Jambudvīpa* because the descriptions of the different parts of this *dvīpa* (such as there being only one male person in *Ilāvṛta-varṣa* or the duration of life being equal to 10,000 years) do not apply to *Bhārata-varṣa*. In fact, there are descriptions of the other *varṣa* too that differ from *Bhārata-varṣa.* The *Hari-varṣa* for instance is the place where the famous demon *Hiraṇyakaśipu* ruled, and *Prahlāda Mahārāja* continues to live there along with *Lord Nṛsiṁhadeva*. Similarly, *Ketumāla-varṣa* is the place of residence for the demigod *Kāmadeva*, the personality of romance.

Śukadeva Gosvāmī continued: My dear King, Lord Nṛsiṁhadeva resides in the tract of land known as Hari-varṣa. In the Seventh Canto of Śrīmad-Bhāgavatam, I shall describe to you how Prahlāda Mahārāja caused the Lord to assume the form of Nṛsiṁhadeva. Prahlāda Mahārāja, the topmost devotee of the Lord, is a reservoir of all the good qualities of great personalities. His character and activities have delivered all the fallen members of his demoniac family. Lord Nṛsiṁhadeva is very dear to this exalted personality. Thus Prahlāda Mahārāja, along with his servants and all the denizens of Hari-varṣa, worships Lord Nṛsiṁhadeva by chanting the following mantra. [SB 5.18.7]

Śukadeva Gosvāmī continued: In the tract of land called Ketumāla-varṣa, Lord Viṣṇu lives in the form of Kāmadeva, only for the satisfaction of His devotees. These include Lakṣmījī [the goddess of fortune], the Prajāpati Saṁvatsara and all of Saṁvatsara's sons and daughters. The daughters of Prajāpati are considered the controlling deities of the nights, and his sons are considered the controllers of the days. The Prajāpati's offspring number 36,000, one for each day and each night in the lifetime of a human being. At the end of each year, the Prajāpati's daughters become very agitated upon seeing the extremely effulgent disc of the Supreme Personality of Godhead, and thus they all suffer miscarriages. [SB 5.18.15]

From the above specific descriptions of the different *varṣa*, and the general statement that 8 of the 9 *varṣa* are *bhauma-svarga* or heavens on *bhūloka*, we can conclude that at least these 8 *varṣa* cannot be identified with Earth because their details don't match with anything we can find on Earth. It can, however, be said that the part of the *Jambudvīpa* called *Bhārata-varṣa* is what we call the planet Earth because this is also confirmed by the following statement in *Śrīmad Bhāgavatam*.

Formerly this planet was known as Ajanābha-varṣa, but since Mahārāja Bharata's reign it has become known as Bhārata-varṣa. [Śrīmad Bhāgavatam 5.7.3]

> *This earth planet is known as Bhārata, or Bhārata-varṣa, due to King Bharata the son of Ṛṣabha, but according to some this land is known as Bhārata due to the reign of the son of Duṣyanta. So far as we are convinced, this land's name Bhārata-varṣa was established from the reign of Bharata the son of King Ṛṣabha. Before him the land was known as Ilāvṛta-varṣa, but just after the coronation of Bharata, the son of Ṛṣabha, this land became famous as Bhārata-varṣa. [Purport to SB 1.12.20]*

The continents on the Earth are the division of *Bhārata-varṣa* mentioned in the *Matsya Purāna* or with how *Mahārāja Bharata* divided the Earth amongst his sons[4]. The nine divisions of the Earth described in *Matsya Purāna* (mentioned above) are: *Indradvīpa, Kaśera, Tamraparni, Gabhastimāna, Nāgadvipa, Saumya, Gandharva, Varunā*, and *Bharat khand.* The last of these (*Bharat khand*) is identified with India, and parts of its topography, such as Cape Comorin in the south and the emergence of Ganges in the north coincide with India's topography. It should therefore be understood that *Bhārata-varṣa* and *Bharat-khand* are not the same thing in cosmology; the former represents the entire planet Earth, while the latter denotes one of the 9 divisions of this planet. In the modern view, there are 7 continents on Earth (Africa, Antarctica, Asia, Australia, Europe, North America, and South America), but clearly, a part of Asia is viewed in the Vedic description as a separate *khand*[5].

We can draw two conclusions from here. First, *Jambudvīpa* isn't Earth since all the *varṣa* are different places that cannot be found on Earth. Second, the part of *Jambudvīpa* called *Bhārata-varṣa* is Earth. A particular part of this planet is India. The relationship between Earth and India is therefore clear from our present understanding of Earth. However, the relationship between Earth and the other *varṣa* mentioned in the *Jambudvīpa*, as well as the relation between *Jambudvīpa* and other *dvīpa* as part of *bhūloka* has no counterpart in modern knowledge.

Since Earth is a separate planet, other *varṣa* in the *Jambudvīpa* must also be distinct planets. Similarly, the many *dvīpa* in *bhūloka* aside from the *Jambudvīpa* and their subdivisions into smaller parts must also be considered planets. Going from one planet to another involves space travel, not just walking on land. The huge lengths, breadths, and sizes of mountains between the different *varṣa* and the descriptions of oceans between the *dvīpa* do not fit in the dimensions of any planet. The natural conclusion is that these descriptions are about different planets.

> *The seven islands (dvīpa) are known as (1) Jambu, (2) Śāka, (3) Śālmalī, (4) Kuśa, (5) Krauñca, (6) Gomeda, or Plakṣa, and (7) Puṣkara. The planets are called dvīpa. Outer space is like an ocean of air. Just as there are islands in the watery ocean, these planets in the ocean of space are called dvīpa, or islands in outer space. There are nine khaṇḍas, known as (1) Bhārata, (2) Kinnara, (3) Hari, (4) Kuru, (5) Hiraṇmaya, (6) Ramyaka, (7) Ilāvṛta, (8) Bhadrāśva and (9) Ketumāla. These are different parts of Jambudvīpa. A valley between two mountains is called a khaṇḍa or varṣa. [Purport CC Madhya 20.218]*

The reason these planets are never visible to us is because visibility is based on *karma*, due to which information is exchanged between living entities. This transaction is mediated only through the *Sisumāra*—which comprises the 9 planets, the solar zodiac, and the lunar *Nakṣatra,* and their numerous divisions—and these are the only things we can perceive because only these entities are involved in our *karma* transaction. Everything else, including the 6 higher planetary systems, the 7 lower planetary systems, the 28 hellish planets, the 6 *dvīpa* beyond *Jambudvīpa*, the 8 *varṣa* which are part of the *Jambudvīpa*, and the *Garbhodaka* Ocean are invisible. The question we ask is not why so many things are invisible, but why some things are visible. Unless we grasp the reason why some things become visible, we cannot explain why other things remain invisible.

Modern interpreters of Vedic cosmology struggle with the interpretation of *bhūloka* far more than they struggle with the higher and lower planetary systems, because we assume that the higher and lower planets are expected to be invisible but the parts of the *bhūloka* should all be visible: after all, they are part of our planetary system. How can we not see things that supposed to be part of our planetary system and therefore similar to the things that we can supposedly see? Given the fact that everything in *bhūloka* except the Earth is invisible to us, many interpretations are created regarding the *bhūloka*. These include equating larger and larger parts of *bhūloka* with Earth. As previously seen, some interpreters equate all of *Jambudvīpa* to Earth, while others equate all of *bhūloka* itself to Earth[6]. When discrepancies in these interpretations arise, new ideas must be added, none of which are satisfactory.

My proposal is quite simple. We know that we cannot see any part of *bhūloka* except the present planet Earth. So, let's not pretend that we are seeing something that we haven't realized we are seeing. Let's not try to interpret Vedic cosmology to fit our vision. Rather, let's try to understand *why* we are not seeing most of what Vedic cosmology describes. The subsequent chapters in this book will provide a detailed explanation of why we don't see: the reason is that light is not being distributed all over the universe. Thus, we are not entitled to see everything that exists. Rather, we see what we are entitled to see, based on *guna* and *karma*. Our *guna* prevents us from seeing higher and lower planets: we don't have the advanced perception to see subtle entities. And our *karma* prevents us from seeing different parts of Earth, and other parts of *bhūloka*.

Even all the parts of the Earth are not accessible to everyone. Everyone cannot go anywhere, be situated in any situation of our choice, or enjoy the pleasures that others seem to be enjoying. Therefore, it is obvious that we cannot experience everything that someone else is experiencing. We know about these things based on the descriptions of those who are enjoying. Sometimes we can see those people, and at other times, we simply must accept their claims. Therefore, it is false to assume that we see everything on this Earth or can even hope to see anything we want. Before we can explain why we see or don't see something in the cosmos, we need a better understanding of why I don't see everything on Earth. That is, we need to understand why we see what we see, rather than why we don't see what we don't see. Nobody really wants to suffer like the worst sufferer and not everyone can be the richest or the most powerful person, even though we want to. In that sense, we have no access to practically the majority of Earth's experience. We need a good understanding of why our experience on Earth itself is limited. If this is properly understood, then other things would be automatically understood as well.

The Pangea Hypothesis

Ramayana describes the incidents surrounding the advent of Ganga on Earth, in which the sons of King *Sagar* dig the Earth into many parts, to find a sacrificial horse which was stolen by *Indra* to prevent the king from performing a sacrifice that could have displaced *Indra* from his powerful position. *Ramayana* describes how the sons of King *Sagar* were burnt by Sage *Kapil* and subsequently one of his descendants *King Bhaghirath* performed austerities to satisfy Lord *Śiva* to bring Ganga to Earth. This narration is important because it indicates that at one time the entire Earth was a single landmass surrounded by the ocean but was divided into parts by the sons of King *Sagar*. This idea is presently called *Pangea* and was proposed in 1912 by Alfred Wegener in his theory of continental drift, suggesting that the present-day continents have drifted away from a single very large landmass that existed millions of years before.

The exact form of the *Pangea*[7], and how it drifted into separate continents, is, however, a matter of much speculation at the present. In most pictures of *Pangea*, the congruence of North America, South America, Europe, and Africa seems quite obvious, based on their shapes. However, Australia, Antarctica, and Asia are variously depicted in different models. Since this exercise is quite speculative, and one could derive different associations by bringing together the continents in different ways, I have not included any of these pictures here, but this is an interesting hypothesis from a Vedic cosmological standpoint due to the narrations about the division of Earth into many distinct landmasses. Furthermore, it would also substantiate the idea of *Bharata-varṣa* as a single landmass surrounded by a salt water ocean. Since there are four other *varṣa* which are also surrounded by a similar salt water ocean, if we had information about the topography of those *varṣa* this thesis could be validated.

Traveling in Jambudvīpa

Vedic literature provides descriptions of kings having conquered lands pertaining to the different *varṣa* in the *Jambudvīpa*. In the *Mahabharata*, for instance, there is a description of how *Arjun,* before the battle of *Kurukśhetra,* goes to different parts of the *Jambudvīpa* to obtain different kinds of weapons from the demigods using *mantras* taught to him by his elder brother *Yudhiṣṭhira*. These *mantras* are said to be part of *prati-smṛti* and they were taught to *Yudhiṣṭhira* by *Veda Vyas.* It is evident that much of the knowledge that existed in earlier times was not written, especially if this knowledge was considered dangerous for the times to come. The *Mahabharata ādi Parva* Chapter 25 provides the following description:

> *Taking Arjun aside, Yudhiṣṭhira held him by the hands and said, "O descendent of Bharata, the four divisions of the science of arms are held by Bhīśhma, Drona, Kripa, Kama and Ashvatthāma. They have all received divine instructions and know how to use every sort of weapon. Having been honored, gratified and supported by Duryodhana, they always seek to do him good. We should not doubt that they will support him in battle. The whole world is now under Duryodhana's sway, and he is our avowed enemy. You are our sole refuge. Depending on you we shall regain our kingdom from Duryodhana. Listen now as I tell you what should be done."*
>
> *Yudhiṣṭhira then informed Arjun of Vyasadeva's instructions. He told him that he should leave as soon as possible for the Himalayas and, by meditating on the mantras he was now going to repeat, he should seek the gods' audience in order to receive their weapons. "Allow me to initiate you today, O virtuous one, and go at once to propitiate Indra. Being pleased with you I am sure Indra will give you his weapons and, by his order, so will the other gods."*

Arjun fully controlled his mind and senses. Then, with due rites, Yudhiṣṭhira bestowed the Prati-smṛti mantras on him. When he was finished Yudhiṣṭhira stood up, with tears pricking his eyes as he thought of Arjun's separation. "Now go, dear brother."

Arjun smiled at Draupadi, circumambulated his brothers and Dhaumya, and then began running swiftly along the path, frightening creatures along the way with his speed. By chanting the mantras Yudhiṣṭhira had given him, he felt himself traveling over mountains and forests at the speed of mind. By the end of the first day he arrived at the great Mandara Mountain. Arjun stopped and looked around. The mountain was beautiful with its bluish stone rising up into the clouds. It was covered with blossoming trees, their many-colored flowers creating rich tableaus and their scent captivating his mind. The sound of peacocks, cranes and cuckoos filled the air, and he could see Siddha and Chārana sporting on the mountain slopes. Arjun decided to climb the mountain and begin his austerities there.

Upon reaching a plateau high on the mountain, he suddenly heard a voice resounding in the sky. "Stop!" Arjun looked around and saw an ascetic sitting at the foot of a tree. The tawny-colored Brahmin had a brilliant aura. His lean body was covered in deerskin and his matted locks hung down to his shoulders. The ascetic said, "O child, who are you? You appear to be a Kshatriya. Do you not know that this is the abode of peaceful Brahmins who are free from anger? Even to have been able to reach this spot indicates that you already attained a high state of purity. Now perfect your life. You have no need of weapons here. Throw them away."

Mahabharata goes on to describe how *Arjun* meets all the demigods and obtains weapons from them, many of which are eventually used in the battle of *Kurukśhetra*. The key point is that travel to different parts of *Jambudvīpa* is described in the Vedic texts, although it involves a special type of knowledge, such as that imparted to *Arjun* by *Yudhiṣṭhira*. The *Śrīmad Bhāgavatam* describes how King *Parīkṣit* conquers *Jambudvīpa*.

> *Maharaja Parīkṣit then conquered all parts of the earthly planet – Bhadrasva, Ketumala, Bharata, the northern Kuru, Kimpurusa, etc. – and exacted tributes from their respective rulers.*
>
> *Purport: Bhadrāśva: It is a tract of land near Meru Parvata, and it extends from Gandha-mādana Parvata to the saltwater ocean. There is a description of this varṣa in the Mahābhārata (Bhīṣma-parva 7.14-18). The description was narrated by Sañjaya to Dhṛtarāṣṭra. Mahārāja Yudhiṣṭhira also conquered this varṣa, and thus the province was included within the jurisdiction of his empire. Mahārāja Parīkṣit was formerly declared to be the emperor of all lands ruled by his grandfather, but still he had to establish his supremacy while he was out of his capital to exact tribute from such states. [Śrīmad Bhāgavatam 1.16.12]*

From these descriptions we can understand that it is possible to travel from one part of *Jambudvipa* to another although this travel is not walking around on the present planet. *Mahabharata* also describes how Arjun travels to different parts of *Jambudvīpa* to conquer the lands on behalf of his elder brother *Yudhiṣṭhira* during the *Rājasūya Yajña*:

> *Finally, Arjun arrived in Hari varṣa, the land where the Northern Kuru dwelt. At the border, a number of powerful, large-bodied guards stopped him. They said, "O Arjun, this land cannot be entered by humans. If you try you will perish along with your army. Indeed, even if you were able to enter, you would not see anything,*

> *because human eyes cannot see this land or its residents. Go back. There is nothing to be conquered here. Your conquests are already sufficient. We are pleased with you and will happily offer you a gift. What would you like?"*
>
> *Arjun bowed respectfully to the divine beings and said, "I desire Yudhishthira's imperial dignity. If you accept him as the emperor of this wide earth, then please give something as a tribute."*
>
> *The Northern Kuru immediately offered Arjun a large number of celestial clothes and ornaments, saying, "We know you and your brothers to be great servants of the Supreme Lord. Go now with our blessings. May you always gain victory!"*

We can see that the different parts of *Jambudvīpa* are not meant for humans, but for certain types of demigods, and entry to these parts is forbidden for humans. And yet, with advanced knowledge, some humans like *Arjun* have traveled to these parts to meet the celestial beings. What is this advanced knowledge by which humans are able to travel?

According to *Śrīmad Bhāgavatam*, the *Himakūṭa* is 10,000 *yojana* higher than *Bhārata-varṣa*. To cross this mountain, one must go 10,000 *yojana* above the Earth surface, and then descend 10,000 *yojana*. *Arjun* covers this distance in roughly half a day (assuming he bade farewell to *Yudhiṣṭhira* at noon, and reached the destination by the end of day, we can say that this time is about 6 hours). Thus, he must travel more than 20,000 *yojana* (160,000 miles) in 6 hours, or about 7.4 miles per second. This travel is against the Earth's 'gravity', and the traveler's speed must exceed the 'escape velocity' of rockets, which interestingly, is about 7 miles per second. However, unlike the rockets which burn large amounts of fuel during launch, *Arjun* travels by the power of *mantra* which implies that he overcame gravity by a *mantra* and went to a place that cannot be sensually perceived, until we enter the atmosphere of that place.

In *yoga* literature eight *siddhis* are described, which include *laghimā* (the ability to become weightless) and *garimā* (the ability to become heavy). On his ascent, *Arjun* would have to use *laghimā* and on descent he would have to use the process of *garimā*. Of course, *Arjun* did not have the mystic perfections of *laghimā* and *garimā* but he still attained their results by the use of *prati-smṛti mantra*. Similarly, when other kings established their rule over *Jambudvīpa*, or sometimes over the entire *bhūloka*, they traveled to these planets by *mantra* or mystic powers.

To understand this space travel, we must recall that space in Vedic cosmology is semantic. The enormous mountains in *Jambudvīpa* are also therefore not huge rocks. Rather, a mountain between two *varṣa* is a semantic barrier of eligibility, which must be crossed before entry into a new realm. This idea might seem naïve or ridiculous, but it has nearly exact counterparts in modern science. When phase space is used to denote the complete state of an object, then transitions between states often involve jumping over energy barriers such as those shown in Figure-29. The implication of these barriers is that the phase space is not 'flat'. Instead, going from one state to another involves two kinds of distinctions: (1) the energy gap between the initial and the final state, and (2) the energy barrier that must be crossed to transition the states.

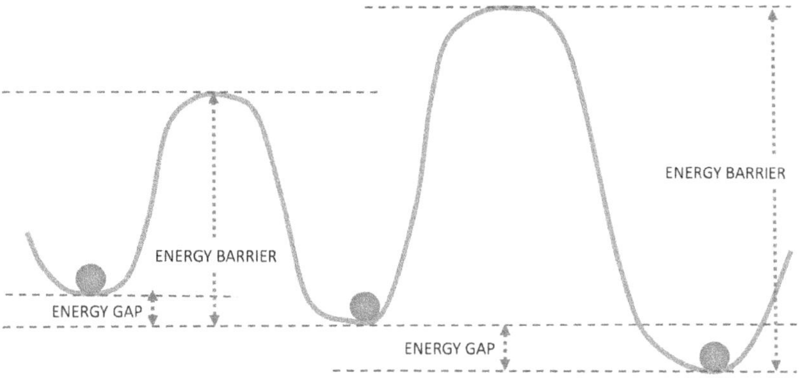

Figure-29 Energy Barriers in State Transitions

The different *varṣa* are not physical heights but levels of semantic information. The *varṣa* on the inner part of *Jambudvīpa* are more abstract informational levels. To go to that level, one must shed the material details. This shift from one state to another is like the energy gap between two states. However, to perform this energy transition, there is a much bigger energy barrier to be crossed. As compared to the energy barrier, the energy gap appears quite small, which means that sometimes to perform a small change, a much larger effort is needed. The energy barrier confines objects in each of the *varṣa* to those *varṣa* unless a much bigger barrier is crossed. These barriers are the 'mountains' of *Jambudvīpa* while the *varṣa* are the 'valleys' in between these 'mountains'.

If we were to think of the mountains in *Jambudvīpa* as gigantic rocks, we would never find them, because these mountains aren't rocks. In fact, they aren't even physical objects. They are rather the energy barriers for an object to be crossed in going from one domain to another. The mountain called *Himavāna* is not a huge mountain called the *Himalayas* in the north of India. It is rather an informational barrier of temperature. Heat, as we have seen earlier, arises when information is added. By contrast, cold is the absence of information. The height of the mountain therefore indicates a tremendous loss in information, and to cross this mountain, an object must lose a lot of information, and thereby become cold. The fact that this mountain is 10,000 *yojana* is thus a measure of the loss in information, not a measure of the physical height of a rock.

This kind of space travel cannot be achieved simply with a rocket that moves away from a physical Earth, while the bodies of the astronauts remain intact as Earthly beings (they don't lose information and become cold). This kind of space travel would indeed surprise most travelers unless they are advanced in understanding how the gross body is simply a manifestation of subtle body, and loss in the body's information is not death of the body, although it makes the body less detailed. When the body loses information, it becomes 'lighter', rises above the Earth's surface (which is a place for macroscopic detailed material objects), until it crosses the informational barrier. It will then descend downwards and manifest a new kind of gross bodily details. When it reaches a different *varṣa* it will also have a different kind of body, although produced from the same subtle body, suited for the new type of planet atmosphere.

The difference between the energy crests and troughs shown in

Figure-29, and the informational transition described above, is that higher type of information naturally entails lower physical energy. When an astronaut performs space travel, he goes over the gravity force by adding energy to himself (through the motion of a rocket). In the informational movement, the traveler loses energy and therefore rises. The mountains therefore are not high energy states, as they would become obvious through physical measurements. They are rather low energy states signifying abstract information. The subtle body can penetrate these mountains directly as the subtle body is even more subtle than the mountains. However, the gross body cannot pass these mountains, so if one has to travel to another *varṣa* without discarding the subtle body, then, at the least, one must discard many of the gross bodily details.

These descriptions appear fantastic today because we don't understand how the gross matter manifests from the subtle matter, and how our body is changing with time. Like a succession of bulbs in a neon display go on and off in succession, which creates the impression of a moving light, similarly, our body is also manifest due to the *karma* manifest at a time. If a living being has the requisite *karma*, understands the process by which gross body manifests from the subtle body, and has the desire to travel to another part of the universe, he can move the body to a different part just like a neon light switches off at one location and switches on at another. The 'continuity' in motion is established in this process by the subtle body and not the gross body, because this subtle body is the real cause of change, not the gross body. Due to a lack of understanding of this process, and lack of requisite *karma* to perform such feats, this process appears mysterious, although it is only mystical.

Similarly, the oceans and rivers are also barriers to going from one part of the geography to another. The oceans separating the *dvīpa* are not water (or milk or yogurt) bodies in the ordinary sense that we currently think of them. They are rather regions of space that denote a different kind of information, and to cross this region of space either the body must be built upon that information or must be subtler than that information. In a simple sense, the different living habitats are strictly demarcated for different types of living beings such that moving from one habitat to another is very difficult. The levels of difficulty are hierarchical and decrease from oceans to mountains, to rivers: it is easier to cross a river, harder to cross a mountain, and even harder to cross an ocean. This difficulty represents the hardship in going from one domain to another.

We earlier discussed the theory of *modal realism* in which demigods and our bodies are shared, although we view this reality from different perspectives. The different parts of *bhūloka* are also different perspectives although not shared. Think of a factory that produces parts of vehicles—such as chassis, engine, steering, wheels, seats, body, etc.—and assembles them into vehicles. We can now envision two kinds of living beings: (1) those who drive the individual vehicles, and (2) those who produce the separate parts of each vehicle. The demigods are in control of the parts, and we are in control of the vehicles. Alternately, the demigod vehicle is the collection of all the parts of one type (e.g., all steering wheels or all motors), while our vehicle is the collection of all types (e.g., one car with all its different parts). A vehicle is built from many parts, and the parts span many vehicles. The creator of the part therefore defines all the vehicles, but only a certain aspect of each vehicle. Similarly, the driver of a vehicle consumes all the parts, produced by the individual creators, but only a small fraction of all the individual parts being consumed.

In the above example, the demigods are producing the parts of the vehicles, but there are many types of vehicles, such as cars or trucks. The demigod's existence shares the car and the truck, and we share a part of the demigod's existence by being a car. However, the car and the truck don't share anything with each other, except through the demigods. Therefore, if we must see a different type of vehicle, then there must be *karma* due to which the information can pass through the demigod (up and down the tree). This *karma* can be obtained by rituals, but unless it exists, we cannot perceive all parts of *bhūloka*. Formerly, the demigods endowed pious kings with the power to conquer many parts of *bhūloka* so that the worship of demigods, and the general principles of religiosity, can be maintained in all parts of *bhūloka*. The demigods thus played an important role in endowing the rulers with powers that ultimately facilitated their own well-being. This process is not spiritual, although it is an advanced form of materialism, beyond current materialism.

Flat vs. Round Descriptions

Another important issue in accepting the Vedic cosmic model concerns the fact that the Earth is described as a flat body rather than a sphere. There are many reasons why Earth is believed to be round today:

- We see that all celestial objects are observed to be spheres rather than flat surfaces. Why should Earth be any different? Aren't we postulating a unique fact about the Earth by supposing that Earth is flat, when every other celestial body is spherical?
- Different parts of the Earth undergo day and night at different times. We are familiar with time zones, and if you travel to the diametrically opposite part of the Earth, you see that there is day when it should have been night according to the clock you are carrying.
- You can keep moving on the Earth on a straight line path and you will eventually arrive at the same point from where you started; this is affirmed by aircraft travel, but it is impossible to achieve if you are on a flat surface; you will simply fall off the edge of the Earth.
- The Earth has been photographed from space and seen to be a sphere. From all these observations, it appears that Earth is round, and any theory of flat Earth must be flat out wrong.

There are, however, other reasons why we might suppose that the Earth is flat. For instance, through actual observations we only know about the *surface* of Earth which is two dimensional, and any two-dimensional surface can be mapped to a plane. In fact, all maps of the Earth are flat, and projections are used to convert the sphere to a plane. In all these projections, we utilize only two numbers: latitude and longitude.

The Vedic model of flatness steps aside these issues, because both spherical and flat Earth models are based on a *physical* picture of nature, not a semantic one. Here, I will describe why the Earth is spherical to all our sensual *observation* and yet flat in a semantic sense. But, before we get into that discussion, let's first try to understand how a sphere can be reduced to a lotus structure, which is widely used in Vedic philosophy as a model of space. Figure-30 illustrates how a *hollow* sphere can be converted into a lotus structure by slicing the surface of a sphere, keeping the slices joined at one end, while spreading them at the other. We frequently use this technique to peel an orange or other fruits, where a knife is used to cut a skin deep groove, and the skin is then peeled from one end. The peeled skin can then be spread on a flat surface. After all, the *surface* of a fruit has only two dimensions, so, although it appears to be spherical, it can be converted into a two-dimensional picture. Maps of Earth use variations of this technique; the variation depends on the point at which you start slicing the spherical surface (e.g., North Pole vs. South Pole), the number of slices you wish to produce in the process, and the extent to which the slices are allowed to be stretched or compressed.

Once you convert the sphere into a flat surface, the two end points of the slicing (e.g., the North Pole and the South Pole) become the center and the circumference of the circle. If you thought that the South Pole was the origin, then it would become the center in the flat structure, while the North Pole would become the circumference, or vice versa. Now the key problem arises in interpreting this flat surface: one of the *points* on the sphere has now become a *circle*. Practically speaking, if the sphere is real, you will observe a point, although in the representation, it is a circle. The flat representation may describe the spherical surface as well as the spherical representation, but we have the practical difficulty of reconciling the point with the circle. If we *observe* that there is a point, but our representation says that it is circle, then there is clearly a gap between what we observe to be real vs. how we describe it in a model.

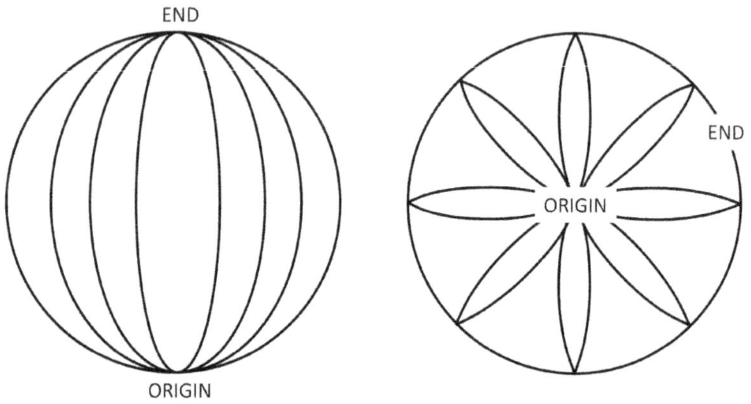

Figure-30 Spherical vs. Lotus Models

This problem, however, does not arise in a semantic scheme if the point that becomes a circle represents a *set* that contains the other points on the spherical surface. In fact, if the point that becomes a circle denotes a set, then our understanding of the sphere is considerably improved because the other parts of the sphere can be seen as *members* of the set denoted by the boundary of the circle. The point that became a circle would be treated as yet another physical entity in the sphere model. However, in the flat representation, we are compelled to treat it as a circle that *contains* all the other points. The conclusion therefore is that the flat model fits better with the reality *if* one specific point on the spherical surface contains all the members on a surface. For instance, if the sphere was used to represent various types of colors, then one point on that sphere (the *origin*) would denote the idea of color, which we might symbolize by white, which is a color, and yet devoid of any particular hue. Similarly, the end of the sphere would be black, which is also a color, but obtained by the complete saturation of all colors, and produced *after* all other colors have been created. This color, now, contains all the other colors in complete saturated form. If we remove some colors from black, we obtain a particular hue. If we remove all the colors, then we obtain white. Thus, while white and black appear to be colors, and they are therefore on the color surface, they would represent the *origin* and *end* of the color space. The origin of the space (white) would represent the *idea* of color, while the end of the space (black) would represent the *set* of all colors.

The difference between the spherical and the flat models therefore hinges on whether the origin and end of the space is treated physically or semantically. If we treat all points on the surface of Earth physically, then the Earth is a sphere. If, however, we treat all the points on the Earth's surface as ideas, then one specific point on that surface is the symbol of a more abstract idea, and thus becomes the origin of that symbolic domain. Similarly, the point on the opposite side of the surface represents the collection of all the points, even though it is just a point. Since the origin and the end look just like any other point on the surface from a physical standpoint, we need a semantic view of nature to treat some points as representations of an idea and a set of members. Since representations are perceived only by the mind and not the senses, if you see the Earth with your senses, you will see a sphere. If, however, you see the Earth with your mind, you will see a flat lotus structure, originating in an abstract idea.

It is therefore true that the Earth is a sphere, when seen by our eyes. It is also true that the Earth is flat, when seen by the mind. As we have noted previously, the semantic description is superior to the physical description because only this description is consistent and complete. Therefore, the flat description is a superior description even though to our senses the world appears spherical. Similarly, every luminary that we can see in the sky appears as a sphere to our eyes, but all these luminaries would be perceived flat through the mind, provided we have developed a semantic perception of the world. The semantic perception appears to contradict the physical picture, but the physical picture is theoretically inadequate. If we are speaking about how the world *really* is rather than how it *appears* to us, then the flat description is reality while the sphere is appearance. This appearance can be used to confirm the theory, even though superficially there is a contradiction between the theory and observation. The confirmation, in this case, for instance, would involve the ability to predict and explain common phenomena such as day and night, the passing of the seasons, the flipping of the poles, and so forth.

Most current discussions of the flat vs. spherical models appear to be contradictory because both describe the world physically in which all points on Earth are just material objects. When you take that viewpoint, then clearly, the spherical model is superior, because we cannot reconcile the circle with the point in a physical numbering scheme. This reconciliation is possible in the semantic numbering scheme where the origin of the space denotes a more abstract idea from which its instantiations are created. Many cars can be created from the idea of a car, but there is one particular car in this set of cars which can be called the "perfect car" from which all the other cars are produced by replicating parts of the "perfect car" in various ways. The perfect car is also a car, but due to its perfect denotation of the idea, it is the very epitome of the idea itself.

In Vedic philosophy, every planet is ruled by a deity, who appears to be just like all the other beings on the planet, and yet that deity is the perfect example of the embodiment of the idea represented in that space. Like the set of all cars also includes the perfect car, similarly, the planet comprising different living beings also includes the perfect living being who embodies the planetary attributes. Thus, for instance, the Sun, the Moon, Jupiter, Mercury, etc. are planets predominated by different qualities, but those qualities are perfectly represented by a demigod who is the "origin" of the space of that type. The demigod lives on the planet, and he has many similarities to the other living beings on the same planet, but he is also the perfect embodiment of the attributes of that planet.

The place of residence of the demigod on the planet is the *origin* of that space. In the flat representation, this origin is the center of the planet, so the demigod is situated at the center. Ultimately, the planet can also be called a sphere, as long as we understand that the origin of the sphere represents an abstract idea, and the end of the sphere represents a set or collection. When two points on the sphere are representations, every other point must also be a representation; in fact, these denotations must be consistent with the two points being an idea and a set. If this accommodation has been made, then it doesn't matter whether we call it a sphere or a flat surface. The planet will appear spherical to our senses, and flat to our mind, but if the correct mental picture has been formed, it can be unified with the spherical model, and we can say that a demigod lives on a particular place on a sphere, which is his "residence" as well as the origin of all the instantiations of the qualities embodied in him.

We have seen (during the discussion of the *Lokāloka* Mountain) how the outer boundary of the *loka* space represents the number 0. We have now seen why the center of the space denotes the foremost entity in that space, and if we were to count all the entities in this space, the center would be counted as the first entity. The center can therefore be seen as a representation of the number 1, while the circumference is 0. The numbers 0 and 1 are the most important numbers in semantic numbering as they denote the origin and end of the space within which we count. Once the outer bounds of space and its center have been defined, the successive members can be created by dividing this space into cardinal directions (East, West, North, and South) which can then be divided by the three modes of nature, producing 12 divisions. Together with the center and the boundary, we can now envision 14 regions, arising from some basic ideas about types and the structure of semantic space, which are seen both in the vertical and the horizontal divisions of space.

These are certainly not the only possible way to construe the division of space. For instance, when space is divided into 12 parts, the division is produced by dividing 4 by 3, and it is possible to think of the universe as divided into 3 or 4 parts. For instance, the 12 houses in astrology are described sometimes in groups of 3, and at other times in groups of 4. Similarly, the 14 planetary systems are divided into 3 parts, namely, the upper, middle, and lower systems, and the universe is sometimes described as 3 parts called *bhūloka*, *bhuvarloka*, and *svargaloka*. Likewise, the *bhūloka* is divided into 9 parts, which is the outcome of successively dividing 3 by 3 but ignoring the 4-fold division. The exact number of divisions used in each such description is only indicative of what type is being prioritized and which type is being contextualized. The significance of these numbers is therefore not quantitative, but qualitative.

Parity Inversion in the Sphere

You might have noticed that in drawing the lotus structure in Figure-30 I arbitrarily picked one of the points on the sphere as the origin.

The origin might be, for instance, the North Pole or the South Pole. I also described that if we envisioned this sphere as a domain of colors, the origin would be white, and the end would be black. The choice of the origin, Vedic cosmology states, is indeed arbitrary, and the color of the poles reverses every 6 months. Due to this reversal, there is 6 months of day on the North Pole when the Sun passes through a phase called *Uttarāyaṇa* during which time there is 6 months of night on the South Pole. Similarly, when the Sun passes through a phase called *Dakshināyana*, there is 6 months of night on the North Pole and 6 months of day at the South Pole. This day and night are explained in science by postulating a *tilt* in the Earth's axis due to which the North Pole is *inclined* towards the Sun for six months and the South Pole inclines towards the Sun for the remaining 6 months in a year. In Vedic cosmology, the same phenomenon must be understood as the inversion in the origin of the Earth's semantic space.

The Sun's phase is called *Uttarāyaṇa* when it passes through the constellations Aries, Taurus, Gemini, Cancer, Leo and Virgo. It is called *Dakshināyana* when it passes through the constellations Libra, Scorpio, Sagittarius, Capricorn, Aquarius, and Pisces. This passing coincides with the day and night of demigods, which are 6 months long each. The day of the demigods is the night of demons, and the day of demons is the night of demigods. The *Uttarāyaṇa* or "northern movement" is the day of the demigods, and *Dakshināyana* or the "southern movement" is the day of the demons. Since the North Pole and the South Pole days and nights coincide with this change, the North Pole is identified with the demigods and the South Pole with the demons. Thus, the Sun's passing through the 12 constellations in the zodiac represents one day and night of the demigods and demons, their days and nights being opposite of each other.

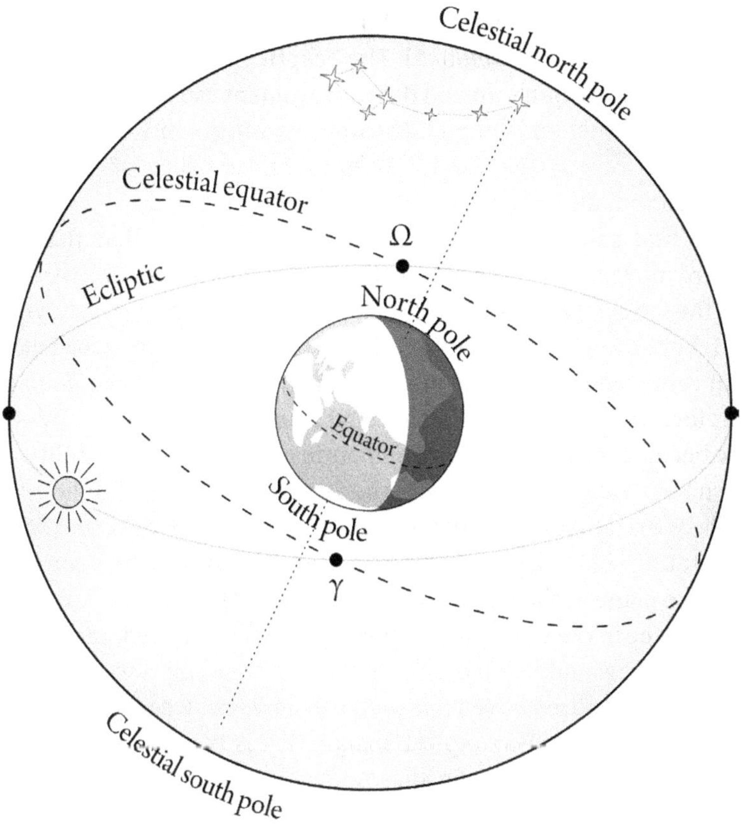

Figure-31 The Equator and the Ecliptic

The reason that *Uttarāyaṇa* is called the "northern phase" is that the Sun "rises up" in its orbit during this phase, and the reason that *Dakshināyana* is called "southern phase" is that the Sun "falls down" in its orbit during this phase. To those familiar with astronomy, this is not a new idea and is called the *ecliptic* as shown in Figure-31 in which the Sun is seen to be above the Earth's equatorial plane for 6 months and below that equatorial plane for another 6 months. The notion of an *ecliptic* is however only a phenomenon and not reality in Vedic cosmology because the Sun is not in the same plane as the Earth *ever*. As noted previously, the Sun is above the Earth by 800,000 miles and the Earth's diameter is stated to be 12,800 miles (1600 *yojana*) in the *Surya Siddhānta*. Therefore, even if the Sun goes down the orbit, it never falls below the equator of the Earth (which in this case would mean going below the *bhūloka*). The ecliptic plane is only an appearance because the Sun's up and down movement causes the changes in seasons (summer and winter). The upward and downward movement is however responsible for the flipping of the origin of the Earth's space without any ecliptic.

The real explanation of the changing seasons is that the Sun's upward movement represents an increase in *sattva-guna* which means that the origin, which denotes a conceptually more abstract symbol (and therefore *sattva*) is lighted. Similarly, the Sun's downward movement represents a decrease in *sattva-guna* and rise in *tamo-guna* and therefore the end of the Earth's space, which was previously dark now becomes lighted. This is a semantic explanation of causality and doesn't have anything to do with the Sun being in "line of sight" of the Earth, or even in the same plane as Earth. As we have seen, the planets are rotating above the Earth at greater height, so they never come into the same plane as the Earth. And yet, by their effects on the Earth they *appear* to be in the same plane. This appearance is a phenomenon, and not reality. If we take a physical viewpoint, the simplest explanation is that the planets are in the same plane. If, however, we take the semantic viewpoint, then the simplest explanation is that the planets are at different heights from the Earth.

The key import of this notion is that the origin of space on a spherical surface is not fixed. Even in modern science we recognize that the origin of a coordinate system could be anywhere. However, practically speaking we tend to fix it in either north or south poles. This origin changes every 6 months, such that the North Pole is the origin during the *Uttarāyaṇa* period, and the South Pole is the origin during the *Dakshināyana* period. The properties of the demigods and the demons therefore dominate during these two periods. The Earth's magnetic field also reverses once in a while, although there is currently no theory to predict when this field reversal will occur. We just know from fossil records that these reversals have occurred in the past. The magnetic field reversal is a longer duration phenomenon than the yearly phenomenon of seasonal changes, but once we understand that this reversal represents a change in the origin of space, and that this reversal is periodic, then a theory of this reversal based on semantic principles can be used to predict pole reversals.

We can see that the flat model of the Earth used in Vedic cosmology has no innate contradiction with the spherical model in modern science because the Earth is indeed spherical from a sensual viewpoint. However, there is a huge difference in the manner in which the two models explain changes. For instance, seasonal changes are caused by the Earth's tilt in modern cosmology. But these are caused by the Sun's upward and downward motion in Vedic cosmology, which then effects a flipping of the Earth's coordinate system origin. As long as the causal differences are understood, all the phenomenal differences will not matter. Thus, for instance, all observations that seem to suggest that the Earth is spherical would be confirmed in the flat model as well, although their explanation would most likely be quite different. As an illustration, in modern science, the explanation of the passing of day and night is that the Earth rotates, and for it to rotate, it must be a sphere. In Vedic cosmology, the Earth remains stationary and the Sun goes around the Earth once per day (this topic is further detailed in the next chapter). Semantically speaking, the rotation of the Sun illuminates different parts of the Earth because the Sun's properties themselves change as it passes through the zodiac in space, and this change in property resonates with the different parts of Earth (which too have different properties), bringing them into day and night. This explanation cannot be understood in a physical theory but would be easily grasped in a semantic view where meanings cause phenomena.

However, even if you did not know this explanation, and just treated the Earth as a sphere, it would still be consistent with the Sun going around the Earth once per day. The passing of the day and night, therefore, has a different explanation in the semantic scheme; however, since the Earth is still a sphere from the standpoint of sensations, all the explanations that we could construct in the physical view could still be used as phenomenal explanatory tools, although these may not always be true. Vedic cosmological texts also alternate between the causal and phenomenal pictures, sometimes speaking about what is really occurring and then how we happen to perceive these changes. The phenomenal constructs (such as the *ecliptic*) thus exist in Vedic cosmological texts too, and the reader must distinguish between appearances and reality.

The Sumeru Mountain

Once we understand how the flat structure is a semantic representation of a physical world, it becomes possible to understand how the center of the flat surface is more abstract than the edges. The center represents the core idea from which its representations are created while the outer edge is the *set* or *collection* of all these instantiations. The center of the *bhūloka* is called the *Sumeru* Mountain, while the outer edge, as we have already seen, is called the *Lokāloka* Mountain. The four sides of the *Sumeru* Mountain reflect the same four-fold division that we have seen previously (these 4-fold division begins with the four heads of Lord *Brahma* who speaks the four Vedas, creating a ritual structure for everything in the cosmos). The *Matsya Purāna* states the following about the four sides:

> *It (Meru Mountain) has a circular form divided into four quadrants. Its sides (quadrants) are of various uniform colors, with properties conferred upon it by Brahma (the Lord of the creatures). On its navel peduncle (east quadrant) sprung from the self-born Brahma there is white color. Consequently it is said to have qualities of Brahmana. On its southern quadrant, there is yellow color, on account of which it is said to have the properties of the Vaisya class. On its western quadrant there is the color of the black bee, owing to which it is said to possess the properties of Sudra. Its northern quadrant is naturally of red color, therefore it has the properties of Kshatriyas. Thus the four colors and classes have been enumerated. [Matsya Purāna, Chapter 113, Text 13-16].*

If we transformed the entire *bhūloka* into a very large sphere, the *Sumeru Mountain* would be North Pole while the *Lokāloka* Mountain would be the South Pole. The rest of the islands and oceans in the *bhūloka* are instantiations of the *Sumeru* Mountain and the *Lokāloka* Mountain represents the outer boundary which is reached after all the instantiations have been produced. In fact, now, it is possible to identify that the region beyond the *Lokāloka* Mountain as the matter *inside* the planetary spheres.

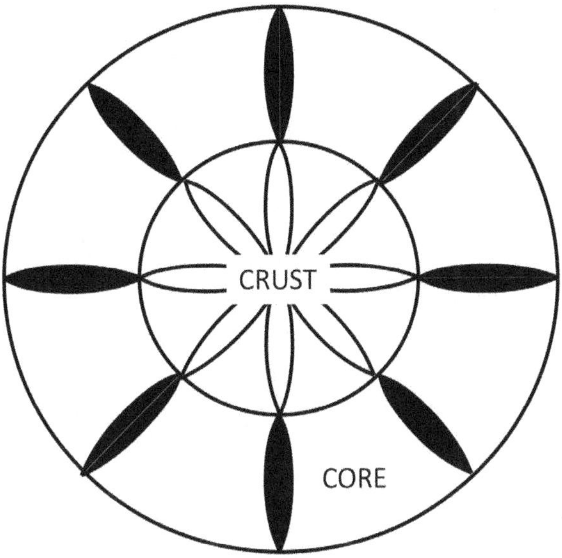

Figure-32 The Crust and the Core of a Sphere

We have previously discussed that the material region beyond the *Lokāloka* Mountain is 3 times larger than the region within this mountain, because when the diameter is doubled, the area is quadrupled. This larger space can be understood as the part of the planets which lies below their 'crust'. In essence, the planets in *loka varṣa* have a "dark" counterpart in the *āloka varṣa,* which is nothing other than what lies within that planet (everything below the visible surface), and therefore remains invisible to sensation or thought. When we flatten a sphere, the part that is within the sphere is therefore not lost; it is just spread beyond the region we call the 'crust'. This region is 'dark' in the sense that it cannot be experienced, and there are no life forms living inside the Earth's core.

The flattening of the sphere illustrates a radically different way in which the world is described in Vedic cosmology where things that we consider physically very close (e.g., the core and crust of a planet) are actually very far. Similarly, the functional parts of living beings (e.g., their eyes) are very close to each other although the living beings appear to be far from each other. The anti-material world exists with the material world, but instead of going 'forward' in time, it moves 'backward' in time (I will discuss the nature of backward movement in the next chapter).

It is important to note that unless a planet is flattened, higher and lower realms cannot be understood in 3-dimensional space. Notably, the higher and lower planets are placed along the vertical dimension *after* the globe has been flattened—i.e., reduced to two dimensions. If we keep the globe intact, then all the higher and lower planets will require another dimension, which is of course impossible in a world where there are only 3 dimensions. The conclusion is that a flat geometry is essential in a cosmology that requires the existence of higher and lower planetary systems, because the higher and lower represents the level of abstraction, and the vertical dimension has to represent abstraction (or detailing) which entails that each planetary system must be flattened.

The *Sumeru* Mountain is the most abstract part of the *bhūloka* and lies in the middle of the *Ilāvṛta varṣa* which, as previously noted, is the planet of Lord *Śiva*. This mountain is said to be made of gold, which is considered the purest material on *bhūloka*. Most illustrations show this mountain to be yellow, presuming that gold is always yellow, but based on what we have discussed previously about the colors and their significance, it is possible that this mountain is golden and yet white. *Sumeru* is said to be 84,000 *yojana* high, and 16,000 *yojana* deep (below the *bhūloka* into the lower planetary systems). It is again noteworthy that we are able to speak about 'below' *bhūloka* only because we have moved the matter 'inside' the planet to a region beyond the *loka varṣa*. Otherwise, if we hadn't flattened the *bhūloka*, then we would not only be required to deal with the dimensionality inside the planet, but also 'below' the planet, which would end up requiring more than 3 dimensions in space.

On top of the *Sumeru* Mountain the 33 demigods reside, which comprise 12 *āditya* (*mitra, aryaman, bhaga, varuṇa, dakṣa, aṃśa, tvāṣṭṛ, pūṣan, vivasvat, savitṛ, indra,* and *viṣṇu*), 11 *rudra* (*ānanda, vijñāna, manas, prāna, vāk, iśāna, tatpuruṣa, aghora, vāmadeva, sadyojāta,* and *atmā*), and 8 *vasu* (*pṛthivī, agni, antarikṣa, apah, vāyu, dyauṣ, sūrya, nakṣatra*, and *soma*), *indra*, and *prajāpati*. These demigods are identified with 33 consonants in *Sanskrit*, as representations of different unique kinds of meanings, and I will elaborate on this aspect of Vedic cosmology further in the next chapter, and why it is crucial to understand the structure of language to understand the structure of the cosmic manifestation[8].

The *Sumeru* is described to be 84,000 *yojana* high, which is 16,000 *yojana* below the Sun, the lowest planet in the *svargaloka*. Therefore, the demigods living on top of the *Sumeru* are not truly the demigods of *svargaloka*. In fact, since the *Sumeru* is rooted in the *bhūloka*, it is treated as a part of the *bhūloka* rather than a part of *svargaloka*. As we have discussed earlier, in a lotus geometry, the center of the lotus represents the *origin* of the space, and therefore the most abstract concept in that space. Due to this abstraction, the location is also higher. The diameter of the *loka varṣa* is 125,000,000 *yojana* so the height of 84,000 *yojana* is a small fraction of the total size of the *bhūloka*, although when compared to the sizes in *Jambudvīpa* this height looks considerable. *Sumeru* should, however, be viewed as the center of the entire *bhūloka*, not merely *Jambudvīpa*.

The demigods on the *Sumeru* should be considered the earthly representatives of the demigods in *svargaloka* who rule the *bhūloka* sitting on a pedestal in the middle of the *bhūloka*. For instance, the center of the *Sumeru* is said to be *Brahmapurī* where Lord *Brahma* resides, although actually Lord *Brahma* resides in the *satyaloka*. Similarly, the *prajāpati* are in the *maharloka* and *janaloka*, Lord *Viṣṇu* is on the polestar, etc. These names and their locations are therefore earthly representations of the higher planetary systems, which can be compared to the embassies of a country in another country, and these demigods are like ambassadors of the higher planets on *bhūloka*. Just like the ambassadors are often called by the name of country they represent, similarly, these demigods are also called by the same name as the demigods they represent. As the representative of a country, the ambassador is accorded the same respect as the person that he or she represents, but the ambassador is still a representative and not identical to the person that s/he is representing.

The job of the ambassador is to communicate the messages of the ruler in the foreign land. Similarly, the ambassador takes the messages of the foreign land to the ruler. In the same way, the representatives of the demigods accept the offerings of the *yajña* performed on the *bhūloka* and communicate them to the *demigods* and the results of the *yajña* from the demigods are communicated back to the residents of the *bhūloka* through these representatives. The representatives of the demigods should therefore be viewed as the *paths* to sending the offerings of the *yajña* and receiving their results from the demigods. All the offerings of the *yajña* are therefore made to these representatives, who then relay them to the demigods. The connection between the *bhūloka* and *svargaloka* is therefore through the *Sumeru* Mountain although it is not *svarga* per se.

The Big Ocean in the Universe

Vedic cosmology describes that the entire system of higher and lower planets comprises only about half the universe; the other half is filled with a type of primordial "water", which lies below the system of higher and lower planets and is called the *Garbhodaka Ocean.* A form of Lord *Viṣṇu* called *Garbhodakaśāyi Viṣṇu* lies in this water, and then creates the entire cosmos from his navel, quite like a baby is attached to the mother through an umbilical cord. In this form, Lord *Viṣṇu* is both "mother" and "father" of the cosmos, and the cosmos is produced as a "flower" which has both male and female reproductive systems. It is very important to understand the nature of this "water" because it is related to how the entire cosmos is created, maintained, and destroyed, and it is an integral part of the entire cosmic scheme. Why the entire cosmos is treated mystically will also become evident once we understand this "water".

Phenomenally, ordinary water appears continuous to us as we cannot distinguish between the various parts of water quite like we can distinguish between ordinary objects. The notion of a "field" in science was in fact derived from water waves, and a field extends continuously and infinitely just as water appears to be continuous and indivisible. Of course, to know something we must be able to distinguish it from other things, and count (or order) them; if we cannot distinguish, we also cannot count and hence cannot know. The water in the lower half of the cosmos represents an undistinguished or undifferentiated state of matter. In this state, the cosmos lies as *possibilities*, but they have not become reality, and hence we cannot distinguish between the possibilities, although we can say that they exist. This possibility world is said to be "dark", implying that the light of the Sun (which helps us distinguish things) doesn't reach this part of the cosmos and we cannot distinguish the parts in this part of the cosmos. The "water" at the bottom half of the cosmos is thus not the water that we can see and distinguish from other things. It, however, has properties due to which we can analogously call it "water".

The structure of the universe discussed so far is related to the nature of different numbers as shown in Figure-33. Different parts of the universe are different in the sense that they partake in the characteristics of different kinds of numbers. At the bottom of the universe are irrational numbers, which are individuals and yet so close to each other that they cannot be distinguished; this is the reason that they are said to constitute an "ocean" of "water" at the bottom of the universe, because in the water we cannot distinguish parts, even though there are individuals.

Above these irrational numbers lies the domain of demons and the hellish planets where the pleasure is obtained by subdividing matter into smaller and smaller parts, the result of which is that the experience becomes more and more refined although the effort you invest into creating the fraction (i.e., the divisor that creates the fraction) keeps getting bigger and bigger. The higher levels of this domain of rational numbers therefore comprise smaller irrationals such as 1/2, 1/3, or 3/4. As we go lower and lower, we obtain even smaller and smaller fractional numbers.

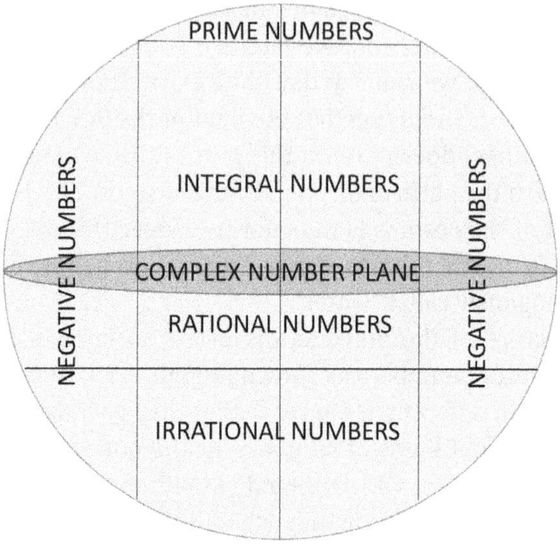

Figure-33 The Universal Structure and Number Types

Above the plane of the rational numbers is the domain of integers, which denote the individual objects that can be counted; these numbers too, can be large or small. At the top of this hierarchy are prime numbers which represent the axioms of the universal construction and they cannot be subdivided or reduced to any other more elementary meaning. As we have noted previously, the *Lokāloka* Mountain separates the domains of positive and negative numbers. These positives or negatives can be natural numbers (integers), rational numbers (fractions), or irrational numbers. The separation between positive and negative numbers therefore extends vertically from the top to the bottom of the universe.

The above structure only represents the *vertical* dimension and is therefore inadequate; additionally, there is the *horizontal* dimension which involves a *plane* comprising two axes. The two dimensions on this plane are objects and activities (which are mutually orthogonal properties), and yet necessary to describe any entity. To model such entities, we need two dimensions represented by two kinds of properties, although the resulting entity is not two separable "parts". The object and the procedure are distinct conceptually and yet they are both necessary to describe any entity in the horizontal dimension. Furthermore, these entities are organized hierarchically from the center of space to the edges, such that the edges are parts of the core. This hierarchical structure requires the use of complex numbers in which the real part denotes the current space, and the complex part is another region of space inside which the current space is embedded. The use of complex numbers has a long history and a deep physical relevance in modern physical theories, connected to the fact that atomic objects are described by complex numbers[9]. This necessity arises because a complex number flattens the hierarchy into a single number and to view a hierarchical world in a flat space, we must use complex numbers. The real and imaginary parts of these numbers could be taken from irrational, rational, integer, or prime number domains. Complex numbers thus span the universe, but depending on the type of components, they can represent different horizontal domains.

While the properties of integers, rational numbers, complex numbers, and primes are easily related to the different types of meanings, some additional discussion is necessary to elucidate the relationship between possibilities and irrational numbers. At the heart of this relationship lies Cantor's theorem on various classes of infinities: the lowest infinity is the cardinality of rational numbers, and the next highest infinity is the cardinality of irrational numbers. It is notable that the set of rational numbers (in Cantor's theorem) includes natural numbers (integers) and primes as well. In the context of the cosmic description, the rational numbers therefore represent the entire manifest universe comprising all the planetary systems. In contrast, the irrational numbers constitute the domain of possibilities "below" this manifest world.

Cantor showed that if the cardinality of all rational numbers is N, then the cardinality of all the irrational numbers is 2^N, which also happens to be the cardinality of the "power set". The power set is defined as the set of all possible subsets of any given set. For instance, if there are N objects in the world, then it is possible to divide these N objects into subsets in 2^N ways, and the collection of all such subsets is called the power set. Cantor essentially proved that the cardinality of the power set is the same as that of the irrational numbers. This means that the members of a power set can be mapped one-to-one to the irrational numbers.

If N represents all the events that can occur individually in the universe, then 2^N represents all the possible subsets of those events that can be enacted at a particular *time*. The power set therefore represents all possible states of the universe *as a whole*, which must, however, occur one after another in time. The fact that the power set has 2^N members means that the possible states of the universe are exponentially greater than the individual states at any time, which is because the *combinations* of states are exponentially high. The real world can now be said to be produced from the domain of all possibilities by a state selection performed by time, which as we can see from above, must pick one out of the 2^N possibilities. Since the selection creates the manifest world from the unmanifest world, the "time" that converts the possibilities into actualities must lie at the "boundary" between the manifest and the unmanifest.

Vedic cosmology tells us that a form of Lord *Viṣṇu* called *Ananta* (also called *Saṅkarṣaṇa*) lies in between the manifest universe and the ocean of water. This form of the Lord represents time in Vedic philosophy. From the above discussion, we can conclude that *Saṅkarṣaṇa* is the boundary between possibility and reality because He represents the time that transforms the unmanifest into the manifest. The manifest is all the *events* that exist in the universe at any time, while the unmanifest is all the possible states of the universe that are currently unreal. We must bear in mind that by fixing the events, the observers of those events are not fixed. The mapping of observers to events is determined by their *guna* and *karma*, and the choice of the state of the entire universe does not override the choices of living beings, although it considerably limits them. We cannot choose any possible event in the universe, although given some events, we can choose from amongst them, subject to the conditions of *guna* and *karma* as discussed previously. Time therefore fixes the events in the cosmos (what will happen at a given time) but does not fix the observers of those events (who will participate in those events).

Since the actuality produced from the possibility is itself very large, Lord *Saṅkarṣaṇa* would have to make as many choices as there are events, if He chose them individually. This fact presents two problems:

(a) *Saṅkarṣaṇa* would be making the same choices that individual living beings would be making, and (b) the question of whether consciousness that chooses many things at the same time can be called "time". A detailed discussion of this topic is out of scope here, so I will just summarize that the above questions become unnecessary if we think of the unmanifest world of possibilities as the *subsets* of all events in the universe. The *subset* is an individual entity, although different from the individual *members* of the subset. In choosing the subset, a single choice is involved (rather than many), and the chooser is not involved with the member events. The choice of all the events therefore doesn't have to be billions of choices of individual events; it can also be a single choice of an irrational number, which picks not individual events one by one, but a *subset* of possibilities, because the number itself represents a set rather than an object.

The idea of time represents the fact that we choose only one thing at any instant, and the sequence of choices creates the "stream of consciousness". This choice can be the time of the entire universe only if a single choice is involved in choosing the entire state of the universe. For such a choice to be possible, there must in fact be one thing that represents all the events that are actualized at any instant in time. This one thing is the *set* of all the events that will become real at any particular time, and *Saṅkarṣaṇa* can choose the set rather than all its individual members. In that sense, *Saṅkarṣaṇa* does not decide who participates in these events, although He decides what will happen. We will see later that the choice of individual participants is based on *guna* and *karma* and two different forms of God are involved in making those choices for the universe.

Irrational numbers are therefore those individual entities which summarize all the events in the universe at any given time. When time chooses these entities, the fate of the universe at that particular instant of time is decided. The choice, therefore, converts the unmanifest world into a manifest world and *Saṅkarṣaṇa* as time who lies in between the manifest and the unmanifest domains controls the destiny of the universe by making choices about its current state. The entire universe is, in one sense, His choice, although He makes just one choice while the numerous living entities in the world make separate choices of each event.

Both God and the living being are therefore conscious because they choose one by one. But there is a huge difference in the *type* of entity they are choosing. Lord *Saṅkarṣaṇa* chooses an irrational number, thereby fixing the state of the entire universe. Living beings in the lower planetary systems choose rational numbers, thus enjoying fractional divisions of any object. Living beings in the higher planetary systems enjoy whole objects, which begin with macroscopic objects in the *bhūloka*. Higher planetary systems enjoy even more abstract wholes. The "water" at the bottom of the universe is therefore a primordial state of the material universe which denotes all the things that can occur in the past, present, and future. This water is produced by *Garbhodakaśāyi Viṣṇu* and called the *Garbhodaka Ocean*. Thus, all the possibilities in the universe are fixed at the creation of the universe itself. However, all these possibilities are not immediately converted into reality. This conversion is done by time.

It is notable that in the spiritual creation, time doesn't exist, which means that everything that is ever possible is also always real, and the conversion of possibility into reality is never required. Nothing that is real ever becomes unreal, and there is hence nothing called possible, so the *Garbhodaka* doesn't exist. There is no sense of past, present, or future, and no notion about manifest and unmanifest. Everything is always manifest, and all forms of God, all their names, pastimes, features, etc. are always manifest simultaneously. Thus, for instance, in the place called *Goloka Vṛndāvana*, Lord *Kṛṣṇa* is simultaneously a baby, a small boy, and a teenager. Different devotees see these pastimes, depending on their inclinations, but all these forms and activities exist continuously.

The material universe is however produced differently because here events become manifest and unmanifest. We don't see all that is possible, and we cannot convert the possibility into reality. It is God who transforms the possibility into reality, and we are therefore secondary enjoyers depending on God's choices. This enjoyment is limited because whatever we see is temporary; if we happen to like and enjoy it, it is bound to disappear. If we don't like it, it will still disappear anyway. Due to this disappearance, there is no permanent happiness or distress in the material creation. The living beings just pass through cycles of happiness and distress.

The Seven Coverings of the Universe

Śrīmad-Bhagavatam describes that the *brahmanda* is covered by 7 layers of elemental matter: *earth, water, fire, air, ether, mahattattva,* and *ego*. Each of these layers is successively 10 times larger than the previous covering. The total size of the universe is therefore 10^7 times larger than the size of the *brahmanda*. These elements are described as follows:

> *Every universe is covered by seven layers—earth, water, fire, air, sky, the total energy and false ego—each ten times greater than the previous one. There are innumerable universes besides this one, and although they are unlimitedly large, they move about like atoms in You. Therefore You are called unlimited [Ananta]. [SB 6.16.37]*

Multiplication Factor	Covering Name
1	Brahmanda
10	Earth
100	Water
1000	Fire
10000	Air
100000	Ether
1000000	Mahattattva
10000000	Ego

Table 8: The Seven Coverings of the Universe

This description is somewhat perplexing because *Sāñkhya* describes eight elements—earth, water, fire, air, ether, mind, intelligence, and ego—which are created from *mahattattva* (which is therefore the 9th element). The difficulty is that the seven coverings of the universe exclude the mind and intelligence, add *mahattattva* and indicate that the *mahattattva* is produced from the ego rather than the ego being produced from *mahattattva* as *Sāñkhya* indicates. The first five coverings (from the inside) have an identical name, but the outer two coverings are different. How do we explain this difference between the two descriptions?

The answer to this problem is that the 24 elements of *Sāñkhya* are limited to matter within the universe, and the elements such as earth, water, fire, etc. do not extend beyond the boundaries of a particular universe (although they are created in each universe). The elemental coverings should not therefore be given the same kinds of meanings as the elements in *Sāñkhya*, although the same words are often used. Fortunately, there are other parts of Vedic philosophy that go beyond the 24 elements in *Sāñkhya*. These elements are described in *Tantra* literature as the "coverings" of the soul. The 24 elements of *Sāñkhya* include the 5 gross elements, the 5 types of sensations, the 5 senses of action, the 5 senses of knowledge, mind, intellect, ego, and *mahattattva*. Lord Brahma is said to be the embodiment of *mahattattva*, and we have seen previously how this element represents moral principles. The *Tantra*, however, describe seven additional layers of covering on the soul, apart from the 24 elements of *Sāñkhya* and beyond the *mahattattva*, which are called *kāla* (time), *kalā* (abilities), *vidyā* (knowledge), *niyati* (place), *rāga* (attachment), *prakriti* (who I am) and *māyā* (what I am not). These coverings create limitations in *Brahman* about what it is, and what it is not, thereby producing a sense of identity or individuality based on many factors.

Niyati is the desire to be in a particular type of place and not in all places, and it creates the impression that the living being is in a particular place. *Kāla* is the desire to be in a particular time and not all times, and it creates the impression that the living being is in a particular time and not all times. *Rāga* is the desire to only be attached to certain things, and not be attached to all things, and it creates the impression that the living being is indeed attached to certain things. *Vidyā* is the desire to know a few things, and not everything, and it creates the impression that the living being has a finite amount of knowledge. *Kalā* is the desire that a living being wants to have some abilities, and it creates the impression that he only has certain abilities. *Prakriti* is idea that the living being has a certain material nature or personality, who likes and dislikes certain things. And *māyā* is the idea that the living being is isolated by his individuality, and because he is an individual, he must be separated from everyone else.

These seven elements are said to "cover" the soul and transform its native properties into material properties. The *chit* of the soul, for instance, has the properties of *icchā*, *kriya*, and *jñāna*, which lead to a tendency to have a desire to know and express itself. The *vidyā* covering affects the *jnana* potency and makes the living being only want to know certain things. The *kalā* covering limits the living being's *kriya* energy to be able to do anything into doing certain limited things. The *rāga* covering limits the living being's *icchā* to desire anything into desiring only limited things. Similarly, the *sat* of the soul has the property of being anywhere and anywhen. The *niyati* and *kāla* place the soul into a particular space and time. Likewise, the *ānanda* of the soul has the ability to enjoy anything and exist in relation to anyone. But *prakriti* and *māyā* cover this potency to only enjoy a certain limited number of things, and relate to only a limited set of individuals, creating a sense of isolation.

When a living being perceives that he is limited in several ways, he considers himself incomplete, which then impels him to obviate this sense of incompleteness. For instance, a person who feels he is in a limited space wants to learn about the universe at large or travel to different parts of the world, physically or mentally. A person who feels he is limited by time develops the urge to do things faster; he may be interested in history or in the future. A person who feels he is limited by his attachments would be tempted to experiment with new things. Individuals who believe they have limited knowledge develop a hunger for knowledge, and those who feel that they have limited capabilities try to learn new skills. Those who feel that they are unable to enjoy all things, are tempted to try new pleasures. The coverings of the soul thus impel it to pursue those things that can help him overcome its sense of incompleteness.

Each universe is a limited region of experience, and to enter this region, one must be satisfying the conditions of that type of limitation. The seven coverings of the universe are the coverings of the soul. These coverings begin in limits to the types of pleasure. They extend into choices, limiting them too. Finally, they extend into our existence, and limit our existence to a certain region of space and time. The universe therefore begins with the outer most covering called *māyā* which represents the desire in the living being to enjoy a certain kind of pleasure, which then develops into a personality called *prakriti*, which then leads to the will to know and express oneself in a particular manner, which then locates the soul in a particular place and time. All these coverings of the soul (and the universe) are therefore developments of the soul's desire to enjoy.

These coverings of the soul (and the universe) represent the deepest recesses of our unconscious and they are logically prior to our entry into the space-time of a particular universe. The soul enters a universe based on the type of its desire. Vedic cosmology describes that there are innumerable universes in the material creation (also called *viraja*, the *kārana samudra*, or the *Causal Ocean*). The seven coverings are called *kārya māyā* or the beginning of activities. In the *viraja* there is no activity and it is the state devoid of *raja* or desire. The seven coverings of the universe are *kārya māyā* because it is the origin of activity and living beings start to become active: their unconscious desires now become manifest.

The coverings of the universe are said to be inhabited by different *Rudra* forms, and their followers. These living beings have renounced various kinds of pleasures of the material universe, by taking shelter of Lord *Śiva* who also leads a renounced life, however, their desires for pleasure have not been destroyed. Such living beings are not perfectly "liberated" although they are free of many material experiences, and therefore better than the living beings who are within the *brahmanda*.

The import of the different layers being 10 times larger is that our desires of pleasure are far greater than the things that we can practically realize at any point in time. The coverings, for instance, represent the ability to interpret or perceive the world from different perspectives, and there are many more perspectives about the world than there is reality available to interpret at any given time. Of course, these perspectives can be realized over time; as our desires are modified, we see the same world differently. The things that we can imagine being realized are thus far greater than the things that would practically be realized in one life. The total realm of the unconscious desires is 10^7 times larger than the total realm of what is practically enacted in the universe as a whole. This only attests to how big our unconscious desires are relative to what can practically be achieved at any time. Regardless of how many experiences a living being is afforded, the realm of desires is 10^7 times bigger!

Studies on the unconscious refer to the "tip of the iceberg" phenomenon indicating that our unconscious is significantly larger than what manifests in our conscious experience. The idea of seven coverings, each 10 times bigger than its inner neighbor, quantifies the size of the iceberg under water. Since all these coverings emanate from *māyā*, we can imagine how big that *māyā* is, relative to the entire manifest universe. Even if you have renounced all the pleasures that a universe has to offer now, you may still not be freed from material desires, and can fall again into the material creation due to unfulfilled desires, when phenomena matching the desires are available for enjoyment. The process of renunciation is thus, practically speaking, forever inadequate. It is practically very difficult to renounce the pleasures of a single planet, let alone all the planetary systems. Then, to give up the unconscious desires for material pleasure is significantly harder. The *ācharyas* thus recommend as the process by which one can be liberated from the influence of *māyā* the development of alternate forms of pleasure, rather than trying to renounce material pleasures. In numerous places in Vedic literature, *māyā* is described as being impossible to overcome. However, for the devotee who has developed affection for the service of God, this freedom is automatic.

Inside, Outside, and the Border

In the beginning of the book I described the three states of primordial matter—*pradhāna*, *prakriti*, and *mahattattva*. We also discussed the nature of *mahattattva* as moral principles, and while elaborating the topic of happiness I noted that there are two ways to connect moral principles to happiness: (1) we can define whatever makes us happy to be our notion of morality, and (2) we can define whatever is moral to be the nature of happiness. We can now connect all these concepts with the three properties of the soul: *sat*, *chit*, and *ānanda*. The *Causal Ocean* or *viraja* is a realm of *material* happiness devoid of activity and objects. It is also called *pradhāna* in Vedic cosmology in which the differentiation between the three modes of nature has not occurred. The material objects, senses, mind, intelligence, ego, and morality too haven't yet manifested.

This realm is said to be created from the sweat of Lord *Mahā Viṣṇu* who "perspires" due to performing austerity. This austerity is Lord *Mahā Viṣṇu*'s self-abnegation or *tapasyā* and He creates the domain of material happiness by engaging in austerity[10]. We all understand that austerity, by definition, is the opposite of pleasure. And yet, there is a sense of happiness even in austerity, quite like we might enjoy exercising or working hard, which causes us to sweat, and that sweat therefore becomes a symbol of our hard work (unless we have sweated, we might not consider our exercising to be hard enough). The material realm, in its most abstract form, is thus a *representation* of God's happiness produced by negating the very definition of happiness. The process of God's sweating externalizes His experience of happiness, into a symbol of His austerity.

The living beings who have developed a perfect sense of renunciation through the performance of austerities, and yet have no real conception of God's true nature of bliss or *ānanda*, enter this realm called *viraja*. Under the ignorance of God's true nature of happiness, they consider this material realm of bliss itself to be the highest form of perfection. In this state, they cease all choices and activities, and they have exited not only all the universal experiences, but also all of the seven coverings. And yet, they are still in the material domain, because they construe austerity and renunciation to be the highest form of pleasure (which is higher than material enjoyment, but not as great as pleasure from God's happiness).

The *viraja* as a whole is the representation of God's renunciation (and therefore God is said to be detached from the material world, even though He creates it), but within this renounced realm there are many types of renunciations. The living being who has developed aversion to God's association, and wishes to enjoy independently of God's pleasure, takes some part of *viraja* as his personal playground (since God has already renounced it, the living being considers this material domain freedom from subordination to God's dominion). The material universe thus begins in the idea that God is dead, or that He doesn't exist in the material world. The choice of a specific part of this domain represents the manner in which the living being wishes to enjoy the material world, and this tendency to enjoy in a specific manner (versus all the possible enjoyments) represents the seven coverings of the soul. In essence, while *viraja* is the domain of all material pleasures, the different universal coverings represent the process of selecting a particular part of the entire material domain of pleasure. These coverings divide God's pleasure into the universes meant for different types of pleasures. This division is then called *māyā*, and the successive categories such as *prakriti* (personality), *kāla* (time), *kalā* (abilities), *vidyā* (knowledge), *niyati* (place), and *rāga* (attachment), are progressive refinements of the pleasure definition.

In the *pradhāna* stage, matter is simply a representation of God's pleasure out of His austerity. In the *prakriti* stage, this pleasure is further refined to produce numerous kinds of coverings of the soul. In a sense, the division of God's pleasure (and therefore participation in a particular type of pleasure) is the outcome of the living being's desires to enjoy material happiness. The living being cannot enjoy the entire *viraja* because his renunciation is never as great as that of God. Some voidists, however, aspire to lead a life of happiness through infinite renunciation, and they are in a sense trying to match God's detachment. Other materialists choose a part of *viraja* for enjoyment. The part chosen is based on the type of desires one has, which are governed by the seven coverings.

Once a particular type of happiness is chosen, then moral principles are defined based on this definition of happiness. In other words, our material notions of happiness subordinate our notions of morality: we don't define happiness as that which arises from moral goodness; we rather define moral goodness as that which makes us happy. This is a hedonistic notion of morality which was defined by Aristippus (a student of Socrates) as the idea that pleasure is the highest form of goodness. As a useful point of contrast, hedonistic morality was opposed by Immanuel Kant, who believed that morality is not the doctrine of how we may make ourselves happy, but how we may make ourselves worthy of happiness.

The notion of morality stemming from material pleasure is called *mahattattva*, which is the first material element of *Sāñkhya* that emerges within the seven coverings of the universe. The *pradhāna* is therefore 'outside' the universe, the *mahattattva* is 'inside' the universe, and *prakriti* is the covering of the universe that lies at the 'border' in between the 'inside' and the 'outside'. The *pradhāna* is almost spiritual because, after all, it is a representation of God's pleasure, even though this pleasure is produced from God's austerity. The *mahattattva* is totally material because it is produced from materialistically conditioned choices of pleasure (given by the seven coverings of the soul). Finally, *prakriti* is between the spiritual and material realms, and it is controlled by Lord *Śiva* who is said to be a form of God who is outside all the material universes and yet the master of *māyā* who creates all the universes. Different Vedic literatures describe this form of God as *Saṅkarṣaṇa*, *Śeṣa*, or *Param Śiva*. They are the same form, called by different names. As earlier discussed, Lord *Mahā Viṣṇu* creates the *Kārana Ocean*, in which Lord *Śeṣa* creates the universes. This creation of universes is initiated by dividing the space-time of the *Kārana Ocean* into individual locations by applying the desires produced from *prakriti*. Thus, a particular living being chooses a part of God's pleasure based on his desire, and thereby enters a universe.

It is worth noting that what we presently call morality, which forms the basis of various types of religiosity, is another form of selfishness, because it is produced from the soul's desire to be happy independent of God. This fact has recently come to light in a big way when materialists have begun arguing that moral principles don't need to be defined in relation to God; rather, we can speak about morality independent of God. This new definition of morality is hedonistic—i.e., we define moral behavior as that which gives us the greatest amount of happiness individually or collectively. Altruism, for instance, can then be defined as that which makes the collective happiness greater than individual happiness. What the materialists are really talking about is *mahattattva* which is indeed a materialistic notion of morality. It should, however, be noted, that following this morality does not free the living being from the seven coverings, because this morality is itself a development of material desire.

The Covering of the Brahmanda

Within the seven coverings of the *brahmanda* (the manifest world), is a layer of 'water' which engulfs the entire *brahmanda*. Like the seven layers of each universe represent the *prakriti*, which determine a soul's desires, the water covering represents their *karma* because the desires cannot be realized unless the *karma* also exists. As the soul is constrained by *prakriti* or *guna*, similarly, even the fulfillment of the *guna* is constrained by *karma*. For instance, we might desire to be some particular type of living entity, to enjoy a specific type of pleasure, but that desire will not be fulfilled unless we have the necessary *karma*. While *guna* represents what we *desire*, *karma* represents what we *deserve*. The *karma* however is layered within *guna* because we must first desire something before that desire can be permitted or denied by *karma*[11]. If *guna* were present under *karma* then only the desires that can be satisfied would appear, and the living being would never be unhappy, since all their desires would always be fulfilled, and they could not desire what could not be fulfilled.

As we have seen, *karma* is produced when our awareness focuses on parts of reality, ignoring the other parts; this focus is caused by desires that seek something in the world, and our perception is distorted when we begin to *interpret* the facts of observation as evidence of the existence of what we seek. For instance, if you are seeking the love of fellow beings, their innocuous behaviors can be interpreted as a sign of their love for you, and if you hate someone, innocuous actions of other beings would be perceived as their hatred towards you. When the perception is thus distorted, it needs to be corrected, and the need for that correction produces *karma*. Since the *karma* is produced from *guna*, it also acts upon *guna*, permitting or denying what we desire due to our acquired *guna*.

Vedic philosophy describes that *karma* exists in three forms: (1) unmanifest, (2) about to manifest, and (3) manifest. The region called *loka varṣa* is the manifest state of *karma*, and the water covering of the *brahmanda* is its unmanifest state. Between these two realms is *āloka varṣa* which is the realm in which *karma* is about to be manifest, although hasn't yet manifested. The region called *āloka varṣa* is considered dark because it cannot be known, and because the energy of the Sun does not enlighten this part of the cosmos. The water covering of the *brahmanda* is even darker and colder because our *karma* is not visible to us[12].

We previously saw how the *āloka varṣa* is the realm of *absence*. In modern science too, antiparticles are modeled as 'holes' instead of 'objects'. The positron, which is an antiparticle of the electron, for instance, is modeled as a 'hole' created by the absence of an electron, and when the electron moves from left to right, the positron moves in the opposite direction, as if it were moving in negative time. We can envision the movement of particles as being *caused* by the movement of holes: when a hole moves from A to B, the particle moves from B to A. Thus, changes can be caused by something that cannot be observed by our senses. Nevertheless, the *effects* of that cause can be perceived. Essentially, when *karma* manifests, it moves in an opposite direction to the effects its produces. This idea needs more elaboration, and I will try to do that now.

One of the classic problems in modern atomic theory is its inability to predict when an event occurs. For instance, if an atomic object goes from state A to B, it must either emit or absorb energy, and for that to occur, there must be another atomic object that does the reverse. This creates the problem of event correlation. Which emission should be correlated with which absorption? This arises because in theories such as electromagnetism, an object exerts force equally in all directions, and the force is produced by the transmission of *bosons* or force particles (these are required due to the problem of locality in relativity where all interactions must be 'local' which then requires all actions at a distance to become local actions by particle exchange). If we cannot predict when a *boson* (a photon in this case) would be emitted, we also cannot predict when a change will occur, since this particle is expected to carry the energy of the cause to the effect. Atomic theory becomes incomplete because of its inability to predict when the events will occur in time.

To overcome this problem, we need a new kind of 'force' that causes changes, because the atomic objects (in any closed ensemble) remain in stationary states. Effectively, this force converts a closed system into an open system, causing energy exchange. In physical theories, there are no boundaries and all systems are open systems, but this open system approach results in loss of semantics, which makes all physical theories incomplete. However, once you postulate closed systems to explain the existence of meanings (which then results in a hierarchical space-time), then we are faced with the problem of how these closed systems are 'opened' to exchange information with other closed systems. The *prāna* is the force that moves matter between closed systems, and it cannot thus be reduced to the matter that creates the closed system. However, we still don't know how the source and destination of any transaction must be fixed. The force of *prāna* can perform a type of activity, provided the source and destination of that transaction has been identified.

In that sense, *prāna* is still inadequate to cause changes, even though it brings us closer to understanding the cause of change. The causality, in the Vedic view, is comprised of four parts: (1) material objects that are changed, (2) the *prāna* force that causes changes, (3) *karma* that decides the source and destination of this change, and (4) time that manifests a particular source-destination event pair. The *karma* of the living beings exists, but the *pairing* of the instances of *karma* across different living beings is created by time, due to which they reap the results of their *karma*. For instance, if you are destined to be educated, which specific teacher will educate you is still not fixed. For the education to occur, a teacher and student must be paired. Each of them have their respective *karma* and they are therefore individually responsible for the consequences of their previous actions, but their pairing is fixed by time. In reaping the *karma*, it appears that a living entity is causing changes to another living entity, although both living entities are only reaping the consequences of their previous *karma* and the mutual relationship is established by time.

We have previously discussed how Lord *Ananta* as time chooses a state of the universe from the possible states, which includes all the events at that time. After the state of the universe has been decided by time, the participants in these events (the living beings) must also be determined. This requires mapping the source and destination of a material transaction (event) to the living beings partaking in that exchange. The fact that living beings (actors) are selected *after* the events (play) has been decided, means that the actors cannot change the play, although they can participate in different roles, if they had the requisite *karma*. The events in the universe represent a series of *roles* while the living beings with their *guna* and *karma* are the actors in those roles. The selection of a living being for a role is based on their *karma*. Given that there can be several eligible actors for a role, the selection of the actor is non-trivial.

The problem is not trivial because of *free will*: there may be a suitable role, and the actor may be qualified for it, but he may not *desire* it. To avoid *karma*, the actor must take another role, which must be available, and the actor must be qualified for it. When such a possibility exists, and the actor is not constrained by the circumstances to take a role, the actor's desire modifies the *karma* being manifested at that time. Most of the time, when *karma* acts, we don't have an alternative role into which we can step into, and therefore we cannot escape the effect of *karma*. But, sometimes, we do have a choice to take a different role, and in that situation, the choice of the role may either manifest the same *karma* or a different *karma*. For instance, we might try to change our situation but even in the new situation, the same *karma* would be reaped. In rare cases, if we change our situation, we would also change the *karma* reaped.

It is this rare case that presents the problem of how to understand the mapping between an actor and a role, and this problem is addressed by the idea of *karma* that is 'about to manifest', which is a byproduct of combining the previously unmanifest *karma*, the circumstancc, and the desire. If the circumstances and the *karma* allow, and we can desire an alternative role, then the *karma* manifested at a particular time could be modified. The 'about to manifest' becomes the stage of *karma* which the living entity has 'agreed' to bear either because there is no alternative, or the alternative fits the native desires of the living being. It is noteworthy that the choices that effect *karma*, do not pertain to the stimulus we receive from the world, but to the actions we can take as a response. The stimulus we receive is out of our control, and therefore free will cannot choose it. Our free will only controls our responses to those events. Therefore, if we have the *karma*, the circumstances permit it, and we desire it, the 'about to manifest' *karma* that pertains to our responses can be modified. In all other cases, where desires cannot control *karma*, the unmanifest *karma* would directly become 'about to manifest'.

The *āloka varṣa* represents the realm of *karma* that is about to manifest. In this realm, the combination of desire and *karma* appears as a trajectory which moves in negative time. This negative time should be understood as counting down to a particular instant in time, like we count backwards during the launch of a satellite, or to welcome the arrival of a new year, or just before a swimmer jumps into a pool at the start of a race. The 'about to manifest' simply means that the event has been decided and we are counting time backwards because we are headed towards a specific goal and the time left to reach the goal is reducing. While the events to be eventually experienced have not yet manifested, we can know that they are about to manifest, since we are heading towards a particular goal and the time left to reach that goal is continuously decreasing.

One of the reasons that modern physics has avoided negative time is because it entails the existence of destiny in the future, and for this idea to be incorporated, the things that exist in the future would have to have an effect on the present. As a result, the postulate that there is a destiny towards which we are headed would entail that the future is 'pulling' us towards that destiny. The same issue exists even for the distant past, because if the past causes the future, then we would be hard pressed to explain how something that no longer exists (because it is in the past) has an effect on the present or the future. These forms of causality create serious issues in science due to the physical model of causality in which the cause must physically be measurable in order to be used in the predictive process. Unlike Vedic philosophy where we consider the unmanifest and the about to manifest, which are not physically real, and yet play a causal role, in a physical theory we cannot speak about these causes because they don't exist physically. All scientific models of causality therefore are based on what exists right now, and its presence can be measured.

Scientists also avoid the causality of the future because if the universe has a destiny, then it is designed with a purpose, which would be a problematic idea in science. Physics therefore only aspires to use positive time, and the causality is based only on what exists presently, not what existed in the past, or what might exist in the future. This notion of time and causality, however, has become inadequate in quantum theory because if we only measure what exists right now, we cannot predict the events; the predictions become statistical, and the time of their occurrence cannot be foretold. Aside from this theoretical problem, with the discovery of antiparticles, there is indeed a necessity to postulate negative time, although physicists don't know how to address the philosophical problems due to which the idea of negative time was shelved earlier. As we can see, negative time implies that there is a destiny towards which we march, and once you induct the idea of destiny, you must also invoke the notion of a past, for symmetry. The past and the destiny thus exist even in modern science, although they are just not adequately recognized due to the philosophical biases against such types of postulates.

The 'about to manifest' is a realm of matter which we cannot observe, and yet it exists as the destiny of the living beings. We march towards this destiny, counting negative time, and this domain of negative time is the part of the universe comprising the 'holes' of information. The goals towards which we are destined may not be what we desire, and sometimes the goals may be compromises we make between our desires and the destiny. Therefore, the use of past and future into the picture of causality makes the theory far more complex. Since the past and the future cannot be measured right now, their causality cannot be based on the measurement of current physical states of visible material objects. *Karma* and *destiny* must be postulated as theoretical entities in science, whose presence can only be confirmed by their effects. The interesting aspect of Vedic cosmology is that it describes natural phenomena which we cannot observe through our senses (e.g., the *āloka varṣa* cannot be measured through any observation), but the *effects* of their existence can be measured, and Vedic cosmology is inadequately understood unless this correlation between cause and effect has been made.

The use of theoretical constructs that cannot be directly measured is not new in science. For instance, theoretical constructs such as an electromagnetic field cannot be directly observed, although its effects can be measured. Similarly, the existence of a gravitational field, or that of a probability wave, cannot be physically measured, although their effects can be detected. Science, therefore, has numerous postulates which cannot be empirically detected, and the theory that employs them is still considered true because the effects of such entities can be measured.

As our perception advances, we can understand which events will occur in the future, and the history that causes it, based on what we see now. With an understanding of the causality, we can extrapolate the current states into the future and the past. Even without an advanced perception, many of us can foresee the effects arising from our actions, and we can consciously modify our actions to avoid those effects. An understanding of *karma* helps us understand how our destiny is determined by our past, and how some consequences can be modified via free will.

Cosmology and Geology

We have discussed how a semantic representation transposes the matter within a globe into the periphery of a circle, when the globe is converted into a flat surface. We have now identified this outer periphery as two kinds of *karma*—about to manifest (*āloka varṣa*) and unmanifest (the water covering of the *brahmanda*). Furthermore, we have noted that the visible part of the universe is called *loka varṣa* and it represents the manifest *karma.* This relationship between the different parts of the universe, the semantic geometry, and the three types of *karma* can now be succinctly summarized: the three types of *karma* are successively 'deeper' parts of each planet in its physical representation. The manifest *karma* is the globe's surface, the about to manifest *karma* lies below the globe's surface, and the unmanifest forms the core of the planetary globe. As *karma* manifests, the core gradually comes up to the surface, and as new *karma* is created, it goes into the core to be manifested in the future.

The planets are therefore not static. Rather, matter from the core is slowing coming up, and new matter being created in a subtle form is compensating for the matter that manifests at the surface. However, this *karma* is not confined to within the globe, but exists in a region outside the *loka varṣa*, due to which this *karma* can manifest in other globes, not just in the globe in which it was previously created. In that sense, the physical analogy is somewhat misleading as it gives the impression that the *karma* created on Earth must always be reaped only on Earth.

It is interesting that even in modern science, the Earth is divided into 3 parts: (a) crust, (b) mantle, (c) core. These parts are in turn subdivided in various ways depending on mechanical and chemical properties. The parts described as *āloka varṣa* and the 'water' covering of the *brahmanda* can be viewed as the parts of planets below their surface. As we have seen earlier, in a semantic representation, the successive spherical concentric regions within a globe are spread into successive disk-shaped concentric regions outside. The 3-dimensional sphere is thus converted into a 2-dimensional flat surface, and the notion of 'distance' is altered: the 'visible' portions of the world are semantically closer to each other than the 'visible' and 'invisible' parts, although the 'invisible' parts are closer to each other too. Since the inner parts of a globe are expanded beyond the *loka varṣa*, the study of the outer parts can be seen as the study of the geology of planets. The Vedas relate the occurrences of natural disasters such as earthquakes, volcanic eruptions, tsunamis, or other normal geological phenomena such as continental drifts, the rising or receding patterns in oceans, to the planetary positions. These are in modern science related to the geological changes under the Earth's crust. These two views of natural occurrences seem dramatically different, but they are also related since the cause of visible phenomena is the invisible world, which lies inside the planets. Of course, the explanations of these phenomena would be radically different, although they are related.

It is already known that the Earth's core rotates opposite to the crust, and these rotations are supposed to create a magnetic field that supposedly deflects the 'harmful' radiation from the rest of the universe. This physical explanation of Earth's magnetism would be explained differently in Vedic cosmology: the radiation being deflected is actually not meant for the living beings, because *karma* only delivers the required information. The opposite rotation (as we have seen) represents negative time, which denotes the existence of a destiny towards which we march. The direction of the magnetic field denotes which of the poles represents the origin and the end of the Earth's space, which in turn defines whether the abstraction is viewed as the foundation of Earth, or the details are considered the basis of all reality. These two, as we have seen earlier, constitute the basis of whether enlightenment or materialism dominates.

The phenomenal surface of our experiences is under the control of the mantle and the core, but that control is semantic rather than physical. Thus, for instance, we should not be describing the mantle and the core in terms of chemistry and mechanics, but as anti-matter which becomes matter. Thus, when collective *karma* manifests, large scale geologic changes also occur: earthquakes, continental drifts, ocean expansion and contraction, islands emerging and submerging, mountains going up and down, rivers being created or dried up, large scale floods, and so forth. The geological phenomena are also therefore the result of *karma* manifestation, although they represent the collective rather than individual *karma.* In Vedic philosophy, this *karma* is called *ādidaivika* and large-scale cataclysmic changes coincide with planetary combinations manifesting the *karma* of living beings collectively. In this process, the theories of geology and cosmology are tightly interrelated through a common theory of *karma.* A better understanding of the nature of material causality is needed before this aspect of cosmology (i.e., *āloka varṣa* or unmanifest *karma*) can be understood within the context of modern science.

Two Notions of Cosmic Time

In case you haven't already noticed, we have been discussing two distinct forms of Lord *Saṅkarṣaṇa*—one lying in the *Kārana Ocean* as the seat of *Kāraṇodakaśāyī Viṣṇu,* and the other lying in the *Garbhodaka Ocean* as the seat of *Garbhodakaśāyi Viṣṇu.* Both these forms are said to be cosmic time, which suggests that there must two kinds of time in the universe. What are these two kinds of time, and why are two notions of time needed?

The time inside the universe concerns the events occurring in the universe, which manifest *karma,* and the time outside the universe concerns the desires of living beings who participate in these events. We have discussed how Lord *Ananta* lying in the *Garbhodaka Ocean* creates the events from the unmanifest, but for living beings to be impelled into participating in these events, those beings too must be motivated. The latter function of the cosmic existence is performed by the time outside, which propels the desires of living beings by directing the *prakriti* or *māyā* that covers them. Recall that *Kāraṇodakaśāyī Viṣṇu* only creates the ocean of material pleasure but does not create the mechanism by which a living being can choose some of these pleasures. This function is performed by Lord *Saṅkarṣaṇa* who creates *prakriti* or *māyā* which forms the seven 'coverings' of each universe, and by choosing a universe, the living being is also covered by the desires of pleasure in that universe.

The matter within the *brahmanda* is the conscious part of the world (comprising the *vaikharī* and *madhyamā*) while the covering of the universe is the *paśyanti,* which remains unconscious. Between the manifest experiences and the unmanifest desires, is the realm of *karma* which converts the desires into experiences. The realm of desires is clearly not static but is also evolving due to the time outside the universe. In effect, like time within the universe moves all particles, similarly, the time outside the universe moves the universes themselves as if they were merely 'particles' in the *kārana ocean*. The effect of this movement is that the universes themselves are passing through different parts of the pleasure ocean, thereby creating new kinds of desires in living beings, which then manifests in the conscious world in a way that we do not currently understand. For instance, during the different ages, the tendencies of living beings are automatically changed due to changes in their desires. Due to the effect of time, they are naturally impelled towards enjoying or renouncing. The effect of the unconscious change is that over time, the entire universe undergoes changes in the desires of its inhabitants. Similarly, what we desire then also changes, and suddenly we might develop new kinds of desires that we thought we never had in us before.

The time inside the universe is the 'external' aspect of time, which decides the phenomena, while the time outside the universe is the 'internal' aspect of time that decides our desires. In between the domains of manifest and unmanifest is the realm of *karma* which constrains our desires on one hand, and places us into situations in the universe, on the other. The external time is thus the controller of the world that we can perceive through our senses, mind, intelligence, ego, and *mahattattva*, while the internal time remains unconscious and controls the evolution of our desires. The conversion of unmanifest *karma* into manifest events is controlled by external time, as we will see in the next chapter.

As we have seen, the unconscious realm of desires is 10^7 times bigger than the conscious realm plus the realm of *karma*. Thus, what we see as the phenomenal thoughts, sensations, feelings, and judgments in our subtle and gross body, is only the tip of the iceberg, and which tips are manifest in which lifetime is decided by the internal time. Effectively, the phenomenal world changes due to external time, and the soul changes its desires due to internal time. The phenomenal world is the reality, and the internal desires are our goals. In between the reality and our goals is our *karma* which decides the destiny, i.e., which goals will be fulfilled.

The desires of a living entity are not limited to a universe; rather the soul can enter different universes as his desires change. There is hence the necessity for a form of time that governs the evolution of the soul in between the universes, and the same time must therefore also govern the soul's desires in a specific universe. Ultimately, therefore, the soul is under the control of *Kāraṇodakaśāyī Viṣṇu* and Lord *Saṅkarṣaṇa* (*Param Śiva)* as time, and he is temporarily delegated to a phenomenal world created by *Garbhodakaśāyi Viṣṇu* and Lord *Ananta* to fulfill some of the desires and *karma*. This 'temporary' phase may last millions of lifetimes, but in comparison to the cosmic durations, it may only be a moment. Since the *karma* is controlled by the external time, a living being must finish his *karma* within a specific universe before he steps out of the universe to fulfill other desires. The desires can therefore transcend a universe, but the *karma* is limited to that universe. Liberation from a particular universe only means that the universe-specific dues have been settled, although it doesn't mean that the living being is free of all the material desires.

The phenomenal time in a universe is subordinate to the causal time that controls all universes, and Lord *Ananta* in the universe is an 'incarnation' or representation of Lord *Saṅkarṣaṇa* outside the universe. They are not separate, although they perform different functions: one controlling the desires of the souls and the other events in a particular universe in the material creation. They are the masters of the material unconscious and the material conscious, respectively. The conscious changes much faster as compared to the unconscious, and therefore the time outside the universe flows much more slowly. As we will see later, the entire lifetime of Lord *Brahma* (which is 100 years of his life) is only one half of *Kāraṇodakaśāyī Viṣṇu*'s breath (when He breathes out the creation).

The Four Forms of God

In the *Pancharātra* texts, *Kāraṇodakaśāyī Viṣṇu* is called *Vāsudeva*, *Śeṣa* or *Param Śiva* is called *Saṅkarṣaṇa*, *Garbhodakaśāyi Viṣṇu* is called *Pradyumna*, and *Kṣīrodakaśāyī Viṣṇu* is called *Aniruddha*. These four forms of God are also called the *chatur-vyūha* or the circle of four, as part of a larger cosmological description that transcends the material creation. In the material creation, *Vāsudeva* is the master of *pradhāna*, *Saṅkarṣaṇa* is the master of *prakriti*, *Pradyumna* is the master of *mahattattva*, and *Aniruddha* is the controller of the *karma* in the material creation.

Vāsudeva is the 'origin' of the material creation not just in the sense of producing it, but also in a more scientific and specific sense of being the *origin* of the space of pleasure in which all the universes, as different playgrounds of material sport (employed to relish material pleasure), are created. This space is not just all the pleasure that the sum total of all the living beings experience at any time, but all the *possible* pleasures ever in the material realm. *Saṅkarṣaṇa* creates *prakriti*, which forms the seven coverings of the individual universes, and the expansions of *Param Śiva* are said to live in these seven coverings as *Rudra* forms. *Saṅkarṣaṇa* is also a form of time outside the individual universes, which means that the universes in the material realm are not permanent; rather, they are created and destroyed. These universes are 'floating' in the *Kārana Ocean* which means that they are slowly traversing different parts of the pleasure ocean, thereby producing different kinds of hedonistic ideas of happiness in each universe. Obviously, this motion is incredibly slow as compared to the motion of the planets within each of the universes.

Within each universe, *Pradyumna* becomes the origin of the universe-specific space, and a 'lotus' sprouts from his navel within which all the planetary systems are situated. This 'lotus' is therefore the space in the universe, whose origin is *Pradyumna*'s navel. Again, this origin is not just in the sense of producing that space, but also in the sense of being at the *origin* of that space as the first and foremost important citizen of the universe. The space comprises all the possibilities within that universe, called the *Garbhodaka Ocean*. A second form of *Saṅkarṣaṇa* (called *Ananta*) within the universe selects from amongst these possibilities and produces the real events within each universe, as discussed earlier.

Different living beings participate in these events, creating their own experiences, but these experiences have the distinction between core and context: we can choose what we want to experience, from within the possibilities that are available to us. The things that we don't experience disappear from our consciousness, but they continue to exist in the awareness of *Aniruddha* who 'maintains' the *phenomenal world* even when no one is observing it. The so-called *objectivity* of the world when we turn our back towards the material objects is because *Aniruddha* continues to observe those objects even when we are not observing them. This observation is essential when the world is phenomena, and not matter.

In the early days of empiricism, when materialists like John Locke were arguing for the reality of objective physical properties that supposedly were to exist independent of our observation, Bishop Berkeley produced a masterful argument stating that even the so-called objective properties were derived from our phenomenal perception of the world. The problem in this argument, however, was that if the world was phenomena, then someone must always observe it for it to exist perpetually. This problem did not arise for the materialists because for them reality was independent of the observer. To address this problem in phenomenalism, Berkeley suggested that God must observe the world even when we don't. After all, Berkeley was a bishop, and he did not have a problem introducing God into the picture of nature. Subsequently, as materialism rose, science gave up on trying to derive material properties based on phenomena, and a distinction between primary and secondary properties was created; the primary properties were objective, while secondary properties were our perceptions. With this distinction, phenomenalism was discarded, and so was the role of God's observation.

In Vedic philosophy, the material world is indeed phenomena and not reality. So, the problem that Berkeley had highlighted comes back into this description of nature. The problem's solution in Vedic philosophy is also similar to that suggested by Bishop Berkeley; the form of God who always observes the world is called *Aniruddha*. Most of what we neglect to see is because our vision is covered by *māyā*. But *māyā* does not cover

Aniruddha's vision and He therefore sees everything just the way it is. Of course, *Aniruddha* only sees the phenomena that are manifested at any particular time, which is the reality produced by *Saṅkarṣaṇa* at that time. In that sense, *Aniruddha*'s consciousness is temporary and exposed to phenomena, even though he is not covered by *māyā*.

In one sense, *Aniruddha* experiences all the reality of the world at any point in time. In another sense, much of this reality is merely a possibility for the individual living beings, who contextualize most of it. *Aniruddha* is thus all that we *can* know although we *don't* know. He is the reason that our bodies are maintained even when we sleep. The universe that begins in the most abstract pleasure of *Vāsudeva* thus ends in the observation of *Aniruddha* when that pleasure has been converted into objects. Due to this fact, *Aniruddha* is said to reside in each atom.

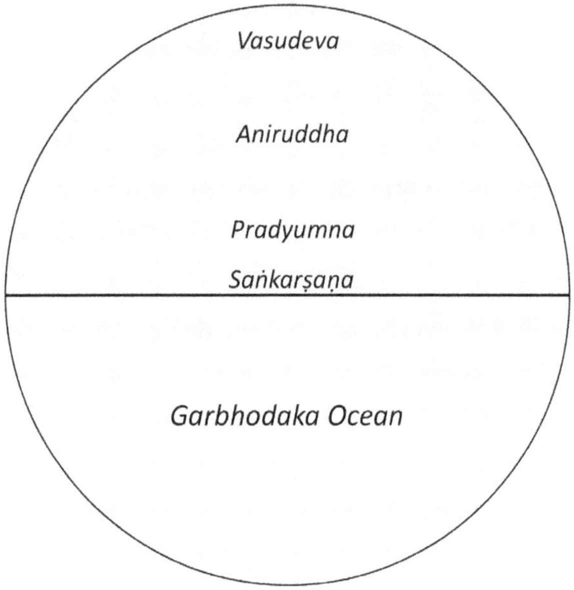

Figure-34 Four Forms of God in the Universe

A form of God (*Vāsudeva*) therefore lies outside the entire material creation and produces space in which universes are just like mustard seeds in an ocean. At the other end of the spectrum is another form of God (*Aniruddha*) who observes each atom, even when we cannot observe it. God is thus bigger than the biggest and smaller than the smallest: the "size" of God is not physical but measured by the amount of information that He holds in His consciousness. By His ability to know the most abstract, He is the biggest. And by His ability to know the most detailed, He is the smallest. He is the creator of space outside, inside, and at the border of each universe. And He is the time that produces the variety, both inside the universe and the creation and destruction of the universe as a whole. Yet, He remains transcendent to all these activities of the creation.

Within each universe too, the four forms of God are present. At the bottom of each universe is *Pradyumna* who creates all the cosmic possibilities, and *Saṅkarṣaṇa* who converts these possibilities into reality. At the top of the universe is a planet of *Vāsudeva* whose feet are washed by the water of the *Karana Ocean* entering the universe (I will discuss this topic at length in the next chapter) and in the middle of the top half of the universe is *Aniruddha* who resides in the polestar and controls the distribution of *karma*, and thereby also controls all the luminaries and demigods. When *karma* manifests, we may be aware of a few things, and unaware of others; the parts that we are unaware of are contextualized from our consciousness, but *Aniruddha* still observes and maintains them.

8

The Motion of Luminaries

The Personality of Godhead is perfect and complete, and because He is completely perfect, all emanations from Him, such as this phenomenal world, are perfectly equipped as complete wholes. Whatever is produced of the Complete Whole is also complete in itself. Because He is the Complete Whole, even though so many complete units emanate from Him, He remains the complete balance.

—*Śrī Īśopanisad, Invocation*

The Movement of the Sun and the Zodiac

In modern cosmology, the distant stars (the 12 star signs) are treated as being stationary and the Earth rotates on its axis, thus causing the day and the night. In Vedic cosmology, the system of 12 constellations rotates around the *Meru* Mountain at an enormous rate. The *Surya Siddhānta* states that the system of stars goes around *Meru* 1,582,237,828 times in the period of a *chaturyugi*, i.e., 4,320,000 years. By dividing the star rotation by the number of years in a *chaturyugi*, we can find the number of times the system of stars rotates around the *Meru* Mountain in a year: 1,582,237,828 / 4,320,000 = 366.2587565. The rising of the star signs is used in Vedic astrology to determine the "ascendant" which represents the star sign that is "rising" at the time of the birth of an individual. The ascendant in turn becomes the first house in the astrological chart, which then determines the placement of the subsequent houses, and the effect of the planets on different aspects of our lives. Therefore, the motion of the zodiac is very crucial because it decides the house placements.

In Vedic cosmology, apart from the rotation of the zodiac, there is also the rotation of the Sun around the *Meru* Mountain. These two motions, however, are different, and their differing rates of motion causes a lag between their motions, which in turn causes the Sun to pass through different signs of the zodiac. Both the zodiac and the Sun move clockwise (east to west) but their speeds are slightly different. To understand the passing of day and night, the changes in seasons, and the passing of years, it is important to understand these two kinds of celestial motions.

> *My dear King, as stated before, the learned say that the Sun travels over all sides of Mānasottara Mountain in a circle whose length is 95,100,000 yojanas [760,800,000 miles]. On Mānasottara Mountain, due east of Mount Sumeru, is a place known as Devadhānī, possessed by King Indra. Similarly, in the south is a place known as Saṁyamanī, possessed by Yamarāja, in the west is a place known as Nimlocanī, possessed by Varuṇa, and in the north is a place named Vibhāvarī, possessed by the Moon-god. Sunrise, midday, Sunset and midnight occur in all those places according to specific times, thus engaging all living entities in their various occupational duties and also making them cease such duties. [SB 5.21.7]*

> *There are many stars located 200,000 yojanas [1,600,000 miles] above the Moon. By the supreme will of the Supreme Personality of Godhead, they are fixed to the wheel of time, and thus they rotate with Mount Sumeru on their right, their motion being different from that of the Sun. There are twenty-eight important stars, headed by Abhijit. [SB 5.22.11]*

Vedic cosmology calculates a *solar month* based on the time it takes the Sun to cross a star sign. A solar year is the time that the Sun takes to cover all the 12 star signs. Since the star signs perform 366.258 rotations in a year, the Sun must perform 365.258 rotations to leave a gap of one rotation in one year, which would then correspond to the

Sun's movement through the star signs. This is nearly identical to how we treat the solar year presently, which is said to comprise 365 days, during which the Sun passes through all the 12 signs of the zodiac, one per month.

The explanations of this passing are however quite different in the modern and the Vedic system. In the modern system, the stars and the Sun are stationary, and the earth goes around the Sun once per year, and rotates on its axis once per day. The rotation around its axis causes day and night, while the revolution around the Sun causes changes in the seasons in a year. In Vedic cosmology, the Earth is stationary, and the zodiac and the Sun are both revolving around the Earth, the zodiac revolving slightly faster than the Sun. Both the zodiac and the Sun therefore go around the Earth every day. Since the zodiac goes a little faster, the Sun appears to lag behind and therefore passes through the signs of the zodiac in a year. The rotation of the Earth around the Sun, and its revolution about its own axis, in modern astronomy, is accordingly replaced by the revolutions of the zodiac and that of the Sun in Vedic cosmology.

Two kinds of time calculations are involved in Vedic astronomy: one based on the rotation of the zodiac and the other based on the rotation of the Sun. A single rotation of the zodiac constitutes a *Nakṣatra Ahorātra* or a *sidereal day*. 30 sidereal days make a sidereal month, and 12 sidereal months make a sidereal year. The sidereal year, however, is not the solar year. A solar year is based on the Sun passing through the 12 signs of the zodiac in 12 months, which is based on differential speeds of rotation between the zodiac and the Sun. As noted above, the zodiac goes faster than the Sun, and the difference in their speeds causes the Sun to lag behind and pass through the 12 signs of the zodiac in a year. The solar year is thus calculated such that there are 365.258 solar days in a solar year, whereas there are 366.258 sidereal days in a solar year. The higher cycles of time such as the demigod year, the 4 *yuga* periods, *chaturyugi*, *manavantara*, *kalpa*, etc. are based on the solar year rather than the sidereal year. Owing to this difference, the *chaturyugi* has 4,320,000 *solar years* rather than *sidereal years*. In a *chaturyugi* therefore the zodiac will undergo 1,582,237,828 rotations while the Sun will undergo 1,577,917,828 rotations, creating an exact difference of 4,320,000 rotations.

The Vedic system explains why there is a leap year necessary every 4 years: the reason is that there should be 365.258 days in a solar year, but we count only 365 days. After 4 years, the 0.258 days add up to an additional day, making the 4th year have an extra day—i.e., 366 days.

The solar year calculation in modern astronomy depends on the distance of the Earth from the Sun, which has no explanation since there is no particular reason why the Earth has a particular distance from the Sun. After all, the Earth could have a slightly lesser weight and have a smaller radius or have a larger weight and have a larger radius. The explanation of the solar day in modern astronomy, therefore, depends on the postulated weight of the Earth, and there is no way to calculate this weight except to reverse calculate it from the Earth's orbit assuming that the gravitational law is true. Therefore, if there were an explanation of the rate of rotation of the zodiac, it would constitute a better scientific explanation of the duration of the year, the passing of the seasons, and so forth.

Solar and Lunar Calendars

Vedic cosmology has a sophisticated explanation for the differential in the motion between the zodiac and the Sun. The explanation is that the zodiac moves clockwise (east to west) while the Sun and Moon move counterclockwise (west to east), but these planets are "dragged" by the movement of the zodiac. Due to this dragging, the planets appear to move clockwise just as the zodiac, but since their actual motion is counterclockwise, they appear to move slower than the zodiac. This slower motion is an apparent phenomenon, and not a real one. The real fact is that the planets are moving counterclockwise and pass the zodiac signs at the rate of their counterclockwise motion. The *Śrīmad Bhāgavatam* provides a very beautiful example of the potter's wheel to illustrate this idea.

> *When a potter's wheel is moving and small ants located on that big wheel are moving with it, one can see that their motion is different from that of the wheel*

because they appear sometimes on one part of the wheel and sometimes on another. Similarly, the signs and constellations, with Sumeru and Dhruvaloka on their right, move with the wheel of time, and the antlike Sun and other planets move with them. The Sun and planets, however, are seen in different signs and constellations at different times. This indicates that their motion is different from that of the zodiac and the wheel of time itself. [SB 5.22.2]

Now the planets (such as the Sun) being on their orbits, go very rapidly and continually with the stars towards the west (clockwise) and fall back (from their places towards the east - i.e., counterclockwise) at an equal rate as if overpowered by the stars (due to their very rapid motion caused by the air). [Surya Siddhānta 1.25]

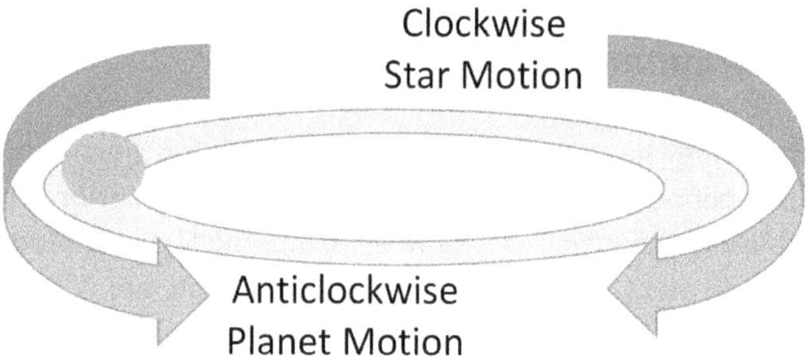

Figure-35 Opposite Motions of Stars and Planets

The explanation of the differential is therefore that the Sun goes around the zodiac once per year in a counterclockwise motion, while the zodiac is itself going clockwise. The motion of the zodiac constitutes the *sidereal day* while the combination of the clockwise motion of the zodiac and the counterclockwise motion of the Sun is the *solar day*. Thus, in a *chaturyugi*, the Sun goes counterclockwise 4,320,000 times, riding on the zodiac's motion that goes clockwise 1,582,237,828 times, like an ant that is moving in direction a opposite to the motion of a potter's wheel.

The Sun is therefore like a passenger on the zodiac train. When the train is moving forward, and the passengers are walking backwards on the train, it appears that the passengers are going forward a little slower than the train's speed. To an observer on the ground (in this case the *bhūloka*), the train just appears to go faster than the passenger, although realistically we must understand that the passenger is walking backwards on the train. The Vedic theory presents the idea of an "ether" that is dragging the planets backwards with the motion of the zodiac. The zodiac, in this case, represents the absolute space reference frame, which moves backwards, and drags the Sun backwards too even though the Sun and the zodiac appear to not be joined or situated on the other.

The *Surya Siddhānta* also describes the motion of the Moon, which goes counterclockwise 57,753,336 times in 4,320,000 solar years. However, the *Surya Siddhānta* states that to find the number of lunar months, we must *subtract* the number of the Sun's rotations from the number of the Moon's rotations. This is interesting because this implies that just as the Sun is dragged clockwise by the rotation of the zodiac, the Moon is dragged by the counterclockwise motion of the Sun. The "real" rotation of the Moon is in addition to the motion caused by the Sun's rotation. If the Sun is an ant on the potter's wheel of the zodiac, then the Moon is an ant sitting on a secondary potter's wheel created by the Sun's motion.

Luminary	Rotations in a Chaturyugi	Direction
Zodiac	1,582,237,828	Clockwise
Sun	4,320,000	Counterclockwise
Moon	57,753,336	Counterclockwise

Table 9: Revolutions of the Sun and the Moon

While we observe the combined effect of the zodiac and the Sun on the Moon, Vedic astronomy does not calculate the time based on this combined motion. Rather, the time is computed by *removing* the effects of the zodiac and the Sun and attributing the lunar time to the Moon's motion alone. Similarly, the solar time is computed by removing the effect of the zodiac on the Sun's movement. It is thus essential to know the zodiac motion to calculate the motions of the Sun and the Moon, because otherwise they would not be removed from the observed motion.

Thus, if the Moon rotates 57,753,336 times in 4,320,000 years while the Sun rotates 4,320,000 times in the same duration, then the real rotation attributable to the Moon must be 57,753,336 - 4,320,000 = 53,433,336 rotations. This number is called *adhimāsa* or "additive month", which implies: (a) the real lunar motion is in *addition* to the solar motion, and (b) their difference is to be viewed as a *lunar month* (rather than a year, as was the case for the Sun's additional motion in relation to the zodiac). The *Surya Siddhānta* goes on to describe the total number of solar and lunar days in a *chaturyugi* which then helps us understand how these months are translated into number of days in that period.

> *There are 1,577,917,828 terrestrial days (solar days) and 1,603,000,080 lunar days in a great yuga. [Surya Siddhānta 1.37]*

The two numbers can be understood from the above description if the number of solar days is defined as the difference between the number of sidereal rotations and the Sun's own counterclockwise rotations (implying that the Sun is dragged by the zodiac in a clockwise direction, and the real motion attributable to the Sun is given by the difference between the zodiac and the Sun's rotations). Similarly, the number of lunar days equals to the number stated in *Surya Siddhānta* if the number of lunar months computed above (as the difference between the number of the Sun's and the Moon's rotations) is multiplied by 30. That is, to obtain the number of lunar days in a *chaturyugi* we must multiply the number of *adhimāsa* by 30.

- 1,582,237,828 – 4,320,000 = 1,577,917,828 solar days
- 53,433,336 x 30 = 1,603,000,080 lunar days

Thus, a solar year has 365.258 days, but the lunar year has 12 * 30 = 360 days. This fact appears confusing if we take the rotations of the Sun and Moon as the basis of calculating the number of days, because the lunar rotations (57,753,336) are far greater than the solar rotations (4,320,000). Similarly, this appears confusing if we see that there are more lunar days (1,603,000,080) than solar days (1,577,917,828) in the same duration of a *chaturyugi*. How can the lunar year be smaller than the solar year when the Moon has more rotations than the Sun and more lunar days than solar days in a *chaturyugi*? The answer to this paradox is that (a) the motion of the Moon is *additional* to the Sun's motion and therefore the solar motion is subtracted from the lunar motion, (b) this additional motion of the Moon is interpreted as a month rather than a year, and (c) the month is defined to have a fixed number of 30 days. The calculation of a lunar year is thus more complex than simply measuring the rotations of the Moon around the Sun, and it arises because the Moon's motion is viewed as an ant riding upon the Sun's potter's wheel, just as the Sun's motion is viewed as riding on the zodiac motion.

The solar and lunar motions create two calendars, which are widely employed at present. Much of the Western world uses the solar calendar, while the traditional Vedic calendar is based on the motion of the Moon. Of course, from the perspective of measuring the passing of days and years, either method of calculation works perfectly well. However, if you are trying to determine birthdays and anniversaries, you would need to know whether a year has 365.258 or just 360 days, since the date would recur after a different number of days. There is, hence, a difference between the two calendars as far as repetitions in time are concerned, although no difference if we only have to measure time linearly.

The Vedic view is that the birthdays or anniversaries are accurately defined by the lunar calendar (and not the sidereal or solar calendars). The reason for this becomes apparent when we see (in the later sections) that the other planets are also like the Moon, and are therefore dragged by the Sun, which is then dragged by the zodiac. In effect, the time used for birthday calculation is based on the cumulative motion of Moon, Sun, and the zodiac, rather than their separate individual motions.

The Passing of Day and Night

The flat geometry of the *bhūloka* creates problems in the explanation of day and night, even though we can compute the calendars and the rotations of the Sun and the Moon, and despite the fact that the flat geometry can also be converted into a sphere. The problem is that the causal explanation of day and night must involve a flat geometry rather than a sphere (the sphere is a sensual appearance, but the causal picture is based on a flat surface). Some modern interpretations of Vedic cosmology try to overcome this problem by the idea that light from the Sun is 'obstructed' by the *Sumeru Mountain*, which actually doesn't solve the problem when the Earth is identified with *Bhārata varṣa* rather than with *Jambudvīpa* (recall from the last chapter that the Earth is *Bhārata-varṣa*).

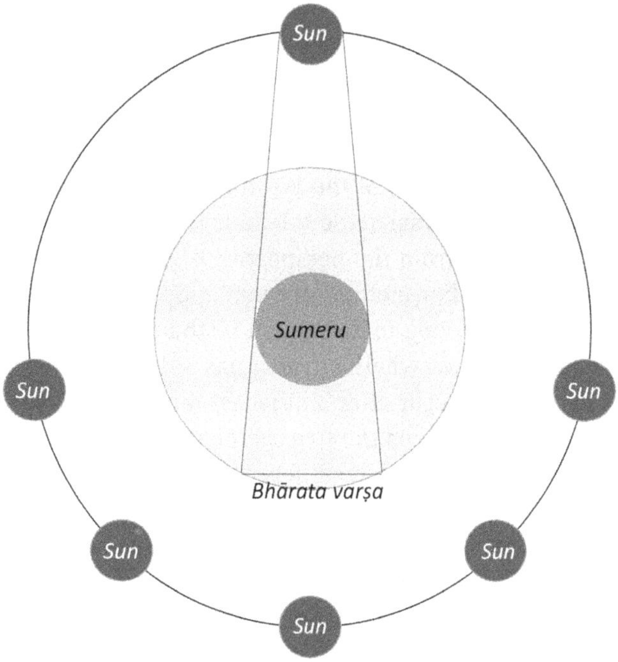

Figure-36 Day and Night in the Physical Model

The problem is that if we use the physical theory of light, then for nearly half the day, all parts of *Bhārata varṣa* would be under light, and *Sumeru* can only cast a shadow for less than half the time. Furthermore, since the *Sumeru* is 32,000 *yojana* at the top, and *Bhārata varṣa* is only 9,000 *yojana* broad, when the *Sumeru* casts a shadow on *Bhārata varṣa*, it should cover the entire planet into darkness (Figure-36 illustrates this point, although due to space constraints, the picture isn't to scale). The result of this explanation of day and night by shadows is that sometimes all of Earth will have a day, and at other times, the entire Earth will be plunged into darkness. Clearly, this isn't true. Some other interpreters also try to address this issue by supposing that the different *dvīpa* and *varṣa* are situated at different heights (which is indeed true, although the heights aren't significant to matter), but no matter how you look at this, you will always find contradictions against observations. Through the remaining chapters, we will come across many such issues, which can only be resolved if a different theory of matter, light, space, and time is adopted. If we take the Vedic cosmological model, and try to apply a physical theory of matter, we will always run into contradictions.

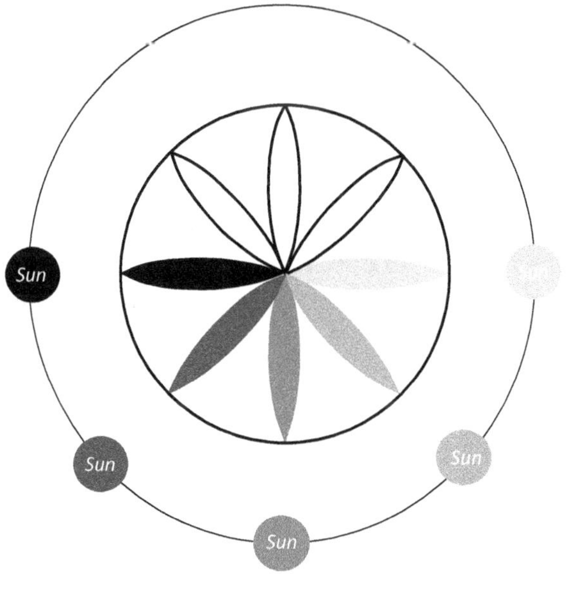

Figure-37 Day and Night in the Semantic Model

The semantic explanation of day and night is that Sun's light is not the same at all zodiac locations. The parts of the Earth too are conceptually different, and they are lighted at different times by the Sun's motion, when the type of the Sun given by its location and the Earth type become similar. The correct physical analogy of this type of causality is *resonance* in which a vibrating string causes another string to vibrate if their frequencies are similar. To understand this type of causality, therefore, both Earth and Sun must be viewed as sound vibrations, such that these vibrations are representations of meanings. The Sun illuminates the Earth when the meaning in the Sun matches the meaning in the Earth. This model of causality exists in atomic theory (where objects are modeled as waves), although this model is inadequately understood at present. For instance, the vibrations in atomic theory can be applied only to atomic objects, not to macroscopic objects. Also, how an atomic object will change its state by motion through space is not clearly understood.

In the semantic model, each *varṣa* in *Jambudvīpa* is a lotus, whose petals are of different types (this point is further elaborated in the next chapter while discussing the *chakra* system in *yoga* philosophy which describes each *chakra* as a lotus whose petals are different letters and represent different kinds of meanings). The day and the night arise because the parts of space (and material objects in them) are 'excited' into a different sematic state through interaction with the state of the Sun, which is called 'entanglement' in modern quantum physics. The Vedic causality of day and night, therefore, is not unscientific, although it needs a proper understanding of atomic theory such that the theory is consistently applied to both macroscopic and atomic objects, not selectively to the atomic objects. Given a misunderstanding of mysterious phenomena such as entanglement, uncertainty, complementarity, non-locality, and probability in current quantum theory, the theory cannot be extended to macroscopic objects, since ordinary objects seem to be independent, have a fixed classical state, and not apparently entangled. However, this view of the ordinary world is itself a mistake, which needs to be corrected[1].

The key point is that the Vedic cosmological model is inconsistent with physical theories of matter, and before this model can be understood, a theory of matter that explains a new kind of causality must exist. Interpreters of Vedic cosmology miss this point, and try to extend the modern theory of space, time, matter, and light, into an explanation of the Vedic cosmological model, which is not only a mistake, but will also not produce a consistent understanding of Vedic cosmology.

The Motion of the Five Planets

Vedic astronomy describes the motion of the five planets apart from the Sun, the Moon, *Rāhu*, and *Ketu* (Mercury, Venus, Mars, Jupiter, and Saturn) differently than the motion of the Moon: we begin to see the use of epicycles. An epicycle employs two kinds of motions: (1) a *deferent* which represents the bigger circle on which a planet moves, and (2) a smaller circle called *epicycle* that drags along with this bigger circle. The apparent movement of the planet is a combination of these two movements, but the explanation is based on two different kinds of movements.

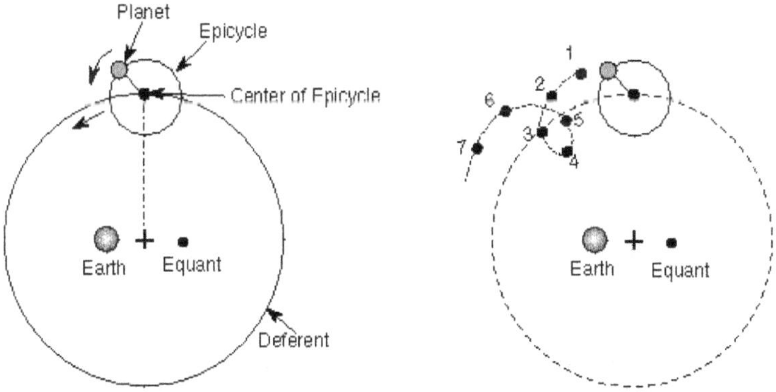

Figure-38 The Deferent and the Epicycle

When Ptolemy employed epicycles to explain planetary motion, the satisfying part of the explanation was that everything was explained in terms of circular motion, but the dissatisfying part was that the Earth had to be moved off-center; this off-center place was called the *eccentric* and the point directly opposite to the eccentric was called *equant*. The observation was that the epicycle rotation remains constant only from the perspective of the equant, when the Earth is placed at the eccentric. This problematic feature of the epicycle scheme does not remain problematic in Vedic cosmology since the Earth planet is identified as *Bhārata-varṣa*, which is a tract of space on the south of *Jambudvīpa* and therefore off-center (the center place in *Jambudvīpa* is *Ilāvṛta-varṣa*). Correspondingly the *equant* in Vedic cosmology is *Kuru-varṣa*, and all epicycle movements are therefore constant in relation to *Kuru-varṣa*.

LUMINARY NAME	DEFERENT REVOLUTIONS	EPICYCLE REVOLUTIONS
SATURN	146,568	4,320,000
JUPITER	364,220	4,320,000
MARS	2,296,832	4,320,000
MERCURY	4,320,000	17,937,060
VENUS	4,320,000	7,022,376
SIDERIAL	1,582,237,828	
MOON	57,753,336	
SUN	4,320,000	

Table 10: The System of Epicycles

Table 10 lists the epicycles mentioned in the *Surya Siddhānta* from which we can discern two kinds of epicycles. The first kind involves the epicycles of Mercury and Venus in which the deferent follows the Sun's rate of revolution, and the second kind involves the epicycles of Mars, Jupiter, and Saturn, in which the epicycle follows the rate of the revolution of the Sun. Accordingly, Mercury and Venus have their own epicycle periods, while Mars, Jupiter, and Saturn, have their own deferent periods. The reason for this difference between two kinds of epicycles is that Mercury and Venus have smaller orbits than the Sun, while Mars, Jupiter and Saturn have larger orbits than that of the Sun as shown in Figure-39. Therefore, the Sun's orbit is the bigger orbit in case of Mercury and Venus and therefore becomes their deferent. Similarly, the Sun's orbit is the smaller orbit in the case of Mars, Jupiter, and Saturn, and therefore becomes the epicycle in their rotation. All the planets use the epicycle model but depending on sizes, the epicycle and deferent differ.

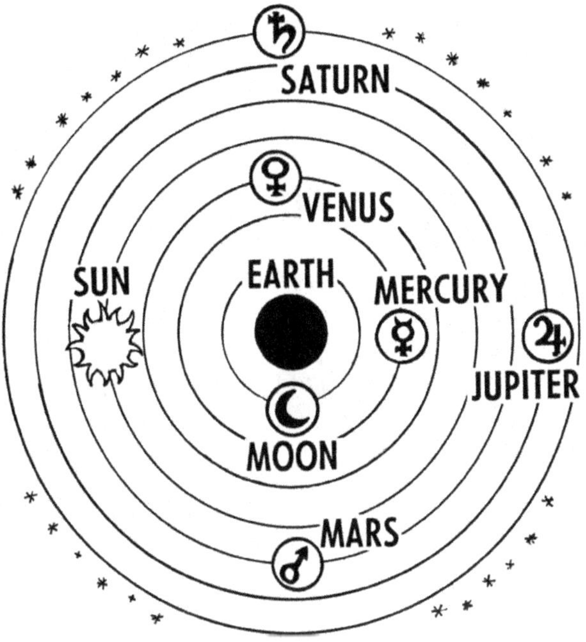

Figure-39 Orbits of Planets in Ptolemy's System

One way to understand this epicycle system is to think of the orbits as two vibrations: the vibration with the bigger wavelength is the wave that is *modulated* and the vibration with the smaller wavelength is the wave that *modulates* the bigger vibration. The bigger wave becomes the deferent and the smaller wave becomes the epicycle. In the case of Mercury and Venus, the bigger wave is the Sun, and therefore becomes the modulated wave, or the deferent, which is then modulated by the smaller periods of the planets creating an epicycle. In the case of Mars, Jupiter, and Saturn, the cycles of these planets are the bigger waves and they become the deferent, and are then modulated by the motion of the Sun. The Sun is still "dragging" the planets in their orbits, although in the case of Mercury and Venus, this dragging appears as the deferent, while in the case of Mars, Jupiter, and Saturn, this dragging appears as the epicycle. In effect, the zodiac drags the Sun, which then drags the other six planets. The motion of the planets is therefore the combination of the drags caused by the zodiac, the Sun, and their own motion. If, however, we calculate time based on the planetary motions, we would remove the effect of the zodiac and the Sun and use only the planetary motion.

Planetary Period and Radii

An interesting fact about Vedic cosmology is the comparison between the orbital periods between the Vedic and modern calculations. This comparison is illustrated in Table 11. The Vedic periods are computed by dividing the period of the *yuga* (4,320,000 years) by the number of planetary revolutions in that *yuga*. This comparison is interesting due to the agreement between the Vedic and modern calculations, but that isn't the primary reason for illustrating them here. The key reason is that in calculating these periods, I removed the Sun's effect: for Mercury and Venus, I removed the deferent, and for Mars, Jupiter, and Saturn, I removed the epicycle, both of which are caused by the Sun, leaving only a planet's "own" revolution. Since the modern calculation is done with the Sun in the center, its effect on the planets is discarded. When the calculation is done with Earth as the center, these effects must be considered.

Planet	Revolutions in a Yuga	Vedic Period (Years)	Modern Period (Years)	Variation
Mercury	17,937,060	0.2408	0.2408	-0.00039%
Venus	7,022,376	0.6152	0.6152	-0.00216%
Mars	2,296,832	1.8809	1.8808	0.00515%
Jupiter	364,220	11.8610	11.8618	-0.08368%
Saturn	146,568	29.4744	29.4571	1.72737%

Table 11: Planetary Period Comparison

The *Surya Siddhānta* also describes the method for calculating the planetary radii, based on the principle that all planets move at a constant speed, and thus their circumferences are inversely proportional to the number of revolutions they perform. The *Surya Siddhānta* states that the circumference of the universe is the number of revolutions performed by the Moon in a *kalpa* (1000 *chaturyugi*) multiplied by the length of the Moon's orbit (324,000 *yojana*). That is, the distance that the Moon travels in a *kalpa* is equal to the circumference of the universe. All the other planets move at the same speed, and therefore they too travel the same distance as the Moon in the *kalpa*. The difference is only that they perform a different number of revolutions and therefore to know their planetary orbits, we must divide the total distance traveled in that time by the number of revolutions (circumference = $2\pi r$). It is notable that *Surya Siddhānta* treats π as $\sqrt{10}$ which comes to 3.1622 rather than the modern value of 3.1415. The reason for this is not clear to me, but to be true to the Vedic description, I have used the value stated in *Surya Siddhānta* rather than the modern value. The resulting calculation is shown in Table 12. *Surya Siddhānta* also states that the circumference of the zodiac (both 12 and 28 stars) is 60 times the orbit of the Sun.

Planet	Revolutions in a Yuga	Circumference (Yojana)	Radius (Miles)
UNIVERSE		18,712,080,864,000,000	23,669,699,404,212,300
STAR DISC	1,582,237,828	259,890,000	328,745,810
SATURN	146,568	127,668,255	161,492,955
JUPITER	364,220	51,375,764	64,987,369
MARS	2,296,832	8,146,909	10,305,368
SUN	4,320,000	4,331,500	5,479,097
VENUS	7,022,376	2,664,637	3,370,611
MERCURY	17,937,060	1,043,208	1,319,597
MOON	57,753,336	324,000	409,841

Table 12: Planetary Radii Calculation

Surya Siddhānta doesn't explain why the circumference of the universe equals the distance covered by the Moon in a *kalpa* which is something to be known separately. The key insight, however, is that all the planets are moving at the same speed, and therefore cover the same distance as the Moon. Of course, they do perform a different number of revolutions, and therefore their radii are computed by using the total distance travelled. Clearly, the idea that planets move at a constant speed goes against the gravitational theory. But the readers can recall the discussion of the problem of "dark matter" which arises precisely because we observe the outer parts of the universe moving at a constant rate, which violates the law of gravitation, and creates an anomaly that science is still unable to resolve. The idea that all parts of the universe are moving at a constant rate, although at different radii, might thus be a useful approach to resolve the problems underlying cosmology today.

The Size of the Universe

The *Surya Siddhānta* states that the universe extends to the place till which the light of the Sun reaches, and the size of the universe (as seen in the previous section) is the distance the Moon (or the other planets) travel in a *kalpa*. This appears to be at odds with the idea of *loka varṣa* discussed in the previous chapter, which is the place described in *Śrīmad Bhāgavatam* as the place until which the light of the Sun reaches. Beyond the *loka varṣa*, according to Śrīmad Bhāgavatam, the light of the Sun is blocked by the *Lokāloka* Mountain. The confusion therefore arises about whether the Sun spreads its light only within the *Lokāloka* Mountain which is 1,000,000,000 miles in radius, or to the entire universe which is mentioned to be 23,669,699,404,212,300 miles in radius.

The resolution of this issue requires three steps. First, in estimating the size of the universe, we need to take into account the seven coverings of the universe. Second, we must consider the 'water' covering between the manifest part of the universe, and its seven material coverings. Third, we need to understand how the light of the Sun goes beyond the *Lokāloka* Mountain although *Śrīmad Bhāgavatam* states that light is confined to within the *Lokāloka* Mountain. The following paragraphs try to address these issues one by one. The seven coverings of the universe grow 10 times in size successively, and by this estimation, the total radius of the universe (including the seven coverings) should be 2 x 10^{16} miles. However, even if these layers are taken into account, there is still a difference of 3,669,699,404,212,260 miles between the two methods. The resolution of this gap is that what *Śrīmad Bhāgavatam* calls the "universe" is actually the "golden egg" or the *brahmanda* which is said to lie inside a layer of 'water' which is then covered by the seven layers.

> *The Supreme Personality of Godhead, the virāṭ-puruṣa, situated Himself in that golden egg, which was lying on the water, and He divided it into many departments. [SB 3.26.53]*

The *virāta puruṣa* is inside the manifest universe, excluding the seven layers of covering. Therefore, the *brahmanda* should not be treated as the entire universe (with the seven coverings), although in some places in Vedic literature, the latter nomenclature is also adopted. The context of description generally clarifies the meaning being used in this nomenclature. Given that there is a layer of 'water' in between the *brahmanda* and the seven layers, we can infer that the width of this 'water' layer must be about 366,969,940 miles, which must be added to the size of the "golden egg" before we calculate the sizes of the 7 successive coverings. The resulting structure of the universe, therefore includes the seven outer coverings, inside which is a covering of water, inside which lies the "golden egg" into which Lord *Viṣṇu* appears as the *Hiranyagarbha*. This structure of the present universe is shown in Figure-40.

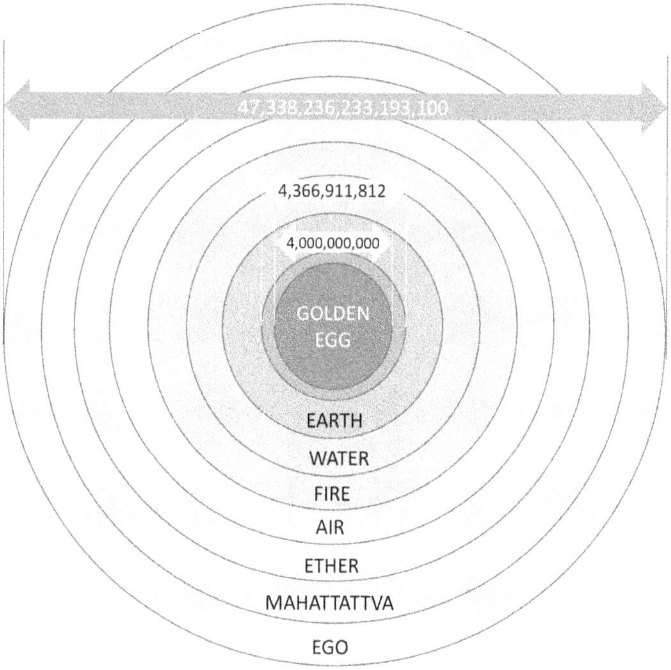

Figure-40 The Structure of the Present Universe

The presence of an ocean of "water" outside the "golden egg" is confirmed in numerous places in the *Purāna* and in the four Vedas. An incarnation of Lord *Viṣṇu* called *Vāraha* is said to have pulled the "golden egg" out of water twice: once in the beginning of the *Svayambhū Manavantara* when *Brahma* requests Lord *Viṣṇu* to take the globe out of the water to begin creation, and next when the demon *Hiranyāksha* submerges the *brahmanda* into the water. *Śrīla Viśwanāth Chakravarty Thākur* has provided a similar picture in his commentary to SB 5.20.38, although he indicates that the entities in the 4,000,000,000 miles sphere add up to 3,968,000,000, which leaves a gap of 32,000,000 miles and in this gap is the ocean from which Lord *Vāraha* rescues the *brahmanda*. Both the above pictures may be true; the "golden egg" may be smaller than the 4,000,000,000 figure such that the gap is filled by the water to complete the size, and there can be water even beyond 4,000,000,000 miles as suggested by the sizes of this material world in the *Surya Siddhānta*.

There is, however, yet another issue in understanding how the light of the Sun goes to the outermost covering of the universe, when it is not supposed to escape beyond the *Lokāloka* Mountain. What we call 'light' as something that we can see, is not the ultimate description of light. The real material entity is not light but *karma*. This *karma* manifests at various levels, including our vision of the world, when it is called 'light', although *karma* is also involved in the manifestation of all the five elements called Earth, Water, Fire, Air, and Ether. The 'light' is the Fire element, but *karma* includes the other four elements as well. The 'light' that doesn't escape the *Lokāloka* Mountain is the manifest experience (i.e., the Fire element), beyond which lies a covering of *karma* and the seven coverings of *guna*. The 'light' that escapes the *Lokāloka* Mountain is *karma* which causes a change to our *guna*, when our desires are altered due to suffering or pleasure. The manifest part of *karma* is 'light' in the sense of things that we see. *Karma*, however, goes outside the manifest realm to alter the *guna*. Since *karma* is originally created from the *guna*, this escaping is the process of reversing the *guna* that produced the *karma* in the first place. The descriptions in *Śrīmad Bhāgavatam* and *Surya Siddhānta* regarding the extent of light are therefore not contradictory. However, they require a deeper understanding of light, which I will discuss later.

The number given in *Surya Siddhānta* is compelling because it equates the size of the universe to the distance travelled by the luminaries in a *kalpa*. This idea is of deep scientific merit because it suggests that the size of the universe (as the set of events) is related to the time it takes to enact the events. We cannot empirically confirm the size of the universe from our current state of observation, but if there is a theoretical connection between the size of the universe and the fact that this size represents all the events which are exhausted over a certain long time period, then we can calculate the galactic size from the radii of the luminaries and the number of rotations they perform. Since all luminaries travel the same distance, the difference between the planets can be associated simply by their radii. This is another important scientific fact which can be the basis of an association between the radii of the planets with the types or functions that they represent in the universe.

In this regard, it is important to note that when Newton formulated the theory of gravitation, he based it upon an observation previously made by Galileo, namely that in the heliocentric model, all the planets sweep equal amounts of *area* in the same given time. Newton's law mathematically formalized this insight from Galileo. The geocentric model given in the *Surya Siddhānta* similarly provides a theoretical principle in which all celestial objects move equal distances in the same time, and the entire universe is equal to the distance traveled by *any* luminary in a *kalpa*. This is a stronger principle than the one formulated by Galileo, because it connects the motion of the planets to the size of the universe, and the time in which the universe is almost annihilated (we will see in later chapters how a *kalpa* is a day of Lord *Brahma* after which the lower planets, including all the above mentioned luminaries, are destroyed).

There is a small difference between *Surya Siddhānta* and *Siddhānta śiromaṇi* regarding the circumference of the universe which should be noted. In the purport to *Chaitanya Charitāmṛta Śrīla Prabhupāda* writes:

> *Śrīla Bhaktisiddhānta Sarasvatī Ṭhākur, one of the greatest astrologers of his time, gives information from the Siddhānta-śiromaṇi that this universe measures 18,712,069,200,000,000 × 8 miles. This is the circumference of this universe. According to some, this is only half the circumference.*

The difference between the two descriptions is:

- 18,712,080,864,000,000 *yojana* in *Surya Siddhānta*
- 18,712,069,200,000,000 *yojana* in *Siddhānta Śiromaṇi*

It is not clear how this difference arises: it amounts to a difference of about 1475 miles in the 'water' covering, which is quantitatively insignificant, although none of these numbers should be viewed as empirical measurements; they are all based on theories and concepts.

The size in *Siddhānta Śiromaṇi* is said to be the distance to the outer covering of the 'kettle' of each universe, which may imply that there is actually no disagreement between the two descriptions, although there is a subtle distinction which needs to be incorporated in our understanding.

Regarding the question of whether this size is full or half, both possibilities can be understood based on the fact that the half size is presented as the distance traveled by the Moon during a *kalpa* which is the day of *Brahma*, equal to his night. If we take the total number of occurrences actualized during the day of *Brahma*, then an equal number of occurrences would never be actualized, although they would 'pass' because the time in the universe is still passing even though *Brahma* sleeps. We might say that these occurrences are realized only in the dream of *Brahma,* but they never become real in the lives of other living beings. In that sense, both descriptions (that take the day, or the day and night) are equally true, depending on how we compute the sizes: either as what can be manifest, or what can be manifest plus what will remain unknown.

Period and Radii Comparison

When we compare the planetary orbital radii computed in the Vedic system with those in the modern system, stark contrasts appear. It is therefore instructive that there is, on the one hand, a huge amount of agreement between the modern and the Vedic system on the periods of the planets, and a huge difference when it comes to the radii of their orbits. This is instructive because, it has been said, by no less than Einstein, after the dawn of the theory of relativity, that heliocentric and geocentric models are merely a matter of our "perspective", and no model could be superior. The geocentric model in the Vedas disproves this view because despite an enormous agreement on the planetary periods, there is no agreement on their radii. As we have previously discussed, distance measurements are subject to the theory of nature involved: e.g., that space and time are linear, that light travels in straight lines, that there are no boundaries in space and time, etc. If these theories are altered, all the distances would be changed.

Similarly, the distances also depend on our theory of geometry; e.g., if the geometry is Euclidean, then the distances are different than if we discarded Euclid's first postulate and constructed a hierarchical space-time model.

We can clearly see that it is one thing to measure the orbital periods based on the fact that we can observe how frequently the planets go around in their orbits, and quite another to know how far these planets really are. As we have previously discussed, the radius measurement is based, in modern science, on the parallax method, which, employs a theory of light, space, and time inconsistent with the Vedic views about them. Even the modern idea that different planets move at different rates, depending on how far they are from the center of the solar system, is also an area of difference. Therefore, the derivation of radii either from the law of gravitation, or based on the parallax method, would never agree with the Vedic calculation. Table 13 illustrates this disagreement.

Planet	Modern Calculation			Vedic Calculation
	Aphelion (Miles)	Perihelion (Miles)	Average Radius	Radius (Miles)
Mercury	43,384,153	28,585,107	35,984,630	1,319,565
Venus	67,694,680	66,786,182	67,240,431	3,370,528
Mars	154,871,360	128,414,944	141,643,152	10,305,115
Jupiter	507,089,363	460,178,958	483,634,161	64,985,773
Saturn	937,594,560	838,871,040	888,232,800	161,488,989

Table 13: Planetary Radii Comparison

This disagreement is an example of what philosophers of science call the *underdetermination* of models and theories by observations: several distinct models and theories can be used to explain the same facts, and to choose a particular model or theory, we must find additional facts. As we go on expanding the observations, many theories and models fail, but this process is limited by our ability to observe new phenomena. If our perception is limited to sensual observation, then our ability to expand the phenomena is itself limited. In this case, the periods of planets are observations which are explained equally well by two distinct models, which differ in terms of the planetary orbits. The orbits themselves are determined in science by the parallax method, which then assumes a theory of light, space, and time. If the theory is changed, the same observations would be explained by constructing a different model of the cosmos.

A similar type of disagreement also exists with regard to the size estimations of the universe. Modern astronomers estimate the size of the Milky Way Galaxy to be about 100,000 light-years, and the universe is supposed to be many millions of light years more. A light-year is the distance light travels in a year, and this is $5.9 * 10^{12}$ miles. Thus, the size of the Milky Way turns out to be about $5.9 * 10^{17}$ miles. The size of the present universe according to *Surya Siddhānta* is 47,338,236,233,193,100 miles, which is an order of magnitude smaller than the size of the Milky Way. If we include the sizes of the other galaxies according to modern estimations, the size of the Vedic universe would be much smaller. So, we must examine the *methods* by which we are measuring distance, in addition to the *notion* of distance itself, before we can compare these two numbers. For instance, distance in Vedic cosmology denotes conceptual difference, which is hierarchical, and not linear. Furthermore, the estimation of galactic distances based on light intensities (as we have seen earlier) can be viewed as *pictorial* rather than real depth. The differences in theories of nature therefore alter our *interpretations* of observations, and all cosmic length measurements are interpretations. The key point is that when the theories used to estimate these differences are radically different, then these distances cannot be compared. We must rather try to validate the theory without such interpretational difficulties and decide which theory is correct, before we use it for distance estimation.

Phases of the Planets

All planets except the Sun undergo "phases" in which only part of the planet is visible, interspersed with full and no visibility. In modern cosmology, this is explained by the rotation of planets around the Sun, but the *Surya Siddhānta* provides a different explanation for this fact.

> *The Moon's deflection to the north and south from the end of the declination of her corresponding point at the Ecliptic is caused by her node. The measure of her greatest deflection is equal to the 1/80th part of the minutes in a circle. [Surya Siddhānta 1.68]*

> *The measures of the greatest deflections of Jupiter and Mars caused by their nodes are respectively 2/9 and 3/9 of that of the Moon, and that of Mercury, Venus and Saturn is 4/9 of the Moon's greatest deflection. [Surya Siddhānta 1.69]*

> *Thus the mean greatest latitudes of the Moon, Mars, Mercury, Jupiter, Venus, and Saturn are declared to be 270, 90, 120, 60, 120, and 120 minutes respectively [Surya Siddhānta 1.70]*

> *The Deity node draws the planet to the north or to the south (from the ecliptic) according as the node is west or east of the planet at a distance less than six signs [Surya Siddhānta 2.7]*

The above verses describe the movement of the planets upwards and downwards in relation to the ecliptic, just as the ecliptic is itself created by the Sun moving upward and downward in relation to the plane created by the zodiac (previously described as the *Uttarāyaṇa* and *Dakshināyana* that causes the changes in the seasons on the Earth). The pattern in these deflections is consistent with the dragging of the Sun by the zodiac and the dragging of other planets by the Sun (creating the deferent or the epicycle). The phenomenal outcomes of these deflections are also similar. Just as the Sun creates "seasons" of winter (dark) and summer (light) on Earth as it goes up and down, it similarly changes "seasons" on other planets. The changing seasons on these planets become the phases of the planets as seen from Earth, where some parts of a planet become lighter or darker, and therefore visible or invisible to our sensual perception. Depending on the periods of the planets the seasons come faster or slower. The phases of the Moon, for instance, change faster than those of the other planets because the Moon has the fastest orbit.

As discussed previously, all planets are spheres from a sensual perspective and flat from the mental viewpoint, therefore, we can describe the phase changes as the flipping of the origin of the space on the planet caused by upward and downward motion of the Sun which causes "summer" and "winter" on the planets. While the overall day and night for the demigods is said to be 6 months due to the Sun's motion around the zodiac, the planets undergo faster or slower changes in seasons. For instance, the seasonal changes on the Moon in 6 months are much faster than on the Earth. Similarly, the seasonal changes are much slower on the other planets such as Saturn or Mars. Effectively, on Moon, Mercury, and Venus, there are many seasonal changes within a single day of the demigods, while on Mars, Jupiter, and Saturn, the seasonal changes occur after multiple days of the demigods. The "summer" and "winter" therefore occur within a single day of the Moon's demigod called *Chandra*, while they occur after several days for the Saturn's demigod called *Shani*.

Since each planet is both a sphere and a plane, the phenomenology of the planetary phases can be understood in a similar way as in modern science, although the *explanation* of this change is quite different. The explanation of the planetary phases in science is that the Earth has a tilt and goes around the Sun, such that all the planets are roughly in the same "plane". The Vedic explanation is that the planets are situated at different heights above the Earth, they go around the Earth, and the changes are caused by shifts in the origins of space on that planet which then creates phases of dark and light, similar to the seasons on Earth. These seasons are perceived as phases. We cannot mix the heliocentric model of modern science, and the Vedic explanation of the phases of planets. If the planets are always above *bhūloka*, then they should not become invisible or only partially visible in the physical model of the cosmos. Therefore, just changing the model of the cosmos doesn't help us understand the phenomena until the causality underlying this model is also changed.

Heights of Planetary Orbits

There are some important differences in the heights of different planets from *bhūloka* as indicated in the different Vedic texts. According to *Surya Siddhānta,* the heights of the planets from *bhūloka* are in the same order as the increasing size of their orbits, which is inversely proportional to the number of rotations they perform, since all the planets move with a constant speed. Thus, the Moon has the smallest orbit and is therefore closest to the Earth. The zodiac has the largest orbit and is therefore farthest from *bhūloka*. This order of planets is given in Table 14.

Planet	Revolutions in a Yuga	Circumference (Yojana)
STAR DISC	1,582,237,828	259,890,000
SATURN	146,568	127,668,255
JUPITER	364,220	51,375,764
MARS	2,296,832	8,146,909
SUN	4,320,000	4,331,500
VENUS	7,022,376	2,664,637
MERCURY	17,937,060	1,043,208
MOON	57,753,336	324,000

Table 14: The Relative Order of Planets

This order of planets is identical to that in modern astronomy, but it varies from the order in *Śrīmad Bhāgavatam* (shown in Table 6). Following are some differences in the two descriptions. First, in *Śrīmad Bhāgavatam* the Sun is closer to the Earth than the Moon, but in *Surya Siddhānta* the Moon is closer than the Sun. Second, the zodiac is above the Moon in *Śrīmad Bhāgavatam* and it is above all the planets in *Surya Siddhānta*. Third, *Śrīmad Bhāgavatam* notes that Venus is below Mercury but the *Padma Purāna* describes that Venus is above

Mercury. These are likely not the only differences, and as we broaden our study, other variations would also likely be discovered. While there is a broad consensus amongst the various texts about the 14 planetary systems, the divisions of the *bhūloka*, the system of planets and star signs, it is also important to recognize that there are some differences which cannot be ignored.

How do we understand these differences? Based on what we have discussed so far regarding the nature of space and time, it is possible to understand why these kinds of differences will arise in any description of the cosmos. The key fact that we need to bear in mind is that distances in Vedic cosmology are not measured along a straight line between any two points in a flat and linear space (as is the case in modern science), but by the length of the *path* one has to take to transform one object into another in a hierarchical and closed space. As we noted earlier, the distance between two cities can be measured physically and semantically: (a) the straight-line path which is based on the physical notion of space, and (b) the length of the road between the cities which is based on the actual procedure needed to go from one place to another. The heights and order of the planets can be different in these descriptions if there is more than one path to a destination, such that one path is shorter and passes through some locations which are destinations on the other paths. In a hierarchical space-time, the paths are never straight. Furthermore, there are many paths to a destination which rise to different abstract locations and then descend from those abstractions to details. One path can begin in the Sun and pass through the Moon, while another path can begin in the Moon and pass through the Sun. Depending on which path we measure the distance on, the distances would be different, besides giving the impression that the Sun comes before Moon on the first path, while the Moon comes before the Sun on the second path. We should not consider these descriptions contradictory; it is rather a matter of understanding the path being used to measure the distance to a specific destination.

All these paths represent different procedures to transform one type of object to another, and distances measured based on these procedures represent the number of steps involved in the procedure. Depending on the number of steps in the procedure, the distance to that destination will also be different. A formal theory of hierarchical space-time is needed to explicate the relationship between distance and the path on which this distance is being measured. The differences between the various orders and distances are not necessarily contradictory; in fact, they are likely outcomes of describing the distances on different conceptual paths.

Vedic cosmology describes the existence of *ākāsh mārga* or roads in space on which space travel occurs. The two paths of the zodiac called *Uttarāyaṇa* and *Dakshināyana* are, for instance, described as two different roads during the times when the Sun passes through two different halves of the zodiac. The light of the Sun is said to go to the upper half of the universe (on and above *bhūloka*), so there is a path from the Sun to the other parts of the universe, and the Sun is worshipped in the Vedic tradition to illuminate these paths and is said to be in the middle of the universe. Effectively, in these descriptions, the Sun is akin to the central square in a city where all the roads meet, and you can go to any part of the city if you reach that square. That doesn't necessarily mean that other roads don't exist. The *Surya Siddhānta* appears to describe all the roads that pass through the Sun, but it is very likely that there are other roads that pass through the Moon, Venus, Mercury, etc. on which the distances to different parts of the universe would be measured differently. The *Surya Siddhānta* goes on to describe many consequences of the order of planets mentioned above resulting from the size of their orbits.

> *The circumference of the middle of the Brahmanda is called Vyomākāsha and in it all the stars revolve. Beneath them Saturn, Jupiter, Mars, Sun, Venus, Mercury and Moon revolve one below the other; beneath them the Siddha, the Vidyādhara and clouds are situated. [SS 12.30-31]*

> *Every fourth of the planets (in the order of their orbits mentioned in 12.30-31) reckoning from Saturn is the ruler of a day (of the week) in succession. In the same manner every third of the planets, reckoning from Saturn is the ruler of a year. [SS 12.78]*

Reckoning from the Moon, the planets above her are called the rulers of the months successively. And from Saturn the planets situated one below the other are successively the rulers of the hours [SS 12.79]

The succession of the 4th of the planets from Saturn in the above list is Sun, Moon, Mars, Mercury, Jupiter, Venus and Saturn, which form the planets ruling the days of the week—Sunday (Sun), Monday (Moon), Tuesday (Mars), Wednesday (Mercury), Thursday (Jupiter), Friday (Venus), and Saturday (Saturn). Similarly, the succession of the 3rd of the planets from the Saturn is Mars, Venus, Moon, Jupiter, Sun, Mercury, and Saturn, which implies that every 7th year is dominated by a particular planet's effects. The above verses illustrate the idea that time has a cyclic structure and it goes through type influences at several levels—hours, weeks, months, and years—and these may not be the only levels.

How Many Solar Systems?

Modern descriptions of the universe suppose that since there are millions of stars in the present universe, some percentage of these stars must also have associated planets, and they would then be like "solar systems", assuming that the Sun in the present universe is a star. This leads to the question of whether the Sun is yet another star, or whether it has a special position amongst all the luminaries. In Vedic cosmology, the Sun is special, and the stars are just like the Moon and other planets, which reflect the light of the Sun. However, to understand this viewpoint, we must look closer at the entire process of how light is produced and reflected.

The scientific claim that there are many solar systems in the universe begins in the view that some stars have wobbly trajectories, and one way to explain that wobbling would be to postulate that there are planets around these stars, although we cannot see these planets. If planets rotate around the star, then they would cause a wobbling in the trajectory due to the gravitational effect of the planets. Similarly, it is observed that sometimes these stars are invisible to us, and then visible again, and one way to explain it is to suppose that there are planets revolving around the stars, and sometimes these planets come in the line of sight between our planet and the star thus hiding the star. The postulate of many solar systems thus arises when we try to explain all observations using gravity, and the failure to do so is overcome by postulating things we cannot observe. Whether or not there are planets revolving around the stars remains an unverifiable hypothesis because we cannot observe those planets, and their existence is *deduced* from other observations.

Clearly, these explanations are not the only possible ones. Since the wobbling trajectory is a result of the parallax method, understanding the real distance to these supposed solar systems is in question. Furthermore, a wobbly trajectory can be effected by a hierarchical time as well, due to which the object will appear to move not just forwards but also backwards sometimes. Similarly, the star may become invisible sometimes when it is not communicating with us, again due to a cyclic time. Under these explanations, the hypothesis of a solar system would be unnecessary. The key point is that the evidence that leads to the postulate of multiple solar systems can also be explained in a different way in a semantic space-time, rather than by assuming gravity and more planets.

In Vedic cosmology, there is only one Sun in the entire universe, which distributes light to other stars and planets, which then redistribute that light in many ways. Light in Vedic philosophy is not photons whose sole relevant quality is frequency. Rather, the Vedas state that there are 100,000 varieties of light, each denoting a different kind of energy. These varieties of light should be viewed as different kinds of meanings, which are transformed by the planets and stars to create even more variety in meaning. The light that we receive from the stars and planets should be seen as meanings that originated in the Sun and were modified by the other planets before being transmitted to the Earth. This modified light transmission is akin to the reflection of light from the Sun, but the reflection is semantic and not physical. That is, the light that is reflected by a star is not identical to the light that was received from the Sun.

We should understand that light never 'travels' in space like material objects, although light causes *changes* which have been modeled in science as the motion of light. The time we suppose it takes for light to go from one point to another is the time it takes to perform a change. To understand this property of light, we again invoke the example from the previous chapter of the teacher trying to educate a student about a topic the student doesn't know. The teacher can finish the lesson quickly, if the student already has most of the background information needed to learn the new concept. The teacher will require a longer time, if the student lacks in the elementary concepts. The extent to which the student knows what the teacher is imparting thus determines the time it takes for a new concept to be grasped. In a semantic space, the distance between the teacher and the student is large if the student is ignorant, and less if he is knowledgeable. The new idea therefore takes less time if the distance is less (the student already knows) and more time if the distance is large (the student is ignorant).

The time taken by light to go from one luminary to another is, similarly, based on their semantic difference. The greater the semantic difference, the greater is the time taken for light to cause an effect. This has little to do with light traveling, and everything to do with how long it takes to transform an object type into another. Light doesn't move in a semantic space because by that motion it will be transformed by the time it reaches the destination, effectively adding no information. Light should be viewed as "action at a distance" which is not "instantaneous".

If one looks into the history of science, classical physics assumed instantaneous action at a distance, and modern physics replaces it with motion of the action (the "force" travels from cause to effect as a "boson"). Both these ideas are wrong. There is action at a distance, which does not move, and is not instantaneous. There is transfer of information which causes changes, which takes time (like a student takes time to assimilate new ideas), which makes us think that the change (i.e., learning) is instantaneous but it takes time for the ideas to "travel" to the destination (i.e., the sound from the teacher's mouth to reach the student's ear). This idea about learning is wrong because the time it takes to learn something depends not on the words reaching our ears, but whether we are capable of comprehending those words. The teacher can speak knowledge in our ears, but the student is not going to learn them faster, if he lacks in basic concepts. The time taken to learn is therefore not based on the physical distance, but on the semantic difference. The distance between the teacher and the student is not physical; it should rather be measured semantically as the gaps in the levels of their respective knowledge.

The light is therefore not traveling from the Sun to the Earth. Rather, the Sun is transforming the Earth without the light moving through the intervening space. Which parts of the Earth are lighted and which parts remain dark depends on the *karma* fructifying at that time and the light that causes changes is a product of that *karma* fructifying. If the *karma* is absent, no changes will be effected, and we remain in 'darkness'. Whether we receive light or remain in the dark, therefore, depends on the effects of *karma* which is a deeper cause that decides who receives the effects of light, and who remains without light. When we receive this light, and its effects are perceived through the senses, we naturally 'project' the cause in a straight-line path although the effect wasn't created in that way.

To change our body, for instance, it is not sufficient to merely push it physically. Rather, a hierarchy of abstract entities must be changed prior, and the process of pushing also involves a hierarchical change, which is not understood in modern science. Many scientific explanations therefore fail because they model the cause-effect relationship in a flat space when, in fact, the space is hierarchical. Light is not traveling to our body, and a hierarchy of changes are effected before our body is changed. The key scientific import of this idea is that numerous objects are being altered one after another before the effect of light is seen by our senses.

The Cycle of Water

The Sun in Vedic cosmology 'absorbs' the water from the *bhūloka* and converts it into rain which then falls on Earth. *Śrīmad Bhāgavatam* vividly describes the cycle of water and the Sun's role in this cycle.

> *During the rainy season, water is generated from the Sun, and in due course of time, during the summer*

season, the very same water is again absorbed by the Sun. Similarly, all living entities, moving and inert, are generated from the earth, and again, after some time, they all return to the earth as dust. Similarly, everything emanates from the Supreme Personality of Godhead, and in due course of time everything enters into Him again. [SB 4.31.15]

Just as the Sun evaporates large quantities of water by its potent rays and later returns the water to the earth in the form of rain, similarly, a saintly person accepts all types of material objects with his material senses, and at the appropriate time, when the proper person has approached him to request them, he returns such material objects. Thus, both in accepting and giving up the objects of the senses, he is not entangled. [SB 11.7.50]

The ordinary understanding of this process is that the heat from the Sun causes the 'evaporation' of water into vapor, which then forms the clouds, which are then converted into rain. This understanding of the cycle of water is not exactly how the Vedic literature describes the water cycle. The Vedic description of this process is that the water being spoken of in the above verses is not the water that we sensually perceive, but the *element* of water which objectifies the property of taste in matter. The word used to describe this 'absorption' is *praviśanti* and *grasanti* which, if literally translated, mean 'entering' and 'eating' respectively. This process of absorption can be understood in view of the other descriptions of matter in *Sāñkhya* where the element of water is produced from fire, fire is produced from air, air is produced from ether, and so forth. The reverse process of absorption occurs during the dissolution of the cosmos.

The element fire then seizes the taste from the element water, which, deprived of its unique quality, taste, merges into fire. Air seizes the form inherent in fire, and then fire, deprived of form, merges into air. The

> *element ether seizes the quality of air, namely touch, and that air enters into ether. Then, O King, false ego in ignorance seizes sound, the quality of ether, after which ether merges into false ego. False ego in the mode of passion takes hold of the senses, and false ego in the mode of goodness absorbs the demigods. Then the total mahattattva seizes false ego along with its various functions, and that mahat is seized by the three basic modes of nature -- goodness, passion and ignorance. My dear King Parīkṣit, these modes are further overtaken by the original unmanifest form of nature, impelled by time. That unmanifest nature is not subject to the six kinds of transformation caused by the influence of time. Rather, it has no beginning and no end. It is the unmanifest, eternal and infallible cause of creation. [SB 12.4.15-19]*

The correct understanding of how water is absorbed by the Sun is not therefore evaporation; rather, the property of taste is absorbed into the property of form, which is then absorbed into air, which is then absorbed into sound, which is then transferred to another place in the universe through the action of *prāna*. This transfer mediated by *prāna* is called the 'ropes of wind'. The reverse process occurs on reception: the force of *prāna* is converted into grosser elements, such as Ether, Air, and then Fire, which appears as light and form that we can see. The light is then objectified into taste, which becomes water, and then falls as rain. The water cycle is therefore not based on the transformation of water from liquid to gaseous state, as modern science describes it, but on the transformation of the water element into the fire element, the transformation of fire into air, which is then transferred through paths in space called the 'ropes of wind'. On receiving this subtle information, it is converted into gross forms, and manifest as light and water.

Many Vedic literatures describe how the universe is annihilated by the Sun blazing for many years without resulting in any rain, which destroys all life forms, following which there are many years of incessant rain during which all the planets are flooded with water. This type of annihilation is impossible with the 'evaporation' theory, because at a certain point in evaporation, precipitation must occur, which must then cause rain; we cannot conceive water being evaporated for years without precipitation. This process is possible only if water is converted into light, is absorbed by the Sun, reinjected and objectified as clouds, followed by rains. But this description also entails that the Sun is not merely emitting light, but also absorbing it, and that it can store vast amounts of light after absorption, before releasing it during annihilation.

Modern science estimates that the Sun is about 4.6 billion years old, and it will die after a similar duration. The Sun is described as a star that performs thermonuclear reactions which emit energy, although the Sun never absorbs energy. In Vedic cosmology, the Sun is both emitting and absorbing energy, and its life is significantly more. In fact, the role of the Sun is not just providing energy but maintaining an *energy cycle*.

The modern theory of thermodynamics shows that as energy is consumed for work, the *quality* of that energy lowers and the energy can no longer be used for work; this degradation of the energy's quality is called an increase in 'entropy', which denotes a growing 'disorder' in matter. To rejuvenate that energy, it must be reconstituted into an ordered form. The ordering has no explanation in modern science, and the thermodynamic law only speaks about an ever-increasing entropy, which eventually results in the 'heat death' of the universe. The semantic view, however, gives us an understanding of this rejuvenation: energy *represents* information, and energy in a disordered state is abstract information from which details have been removed. This energy cannot be used to do work if work is done by information. To rejuvenate this energy, it must be reconstituted into useful information, so that it can be utilized again. This reordering is like filling the abstraction again with the details, which involves the addition of information. This explains why disordered states cannot be automatically ordered without more energy, because the additional energy is the information that organizes the abstract state.

The Sun, therefore, is not about to die after 4.6 billion years, the universe is not headed towards a heat death, and the Sun is not just one of the many stars in our universe. The key role of the Sun is in recycling the energy: i.e., converting it from a disordered to an ordered state. The Sun absorbs disordered matter from different planets and transforms it into ordered matter. This fact is recognized in modern times where rain water is considered better than ground water for watering plants, or growing crops. The reason is attributed to the ground water having become 'hard' and contaminated with impurities while the rain water is far purer. While these are not entirely inaccurate, they miss the key point that to create life, we need information, not just matter. This information is created and destroyed and has to be rejuvenated. The Sun has the crucial role in the universe to rejuvenate information in our habitat by which life is created. The nature of this rejuvenation is described in the next section.

The Transmigration of the Soul

The Vedas describe that the living beings reborn on the *bhūloka* come to these planets through rain, produced by objectifying the light of the Sun, are absorbed in the soil, which is then converted into the food that a father consumes. When the food is digested, the soul (originally present in the light, then in the water, and then in the earth) is carried to a mother's womb, where it is reborn into a type of living form. The body of the father has seven *dhātu* or types of materials in the body, of which the innermost material (the most essential part of the body), is called the *shukra dhātu*, which maintains the reproductive system. The successive stages of the digestion of the food, therefore, ultimately produces the reproductive tissue in which the soul to be reborn is transferred. When the mother conceives the child, the soul in the *shukra dhātu* is already present in the father's semen and it fertilizes the mother's egg. If the egg is fertilized, the soul is incarnated into a new body after conception. The entire process of the transmigration of the soul thus depends on the cycle of water, its absorption by the Sun, and its reinjection as rain and then its consumption by different types of living beings. The soul that enters a mother's womb depends on the type of food that the parents consume, so the purity of the parent's life is considered essential to procreate pious children.

The water that the Sun absorbs is not originally created by the Sun.

Rather, this water enters the universe via an 'orifice' at the top of the universe through which the water of the *Kārana Ocean* flows in. As we have seen earlier, this primordial water represents different types of material pleasures that a living being wishes to enjoy in the material creation, and this water is continuously flowing into the universe through a 'hole', implying that new kinds of material pleasures are being continuously injected in the universe, and new living beings are constantly entering in the material creation desiring these kinds of pleasures.

The water from the *Kārana Ocean* passes through the seven coverings of the universe, until it enters the 'water' layer above the *brahmanda*, which (as we have seen), represents a soul's *karma*. When the *guna* and the *karma* can be manifested, because the appropriate time for their manifestation has arrived, the soul leaves the water covering of the *brahmanda* and enters the universe to be born into a life form.

From there, the water passes through *Viṣṇuloka* at the top of the universe, where it washes Lord *Viṣṇu*'s feet, forming what is then called the *ākāsh ganga* (or the Celestial Ganges) which traverses the various higher planetary systems. The water then rains on top of the *Sumeru Mountain*, divides into four main rivers in the four cardinal directions (and many rivulets), and drips down the sides of the *Sumeru Mountain*, eventually reaching the *bhūloka* where the rivers become parts of the structure of the *Jambudvīpa*. When the water reaches *Jambudvīpa*, it first falls into *Ilāvṛta-varṣa*, which as we have seen, is the realm of Lord *Śiva*. The *Purāna* describe how this celestial water was held in the matted locks of Lord *Siva*[2] after its descent into the *bhūloka*, who then released it for the rest of the *Jambudvīpa* by dividing it into many rivers.

The descent of the Celestial Ganges onto the *bhūloka* means that prior to this descent living beings entering the universe could have only been born in the higher planetary systems (including the planet of Lord *Viṣṇu* at the top of the universe, where they would have served the feet of Lord *Viṣṇu*), although never lower than the *svargaloka,* after which they may have descended into the lower planetary systems, or gone higher up. Following this descent, the living beings can potentially enter the universe directly into the *bhūloka* and even the lower planetary systems, since this water also goes to the lower planetary systems. There are hence two paths for the living entity to go to the different planets in the universe: (1) through the rays of the Sun, and (2) through the water of the different rivers. Since the water of the Ganges flows 'downwards' (from higher to lower planetary systems), the descent into lower planets can be easily achieved by following the path of this water flow.

Of course, the living entities can also go to the higher planets, governed by the Sun evaporating the water of the Ganges, and releasing it as rain in the upstream part of the same river. Many Hindus thus worship the Sun while standing in the Ganges waters even today, by chanting the *Gāyatrī mantra*, which glorifies the Sun. Similarly, in the Vedic tradition, after a living body dies, the ashes are immersed in the water of the Ganga. These rituals might appear inexplicable today, but they are based on a deep understanding of the process of the soul's transmigration.

After entering the *Ilāvṛta-varṣa*, the rivers flow in different directions to the other *varṣa*, eventually falling into the salt water ocean around the *Jambudvīpa*. From there, this water goes to the six successive islands and oceans, thus carrying the living being through different parts of the universe, where they are born into many living forms. When the living being dies, the soul is again carried to the water, from where it is absorbed by the Sun, and then released back into the different planetary systems through rain, based on the process just described above.

The Sun has a central role in this transmigration process because the light of the Sun is sent to all parts of the cosmos, and even the stars and planets only 'reflect' the light of the Sun, which means that they originally receive the light from the Sun[3]. When a living being dies, the soul is carried to a different part of the cosmos by the Sun absorbing this light, converting it to air, transmitting this air to other parts of the cosmos, where it is reconverted back to light, and then to water, carrying the soul to a new body. The Vedas state that the living being is carried by *prāna* and the gross element of air. The *prāna* sustains the subtle body's connection to the gross body, which in this case comprises simply of air. In this form, it is possible to touch the living being, although not see it. When some living beings report having out of body experiences, they are being carried out of the body in another type of gross body comprised only of air. Sometimes, these forms of air have also been photographed, i.e., converted into a visible form by adding light information into it.

The living beings who die during *Uttarāyaṇa* are said to rise to a higher life form, while those dying during *Dakshināyana* enter a lower type of life form. In the case of humans, those dying in the *Uttarāyaṇa* phase are said to enter the realm of demigods, while those dying during the *Dakshināyana* phase enter the realm of demons. The light of the Sun, and its behavior during the different phases of the year, is therefore also the controller of the soul's reincarnation into different kinds of living forms. This reincarnation depends on the understanding of how matter exists as subtle and gross information, and the soul is carried to different parts of the cosmos through the energy absorbed by the Sun.

The Sun is vertically in the middle of the *loka* realm in Vedic cosmology. The Sun's centrality is given in that it absorbs and distributes light throughout the cosmos, which has a central role in the creation of life. In effect, the Sun is like the central square in a city through which every part of the city can be reached, and the living being must pass through the Sun in the process of being reborn into a different form.

The Leaky Bucket

The water that falls from the *Kārana Ocean* gradually objectifies into grosser forms, similar to how the lower planetary systems are objectifications of the higher systems. It becomes the Celestial Ganga after descending fr om the *Viṣṇu loka* and in this form it passes through the upper planetary systems. It then enters the *bhūloka* where it is divided into many rivers, which fall into the oceans, and again become rivers for the successive *dvīpa* in the *bhūloka* (the term *dvīpa* means surrounded on two sides). The Ganga also enters the lower planetary systems where it is called *Bhogavati* (the term *bhoga* signifying the predomination of sensual pleasure in these places). Similarly, Ganga also goes to the hellish planets where it is called *Vaitarani*. Eventually, this water exits the universe through an orifice at the bottom, just as it had entered through an orifice at the top. The universe is therefore just like a leaky bucket that is half-full, and into which the water is constantly being poured at the same rate at which the bucket is leaking out from the bucket.

The rate at which water flows in and out of this bucket decides the rate of time flow in the universe; a faster water flow indicates more events transpiring in a given duration. We have seen how the universes have different sizes and are governed by a *Brahma* with a different number of heads, which then represent a different number of subdivisions of space. Similar kinds of subdivisions of time must also exist in these universes. However, regardless of how big or small the universe is, all these universes are created and destroyed at the same time, aligning with the breathing of *Kāraṇodakaśāyī Viṣṇu*. Therefore, whether the universe is big or small, it exists for the same duration, and the lifetime of Lord *Brahma* in different universes is the same duration regardless of how time is divided into parts. Effectively, in the bigger universe, there will be more hours in a day, more days in a month, more months in a year, and even more years in a lifetime, than the smaller universe. However, the total duration for which each of the universe lives is still the same.

The consequence of this fact is that time must flow faster in a bigger universe; i.e., there must be more clock ticks in the same duration in a larger universe than in a smaller universe, although the duration of each tick gets smaller in the bigger universe, such that all universes last the same duration. The larger universe must thus squeeze more events within the same duration than a smaller universe. We can say that the water through a larger universe flows faster, and the experiences are thus changing faster, and therefore one can encounter more experiences in the same duration. The bigger universe is therefore a bigger leaky bucket in the sense that its input and output of water is much faster.

> *According to Śrīla Jīva Gosvāmī, all the universes are clustered together up and down, and each and every one of them is separately sevenfold-covered. The watery portion is beyond the sevenfold coverings, and each covering is ten times more expansive than the previous covering. [Purport to SB 2.2.28]*

Based on the above, we can envision the entire material creation as the moving hand of a clock as shown in Figure-41. All the universes are stacked linearly, and their sizes grow gradually. The size of the universe is the basis of counting in these universes, which is the position of the universe on the moving clock hand. That is, the farther out the universe from the center, the larger is its position and therefore larger is the basis of counting in this universe, and correspondingly this universe has a greater number of divisions in space and time. However, like the moving hand of a clock sweeps the same duration of time, even though the outer parts of the hand move faster, similarly, all these universes are also moving at different rates, but they are sweeping the same duration in time. Effectively, all the universes cover a revolution in the same duration, although the outer and larger universes sweep more distance in the pleasure ocean, and therefore more water from this ocean must enter and exit the universe. The time in the farther universe therefore appears to go much faster, but due to a higher number of time divisions, this time is merely a larger number of clock ticks rather than a larger duration.

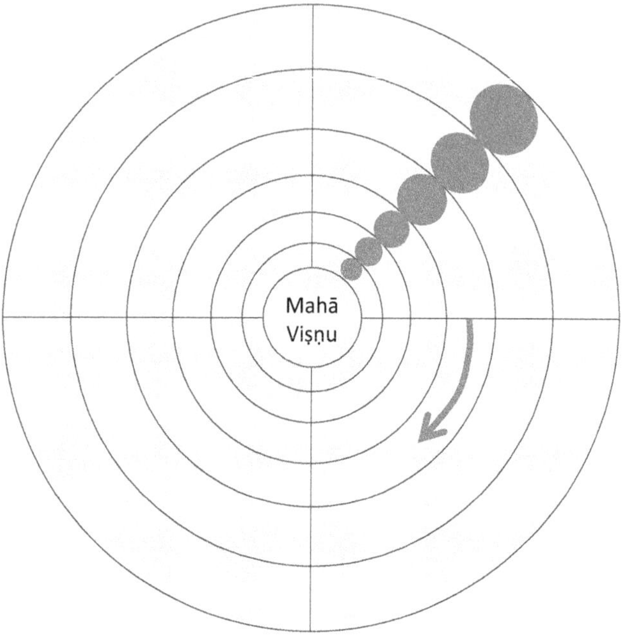

Figure-41 The Structure of the Material Creation

All these universes are circumambulating *Mahā Viṣṇu* in the center of the material creation, like pilgrims go around the deity in a temple. Each of these universes is a living body whose soul is *Garbhodakaśāyi Viṣṇu* and they worship *Mahā Viṣṇu* even in the material creation by going around His place. They begin and end the circumambulating at the same time, which coincides with the creation and annihilation of the material creation. During their existence, all the universes traverse the entire pleasure ocean created by *Mahā Viṣṇu* and once this traversal is over, the material creation is annihilated. The entire process of material creation and annihilation is a single clock tick for *Mahā Viṣṇu*, and the Vedas describe that this period of existence corresponds to His single breath.

The water of Ganga that passes through the different planets in the universe is the same, at the subtle level, as the water that exists in the *causal ocean*. However, as this water traverses the different parts of the universe, it is covered by grosser levels of material energy and therefore manifests in different ways. In one sense, the river Ganga is the same everywhere, and in another sense, the river appears quite different in the different places. As *Vaishnava ācharyās* have described, all living beings in this cosmos enjoy eating, sleeping, mating, and defending, although these may be performed by the senses, mind, intellect, ego, or morality. The *expression* of these activities can be subtle or gross, but the *pleasure* derived from these activities remains the same. In other words, it doesn't matter whether you have sex with the body or the mind; the pleasure of sex is *qualitatively* the same (the quantity and expression of this pleasure may differ). Of course, to even see that the pleasure is the same, one must have developed the ability to enjoy with different kinds of senses. For instance, for one whose mind isn't well developed, sex with the mind may appear not as pleasing as the sex with the body, or vice versa. Assuming that the method of enjoying has been mastered, the pleasure through that method is identical. The pleasure attained by an animal, human, demon, or demigod, from a spiritual viewpoint, is therefore the same, as long as these beings are engaged in eating, sleeping, mating, and defending.

Similarly, renouncing sense pleasures by the gross body, while dreaming and thinking about them in the mind, or sublimating the desire for sex into other activities such as sport, is not true renunciation. Sex and sport may appear to be different from a gross vision, but they are driven by an underlying desire which is very similar, and sometimes the same. In the same way, the river Ganga flowing through the different planetary systems in the universe is the same river of pleasure types, although depending on which planet it passes through, the pleasure is manifested differently, such as the difference between sex and sport.

Every living being in a given universe aspires for the same kind of pleasure, and some of them get it while others don't, depending on the extent to which this pleasure is covered up by the *prakriti* and *karma*. When one is freed from *guna* and *karma* the pleasure is never ending. Similarly, the various living beings are only enjoying the different subtle and gross manifestations of the same qualitative pleasure, although they imagine it is a different kind of pleasure. Thus, both demigods and demons think they are superior to each other, because they have different manifestations and ways of enjoying, although that enjoyment is built upon the same kind of pleasure. In that sense the river Ganga that flows through the universe is the same river everywhere, although it just appears differently to everyone, based on their method of perception.

The key point is that we should not view the river Ganga, and her numerous tributaries, merely as water bodies in which we can take bath or use for watering crops. The river is actually the symbol of material pleasure, as it was originally produced as the sweat of Lord *Mahā Viṣṇu*. It is not perfectly spiritual because it represents His austerity. Nevertheless, it is, in the most subtle form, an emanation from the body of Lord *Mahā Viṣṇu*, and by taking bath in the Ganga, one can purify oneself from the layers of *guna* and *karma* that have covered us in the universe.

The Rotation of the Sisumāra

In the previous chapter, I described two kinds of time (internal and external), which pertained to the evolution of the universe events and that of the living beings. The time in the universe has several components, but the most basic component is the clockwise motion of the zodiac. Based on the information about the rotation of universes, it is possible to see the relationship between the galactic and the zodiac motions. To develop this understanding, we need to bear two things in mind: (1) the zodiac is a wheel on which the water of the Ganga is said to flow, and (2) that the water of the Ganga flows from the top to the bottom of the universe. These two motions can be correlated if the wheel of the zodiac is viewed as a *fan* on which the water falls and drives the fan quite like a water turbine is driven by the motion of water falling on its blades. An ordinary propeller motor—such as that in the case of a boat—drives the boat forward, and we can invert the process such that the motor becomes a turbine. The water falling on the blades of the fan would then drive the rotation of the flan blades, rather than the fan rotation driving the motion of water.

Figure-42 Fan Blades Driven by Fluid Flow

Figure-42 illustrates a fan. We can see that it has the structure of a lotus, which is a flat representation of a sphere, as we have previously discussed. In the universe, the rotating zodiac is the fan, which produces the 'wind' which then drags the other luminaries such as the Sun and causes the periodic appearance and disappearance of phenomena on all the planetary systems, *as if* these planetary systems were also rotating. The fan's rotation can be seen as being caused by the flow of water perpendicular to the fan's surface, when the water's inflow into the universe is caused by the universe's rotation in the causal ocean.

The criterion for the falling water to cause the fan's motion is that some parts of the fan are 'higher' than the others, which creates an 'incline' on which the water can 'push' the blades of the fan clockwise. To achieve the 'higher' and 'lower' position of blades, the blades in the celestial zodiac would require the alternate star-signs to be conceptually more abstract, which would then 'raise' them in the vertical dimension, since higher and lower in the vertical dimension represent abstraction. In the next chapter we will see how the alternate signs are indeed higher and lower and represent the flow of *prāna* in two alternating paths.

The fan's rotation represents sidereal time, and this motion can be understood as being caused by the movement of the universe in the causal ocean which forces the water into the universe and causes the living beings to enjoy. The universe's rotation impels the living beings to develop new desires, while the rotation of the wheel manifests the basis of the other kinds of events in the universe. These can appear unrelated, although they are produced from a single cause: the universe's rotation. The changes caused within the universe are influenced by the time outside the universe, although to see this connection, we must understand the role played by causal water in transforming the rotation of the universe into the rotation of the wheel of time inside the universe. With the above understanding, each universe is like a boat dragged in an ocean, such that the fan in this boat is rotated by the boat's motion, and this rotation generates the energy that in turn powers the life in the boat.

While all universes follow the same basic principle, the number of fan blades in each universe can differ. A fan with 15 blades, for instance, would create 15 hours in a day instead of 12, and a 15-fold division of space instead of a 12-fold division, thereby altering the space-time structure. Similarly, the fans can rotate faster or slower, such that the duration of 15 'hours' in a different universe can be equal to, less than, or greater than, the duration of 12 hours, in our universe. Accordingly, the living beings in the other universes may consider themselves living for greater or fewer number of years, with longer or shorter days, although the lifetime of the universe measured from outside the universe (i.e., from the perspective of *Mahā Viṣṇu*) remains identical for all universes.

It should be remembered that while we have described the rotation of the *Sisumāra* in analogy to the motion of a fan rotating due to falling water, the causality in this process is not physical but semantic, because the water represents pleasure, and the spatial divisions represent meanings. We aren't therefore speaking about the 'force' of ordinary water causing the motion of a physical fan, but how shifts in the type of desires change the type of meanings. The mechanism involved in the rotation of the space is therefore quite different from that of motion of fan, although it is possible to understand the spatial motion analogously.

The Counterclockwise Rotation

Of course, this description of the rotation of the zodiac by itself is inadequate to understand the passing of time because the planets, as earlier discussed, are moving in the opposite direction to the motion of the zodiac. The calendar times—both solar and lunar—depend on the motion of the planets rather than that of the zodiac. Therefore, if the water is falling from top to bottom, and causing the zodiac to move clockwise, there must be another 'force' that is moving bottom to top, and causing the planets to move counterclockwise, superimposed with the zodiac motion. This additional force is Lord *Ananta* above the *Garbhodaka Ocean*. He is the cause of event time in the universe, and as we have seen above, this time is measured by the motion of the planets rather than the motion of the zodiac. The planets are dragged by the motion of the zodiac, but they also have their own motions. In fact, the other planets are also dragged by the Sun's motion. Nevertheless, all planets are moving at the same speed, although they have different radii orbits. The force driving the counterclockwise motion of the planets therefore moves them at a constant speed, resulting in different rotations per *chaturyugi*.

To see the significance of the counterclockwise motion, we must recall that the internal time controls desires, but these desires are constrained by *karma*. If the internal time was the only time, then it would manifest the *karma* that represents our abilities, and our desires would only be constrained by our abilities. If we have the abilities, and we perform the necessary actions, the results of those actions would be guaranteed, since the outcomes would depend only on our ability. In this case, the only reason for our desires to be frustrated *after* we have performed our actions would be someone overturning what we had done, and the reasons for our failures would then be attributed to others.

This is not how Vedic philosophy actually describes natural causality. Even if someone else frustrates our desires, after we have done the due diligence, the cause of the frustration is still *our karma*. Thus, both success and failure of endeavors is attributed to the individual actor, not to actions of others. Furthermore, there is a second type of *karma* which manifests even though we don't desire it. For instance, no one desires to be mistreated or misjudged. But these things happen automatically. If causality was limited to internal time, this kind of *karma* would never manifest as we would never desire such things.

The causality based on internal time alone thus proves inadequate for this reason too.

To address the above issues, we need another time—the external time—which manifests the *karma* independent of the desires of the recipient, although they can be someone else's desires. For instance, if my *karma* entails mistreatment, then someone will desire to mistreat me, although I won't. The desire to mistreat is caused by internal time, while the fulfillment of that desire is caused by external time. Both the above issues in moral causality are addressed by a second type of time. For instance, when we have performed our duties, the results of those actions may not be obtained due to someone else's actions, although we cannot blame those individuals as the cause of our failures. We must rather recognize that these failures are the result of our own *karma*, the manifestation of which does not depend on our desires, although it can be realized through someone else's desire. We can therefore choose to act, but we cannot choose the outcomes, because those depend on *karma*, the manifestation of which is not in our control. Similarly, when we undergo situations that we haven't desired or anticipated previously, they too are caused by external time. Thus, mistreatment or misjudgment by other people are caused by external time, without regard to our desires.

Thus, we can distinguish between two kinds of *karma*: (1) that which exists as abilities in us, and (2) that which appears as the destiny of living beings. The former type of *karma* is under the control of our desires, and we can choose not to act even though we can. The latter type of *karma* is not under the control of our desires, and it will act, regardless of our desire. Both kinds of *karma* are manifest by external time, although the *karma* as abilities can be controlled by our free will. Thus, Lord *Saṅkarṣaṇa* impels us to desire, while Lord *Ananta* delivers the results of *karma.* We can control the *karma* created as abilities, but we cannot avoid the results of involuntary *karma* or the abilities in other individuals.

The internal and external times are two sides of a coin, because when I'm acting voluntarily, I can be producing the outcomes that are involuntary for the others. Similarly, if I'm receiving something involuntarily, it is caused by the voluntary actions of the others. Regardless of whether the events are caused voluntarily or involuntarily, the events are always attributed to the *karma* of the individual involved in that activity. Thus, whether I do something, or I'm at the receiving end of the actions performed by another person, it is my *karma* that causes it.

The distinction between internal and external times can be understood if the internal time is seen as manifesting the *guna*, while the external time is seen as manifesting the *karma*. The creation of desires represents 'forward' time while the creation of consequences represents 'backward' time. The present moment is created as the outcome of these two opposite directions in time. The forward time is given by the clockwise motion of the zodiac which defines our *prakriti* or *guna*, and when a soul is born, his Ascendant in the astrological chart along with the position of the 12 houses is fixed. The time of birth also fixes the *daśā* (more on this later in the book) which propels the soul forward in the sense that as time passes, different desires will manifest. The backward movement is represented by the counterclockwise motion of the planets, which controls *karma* manifestation and how much success or failure a living being will achieve with regard to his desires in the different phases of his life.

Most modern Vedic astrologers consider the zodiac fixed, and calculate only the planet motion, *relative* to the zodiac: both solar and lunar calendars are based on the relative motion of the planets, although the zodiac is not fixed in Vedic astronomy. The zodiac drags the planets clockwise, while the planets move counterclockwise. If we are on the zodiac, then we see the counterclockwise motions of the planets, but if we are outside the zodiac, then we see only the *slower* clockwise motion of planets. Both views are partially inaccurate, because there are two motions—clockwise and counterclockwise—and they must be combined for the total effect. Since the zodiac moves faster than the planets, the forward movement of time appears dominant and we think that we are going forward in time. However, if we have to understand *karma* and how it manifests due to the motion of planets, then we have to take into account the backward time as well. In short, Lord *Saṅkarṣaṇa* is the forward time and causes changes to our *guna*, while *Kṣīrodakaśāyī Viṣṇu* is backward time and manifests our *karma* by manifesting the events in the universe.

The forward time denotes what we desire, and backward time

denotes our destiny. We count forward seeking goals in life, and we count backwards to destiny. The forward and backward counting is two clocks moving in opposite directions: the clockwise motion is the evolution of desires under the control of Lord *Saṅkarṣaṇa* and the backward time is given by the counterclockwise motion of the planets under the control of *Kṣīrodakaśāyī Viṣṇu*. The mystery of the cosmos is apparent, when this cosmos is understood as being produced due to *guna* and *karma*.

The events produced by Lord *Ananta* do not fix the participants, which are fixed by *Kṣīrodakaśāyī Viṣṇu* or Lord *Aniruddha*. If, however, no such participant exists, then Lord *Aniruddha* Himself incarnates into a role. Thus, all incarnations of God in the universe occur through Lord *Aniruddha*. Our *karma* is also delivered by Lord *Aniruddha*, who ensures that our destiny is part of the cosmic destiny. We can think of these two forms of God as the director and producer of a movie. Lord *Ananta* is the director of the movie and He controls all the events in the universe. Lord *Aniruddha* is the movie's producer who identifies which actor will play which role. The show will go on even if there are no suitable actors, because the producer will Himself incarnate to play a role that cannot be enacted by any actor. Similarly, the producer can reshuffle the roles between the actors, if the need so arises, to keep the show going.

Vedic cosmology is a great science that weaves principles of matter, time, causality, consciousness, morality, and God into a single picture. This science is perfect, but our understanding is imperfect. As we develop our understanding, by studying under the guidance of an enlightened master, we can see the perfection even in this imperfect world.

9

The Theory of Language

The Supreme Lord Personality of Godhead is Himself this cosmos, and still He is aloof from it. From Him only has this cosmic manifestation emanated, in Him it rests, and unto Him it enters after annihilation. Your good self knows all about this. I have given only a synopsis.

— *Śrimad Bhāgavatam* 1.5.20

The Universal Mind-Body Divide

The above description of Vedic astronomy is by no means exhaustive. Texts such as the *Surya Siddhānta* describe many details about the planets, which I will not cover here as these descriptions represent the *phenomenology* of planetary observations, and methods to *derive* these phenomena using formulae, geometry, and associated numerical calculations. While these calculations and methods are useful practical utilities in determining the exact locations of planets, the times at which planets would appear and disappear at a certain place on Earth, beyond a certain point addition of these details only refine the cosmological *model* while leaving the *theory* that explains why precisely these methods are to be used unclear. Therefore, rather than elaborating the cosmic *model* in even greater detail, I will now turn to describing the *theory* that can be used to understand this model. As we have previously discussed, the models in science must be explained by theories: i.e., the theory must explain why we use a particular model and not a different model. The models may be practically useful, and empirically verifiable, but unless the theory can explain and predict the model, there is a lot left unanswered.

Some difficulties arise in the understanding of Vedic cosmology when the *Sisumāra* planetary system is taken into account. Why, for instance, do we count only seven planetary systems, when the *Sisumāra* planetary system also exists, and is, in fact, the 4th planetary system from *bhū-mandala*? The difficulties are also created when in several places, the universe is described as comprising only three "worlds": *bhūloka*, *bhuvarloka*, and *svargaloka*. What about the remaining four planetary systems, even if we don't count the *Sisumāra* planetary system? Why are these sometimes not counted as part of the overall universe?

This requires us to recall that the sevenfold division of the upper planetary systems represents the seven layers of matter: *mahattattva*, ego, intelligence, mind, senses, sensations, and sense objects. The *bhūloka* is the planetary system for sense objects, *bhuvarloka* for sensations, and *svargaloka* for senses. Together these three planetary systems constitute the manifest "body" of the universe. The lower planetary systems are greater details or elaborations of this "body" which is experienced by the demons but not by earthly beings or by the demigods in the *bhuvarloka* or *svargaloka*. When faced with such details, our senses will discard them as "noise" rather than "information" because we cannot decode the intricate modifications to abstractions. The universe is described as three worlds when the description concerns the "body" of the universe.

Beyond this "body" there are four other planetary systems which correspond to mind, intelligence, ego, and morality. We might collectively term them as the "mind" of the universe, which is above the body because it is semantically more abstract. The "mind" and the "body" of the universe are joined by the *Sisumāra* planetary system, and in analogy to the mind and the body in a living body, this planetary system is representing the *prāna* or "life air" of the universe. As we have previously discussed, matter is divided into three categories: concepts, activities, and objects, which correspond to the three modes of nature. The subtle body of a living being (loosely called the "mind") predominates in *sattva-guna* or idea-like entities, the gross body (which we normally consider the "body" but which also includes the senses and sensations, beyond the organs) predominates in *tamo-guna* or thing-like entities, and a body of "activities" that lies between the gross and the subtle bodies predominates in *rajo-guna*. The body of activities is created by *prāna* and it connects the gross with the subtle body. In many places in Vedic literature, the *prāna* is also considered part of the gross body, and sometimes it is described as being part of the subtle body; these ways of aggregating the gross and subtle body parts aren't very important, so long as we can see what *prāna* does.

The four higher planetary systems (*maharloka, janaloka, tapaloka* and *satyaloka*) represent the subtle body of the universe. The three lower planetary systems (*bhūloka, bhuvarloka,* and *svargaloka*) represent the gross body of the universe. And the *Sisumāra* planetary system represents the "field" of activities that joins the gross and the subtle worlds. The role of *Sisumāra* thus becomes evident when seen in analogy to the construction of a living body. The role is that just as *prāna* translates the ideas in the mind into words that are sensually accessible, and then the words back into ideas, similarly, the *Sisumāra* connects the subtle and the gross realms in the universe. The subtle and the gross realms are distinct, and yet, the subtle realm can control the gross realm, quite like the mind can control the body, although the body has its own distinct existence.

Ideally, the upper planetary system should be counted as nine systems, including the *Viṣṇu Loka* representing pure consciousness, and *Sisumāra* representing *prāna* or the field of activities, rather than seven systems. Similarly, in the *bhū-mandala* system, there are nine divisions including the inner 7 oceans and islands, the 8th "golden land" and the 9th "diamond land", although seven of them are prominently described. The *Jambudvīpa* is similarly divided into nine *varṣa* (as we saw earlier) of which only the *Bhārata-varṣa* is said to be the place of performing activities, while the other 8 *varṣa* are for much higher enjoyments.

The key point is that the universe is also a mind-body-activity complex built from the three modes of nature, and parts of Vedic literature describe either the body, or the mind, or the *prāna* joining body and mind. All these are partial understandings. Only when all these tiers of systems together with a realm of pure consciousness in the universe are taken together do we get a complete understanding of the universal structure.

The correlation between *Sisumāra* and *prāna* in the body gives us new insights for understanding how the motion of planets and stars controls our lives: the insight is that the *Sisumāra* controls our *prāna* and thereby the expression of the mind into the body, quite like *prāna* converts meanings into words. We will see later how this *prāna* brings the *karma* of the living being from which the gross body is developed. The lower three planetary systems (*bhūloka*, *bhuvarloka*, and *svarga-loka*) can thus be said to be the body of the universe, also known as *vāk* in *Sāñkhya*, while the higher three the planetary systems (*janaloka*, *maharloka*, *tapaloka*, and *satyaloka*) can be called the mind of the universe, also known as *manas* in *Sāñkhya*. Together, the upper seven planetary systems represent the *manas*, *prāna*, and *vāk*, or concepts, activities, and things.

Since the *svargaloka* is below the *Sisumāra*, the demigods are also under the control of the *Sisumāra*. After all, they are part of the "body" of the universe, although more subtle than us. The planetary systems above the polestar are free of this control, because they constitute the "mind" of the universe. Therefore, when a *manavantara* (described later in this book) expires, everything from the bottom of the universe until the polestar is destroyed. Dhruva, a devotee of Lord *Viṣṇu*, lives on the polestar and his planet is not destroyed at the end of the *manav-antara*, along with other higher planetary systems such as *maharloka*, *janaloka*, *tapaloka* and *satyaloka*. All the planets are 'hooked' to the polestar through *prāna* and they move governed by the 'ropes of wind'. The end of the *manavantara* is in effect like the death of the body in which the subtle body is carried by the *prāna* to a new gross body. The beginning of a new *manavantara* is similarly like the childhood of a new born when a new gross body is developed based on the preexist-ing subtle body. The subtle body comprising mind, intelligence, and ego is also destroyed at the end of a *kalpa* (as we shall see later, a *kalpa* is the day of Lord Brahma) and only the realm of *satyaloka* compris-ing morality remains at the end of each day of Lord Brahma. Finally, even this realm of morality is destroyed at the end of the life of Lord Brahma (100 years of his life).

The universe is also a gross body which keeps dying and a new gross body is acquired at the end of a long period, carrying forward the *prāna* and the subtle body. The subtle body is produced from the principles of morality which change from one *kalpa* to another, and this subtle body is destroyed at the end of each *kalpa*. The polestar and the higher planetary systems, which represent the *prāna* and the subtle body, are preserved when the gross body is destroyed at the end of each *manavantara*. Thus, we might say that the universe's gross body is dead although the subtle body is alive. Similarly, the *mahat-tattva* or "contaminated consciousness" which is the realm of ideals based on material morals is preserved when the subtle body comprising of mind, intelligence, and ego is destroyed, at the end of each *kalpa*. The *Viṣṇu Loka* at the top of the universe is the "soul" of the universe, which never dies, and at the end of Lord Brahma's life, this soul is merged within the body of Lord *Mahā Viṣṇu*.

In Vedic cosmology, the top tiers of the universe down to *bhūloka* comprise the upper half of a form called the *virāta puruṣa* while the lower planetary systems are his legs and the hellish planets are his toes. This form is imaginary because the "head" of a material body is not morality, even though every system begins in some moral values which are the "root" of that system. As the "highest", most subtle, and abstract principles of the system, they can be called the "head" although this head is not like a real body that we can envision. The *virāta puruṣa* is thus a conceptualization of the universe in analogy to a system that has a head and a toe, and the various parts of the universe are described analogously.

Sisumāra and the Field of Activities

We previously noted that the 28 lunar mansions, the 12 zodiac signs of the Sun, the 7 stars of the *saptarishi*, and the polestar together constitute 48 stars. With the Sun and the Moon, which are used to calculate time, there are 50 key luminaries. There are additionally 7 other planets, namely, Mercury, Venus, Mars, Jupiter, Saturn, *Rāhu*, and *Ketu*. We also discussed in the previous section how the *Sisumāra* should be viewed as the field of activities which translates the meanings, judgments, intents, and morals into the behaviors of all the lower planetary systems. Taken in this way, it is possible to unify the study of *prāna* in the living body as given in the *yoga-sutras* with the astrological entities as described above, thus creating an understanding of why the system of luminaries exists, what it does, its internal structure, and its relation to the rest of the universal system. Such an understanding can then be viewed as a *theory* of the cosmos in addition to its *model*. Table 15 illustrates the relationship between the 12 signs of the zodiac and the 7 chakras in the *yoga* system. The signs alternate between the two sides like how *prāna* flows from one side to another as shown in Figure-43. This is important because, for the falling water of the Celestial Ganges to cause the rotation of the zodiac, there needs to be an 'incline' on which this water can 'push' the zodiac. The alternate positions of the zodiac signs create this conceptual 'incline', implying that the *prāna* is ultimately under the control of time.

Left Sign	Chakra Name	Planet Name	Right Sign
	Sahasrāra	Sun	
Aquarius	Ajna	Mercury	Pisces
Sagittarius	Viśuddha	Venus	Capricorn
Libra	Anahata	Moon	Scorpio
Leo	Manipura	Mars	Virgo
Gemini	Svadhisthāna	Jupiter	Cancer
Aries	Mulādhāra	Saturn	Taurus

Table 15: Chakras and the Luminaries

Yoga texts describe the presence of 72,000 'channels' called *nādi* in which the *prāna* flows through the body. Of these, there are three main channels called *idā* (which represents the body), *pingalā* (which represents the activities), and *sushumnā* (which represents the mind). This division of *prāna* may appear confusing since we already said that *prāna* is separate from the body and the mind, and so it helps to cast this division in a more modern terminology. The *sushumnā* is a representation of the mind because it carries the impulses of the somatic nervous system, to and from the senses of perception and action; the mind is the controller of the senses because it extracts the meanings from the sensations, and in that sense the activity of the *sushumnā* is said to be a representation of the mind even though it is a flow of the *prāna.* Similarly, *idā* carries the emergency "fight or flight" impulses to and from the various parts of the body, and it is associated with the body; this function is called *sympathetic nervous system* in modern physiology. The *pingalā* carries the force to perform the functions like digestion, circulation, assimilation, elimination, and expression, and it is thus the carrier of *prāna*; this is called the *parasympathetic nervous system* in physiology. The fact is that all three are *prāna* because they drive the different functions in the body, and often all three are present in the same part of the body. For instance, our hands and legs are involved in fight or flight, in common expression such as music or painting, and in assimilating and eliminating. The division of *prāna* into *idā, pingalā* and *sushumnā* controls the various types of functions.

The key *nādi* responsible for the *prāna* is thus *pingalā. Idā* connects these activities to the body, while *sushumnā* connects them into the mind, in the sense that if the parasympathetic functions are stopped, then other somatic and sympathetic functions also cannot work. *Idā* originates on the right, *pingalā* originates on the left, and *sushumnā* lies in the middle. Thereafter, the *idā* and *pingalā* crossover to the opposite side at every *chakra* as shown in Figure-43. Only 6 *chakras* are involved in this process, and the 7th *chakra* called the *sahasrāra* is "above" the flow of *prāna.*

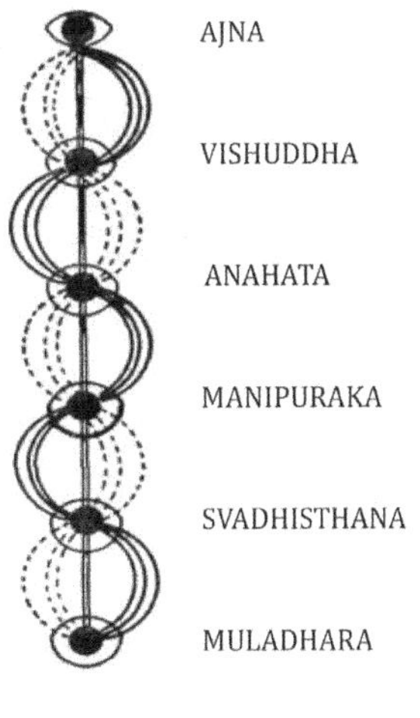

Figure-43 The Alternating Flow of Prāna

The *Śrīmad Bhāgavatam* also establishes the relationship between the left and right sides of the *Sisumāra* and the 28 *Nakṣatra*, although the relationship is different than the 12 signs of the zodiac because the alternating behavior of the 12 signs is absent in the *Nakṣatra*. This description entails that the 14 signs on the right have *idā* flowing through them, while the 14 signs on the left have *pingalā* flowing through them. This difference arises because the 12 zodiac signs are solar mansions while the 28 *Nakṣatra* are lunar mansions. I will return to this distinction after we have discussed the differences between the Moon and the Sun.

> *The coiled body of the Śiśumāra-cakra turns toward its right side, on which the fourteen constellations from Abhijit to Punarvasu are located. On its left side are the fourteen stars from Puṣyā to Uttarāṣāḍhā. Thus, its body is balanced because its sides are occupied by an equal number of stars. [SB 5.23.5]*

The relationship between the various star signs, and the *chakras* in the living body helps us see that these star signs and planets are not merely in the outer space, but they are also in our body because the *types* indicated by the planets and star signs are in our body too. The *Sisumāra* system is also modeled as the body of a dolphin, and it is said to be coiled in the sense that it moves cyclically. This relationship between our body and the cosmic system of time forms the basis on which we can study the properties of the cosmic system in analogy to the study of *prāna* in a living being. That is, like how the *Sisumāra* rotates in time, similarly, the *prāna* is also circulating through our bodies. The zodiac rotation defines a pattern according to which our lives must be molded; for instance, the passing of seasons, the day and the night, etc. are produced by the effect of the *Sisumāra*, which then effects the working of the living body.

Luminaries and the Sanskrit Language

A profound understanding of the relationship between the living bodies and the cosmic system can be established if we recognize that each *chakra* is said to represent a different set of sounds given in the Sanskrit alphabet, and these sounds too form a lotus-shaped space. As we have seen previously, the lotus structure is synonymous with a semantic space formulation because the center of the lotus represents the origin or the abstract concept from which the petals of that lotus are produced while the petals of the lotus denote different *types* of division of the abstraction. Effectively, the abstraction of the space is *subdivided* into many types by adding the information denoted by those types. Each *chakra* therefore denotes a type, similar to the types represented by the seven planets. Furthermore, each such type is further divided into subtypes by the addition of information denoted by the 50 alphabets of the Sanskrit language. The petals on the seven lotuses vary. *Mulādhāra*, *Svadhisthāna*, *Manipura*, *Anahata*, *Viśuddha* and *Ajna chakras* have 4, 6, 10, 12, 16, and 2 petals, respectively, each of which is also denoted by a particular Sanskrit letter, and the 50 Sanskrit letters are present on the 50 petals.

It is said that when the *kundalini* is not awakened, the petals on the lotuses "hang downwards" and then when the *kundalini* is awakened, the petals are "turned upwards". From what we have discussed previously about the lotus structure, this is not difficult to understand now: the upward and downward direction represents the shift in origin and end of the space. When the petals are pointing upwards, the abstraction is the origin of the space, and when the petals are hanging downwards, the abstraction is the end of the space. In the upward state, we understand that the material world is created from ideas, and in the downward state we believe that the ideas are created from matter. When the lotus is turned upwards, and the *kundalini* begins to rise, we rise above the material phenomena and seek their origin. Conversely, when the lotus is turned downwards, we think that matter is the origin of all higher "epiphenomena".

Modern science can be viewed as seeking the most basic axioms of the material world, which in the materialistic view, can be denoted by the 4 symbols found on the lowest *chakra* called *Mulādhāra*. In modern science, for instance, we seek the fundamental properties of nature, which are described as the properties of space and time[1]. The petals of the *Mulādhāra* (and other lotuses) are also dimensions of a conceptual space, and these petals can thus be viewed as fundamental properties or concepts in terms of which the phenomena of that level must be described.

Of course, since *Mulādhāra* is not the only *chakra*, even if science were to be in possession of the four key concepts present in *Mulādhāra*, it would still not be able to explain the phenomena manifesting at the higher levels. However, if an understanding of the four concepts in *Mulādhāra* is developed in science, it will open the doors to the higher conceptual spaces. A proper knowledge of the space of gross material phenomena can thus be compared to the lotus turning upwards and initiating the rise of *kundalini*. Since *Mulādhāra* denotes the *bhūloka*, a proper knowledge of the present material world would open the doors to the higher planetary systems, where those who have acquired this understanding can go to *bhuvarloka*. As they understand the working of the *bhuvarloka*, then can go to *svargaloka*, and so forth. The gradual process of *kundalini* rising is also the process of knowledge advancement.

The rising of the *kundalini* toggles the origin and the end of the space denoted in each of the *chakras*. That is, as the *kundalini* rises, one begins to understand that the new *chakra* is the foundation of the previously discovered *chakras*. This toggling can be seen as the conversion of the phase of "darkness" into the phase "light" (similar to the changes in the seasons of winter and summer on Earth) and the rising of the *kundalini* therefore makes the petals "visible" whereas they previously lay "invisible".

It is noteworthy that this identity between the *chakras* and the planetary systems is not physical but semantic. That is, the seven *chakras* are like the *types* represented by the seven upper planetary systems. The number of alphabets seen in each of the *chakra* symbolizes the essential ideas from which the higher planetary systems are created. By identifying the *chakras* with the planetary systems, therefore, we can understand how the different planetary systems differ in terms of their concepts, activities, and things. Of course, since the *chakra* exists in our body even in this world, the concepts, activities, and things found in higher planets are also present in a subtle form in our body, and by understanding these forms, we can therefore visualize the life in those planets. The mapping between planetary systems and *chakras* is shown in Table 16. This mapping should be seen semantically rather than physically; the *chakras* in a body are symbols of the *types* existing in the higher planetary systems.

Chakra Name	Loka Name
Sahasrāra	Satyaloka
Ajna	Tapaloka
Viśuddha	Janaloka
Anahata	Maharloka
Manipura	Svargaloka
Svadhisthāna	Bhuvarloka
Mulādhāra	Bhūloka

Table 16: The Planetary System to Chakra Mapping

The *Tantra* literature describe that the 50 letters of Sanskrit are worn as a garland by Goddess *Kāli* and those practicing the *Tantra* methods to attain a rising *kundalini* therefore worship and meditate on this form of God's *śakti*. The mapping between the *chakras*, the petals of their lotuses, and the alphabets of the Sanskrit language are shown in Figure-44. All these alphabets are different kinds of *śakti* that man ifest in different types of activities. The 50 key luminaries (28 lunar signs, 12 solar signs, 7 stars in the *saptarishi*, the polestar, the Sun and the Moon) are representations of the 50 letters of Sanskrit. Like the luminaries are different types, similarly, the alphabets are representations of different types. Those who have perfected yoga perceive the alphabets to be of different colors in their mystical trance. The alphabets are actually not colors, however, when the different energy types are converted into gross perception, their type differences appear as color differences.

Figure-44 The Sanskrit Alphabet in the Chakras

The purpose of establishing the above relationship between the cosmic system, the human body, and the manner in which this body works due to *prāna* is to illustrate that underlying the cosmic *model* is a *theory* that everything in the universe is a manifestation of *language* and to understand the cosmic structure, we must understand the nature of language prior. The material creation is described as *śabda brahman* or words, *artha brahman* or meanings, and their relationship established by *prāna*. The meanings here are the concepts, and the words are the things. Concepts are converted into words by *prāna* through a process of instantiation in which the word becomes a symbol of the concept. To create such a word, we must add information to the concept, which then details the concept, and if sufficient level of detailing has been achieved, then the concept becomes perceivable through the senses.

The objects that we see are also concepts; they are just more detailed symbols of the original idea. The letters of Sanskrit can denote the concept, the process of detailing by *prāna* or the symbol or word produced by that detailing. As we have seen before, these are respectively the three modes of nature, which are also called *manas*, *prāna* and *vāk*. The succession of these three modes creates the hierarchical tree structure in which abstract ideas are converted into symbols of those ideas, which are then further detailed. The things that we perceive with our senses are therefore abstract ideas that have undergone numerous stages of detailing. To know their true nature, we don't just have to perceive them through our senses, but also through the mind, intellect, ego, and the moral sense. Underlying this hierarchy of detailing, and the three modes of nature which construct the semantic tree, are the elementary memes which are being detailed. These memes are represented by the alphabets of Sanskrit.

Meanings and Sound Vibrations

It is noteworthy here that the alphabets of Sanskrit are unlike the alphabets of other languages such as English because the Sanskrit alphabets are *phonemes*. In English, by contrast, multiple alphabets must be combined to produce a phoneme. The first consonant in Sanskrit is the sound *ka* as used in cat, car, corporation, etc. which comprises of two letters 'k' and 'a', but is generally being written as 'c' which becomes inconsistent when 'c' is used to denote another phenome called 'cha' as in chair, chance, choice, etc. The idiosyncrasies of English are well-known, and they begin in the arbitrary manner in which the relationship between alphabets and phonemes is established. This idiosyncrasy does not exist in Sanskrit and the language is spoken exactly as it is written.

Through studies in phonosemantics[2], it has been established that the meaning in language comes not from how things are written but from how they are spoken. The famous Bouba-Kiki effect[3] is an illustration of this fact where two seemingly meaningless words (Bouba and Kiki) can be associated with two kinds of forms: Bouba with a round and smooth shape, and Kiki with an angular and jagged shape. The forms of sounds can be associated with meanings while the form of the text cannot be associated with meanings in any simple manner, given the idiosyncrasies of the modern written languages. Thus, when nature is described as the form of language, we must understand that this is a language in which sounds are themselves expressions of meanings. These meanings are refined by the application of context, and the same word acquires different meanings in different context, however, there is some native meaning to begin with. The context is the higher or the more abstract concept. For instance, when we refine the idea of a 'shirt' with the idea of 'black', then the context is 'shirt' and the refinement is 'black'. This refinement produces the idea of a 'black shirt'. The concept of 'black' already has a meaning, but it is given a context of the 'shirt' to create the notion that the blackness is being spoke of in the context of something that can be worn.

The hierarchy of the concepts present in the seven stages of *chakras* imply that the material world begins in abstract ideas which are gradually refined by more ideas, and as we descend the hierarchy of concepts, new concepts are discovered. These new concepts cannot be understood unless the higher concepts have been grasped, just like we cannot understand 'black' unless we grasp the notion of objects (like a 'shirt') of which the blackness is a property. In the hierarchical space-time, the higher nodes are objects, and the lower nodes are properties. Thus, for instance, redness is the property of the object called color. Similarly, color is a property of the object called sight; sight (and other senses) are properties of the object called meaning in the mind, which is a property of the object called judgment in the intellect, which is a property of the object called intent in the ego, which is a property of the object called morals.

This hierarchy of object-property relationship continues all the way to *Kṛṣṇa*, and everything ultimately is a property of *Kṛṣṇa*. However, to reach that conclusion scientifically, one would have to understand the deeper tiers of object-property relationships. Unless that hierarchy is traversed, the ultimate conclusion cannot be obtained, and we might prematurely terminate the hierarchy thinking perhaps that meanings or morals are the ultimate objects. Modern science, for instance, terminates the hierarchy at the gross material entities themselves, treating everything else to be an epiphenomenon, although we can't explain even the experience of sensations, let alone meanings or morals.

Language as the Foundation of Nature

To formulate a theory of nature, we must go beyond the models. In cosmology, the model comprises the various planetary systems that we have so far discussed. But to go beyond these models, we must understand how these models are only reflections of the properties inherent in language. Like modern cosmology tries to explain the structure of the universe based on gravitation and other physical theories, similarly, the Vedic philosophy explains everything based on the nature of language. The "atoms" of the universe are fundamental particles in modern science, and the "atoms" in Vedic philosophy are the alphabets of Sanskrit.

The universe is created as a hierarchical space-time, and nodes on this tree are produced from language. To describe these nodes, we must obtain an understanding of language. All forms of knowledge, thus, reduce to the study of language. The education of a *Brahmana* in ancient times laid an extraordinary emphasis on the study of language. The *Siddhānta śiromaṇi* (a classic text in Vedic astronomy) describes the preeminent role of language in the study and understanding of nature:

> *He who has acquired a perfect knowledge of language, which has been termed Vedavadana–i.e., the mouth of the Vedas and domicile of Sarasvati, may acquire the knowledge*

> *of every other science, nay of Vedas themselves. For this reason it is that none, but he who has acquired a thorough knowledge of language is qualified to undertake the study of other sciences. [Siddhānta Śiromaṇi 1.8]*

This emphasis on the study of language is largely missing in modern times. We don't expect mathematicians, physicists, or chemists to be experts in English, Greek, or Latin (although biologists and physiologists do undergo a course in Latin to grasp the body part nomenclature that originated earlier), and those interested in science generally steer clear of studying language arts and literature. The Vedic view emphasizes the study of language because everything ultimately reduces to the structure of language. If we know that structure, we can see aspects of that structure being reflected in every domain of scientific inquiry.

While the study of language is independent of cosmology, it is important to know why language is essential even for cosmology. As we get deeper into cosmology, we will begin to ask questions such as: Why are there 28 star signs? Why are there 12 signs in the zodiac? Why are there 7 planets? Why are there 14 planetary systems? Why is *bhūloka* divided into 14 oceans and islands? Why is *Jambudvīpa* divided into 9 *varṣa*? Why do the Sun, the Moon, and other planets perform a certain number of revolutions? Why do they have a certain radius? Why is the cosmic age a specific number? The model of the cosmos only describes these numbers but does not explain them. The problem is not unique to Vedic cosmology but exists even in science. For instance, why do the laws of science have a formula? Why do constants of nature have one value, and not another value? How will we explain the laws and the constants?

The Vedic explanation of these facts is that they emerge from the structure of language. That different *chakras* manifest a different number of ideas entails that these ideas in turn define the *form* of the theory, and the space-time properties themselves are those ideas. The objects and activities produced in that space-time therefore manifest a different type, because the space-time is formed from those ideas. The dimensions of that space-time are therefore ideas, and not physical entities. Different locations in these space-times are also different types of entities. As they are built from language, they can be described by language. Our ability to know and communicate the state of the world itself means that the construction of the world follows the construction of language. Unless these two were similar, we could not communicate or know about the world.

The Origin of Language

The study of language is the Holy Grail of all science, in the Vedic view. We cannot *describe* this language because all descriptions require language. The language can, however, be *demonstrated* in the sense that its structure pervades everything in the universe. In the context of science, this means that the structure of language is the structure of space-time. We cannot describe space-time through objects in *that* space-time. However, if the space-times are constructed hierarchically, then a lower space-time can be described in the higher space-time. In that sense, to even know the lower space-time, we must know at least the next higher space-time before we can describe the lower space-time. Ultimately, all these space-times are manifested from the original object: God.

Vedic philosophy offers further insights into the origin of language: all language is a manifestation of consciousness, and the structure of language is therefore produced from the nature of consciousness and its choices. The alphabets of language are therefore ultimately different kinds of choices that *all* conscious beings are capable of. We may or may not make all those types of choices, but if someone has made that choice, we are capable of understanding it. All living beings are therefore fundamentally similar because of their native ability to process the same kinds of meanings encoded in a common and shared language.

It is due to the ability to share language that we can communicate. If there was only matter as science describes it, then we could not *represent* facts into symbols. Even if there were symbols that could represent facts, we still could not communicate with each other unless there was a shared *convention* of encoding meanings. A material universe would therefore only be perceivable by the senses, but not understandable by the mind. Even a semantic universe without a shared language could be understood by the mind, but there would be no way of knowing if that understanding is true. Furthermore, we could not communicate our meanings to others because we could never agree upon a universal language.

The possibility that the world has meanings beyond objects, that these meanings can be true, and that this truth can be communicated to others, requires the existence of a universal language. The properties of language must therefore emerge from the nature of the observers involved in communication. This is the point at which Vedic philosophy goes from the study of material world into the study of consciousness. This consciousness, by definition, cannot be *described* in any material space because it is the *origin* of language which can only be *demonstrated*. To describe our consciousness, and to know ourselves, we must find a deeper space-time than our existence, and this space-time is God. This connects the study of the world to the study of God, because the study of the world can be connected to language, which can then be connected to our consciousness, but our consciousness itself cannot be described by us unless put in relation to God's consciousness. We know ourselves when God knows Himself, and our knowledge of ourselves is produced in relation to God's knowledge of Himself. This means that to even know ourselves, we must establish a relationship to God, through which we can then describe ourselves, in just the way God would describe us.

The key point is that while all forms of consciousness (living beings and God) employ the same language, the living beings are objects in the space-time of God's consciousness, which represents language, and to describe ourselves, we must know which part of that space-time we are *located* in. God, in this sense, cannot be described, because He is the space-time of all descriptions. He is the whole of which everything else is the part. God is *demonstrated* in everything, if we can connect all these things to God by giving them a location in God. Our relation to God is our description, and everything else in the universe is similarly to be described in relation to God. This is not merely a religious viewpoint, it is also a natural outcome of seeking the origin of language and of ourselves.

It also follows that while the soul can be demonstrated in the material world through bodies, minds, and activities, these material entities are not a description of the soul. Like the idea of a triangle can be expressed through many triangles, which are demonstrations of the idea, but no triangle is a description of the *idea* of triangle, similarly, all our thoughts, actions, and bodies obtained through repeated incarnations are not the true description of the soul. They are merely expressions of the existence of the soul, like a triangle is the expression of the idea of a triangle. We can get an inkling of the soul from the body, mind, and activities, but these are not the soul itself. No amount of material science can, therefore, 'reduce' the soul to the body, mind, or activities, although the soul is demonstrated in all these bodies, minds, and activities.

Language and Consciousness

With this background, we can now understand how the structure of language emulates the structure of the soul, with three aspects: *sat* or awareness, *chit* or cognition, and *ānanda* or pleasure. The structure is that the existence, choices, and pleasures are themselves of different types.

There are six basic forms of cognition called knowledge, beauty, renunciation, wealth, power, and fame, which become the cognition of that thing. There are also six kinds of pleasures obtained through different kinds of relationships: relationship to self[4], appreciation of others, service to others, friendship with others, parental affection for others, and conjugal association with others. There are also six kinds of awareness, which result in the questions of what, why, who, how, where, and when: what we should do, why we should do it, who needs it, how it can be done, where it should be done, and when must it be done. These 18 divisions of the soul are the *parā* state of language, in which the observer is *capable* of experiences, although no such experiences have yet begun. This state is further developed through *paśyanti*, *madhyamā*, and *vaikharī*.

In the *paśyanti* state, activity originates as desires for pleasure. In the material creation, these desires are the choices of the soul, although the soul itself never creates these desires; these desires are rather a form of subtle matter, which is *chosen* or *accepted* by the soul.

This is a very instructive aspect of Vedic philosophy in which material desires are never created in the soul, and exist in a form of subtle matter which 'covers' the soul; it is instructive because it means that the soul is never actually in matter, although he accepts the desires in matter, just like we might observe an apple. These desires therefore follow the six-fold division of our awareness into what, why, who, how, where, and when.

This structure of choice is seen in all material activities. For instance, we ask ourselves: "What are we doing?" the goal of which is to describe the output of our activity. Once this output is defined, we must ask: "Why should we do it?" and in asking this question we seek to find the benefits of doing something; for instance, the benefit of a book can be that someone will acquire knowledge. This is, of course, not enough. We further ask: "Who is benefitting?" in the sense of who the consumer or beneficiary of the benefits is. Once we have decided the nature of the activity, that it is beneficial, and the consumer of that benefit is identified, we ask the more prosaic questions of how, where, and when.

These six types of questions follow from the basic desire to do "something", because if we don't wish to do anything, then the successive questions of what, why, who, how, where, and when cannot arise. That basic desire to do something in the material world is called *māyā* which develops into *prakriti* that defines what to do, which evolves into *vidyā* that represents why something should be done, which evolves into *rāga* that denotes for whom it must be done, which evolves into *kalā* or how it is to be done, which develops into *niyati* that defines where it is to be done, which develops into *kāla* that defines when it must be done. All these are choices, and the soul does not produce the alternatives (as they exist materially) but he chooses them. If the soul prematurely terminates these choices, and does not carry them forward, the manifestation of the material existence terminates prematurely. As we have seen earlier, these seven desires of the soul—beginning with *māyā*—are present as coverings of the universe. In other words, the universe is covered with all the *alternatives*, and the soul picks some of the alternatives, and is situated there. These desires constitute the *paśyanti* state of language.

In the *madhyamā* state, the native propensities of the soul, which were previously developed into material desires, are now further developed into conscious experiences. These conscious experiences are created from *karma*, and when the soul that was already covered by desire is further covered by *karma*, he is called the *puruṣa* or the 'enjoyer' because he is now going to reap the results of his past activities. From *puruṣa*, successive elements such as the *mahattattva* (morality), ego (intentionality), intelligence (judgment), mind (meaning), senses (of action and knowledge), and sensations (of action and knowledge) are produced. There are 5 senses of knowledge, 5 senses of action, 5 sensations of action and knowledge, mind, intelligence, ego, *mahattattva*, and *puruṣa*, which together constitute the 25 elements of *Sāñkhya* philosophy.

The 18 native properties of the soul, covered by 7 types of desires, covered by 25 categories of experience constitute the 50 essential categories of language. These categories are *meanings* that can be objectivized as material symbols to create the *speech* or alphabets used in Sanskrit. These alphabets are the *vaikharī* or gross form of language. These categories are common to all universes, and they exist even in the spiritual world. Thus, if we are looking for the structure of a universe, nothing of interest has so far happened. We have defined the categories that the soul needs, but the variety in that experience is yet to be created.

Categories vs. Concepts

The above 50 categories are subdivided in many ways. For instance, the sensation of sight is divided into form, color, and size; color is divided into brightness, saturation, and hue; hue is divided into red, green, and blue, etc. The three modes of nature continue subdividing each of the categories, producing many varieties, but this division into variety is not common across all the universes. The crucial difference in these divisions is injected by a prime number that subdivides all the divisions performed by the modes of nature. The smallest, non-unitary prime number is 2, and since the present universe is said to be the smallest universe, this prime number can therefore be supposed to subdivide all the variety. For instance, the space of the three modes of nature has 3 dimensions, but this space is subdivided by 2 to create 6 cardinal directions (4 directions in a plane): east, west, north, south, up and down. As we have discussed previously, this need not be the only way to divide space; we could for instance, divide a dimension by 5, creating a pentagonal geometry, or by 7 creating a heptagonal geometry. We can presume that the bigger universes in the material universe are performing these higher divisions.

The point of a prime number is that it cannot be produced by any other number, which means that the universe that subdivides by 2 will have mutually exclusive experiences than the universes that subdivide by 5, 7, 11, or 13. All these universes put together, thus, constitute mutually exclusive material experiences. Furthermore, the universes that use larger subdivisions by larger prime numbers will also be much larger than the present universe. The prime number 3 will be common across all the universes, but all the other primes are used for creating exclusive variety. This variety can then, for sake of distinguishing it from categories, be called *concepts* which are unique to a specific universe.

While the categories in all universes are common, concepts are exclusive, such that all the universes together represent all possible material experiences. If concepts are produced by a prime number division, then we can never construct many of these concepts in the present universe. For instance, we can divide the color palette in our universe by 3, 6, 9, 12, or any other multiple of 2 and 3, but we cannot create the palette by dividing in multiples of 3 and 5 because these divisions cannot be achieved in nature, and attempts to find such divisions would only *approximate* to the closest possible division that can be produced by multiples of 2 or 3: e.g., the division by 15 can be approximated to 16.

In modern computers, for instance, all numbers are denoted by binary digits—1 and 0—which represent 'up' and 'down' quantum spins. We can further qualify these by the 3 spatial dimensions, which would then give us 6 discrete values to represent all numbers. Any fractional number must always be approximated to these alternatives. Although we can imagine a division by 5, 7, 11 or 13, these divisions can never be accurately realized in this universe, although they can be approximated. Other universes will realize these divisions naturally, but they would not achieve the kinds of divisions that we can naturally represent.

We previously discussed how the lower planetary systems are enjoying 'fractional' material objects, and we can now qualify that statement further: the fractions available in the present universe are only those that divide by 2 and 3. This is a much smaller number out of all possible fractional numbers, but those other possibilities cannot be achieved in our universe. All universes therefore present unique experiences, although they are produced from the same material categories, three modes of nature, the same principles of soul, God, time, and *karma*, and the reason for this uniqueness is how the categories are subdivided into concepts. In one sense, the pleasure in the other universes is higher because they have greater refinement in matter. But in another sense, it is no better, because they too are missing a lot of things that the other universes enjoy.

All the concepts in this universe are thus produced by only two numbers—2 and 3—and when we see other types of numbers such as 5, they are not due to concepts but due to categories—i.e., the five types of senses of perception. Similarly, numbers such as 7 are produced by selecting from a set of 12; e.g., a musical instrument has 12 notes, but we can pick 7 notes (diatonic) or 5 notes (pentatonic) and leave the rest unused. Such selection constitutes what we called core and context: we can ignore some parts, but to ignore we must have a natural basis from which things can be selected, and that basis cannot be constructed in any other way.

We have several times previously encountered a division by a number 7: for instance, there are 7 higher and lower planetary systems, there are 7 oceans and islands in the *bhūloka*, etc. But a closer look always reveals that this is a partial description and a more complete description always involves a multiple of 2 or 3. The 7 higher planetary systems, for instance, are actually 9 planetary systems, when we include the *Sisumāra* and the *Viṣṇu loka* (refer to Table 2). Similarly, the 14 divisions of *bhūloka* are actually 16 divisions when the Golden Land is included (refer to Table 1). Similarly, the 28 *Nakṣatra* are actually 27, and *Abhijit* is an overlaid part of a different system. Other divisions found in Vedic cosmology—such as the 9 divisions of *Jambudvīpa*, the 12 divisions of the solar zodiac, or the system of 9 planets in *Sisumāra*—are aligned with the division by only two numbers: 2 and 3. All further subdivisions, such as the division of 27 *Nakṣatra* by the 12 zodiac signs, or the division of the zodiac by the 9 planets, always produce types in multiples of 2 and 3. Even these methods of division are different tiers of abstractions, and even these systems can be subdivided in many ways. For instance, while *bhūloka* is described as only one of the 14 planetary systems, it is actually subdivided into further parts; while *Jambudvīpa* is a part of the *bhūloka*, it is also subdivided; while *Bhārata varṣa* is a part of *Jambudvīpa*, it too is subdivided. To get to a deeper understanding of the cosmic structure, therefore, we need to step back from these details and understand that divisions arise naturally in a hierarchical system. There are upper and lower limits in this division, and the process of division is well-defined.

While we discussed how the different parts of the universe comprise prime, integral, fractional, complex, and irrational numbers, we can now qualify that claim: the numbers in these parts are always divisible by 2 or 3, barring when they involve the categories that we have previously enunciated, which denote the 50 alphabets of the Sanskrit language. This simplification is quite useful, as it helps us focus only on understanding a single number—two—and what it represents, rather than trying to comprehend the meaning of every type of subdivision, which exists in other universes, but then the subdivision by two will not exist there.

The effect of two in the present universe is that we tend to see things in terms of opposites: bitter and sweet, rough and smooth, before and after, up and down, black and white, empiricist and rationalist, materialist and spiritualist, east and west, liberal and conservative, etc. The wide prevalence of this duality is because two has such a fundamental role in this universe. We see things in triples too: e.g., red, blue, and green, and then in combinations of twos and threes. The multiples of three (trichotomies) are due to the three modes of nature, and the multiples by two (dichotomies) are due to duality. The dichotomies are unique to our universe, but trichotomies are common to all the varied universes.

We earlier spoke about opposites such that knowledge is in the *loka varṣa* and absence is in *āloka varṣa*. The dichotomies here are different from those oppositions in that the opposites in a dichotomy do not represent the absence of each other. For example, the opposition amid bitter and sweet is different, because if we remove bitter, we don't get sweet. However, when we remove light, we get darkness, and light is the absence of darkness. The bitter and sweet are both perceivable, but darkness is not perceivable. When bitter is moved in space, we don't say that sweet was moved in the opposite direction. However, when light is moved in space, we can say that darkness was moved in the opposite direction. The opposition amid percept and non-percept is also a duality, but different than the duality between two kinds of perceivable opposites.

The Exponent Universes

The *Brihat-Bhagvatāmrita* by *Śrīla Sanātana Gosvāmī* describes the travels of one cowherd boy *Gopa-kumar* through many parts of the universe and beyond it. While situated in *Maheśa Dhāma*, Lord *Ganesa* shows the cowherd boy the differences between many universes, which have *Brahma* with 4, 8, 16, and more heads. The living beings in these universes are said to be moving much faster, when seen from the outside (i.e., *Gopa-kumar*'s perspective). We have discussed the reasons for this earlier: time flows faster, although the total duration remains the same. Due to this, one experiences more events produced from a greater division of space. For instance, the universe with a *Brahma* with 8 heads will have 48 hours in a day, and 24 divisions in the zodiac. The 24 zodiac divisions will, however, be twice as large as the 12 zodiac divisions, given the limit in the smallest particle that consciousness can experience. Thus, from the outside, it appears that the living being in the larger universe is traveling twice the distance, but from the inside the living being thinks that he also has twice the time available, since the clock has more hours in it.

> *Just see these other Vaikunṭha companions of the Lord, traveling in this small universe ruled by four-headed Brahma. And further away from those others, moving swiftly in the universe of an eight-headed Brahma, a world twice as large. And those others in the world of*

> *Brahma with sixteen heads, a world twice as large again. Commentary: To show that these visitors from Vaikuṇṭha were indeed extraordinary, śri Ganesa pointed out more of them entering the other side of the universe, a great distance away, on some other mission. And beyond this relatively small universe of four-headed Brahma, still other Vaikuṇṭha messengers were visiting the world of an eight-headed Brahma, which was one billion yojana in diameter, twice as big as this one. They were traveling swiftly (vegatah) because the universe is so large. Ganesa further showed the same thing happening in universes still larger. [Brihat-Bhagvatāmrita Part Two, 3:86-87]*

> *In this way Ganesa showed me many Vaikuṇṭha companions of the Lord traveling with ease in the millions and billions of universes of multitudes of huge Brahmas, who had millions and billions of lotus faces. The Vaikuṇṭha devotees, attractive to the eyes and mind, all had suitable bodies and were suitably equipped for the universes they were visiting. Commentary: One after another, Ganesa pointed out messengers from Vaikuṇṭha in the universes of a Brahma with 32 heads, 64 heads, 128 heads, and so on. Gopa-kumara could perceive no end to these countless universes. [Brihat-Bhagvatāmrita Part Two, 3:88-89]*

In effect, the living being in the universe doesn't feel that he is moving much faster because twice the distance is covered in twice the time, but from the outside one can see that twice the distance is real, but twice the time simply arises due to a larger subdivision in the clock. Thus, all *Brahma* in all the universes live for the same duration—i.e., 100 years—but in that duration they obtain a far greater amount of experience because they undergo many times more events in the same duration.

From the above description we can see that aside from the prime number divisions of space mentioned earlier, there are also higher exponents of that prime number—e.g., 2^2, 2^3, 2^4, etc. Similar exponent divisions must exist even for the other prime numbers. In each such bigger and bigger universe, the Sun, the Moon, and the other planets cover the same number of revolutions, the living beings have the same duration of lives, but they just think they are living much longer, and experiencing much more, by experiencing faster and faster. This increasing speed of experience now sets a limit on the maximum exponent, because as we go through faster and faster experiences, there is a point at which we simply cannot experience any faster, and if the time goes any faster, the experiences would simply be ignored, just like a movie reel that goes too fast would force some viewers to actually miss the pictures in the movie.

This maximum exponent also similarly sets a limit on the maximum prime number that can be employed in the subdivision of space, because at some point the prime number is so large that the resulting speed of experience has become equal to the maximum theoretical limit of how fast we can experience distinct events. This theoretical limit to the speed with which consciousness can experience will then limit the size of the material creation. That is, the material creation is not infinite, even though the prime numbers and their exponents can be infinite, simply because at some point the sizes have reached beyond the ability of consciousness to fathom in terms of the space and time subdivision.

There is hence a limit to the largest prime number, given by the ability in our consciousness to experience. This limit, however, would be discovered only in a semantic number theory, because in the physical theory of numbers, there is no largest prime number[5]. In a physical number theory, numbers are quantities and not ideas. There is hence no correlation between the bigness or smallness of the number and the bigness or smallness of the ideas. Furthermore, there is even no correlation between the size of the numbers and that of the physical limits in the universe—either big or small. Due to these reasons, the physical number theory cannot show why there are limits to the biggest and smallest numbers, and this fact would be seen only when numbers are viewed as ideas. The relationship between numbers and ideas represents an advancement in mathematics that I have separately described as *Type Number Theory* (TNT)[6].

The *Śrīmad Bhāgavatam* provides interesting correlations between space and time, illustrating how the passing of time is measured by movement, and the smallest unit of time is given by a moving body covering the smallest unit of space. In each universe, the smallest unit of time varies, because time gets subdivided into smaller parts. However, the smallest unit of space remains the same, and the larger division universes become larger and larger. Thus, the theoretically smallest unit of time possible would only be found in the largest universe, where things move the fastest, and therefore they must cover the same distance in smaller and smaller durations. Notably, this smallest time would still be *called* the same since the hierarchy of types remains the same, although the subdivisions increase. Thus, the smallest duration of time measured in the smaller universe would not be the theoretically smallest time, although it will be practically the smallest measurable time for that universe.

> *One can estimate time by measuring the movement of the atomic combination of bodies. Time is the potency of the almighty Personality of Godhead, Hari, who controls all physical movement although He is not visible in the physical world. [SB 3.11.3]*

> *Atomic time is measured according to its covering a particular atomic space. That time which covers the unmanifest aggregate of atoms is called the great time. Purport: Time and space are two correlative terms. Time is measured in terms of its covering a certain space of atoms. Standard time is calculated in terms of the movement of the Sun. The time covered by the Sun in passing over an atom is calculated as atomic time. The greatest time of all covers the entire existence of the nondual manifestation. All the planets rotate and cover space, and space is calculated in terms of atoms. Each planet has its particular orbit for rotating, in which it moves without deviation, and similarly the Sun has its orbit. The complete calculation of the time of creation, maintenance and dissolution, measured in terms of the*

circulation of the total planetary systems until the end of creation, is known as the supreme kāla. [SB 3.11.4]

The size of the smallest atom in our universe is also the size of the smallest atom in all universes and represents the smallest possible division of space. However, the smallest time in our universe is many times bigger than the smallest time in the other universes. The smallest unit of space limits the theoretically smallest particle, while the smallest unit of time limits the maximum size of the universe, which in turn limits the maximum number of universes. The material creation in Vedic cosmology is therefore not infinite although it is very, very large. The key principle that decides the limits of the material creation is the smallest space and time that consciousness can experience. The smallest space defines the atoms, while the smallest time defines the entire material creation. The properties of a soul thus set the limits of the material domain.

The living beings in the bigger universes are experiencing far more phenomena in the same duration, which implies that they are much more attentive than us. As the attentiveness improves, more details are grasped. The demons in the lower planetary system in the present universe are more attentive than the earthly beings because they can process far more details than we can. Our consciousness neglects so many finer details that we see only macroscopic objects. Similarly, the living beings in the far bigger universes are millions of times more attentive that the most attentive living being in the present universe. As a result of that attentiveness, their pleasure is also higher, since they can process the experiences much faster, and therefore have more experiences. In that sense, we must understand that going to another universe also depends on the level of attentiveness a soul has developed. As the soul becomes more and more attentive, he becomes eligible to enter the other larger universes too. In that specific sense, the living beings in the bigger universes are naturally far more advanced than in this universe.

The Devi Dhāma

When different universes are constructed via distinct prime number divisions (including their exponent combinations), then many prime number combinations will not exist in any universe. For instance, if two distinct universes have divisions by 5 and 7, respectively, then the division by 35 (and their other multiples) will not exist in any universe. Does this mean that the material creation is not all the possibilities in matter since many such possibilities are missing from all such universes put together?

This issue is resolved in Vedic cosmology by a place called the *Devi Dhāma* which is distinct from all the individual universes. It is also distinct from *Mahesh Dhāma,* which is place of Lord *Saṅkarṣaṇa* who represents internal time, and is sometimes identified with Lord *Śiva* or *Mahesh* (the distinction between *Devi Dhāma* and *Mahesh Dhāma* will become apparent shortly). The *Brahma Samhita* states the following:

> *Lowest of all is located Devi Dhāma [mundane world], next above it is Maheśa Dhāma [abode of Maheśa]; above Maheśa Dhāma is placed Hari Dhāma [abode of Hari] and above them all is located Kṛṣṇa's own realm named Goloka. I adore the primeval Lord Govinda, who has allotted their respective authorities to the rulers of those graded realms. [Brahma Samhita 5.43]*

The *Devi Dhāma* is in one sense the entire material creation although it is not any of the universes. This is perplexing if we look at the universe physically. How can there be separate universes which are distinct from *Devi Dhāma* and yet this place is the whole material creation? This description can be understood if *Devi Dhāma* is understood as the place in which all kinds of subdivisions are simultaneously possible, such that what remains mutually exclusive in the other universes is concurrently available in the *Devi Dhāma*. For instance, if two universes divide the categories by 7 and 5 to produce concepts, which then make them mutually exclusive universes, both methods of division will be simultaneously available in the *Devi Dhāma* allowing living beings to enjoy the pleasure available in both the above universes, without their *karma*.

Indeed, now, we can also say that the individual universes are merely portions of the *Devi Dhāma* such that each portion sees only a particular type of subdivision and many of these divisions are never manifest in any universe, although they at once exist in the *Devi Dhāma*. This place, therefore, can be said to encompass the entire material creation, which is far greater than the sum-total of all the universes put together. The individual universes are parts of this much bigger place, and it is thus possible to describe the entire material creation as a single *Dhāma*.

The idea that different universes are part of a single much larger universe, although each material universe is a separate place, is not understandable in a physical model of the cosmos. It can, however, be understood when each universe is seen as a *perspective* on reality, created by a particular type of perceptual stance. We have discussed this earlier while describing how the modes of nature create a perspective on reality, and I will elaborate on this theme again during the exploration of astrology. These ideas follow naturally from a hierarchical space-time view where each trunk, branch, twig, and leaf is an experience of the root from a specific perspective and the perspective just presents the root although in a different way in each perspective. The nodes of the tree are produced from the modes of nature, which cover the vision of the root. The successive leaves on the tree are therefore produced from many layers of material covering. Each universe is also a certain type of material covering, although the universes are subdivided into different branches because each branch is *causally complete* although *theoretically incomplete*.

Thus, the *Devi Dhāma* is the complete material creation, and we can call it the main trunk from the root, which has subdivided into three branches due to the three modes of nature. This is the domain of the *śakti* which has a three-fold nature. In *Pancharātra* literature, these *śakti* are called *Sri, Bhū and Nilā* and in each material creation they appear as *Lakshmi*, *Sarasvati*, and *Durgā*. The *Shakta* divisions of Vedic *Tantra* describe many form of *śakti* including three-fold and nine-fold divisions.

The Mahesh Dhāma

The *Mahesh Dhāma* is said to be even higher than the *Devi Dhāma* because it represents time—i.e., the *awareness* of past, present, and future. The sum total of all the universes or the *Devi Dhāma* is only the reality manifest at any given time. While Lord *Ananta* converts the unmanifest into the manifest, this conversion is limited to a single universe, and when the universe is destroyed, the memory of all the events is merged into Lord *Saṅkarṣaṇa*. In other words, the *Devi Dhāma* is only the things that exist right now, but *Mahesh Dhāma* is all the things that have ever happened in the past, are happening currently, or will happen in the future. Time in Vedic philosophy has no start and end, and since this time is also consciousness, it means that it is awareness of the past, present, future.

It is notable that there is memory associated with all the living beings too, which exists as their *guna* and *karma*. All our *guna* is due to habits formed in the past, and all the *karma* is due to consequences of previous actions. These exist with us, and we can potentially be aware of our past, although most of the time we lack that awareness. To the extent that we can become aware of this past, the past exists with us as our *objective history*. But this history is constantly being created and destroyed as old habits are overturned, and as old *karma* is reaped, and new habits and *karma* are produced. In that sense, if some habit has been destroyed, and some *karma* has been reaped, *we* have no way of knowing that past, because that past has been objectively destroyed. However, this destruction only concerns *our* knowledge, not the fact of the events themselves.

For the events to be real beyond our memory of those events, there must be an observer who knows the past, present, and future. That observer is Lord *Saṅkarṣaṇa* or *Mahesh* or *Śiva* who remains aware of the activities of all living beings, including when they enter the material creation, or exit it after liberation from the material entanglement. Clearly, this history and future is spiritual knowledge (and not material knowledge), because it doesn't exist *in* matter—either as *guna* or *karma*. Nevertheless, since this is knowledge *about* matter (even though present in consciousness), the form of Lord *Śiva* is considered lower than Lord *Hari*.

> *Just as milk is transformed into curd by the action of acids, but yet the effect curd is neither same as, nor different from, its cause, viz., milk, so I adore*

the primeval Lord Govinda of whom the state of Śambhu is a transformation for the performance of the work of destruction. [Brahma Samhita 5.45]

The *Brahma Samhita* compares *Hari (Govinda)* and *Mahesh (Śambhu)* to milk and curd. Both are spiritual, and their knowledge is also spiritual—i.e., eternal. However, this eternal knowledge itself pertains to two different domains: eternal and temporary. Lord *Saṅkarṣaṇa* is therefore in the position where He possesses spiritual knowledge of the material world. This knowledge is far bigger than the knowledge of all material universes combined at any given time, which exists in *Devi Dhāma*, but it is not as big as the knowledge of the living being's spiritual existence in the spiritual world itself, because a living being's existence in the material world is only a blip in the entire spiritual sojourn. Lord *Hari* remembers the time when we were in the spiritual world, while Lord *Saṅkarṣaṇa* remembers the time from which we entered the material realm. Both are different kinds of spiritual knowledge, and both are eternal. They just pertain to different domains, and since the material domain is temporary, and our existence in it has a start and an end, the spiritual knowledge of the material world is much smaller as compared to Lord *Hari*'s.

Vedic literature describes several subdivisions of Lord *Hari*'s spiritual knowledge of the spiritual world, which then result in several subdivisions of the spiritual world as well, similar to the subdivisions of the material creation, culminating ultimately in the description of the spiritual realm called *Goloka Vṛndāvana*, which is said to be the highest spiritual realm. I will not get into that description here since that requires a book in itself, and this book is focused exclusively on the Vedic description of the material creation. It is just worth remembering that the Vedic descriptions don't end with the description of the material creation.

The goal of the *Śakti Tantra*, which is a part of the Vedic canon of texts, is to take the living being to the *Devi Dhāma*. The goal of the *Śiva Tantra* is to take the living being even beyond, to the *Mahesh Dhāma.* The goal of the *Pancharātra* texts[7] is to take the living entity to *Hari Dhāma* described above. And the goal of *Śrīmad Bhāgavatam* is to take the living entity to Lord *Kṛṣṇa's* place called *Goloka*. Readers new to

Vedic theology and cosmology may feel confused about the different divinities, but a detailed study shows why these different places must necessarily exist.

10

The Vedic Theory of Time

Inexhaustible time, stronger than the strong, is the Supreme Personality of Godhead Himself. Like a herdsman moving his animals along, He moves mortal creatures as His pastime.

—*Śrimad Bhāgavatam* 10.51.19

Time and Consciousness

Time in Vedic cosmology is a type of supreme consciousness called *Saṅkarṣaṇa*. As we have seen earlier, this time selects *sets* of events which become the events of the cosmos at that instant, and these sets of events have to be described differently from the member events: while the member events are countable entities (natural and rational numbers), the sets are to be denoted by irrational numbers. Individual observer experiences also involve time, which is personal to the observer engaged in that experience. Thus, both cosmic and individual experiences are associated with different kinds of times. While the cosmic time represents the evolution of the entire universe (and hence a *trajectory* in the space comprising all the universes), the individual time represents the evolution of an observer (and hence the trajectory of the observer within that universe).

Since these notions of time are different from those used in modern science, some discussion is warranted to explicate the basis of the difference. Time, as we have discussed before, is hierarchical in the Vedic view: there are many higher and lower cycles of time which represent different clocks that function within the higher clock. Our ordinary clocks elucidate this idea quite well: the minute clock works within the hour clock, and the second clock works within the minute clock. Despite these cyclic notions of time employed in the pragmatic methods of computing time, all scientific theories of time employ a linear axis of time. The linearity of space and time is further tied to the conservation of physical properties (the linearity of time is associated with the conservation of energy). The linear vs. cyclic properties of space and time therefore are not merely heuristic tools for calculating time; they are rather deeply enmeshed with our physical theories. Before we adopt a cyclic notion of time, therefore, we must understand the conceptual basis of this type of time.

This chapter discusses such a basis and connects it to the problem of choice. As we know, the world around us presents many possibilities, but they don't necessarily become our experience, because we *choose* a very small subset of all these possibilities to construct our experience. This choice, in Vedic philosophy, has *effects* (experience) and *consequences* (future possibilities of experience). The law of nature is based on the choices that convert some possibilities into experiences. Thus, if nature presents us with the possibility of experiencing A, B, and C, and we choose C, the consequences are different than if chose B or A. These consequences in turn shape our *trajectory* of possibilities, and consciousness therefore enters the law of nature not incidentally but fundamentally: we cannot explain our trajectory without invoking choices.

The Problem of Dualism

To understand the role of consciousness in nature, and how it relates to the issue of time, we must first decouple it from the problem of mind and meaning. In Western philosophy there is a problem of mind-body dualism, which concerns how the mind interacts with the body. Given that bodies are supposed to be physical while the mind has ideas, the interaction between things and ideas becomes problematic. This problem is resolved in Vedic philosophy by describing how even things are symbols of ideas, and they are therefore produced from abstract ideas through refinement. The above resolution of the mind-body duality, however, does not represent a complete solution, because it does not incorporate the idea of awareness: the semantic view addresses the problems associated with conscious *content* but not with *awareness* of that content.

Cartesian dualism lumps conceptual content and awareness into the singular "psyche", and this lumping is problematic because consciousness is sometimes added to content (when we become aware of the content) but the content may exist even when consciousness doesn't. Content includes many everyday concepts—such as houses, cars, countries, cities, and companies—which cannot be reduced to physical states (recall the problems in reducing concepts to physical states noted earlier), and yet these concepts themselves aren't free will or consciousness. After all, we don't expect every ordinary concept (e.g., a house) to also be conscious[1]. Conceptual content and consciousness are therefore quite different and cannot be treated in the same way. This separation, however, brings in a new kind of dualism between consciousness and its content.

Consciousness is our ability to accept or reject the content of awareness. When the content is accepted, we become conscious of it; when it is rejected, we remain unaware. Of course, the acceptance depends on whether the content is *presented* to consciousness for awareness, but this is a somewhat separate issue that I will cover shortly. For the moment, let's assume that the content has been presented to consciousness, and consciousness can choose to be aware of it: we may pay attention to the content, or we might just ignore that content. All meditative traditions are based on the idea that we can focus our attention on some content, while withdrawing it from other contents. This focus and withdrawal is not always easy, but it can be practiced and perfected. The practices of attention focus and withdrawal in semi-controlled meditative practices represent the attempts to comprehend consciousness as choices.

If consciousness is choice, and awareness is a byproduct of applying choices to content, then the consciousness-content duality reduces to that between choice and content. We must now ask: How do choices interact with content to produce content-awareness as a byproduct?

Core and Context in Experience

At any stage in perception, we focus upon a "core" while being peripherally aware of the "context" in the perception. If you are reading this text, you might be peripherally aware of the texture and shape of the chair on which you are sitting, or the type of airflow around you. All the information around you is potentially "available" to you for awareness, but we choose a much smaller subset of that information to be conscious of.

This choice is quite like picking some objects from a set of objects, and the problem of choice—and how it interacts with the objects—is well-known in many areas of science (particularly, set theory in mathematics), although the solution to the problem is not well-known. For instance, *how* do we pick things from a set of things? What *mechanism* underlies the process of selection? The problem of choice is tied to the problem of counting as we have previously seen and leads to the *Axiom of Choice.*

Mathematics could not be applied to things if choices of selection did not exist. If the collection of objects has been structured by drawing a coordinate frame within that set, then objects in the set are naturally ordered, but that ordering is contingent upon the choice of a coordinate system. Furthermore, the use of a coordinate system follows the application of a *metric*, which serves precisely the purpose of *sequencing* although not *ordering*. For instance, you can order the letters of the English alphabet from A to Z or from Z to A. The fact that A is always found adjacent to B is the metric, and whether A precedes or follows B is the order. The key point therefore is that choice is not merely a mystical notion about a mysterious soul but a fundamental conceptual construct in every act of observation, distinguishing, ordering, and counting things.

Materialists often claim that choices are properties of the brain, and that they can be reduced to physical properties. Little do they realize that if choice is an axiom in counting, then every physical or mathematical theory that employs numbers to describe the material world—including the brain—must also have this choice in-built as an assumption. Using such theories to "explain" choice isn't going to be of any consequence, because, at best, we will employ a theoretical explanation that already assumes choice. The manner in which choice interacts with content, therefore, needs a revision to our notion of content, because the current notions of content do not allow an interaction with consciousness without creating the kind of mind-body problem that was described earlier.

Choices, Information, and Time

The interaction between choices and objects can be demystified if objects are treated as information. For instance, in physical information, objects are reduced to bits—1s and 0s. Whether the bit 1 or 0 represents new information is known only when it cannot be predicted by the occurrence of previous bits (Shannon's Information Theory), and the bit represents a choice. The choices that construct concepts would be more sophisticated (at least they must accommodate the 3 directions in space, aside from the distinctions between forward and backward in space) but they would be choices nevertheless. If objects themselves are comprised of choices, then the interaction between objects and choices can be construed more easily than if objects were treated as physical entities.

The meanings and their selection for observation, however, involve different *types* of choices. While content can be completely expressed by locations and directions in space, all observation use time: when consciousness orders things—and when things distinguished in space are being ordered—they must be ordered as events in time. For instance, I might pick letter A at time T_1, then letter B at time T_2, etc. A and B may be symbols at different locations, but they also become symbols at different instances in time when consciousness becomes aware of them.

A simple illustration of this fact is in how we read books. The book exists as symbols in space, but it is only read sequentially in time. The order of the words in the book may not necessarily be the order in which we read them: e.g., we might jump from section to section, chapter to chapter, or read the epilogue before the preface. The author too might not have written the book in the same order in which it is eventually presented to the reader: some chapters may have been written before the others, or they may be reordered after they have been completed.

The spatial and temporal ordering of symbols is connected in each act of observation—we take a path in space, ordering locations in space as successive events in time. The spatial ordering of symbols is what makes those symbols "objective" —i.e., independent of our awareness, while the temporal ordering of those symbols is what makes the very same symbols "subjective" —i.e., contents of our consciousness.

These commonsense facts derived from our everyday experiences indicate the following: the choices of consciousness must be treated as order in time, while the choices that comprise content must be viewed as order in space. Content and consciousness are different, but their duality can be understood as the complementarity between time and space, not a paradox like the mind-body duality. If consciousness cannot be simultaneously aware of everything in space, and awareness must follow a pattern of selecting "core" vs. "context," then another *modality* is necessary to describe our *experiences* as different from *objects*. Things in space are the *objects* but a small subset of those objects ordered in our consciousness becomes our experience. That conscious ordering is time.

Problems in Theories of Space and Time

Is time purely a personal phenomenon? Isn't time also objective like space, and the world is *changing* even when we don't know about it? The short answer to this issue is that there are two key problems in science due to which this classical notion of "passing time"—as the underlying mechanism that forces changes in the universe—has become untenable.

First, all modern theories of science are indeterministic due to a *matter distribution problem* because they describe nature's properties in the aggregate. The total universe can, however, be divided into individual particles in infinite ways, which aren't predicted by these theories. We cannot speak about a deterministic universe, unless we *a priori* suppose that the particles in the universe are immutable—i.e., they do not combine or divide. In any universe where particles themselves are not conserved (due to particle splitting and combining) the universe is never deterministic, even if the physical properties (in the aggregate) are conserved, and the law of motion is deterministic. If the universe is indeterministic, then the idea that there is a "law" of nature that governs the evolution of the universe is itself flawed: if we cannot use this law to deterministically predict the outcomes, how do we even know that the law exists?

Second, the notion that objects exert "force" on each other and cause the other objects to "move" has itself collapsed in a fundamental way: physical properties cause material properties to enter a *stationary* state rather than a *dynamic* state because these stationary states are waves and they can hold different levels of energy without having to dissipate it to other objects. In fact, the mechanism by which energy is transferred from one such vibrating wave to another has itself become mysterious: we cannot predict when and why that transfer even occurs, and the source and destinations involved in such energy transfers. That the universe will remain in a stationary state is therefore easily explainable but that it will change from one state to another has no theoretical explanation!

Two classical ideas in science—namely that change occurs according to a law, and that change can be deterministically predicted—have collapsed in modern science. Since time was the underlying agency that pushed the universe forward according to a law, the forward march of time is itself now controversial given that we have no predictive law and change itself cannot be explained. The only reason we still maintain the idea of time in science is that we *experience* it to be passing, and that the world appears to be changing, not because the idea of time as that which pushes the universe forward is a theoretically sound idea.

The only way in which the universe can be deterministic is if space and time have a predetermined *structure* which dictates a deterministic evolution of the universe. For instance, there must be a natural law that predicts which events will occur at which location and at which instance. Furthermore, the occurrence of such events must represent the appearance and disappearance of space-time locations and instances themselves. Thus a "particle" would disappear at one space-time, and appear at another, and this appearance and disappearance is due to the structure of the space-time, not due to the properties of the objects.

Classical physics modeled the determinism of the universe based on object properties, but since these properties are always described in the aggregate, determinism is theoretically untenable unless particles are immutable. If particles are immutable, then the universe must be eternal—never created or destroyed. This premise is empirically denied due to the fact that objects—e.g., living bodies—are created and destroyed. To recover determinism now, we must attribute it to the structure of space-time, rather than to the properties of objects. If an object emits energy and another object absorbs it, then this "transfer" of energy is not due to a material property that we can find in the source and sink of that energy, but in the space-time structure as a whole[2]. In fact, the idea that energy is being "transferred" from one space-time location to another is itself flawed, because it appears to give a false impression that the objects are the *cause* and *effect* of some *action*. The correct understanding of this change would be that energy disappears at one location and appears at another due to change in space-time structure, and the source and sink of the energy are not causal *agents* in this action. When the causality is attributed to a space-time structure, such problems are avoided. We have seen in previous chapters how such a space-time structure is semantic.

However, even this space-time structure only predicts the *events* not the *trajectories* that sequence events. The trajectories—representing the succession of individual conscious experiences—are still undetermined. The trajectories must be attributed to our *choices* which select from possible events, and the succession of these choices make our experience. The succession also represents our personal notion of time, which *picks* from the space of possible events (they are objectively real because they exist even when we aren't aware of them, but they are possible from the standpoint of consciousness because we become aware of their existence). The space of events evolves according to the predetermined space-time structure, leaving us capable of choosing from amongst the events.

The Stream of Consciousness

The problem of causality in science and its resolution through semantics introduces a role for choice in building trajectories. These are not paths for lifeless particles but rather life-journeys for conscious beings. If our experiences are produced by a succession of choices, then all changes are deterministically effected by the space-time structure, but our conscious participation in these events makes us the *causal agents* of change.

The effects can be described in space-time, but the agent is *responsible* for them. For instance, if you are speeding in a car, the burning of the fuel is the cause of the speeding, but you (as the driver) are responsible for speeding. Accordingly, you may be punished for speeding (if you were speeding on a road) or rewarded for it (if you were speeding on a racetrack), even though the car moved due to the fuel burning. You may argue here that the choice of speeding is again a physical process, and if you do, please go back to the issues in reducing the choice to physical processes, and why choices are assumptions in every physical theory.

William James—an American psychologist—used the analogy of a "stream" to describe the continuous and ordered nature of our experiences. The distinction between conscious and unconscious, the distinction between core and context, the idea that we pay attention to some things to become aware of them, all point in the same direction: there is an ordered sequence of events organized by our choices in time.

To these realizations we can add that the order in events requires an understanding of how consciousness interacts through choices with matter, and that explanation in turn must view consciousness as time. This time is a personal creation and arises from the stream of choices we make, and it is not the pre-existing space-time that "creates" living bodies that can be conscious. In other words, the universe is not a "block" of predetermined space-time that creates living beings, but an evolving domain of possible events which are ordered into actual *trajectories* through the choices of conscious observers. This is not to say that a predetermined block of fixed events does not exist, but only to assert that the block only produces events although not trajectories. Both trajectories and events are underdetermined when causality is attributed to material objects. Events are determined when causality is attributed to the space-time structure, but trajectories are not. To determine these trajectories, another agency is needed, and that agency is our conscious *choice*.

There is, hence, an "objective" time independent of individual observers which defines the actual events—the things that will happen—which become the *set* from which we must choose. There are also individual trajectories produced from selecting and ordering events from the set of possible events, which constitute our individual experiences. This choice represents my ability to focus my awareness upon writing this text, or the touch of the airflow caused by the ceiling fan, or the pressure of the chair in which I'm sitting, or the noise of the children playing in the background, or the sound of the siren from the ambulance in a distant street. All these events are simultaneously present, but they do not all enter my awareness; I have the choice to be able to focus upon some of them, while contextualizing the others. The succession of these choices becomes the order of events in my awareness and constitutes my subjective time. If I stopped choosing and became unaware of everything around me, the subjective time will stop, even though the objective time will continue producing changes in possibilities of observation.

Consciousness therefore interacts with matter by selecting from the available events to create the core and context of our experience. The choices of selection become the *time* of my experience, while the selected (or contextualized) possibilities become the *space* of my experience. The interaction between matter and consciousness to create experience is merely the two different factors—space and time—contributing to create my conscious experience. The noteworthy difference is only that space denotes meanings, and time comprises choices of these meanings.

Free Will and Freedom

Aside from choosing certain facts from our perceptual field, the perceptual field is itself quite limited: we don't see and hear things that are far away, we don't interact with everyone in the world, nor do we know things far into the past or the future. We are "localized" creatures in space-time, such that a very limited subset of all the possibilities in the universe is even available to us. What determines this localization? Why are we situated at a particular location in space, and a particular moment in time? Vedic philosophy has an answer to this question, and the answer is that our choices determine what events we are subjected to.

Our choices on the available possibilities represent our *free will* while our localization in space-time which limits those possibilities is our *freedom*. Our free will operates within the freedom afforded by the circumstances and we cannot choose outside our freedom. Many of us have at one time or another felt constrained by our situation when we wanted something that was clearly outside the limited freedom the circumstances afforded. We often feel "bound" by our circumstances, where merely broadening our choices does not help because what we want seems to lie outside the possibilities themselves. Even if we removed all the filters, some things would still be inaccessible because we are localized in space-time, and certain events are outside that location. We ask: Why am I in this situation, when someone else is in another situation? Why am I poor, while the others are rich? Why am I sick when the others are healthy? Why am I disabled when the others are capable?

Our localization in space presents the situations through which we pass, although we may not be aware of everything. While writing this text, I'm not aware of the pressure of the chair on my back, although it is easily accessible to me. The focus of our experiences helps us determine the *essence* of that experience. Similarly, if you look at a moving planet in the sky and just wish to draw its trajectory, then the color, size, and texture of the planet become irrelevant, and would be contextualized. Through a specific focus on the trajectory alone, we can now reduce the planet to a point particle. The color, size, and the texture of the planet, however, are not unimportant, although they were contextualized due to a specific type of focus. If that core-context splitting always works, then the facts that were neglected from the phenomenon would never enter experience again, since we would believe that the planet is a point particle.

Therefore, if the point particle is not the essence of all experiences, then to bring size, color, and texture back into our experience there must be locations where the particle description becomes unviable. Our localization in different parts of the universe serves such a purpose: it forces us into situations where our theories about nature are challenged, and our core-context divisions are tested at their boundaries. When our assumptions about what is core and context fail, new core-context boundaries can be drawn. However, for these boundaries to be tested, failed, and revised, there must be new localizations to test them.

The new localizations are useful if what was context earlier becomes the core now. A new situation can be useful if it is hard to use particle trajectories—e.g., during the observation of water waves in a pond, or the vibration of strings in a musical instrument. We are presented with a situation in which what was previously considered core and context must change. This change can enforce a contextualized fact into the core of our consciousness, restarting the process of core-context formulation.

As we go through a succession of experiences, previously formed core-context divisions are tested, some of them fail, causing new core-context constructions. Each core-context construction has two parts: the core is the *theory* of nature while the context is the *phenomena* explained by that theory. Which aspect of a phenomena is the theoretical essence, and which other parts are the non-essential facts explained by, and reducible to the theory, depends on the localizations. If we have made a mistake in conceiving the essence, ideally, we would like to suppose that what was previously contextualized must now be brought into the core of our experience. If, instead, the core is correct, then it would be ratified by the experiences anyway. Different localizations, therefore, present us with an opportunity to discover the *real* essence of *all* things.

If nature were not helping us find the truth, then the truth could never be found: we cannot know if a false theory will be falsified by some phenomena in the future. Furthermore, since we cannot know if our theories will not be falsified, we cannot know if they are in fact true. In brief, we can never know if our beliefs about nature are true or false.

However, if nature is helping us find the truth, then we can assume that it will give us opportunities to correct false theories. The law of nature that controls the succession of localizations would—in effect—be controlled not by the previous localizations (as in a deterministic theory) but by our *interpretation* or *understanding* of that situation in terms of what is core and context. If a given situation has resulted in a false interpretation of reality, then repeating that situation again would only reinforce that false view. Conversely, if a given situation has resulted in a true interpretation, then the ratification of that true idea through diverse experiences would reinforce the true interpretation.

Thus, individuals with both true and false interpretations will appear to undergo diverse experiences, but the underlying *rationality* of that journey will differ.

The key difference between such a localization law and the laws of current science would be that the former must consider our *understanding* of nature rather than merely the objective description of the situation itself. To use our understanding as the basis of a scientific law, science itself must be updated to incorporate meanings (as described earlier). If nature is itself meaningless, then interpretations of nature are outside nature, and any theory we formulate about nature cannot alter the evolution of our bodies, and hence of our experience gained via the body.

Three Notions of Time

We now have all the necessary background to distinguish between three notions of time, which I will call *universal, local,* and *personal* times. The universal time represents all the events that can be objectively described. However, this time does not describe which individual observers will pass through which events. The universal time is deterministic and the universe of events—i.e., what will happen at which time—is also deterministic. However, this time does not predict or explain the *trajectories* or the succession of events, by which some events are connected to others and attributed to a specific *object* (or observer). We can compare the predictions of this time like the script of a drama which describes all the dialogues but does not specify which actor speaks which dialogues.

When we add the notion of an observer into the picture, then it becomes possible to speak about the *situations* or *contexts* through which an observer will pass, the transactions the observer will partake in. This time—which we can call *local time*—describes all that will happen to an observer's body and mind, but not if those events will enter a person's awareness, and how that person will react to those situations. The local time closes the gap in predictability created by the universal time by fixing the individuals that must go through some of the events, although it does not fix whether they are aware of those events, and their reactions to that awareness. Now, we can say which character will speak which dialogues, but whether or not they will enjoy speaking those dialogues still cannot be determined. If the actor doesn't enjoy rendering the dialogues, some mechanical utterances can still enact those dialogues, while the actor's consciousness is focused on other interesting activities.

The *personal time* represents the individual choices of a person by which he or she brings different parts of their surrounding or bodily activities into their awareness and interprets the situation into core and context—thereby forming their theories of nature and enjoying or suffering according to those theories. Our reactions to our situations generally depend upon our previously formed habits of dividing the world into core and context, but these habits can be changed by our free will. Common examples of the use of such free will is seeing the glass half full vs. half empty. The facts of the situation remain unchanged, although the interpretation (and whether it makes us happy or unhappy) can be changed. To the extent that we can gradually modify our core-context habits, and their interpretation, we can also alter our reactions to situations. Since our core-context habits determine the subsequent localized situations, our future situations depend on how we interpret the current situation. Since our interpretations can be controlled by our free will, through such control we can alter our future situations, and become free of them.

The personal time defines an individual's experiences as a result of their choices and there are as many instances of this time as there are observers. The local time defines the situations in which an individual participates, and many individuals can participate in that situation. Finally, there is only one universal time, which contains all the situations.

All the three times—universal, local, and personal—are objective, but they cover different facets of the universe and who participates in them. The universal time fixes the events in the universe, regardless of who participates in those events. The local time divides these events into observer-specific events, and the observers that participate in them. The personal time defines if an individual is aware of those situations, and which parts of those situations are considered core vs. context. Our ability to divide a situation between core and context decides whether we are happy or sad in a given situation. These core-context divisions determine an individual's future contexts, and the other individuals he or she will interact with. These contexts are limited by what is possible in the universe controlled by the change in events under universal time.

Each of the three times acts as a "choice" on a different kind of space. The universal space represents all possible events—in the past, present, and future. The universal time selects from amongst these possibilities to create the universal present. The local space represents all the events that can occur in a particular location, at the given moment, which are a subset of the events in the universe occurring at that particular universal time. The local time populates the local event-set with the specific individuals based on their previous core-context divisions and the new situations they must undergo to correct or ratify their previous viewpoints. Finally, the personal time is all the events that will be experienced by a particular observer under a given situation, and the personal time selects a subset of those available experiences—creating a core-context.

The space of all events—in the past, present, and future—is a state of timelessness. It contains all possibilities, but none of the realities—universal, local, or personal. The universal space of all possibilities produces the real universal, local, and personal space-times, when universal, local, and personal times combine with the universal space of possibilities.

The Reality of the Past and the Future

Since the universal space comprises all that is possible those events are "real", as they exist, even though they may not be *manifest* in a universe, in a given situation in a universe, or in an individual's consciousness in a situation. What we are aware of at any given time is a smaller part of what we can theoretically be aware of, due to the core-context division. What a given situation contains is again a very small subset of what is possible in the universe. Finally, the entire universe at the present moment is a very small subset of everything that is theoretically possible.

It is now possible to conceive of multiple "domains" which collectively realize all the possible events during their lifetimes. Thus, when we speak of the past, present, or future, we may not be speaking about a universe, a situation in the universe, or an individual in a situation. Rather, we may speak across the universes, and while such events can be described *qua* events, it is hard to relate to them from within a limited individual, local, or universal perspective. To speak about the past, present, and future, we must also contextualize it via the individual, contextual, and universal divisions within which that event actually occurs.

The material "universe" can now be spoken of as the set of all possible events, as across different universes, the situations in a universe, and the experiences of the individuals in a given situation. That material domain is obviously large and difficult to understand from our current observations. The time it would take for an individual observer to traverse all the universes, all the situations in those universes, and all the possibilities in those situations, one by one, is hence unspeakably large. This is, however, the time that it would take someone to collect all the data necessary to formulate a perfect theory of the universe. It is only when we can accumulate all the possible events that we can be sure our theory is correct—if that theory was being empirically *discovered*. This inordinately large time represents the problem for epistemology: if we need to go through all the *possible* events before we can form a theory then the time required to even collect all the *data* to be described is so high that our method of knowing will need to survive the creation and destruction of many universes! Empirical discovery is still *in principle* possible, but it is practically so difficult that we might consider it impossible[3].

The Determination of Age

The idea of local time decides our "age". It is all that has happened to our body and mind, and therefore has constituted a trajectory. It is obviously much smaller than the universe, and much larger than our conscious experience, since we experience only a fraction of all that happens in our body and mind. Many old people, who haven't become jaded with passing time in terms of their outlook, say that they "feel young", and they are talking about the personal time, rather than their age, which allows them to enjoy even their old age. Similarly, some young people fall into depression and find even a young age unbearable in personal time.

The issue of age is subject to debates in modern science since the advent of relativity theory. The contention is that if an observer is moving fast, then he must age slowly, because the clock that he is carrying would slow down. This slowing of the clock leads to what is now called the Twin Paradox[4] which describes a scenario in which one twin boards a rocket that moves at a great speed for some years, and upon his return from the journey, finds that the twin who stayed back on Earth has aged more.

The Twin Paradox originally arose in response to the time dilation predictions of Special Relativity (SR), and it was considered a paradox due to the symmetry in the motion of the twins: instead of saying that one twin boarded the rocket and therefore moved for many years, we might as well say that the twin on Earth moved in the opposite direction for as many years. Thus, time dilation must be symmetric for both observers, each observer thinking that the other is staying younger, because they cannot know which observer is moving (due to relative motion).

The resolution of this paradox is that the symmetry between the twins is broken when the traveling twin turns back toward the Earth. When the rocket slows down, changes direction, and accelerates again, the moving twin would know that he has been traveling. Accordingly, when he returns, according to relativity, he should have aged less.

Time dilation has been confirmed on atomic clocks and in particle physics experiments. So, it seems that the traveling twin must age less. However, the experiment hasn't been done with twins. To observe a difference between the twin's ages, one twin would have to travel at speeds close to the speed of light for several months to produce a visible difference in age. This might be practically very hard as rockets that travel so fast are far from practical today. But there is an important question which arises if we separate the facts of our body from our *experiences* of those facts. When our bodies are moving faster, and probably changing slower (according to relativity) are we also experiencing fewer things in our consciousness? In other words, do we become aware of our motion?

Clock Time vs. Conscious Time

Time dilation predicts that the clock runs slower as the clock moves faster; conversely, if the clock moves slower then it runs faster. Let's take this for granted and perform the following thought experiments.

- Suppose that I'm in a slow-moving spaceship with a clock. Naturally, we expect the clock to run at a faster rate. If we knew the distance we traveled, we would be able to compute the rate of our motion. If the spaceship is going slowly, the time passed is higher, but the distance traveled is lower. Accordingly, *my rate of change is slow.*
- Suppose that I'm in a spaceship moving near the speed of light. Now, we expect the clock to run slower. If we can measure the distance we travel, we can compute the rate of our motion. Since the spaceship is moving at a high speed, the time passed is lower, but the distance traveled is higher. Accordingly, *my rate of my change is high.*

Now, there are two ways in which we can measure time:

- We can see the clock ticking slower or faster and determine the time that has passed because of the number of clock ticks.
- We can see that our rate of change in conscious experience is higher or lower and determine the time as a function of that change.

If we are going to measure the lifetime of material objects, then we depend upon the results of clock ticks, and the faster the clock moves, the slower the clock goes, and the lifetime of the moving object appears to increase because the clock slows down. For a material object, therefore, the rate of passing time is the rate of clock ticks. Conversely, if we are going to measure *our* lifetime, then we should measure the rate of change in our experience, and the faster we go, the resulting perceived rate of change is thus higher. For a conscious being, therefore, the rate of passing time is the rate at which our conscious experience changes.

Of course, this isn't an apples-to-apples comparison: we are comparing the rate at which the clock ticks to the rate at which my conscious experience changes. However, it is also true that as the rocket speeds up, the clock slows down, but my conscious experience goes faster.

We can now define two kinds of times based on the above:

- Clock Time based on the rate of clock ticks
- Conscious Time based on the rate of change in experience

According to Clock Time, a traveling twin will age less as the clock goes slower. According to Conscious Time, a traveling twin will age more because experience changes faster. Which of these two decide age?

Measuring the Passage of Time

The measurement of Conscious Timc, of course, depends on whether the traveler is *conscious* of the travel—e.g., *sees* that she is traveling by observing the passing planets, stars, or universes. If the traveler sleeps right when the rocket takes off, she would be unaware of the distance traveled and the Conscious Time would thereby be even lesser than the Clock Time because there are fewer changes occurring in her conscious experience. Thus, if the traveler goes into deep sleep, and time is measured according to Conscious Time, the traveler would be far younger when she arrives back on Earth than even predicted by Clock Time.

Conversely, if the traveler is conscious of the entire travel (never sleeps during travel) then the Conscious Time would be much higher than Clock Time, and the traveler would be far older than the twin on Earth who caught many winks while the traveler was on the rocket.

We can also imagine a conscious experience under which Clock and Conscious Time are equal on the rocket, or a level of experience in which the Conscious Time of the traveling twin matches Clock and

Conscious times of the non-traveling twin. Numerous other possibilities can be envisioned too—e.g., that the Conscious Time of the traveling twin equals the Clock Time of the non-traveling twin, but the Conscious Time is much lesser because the non-traveling twin was in deep sleep all along.

What is Aging, Really?

These scenarios present a paradox in which the age of the twins is determined by their respective Conscious Times rather than Clock Times. Depending on their levels of conscious experience, the traveling twin could be younger, older, or the same age when she returns to Earth.

If the traveling twin never sleeps and acquires all the experiences of traveling, she would age must faster according to Conscious Time, but much lesser according to the Clock Time. If this traveling twin happened to look at the mirror occasionally and then at the clock in the rocket, she would find herself suffering from Progeria[5] in which the person appears to age much faster than the clock time stipulates. Conversely, if the traveling twin slept through the entire journey, then she would find that the travel seems to have considerably elongated her life span relative to the people who were leading normal waking-sleeping lives on Earth.

Do we measure our age by the clock ticks, or by the amount of conscious experience? What decides lifespan? The number of clock ticks, or the number of experiences? Of course, if we happen to only look at the clock, and the ticks on the clock was all that we ever experienced, then the two times would be identical. But aside from this possibility, when we actually venture into other kinds of experiences, determining our lifespan presents a serious problem if Conscious Time decides our lifespan.

The Mystic's Viewpoint

Those who have practiced yoga know that by entering stages of trance the yogi is able to elongate their lifespan. Vedic literatures are replete with narratives about yogis who have lived thousands of years—most of this time spent in trance. This might seem far-fetched, and therefore, it helps to cast this problem in the context of the Twin Paradox: the aging of the twin does not depend on the speed at which the rocket moves but on the rate at which the traveler is conscious of that motion. If the traveling twin leads a "normal life" given by the ticking of the clock time on the rocket—i.e., sleeping, eating, and working according to the clock—then she would elongate her lifespan and appear younger when she returns to Earth. But if she observes the changes that the rocket takes her through, then she would be much older relative to the people on Earth.

When the rocket moves faster, the clock times go slower, and that will influence the traveler's biology: e.g., the traveler may eat or sleep less frequently because the time has slowed down. The yoga practices similarly train a person to reduce their eating and sleeping to revector their time. By so doing, they reduce the number of material experiences and since the lifespan is decided by the number of such experiences, the yogi elongates their lifespan. The key idea that the foregoing discussion takes us to is this: there isn't a single time that we call Clock Time. In particular, there are potentially other kinds of times that depend on our conscious experience, and while these times may not be physically empirical, they can be empirical in other ways such as the extent of our lifespans.

Of course, if changing our experience changes our lifespan, then there needs to be a scientific explanation of why our lifespan is not based on the clock time but on how we experience the world. As we have noted previously, Vedic cosmology describes places in which living beings live for 10,000 years. The demigods, similarly, experience a single day when 6 months of our time have passed. In these cases, 6 months is the clock time and 1 day is the conscious time. The extent of life depends not on the clock, but on the conscious time. Therefore, the demigods live longer by the calculation of conscious time, not by the calculation of clock time. Lord Brahma similarly passes only one day while 4,320,000,000 years of clock time (by our measurement) have passed. These descriptions appear fantastic and unreal because we imagine that lifespan is given by clock time rather than conscious time. When lifespan is measured by conscious time, then these discrepancies automatically disappear.

The idea that consciousness plays a role in deciding time, therefore, is not merely a subjective and non-empirical construct about time. The passing of time is definitely a personal and subjective phenomenon, but it has *effects* on the body due to which the body lives longer. As we have noted several times previously, the subtle levels of reality are not knowable directly through sense perception, but their effects can be observed. In that sense, conscious time is also empirical due to its material effects, although consciousness is not empirical to the sense perception.

11

Calculation of Universal Time

My dear mother, O daughter of Svayambhū Manu, the time factor, as I have explained, is the Supreme Personality of Godhead, from whom the creation begins as a result of the agitation of the neutral, unmanifested nature.

—Śrimad Bhāgavatam 3.26.17

Natural Clocks

When time is defined cyclically, there is no difference between the "axis" of time and the clocks that change periodically. That is, the axis of time cannot be linear when the clock measures periodicity—which we commonly represent as a circle; the axis of time must also be the periodicity of the clock that measures it, and therefore, the *form* of time must be a cycle. A smaller time division is a smaller clock that has smaller periods, and each time division must correspond to a natural clock that has a periodicity of the time it measures. In Vedic cosmology, many clocks are defined. The smallest clock is called *truti* which is about 3.08×10^{-7} seconds while the largest clock is Brahma's lifetime which is 9.67×10^{21} seconds.

On a base 10 logarithmic scale, these time scales would require 29 positions, if all these clocks were counting base 10. Of course, the natural clocks are not always counting in base 10. In Vedic cosmology, many different natural clocks are defined which count in different periods of time. This chapter discusses all the units of time and the rates at which these clocks are measuring time. For the larger time periods, the clocks are easily understood as they measure in multiples of years and are related to cosmic time cycles which can be identified with the cosmic events. For the smaller time periods, it is not easy to identify the clocks unless a study of the Vedic atomic theory is done. Modern atomic theory also treats matter as a wave, rather than a moving particle as in classical physics. Therefore, clocks had to be man-made in classical physics since time with linear motion also moves linearly, not cyclically. With atomic clocks, however, it is possible to envision natural clocks which keep time *in nature* even when we don't know the time. This time keeping is essential in biology, and indeed all systems, for that system to know the elapsed time.

For instance, all biorhythms such as breathing, hunger, sleep, circulation, etc. require timekeeping. The things that we aren't aware of, and are outside our conscious control, are still following some clock. Time clocks aren't simply human constructs for our timekeeping. Rather, nature is itself keeping time through many natural clocks. In the following sections, I have divided these clocks into several categories such as atomic clocks, human clocks, cosmic clocks, etc. This division is only for convenience of our understanding and has no natural basis by itself.

Atomic Clock Time

Atomic time is calculated in relation to a *Prāna* which is described as 4 seconds. There are at least 4 subdivisions of this period, each of which divides the previous clock by 60. These are respectively called *Līkṣaka*, *Lava*, *Renu*, and *Truti*. Their measures are shown in Table 17.

Unit Name	RELATION			DURATION	
TRUTI			=	4/12960000	SECOND
RENU	60	TRUTI	=	4/216000	SECOND
LAVA	60	RENU	=	4/3600	SECOND
LĪKṢAKA	60	LAVA	=	4/60	SECOND
PRANA	60	LĪKṢAKA	=	4	SECOND

Table 17: The Atomic Clock Time

Human Clock Time

Larger than the atomic clocks are other clocks that we are familiar with as humans. These include commonplace ideas like seconds, minutes, hours, days, months, and years. It is surprising that many of these measures have remained intact over the millennia and are used in nearly identical form even today, given that so many of the other things such as theories about matter and space have changed. There is no particular reason, for instance, to have the notion of 12 "months" in a year, or 24 "hours" in a day, or to divide an hour into 60 minutes, and a minute into 60 seconds. As arbitrary as these divisions appear to be, particularly from a physical standpoint, it is perhaps not incorrect to assume that they have been carried forward from ancient Vedic times up till the modern time.

UNIT NAME	RELATION			DURATION	
PRANA	4	SECOND	=	4	SECOND
PALA	6	PRANA	=	24	SECOND
GHATIKA	60	PALA	=	24	MINUTES
AHORATRA	60	GHATIKA	=	24	HOURS
MASA	30	AHORATRA	=	1	MONTH
VARSHA	12	MASA	=	1	YEAR

Table 18: The Human Clock Time

It is notable that the year in Vedic cosmology has 360 days—which is identical to the number of *degrees* in a circle used in geometry. This is different from modern definition of 365 days in all years except the leap year which has 366 days. Similarly, all months in Vedic cosmology have 30 days, and the system of 30 or 31 days in the Western calendar with 28 or 29 days in February is not used. Clearly, this method of calculating time is closely aligned with cosmic calculations of planetary movement, since the planets don't move faster or slower in different months. Thus, we can also say that the notion of a "month" or a "year" in the Western system is not a "clock" because it appears to go faster and slower, while these same terms are actually clocks in the Vedic cosmological time system.

Cosmic Clock Time

The Vedic system begins to differ when it comes to larger time scales. In particular, this happens when the cyclic times are extended beyond our everyday notions of a day and year. In Vedic cosmology, the universe undergoes cycles of 4 *yuga* or "ages" in which the 4 legs of *dharma* slowly decline. These ages are also said to be proportionate in duration to the number of "legs" of *dharma* that prevail in that age. Thus, for instance, *satya-yuga* (which is the first age in the cycle of 4 *yuga*) is 4 times longer than the smallest age called *kali-yuga*. Similarly, *treta-yuga* is 3 times as long as *kali-yuga*, and *dvapara-yuga* is 2 times as longer. The sum-total of the 4 *yuga* is thus 10 times as longer as *kali-yuga* (4 + 3 + 2 + 1 = 10). The system of 4 *yuga* is thus also collectively called a *chaturyugi*.

UNIT NAME	RELATION			DURATION	
DEVAVARSH	360	VARSHA	=	360	YRS
KALIYUGA	1200	DEVAVARSH	=	432,000	YRS
DVAPARAYUGA	2400	DEVAVARSH	=	864,000	YRS
TRETAYUGA	3600	DEVAVARSH	=	1,296,000	YRS
SATYAYUGA	4800	DEVAVARSH	=	1,728,000	YRS
CHATURYUG	12000	DEVAVARSH	=	4,320,000	YRS
MANAVANTAR	71	CHATURYUG	=	306,720,000	YRS

Table 19: The Cosmic Clock Time

Central to the definition of a *chaturyugi* is the idea of a *devavarsh* or "demigod year" which is 360 human years (1 year of the humans is 1 day of the demigods). Just as humans live for 100 human years, the demigods live for 100 demigod years. When 12 such demigods have been replaced (1200 demigod years have passed) the *kali-yuga* is said to be completed. Similarly, the other *yuga* are twice, thrice and four times longer than the *kali-yuga*. By this calculation, the age of 4 *yuga* is 4,320,000 years.

There are higher clocks too, and the next clock is called a *manavantara* which comprises 71 *chaturyugi*. A *manavantara* is the period of a

Manu who lives much longer than many of the demigods. There are 14 *Manu* in a single day of Lord Brahma as we will shortly see, and Lord Brahma then lives for 100 years, following the same system of day, month, and year as the humans. The interesting aspect of this description is that there isn't a single day, month, or year in Vedic cosmology. Depending on whether the universe is described from the standpoint of humans, demigods, *Manu*, or Lord Brahma, the durations of these terms can change dramatically. They are, therefore, given names, and identified with the passing of time in the life of a different personality. Like our life goes in cycles of days and years, every higher living being's life too follows the same pattern although their durations are vastly different.

The Four Ages

Each of the four *yuga* are further divided into 12 parts, such that 1 part is the prelude, 10 parts are interlude, and 1 part is epilude. The prelude and the epilude are called *sandhyā* and *sandhyānsha*, respectively. Their durations depend on the total duration of the *yuga* and therefore the prelude and the epilude for *satya-yuga* is 4 times as long as that of the *kali-yuga*. During the prelude, the properties of that age are gradually rising, and during the epilude, they are gradually diminishing. During the interlude they are fully manifest. Therefore, when one age transitions into another there are two periods—one of decline of the previous age and the second of the rise of the next one. Their durations depend on the type of age.

YUGA NAME	DURATION	
SANDHYA	144,000	YEARS
SATYAYUGA	1,440,000	YEARS
SANDYANSHA	144,000	YEARS
SANDHYA	108,000	YEARS
TRETAYUGA	1,080,000	YEARS
SANDHYANSA	108,000	YEARS

SANDHYA	72,000	YEARS
DVAPARAYUGA	720,000	YEARS
SANDYANSHA	72,000	YEARS
SANDHYA	36,000	YEARS
KALIYUGA	360,000	YEARS
SANDHYANSA	36,000	YEARS
CHATURYUGI	4,320,000	YEARS

Table 20: The Four Ages

The changes between the ages don't result in a sudden shift. For instance, if *satya-yuga* ends today, and *treta-yuga* begins tomorrow, we do not expect a dramatic change in the properties at the midnight hour. Rather, there is a gradual period of transition in which the properties of the first age begin to decline and the properties of the next age begin to manifest. The longer the age, the longer it takes for the rise and decline.

The Time of a Kalpa

Beyond the *chaturyugi* is another cycle called the *manavantara* which comprises 71 *chaturyugi.* Each *manavantara* is "ruled" by a different *Manu* and the *manavantara* is called by the name of the *Manu* at that time. For instance, the present *manavantara* is ruled by a *Manu* called *Vaivasvata* and the *manavantara* is therefore called after him. The succession of 14 such *manavantara* or the lives of 14 *Manu* constitutes a *Kalpa.* The sum of these periods constitute 14 * 71 = 994 *chaturyugi.* At the end of each *manavantara*, the universe is said to be partially destroyed, and life in most of the planetary systems is recreated at the beginning of the next *manavantara.* In Vedic cosmology, therefore, life is not directly created by God. Rather, a form of God called *Garbhodakaśāyi Viṣṇu* creates Lord Brahma, who then creates a *Manu* who then creates the living beings.

	NAME	YUGA DURATION		YEAR DURATION	
	SANDHI	0.4	CHATURYUG	1,728,000	YEARS
1	SWAYAMBHU	71	CHATURYUG	306,720,000	YEARS
	SANDHI	0.4	CHATURYUG	1,728,000	YEARS
2	SWAROCHISHA	71	CHATURYUG	306,720,000	YEARS
	SANDHI	0.4	CHATURYUG	1,728,000	YEARS
3	UTTAMA	71	CHATURYUG	306,720,000	YEARS
	SANDHI	0.4	CHATURYUG	1,728,000	YEARS
4	TAPASA	71	CHATURYUG	306,720,000	YEARS
	SANDHI	0.4	CHATURYUG	1,728,000	YEARS
5	RAIVATA	71	CHATURYUG	306,720,000	YEARS
	SANDHI	0.4	CHATURYUG	1,728,000	YEARS
6	CHAKSHUSHA	71	CHATURYUG	306,720,000	YEARS
	SANDHI	0.4	CHATURYUG	1,728,000	YEARS
7	VAIVASVATA	71	CHATURYUG	306,720,000	YEARS
	SANDHI	0.4	CHATURYUG	1,728,000	YEARS
8	SAVAMI	71	CHATURYUG	306,720,000	YEARS
	SANDHI	0.4	CHATURYUG	1,728,000	YEARS
9	DAKSHASAVARNI	71	CHATURYUG	306,720,000	YEARS
	SANDHI	0.4	CHATURYUG	1,728,000	YEARS
10	BRAHMASAVARNI	71	CHATURYUG	306,720,000	YEARS
	SANDHI	0.4	CHATURYUG	1,728,000	YEARS
11	DHARMSAVARNI	71	CHATURYUG	306,720,000	YEARS
	SANDHI	0.4	CHATURYUG	1,728,000	YEARS
12	RUDRASAVARNI	71	CHATURYUG	306,720,000	YEARS
	SANDHI	0.4	CHATURYUG	1,728,000	YEARS
13	DEVASAVARNI	71	CHATURYUG	306,720,000	YEARS
	SANDHI	0.4	CHATURYUG	1,728,000	YEARS
14	INDRASAVARNI	71	CHATURYUG	306,720,000	YEARS
	SANDHI	0.4	CHATURYUG	1,728,000	YEARS
	KALPA	1000	CHATURYUG	4,320,000,000	YEARS

Table 21: The Time of a Kalpa

Similar to the "joining" periods in between the 4 *yuga*, there are joining periods in between the *manavantara* as well. This is the period in which the universe exists but most of the living beings don't. These joining periods are called *sandhi* and they are 40% of a *chaturyugi*. When all the *manavantara* and the *sandhi* in between are added, the clock called *kalpa* equals to 1000 *chaturyugi*. 14 *Manu* pass in this day, and hundreds of demigods are replaced. This period is 4,320,000,000 years long, but it only constitutes a single day of Lord Brahma (his 12 hours)!

Thus, Lord *Brahma* is seeing his own child—*Manu*—being born and dead every 52 minutes of his clock. If it is difficult to see your child pass away during your own life, Lord *Brahma* sees 14 of these children die every day. For all the power invested in Lord *Brahma* to manage the universe, he cannot save his child from death. In fact, as his children die, he must create more of them to manage the worldly affairs. The person who creates various forms of life in the universe himself must die!

The Life of Lord Brahma

The period of 1 *kalpa* constitutes 1 day of Brahma. At the end of that day, the universe is annihilated and only *satyaloka* (which is the planetary system for Lord Brahma) remains. Lord Brahma is said to sleep for the 1 *kalpa* which constitutes his "night". Creation begins again at the dawn of the next morning, and in this way Lord Brahma lives for 100 years. His days and nights follow the same pattern of months and years as the humans (i.e., 30 days and nights in a month, 12 months in a year). The entire universe (including the *satyaloka*) is annihilated at the end of Lord Brahma's 100 years. The entire life of Lord Brahma only constitutes one half of a breath for Lord *Mahā Viṣṇu*: His "exhalation". The entire material creation (comprising billions of universes) is produced when Lord *Mahā Viṣṇu* exhales, and they are annihilated when He inhales.

NAME	KALPA DURATION		YEAR DURATION	
DAY	1	KALPA	4,320,000,000	YEARS
NIGHT	1	KALPA	4,320,000,000	YEARS
MONTH	60	KALPA	259,200,000,000	YEARS
YEAR	720	KALPA	3,110,400,000,000	YEARS
LIFETIME	72000	KALPA	311,040,000,000,000	YEARS

Table 22: The Duration of Brahma's Life

The modern concept that the universe is created due to a Big Bang is not recognized in Vedic cosmology. The universe begins when "life" or *prāna* is breathed into matter by *Mahā Viṣṇu*. Through His breath, *Mahā Viṣṇu* inserts the soul into matter (His *prāna* carries the soul) and the control of *prāna* is called *prānāyāma*. The time in the universe therefore has a beginning and an end— it begins when God inserts His choices in matter, and it ends when He withdraws His choices. Like a body dies when *prāna* leaves the body, similarly, the material universe as a body dies when Lord *Mahā Viṣṇu* withdraws His *prāna* from the cosmos. The death and life of the universe is therefore no different from the life and death of our material bodies. When the universe is annihilated, time doesn't end, although all the phenomena are unmanifest from *our vision*. From the standpoint of *Mahā Viṣṇu*, He has just withdrawn the *prāna* from matter, which makes matter inert, and incapable of producing universes.

The living beings who were enjoying the material creation are sucked back into the body of Lord *Mahā Viṣṇu* as he inhales, and they are injected into matter as He exhales. Inside His body, the living beings are still living, just as Lord *Mahā Viṣṇu* is living, although there are no experiences. The living beings, just like God, are eternal. Matter is also eternal, although the phenomenal universe is created and destroyed.

The Age of the Universe

The total life of a universe—i.e., the age of Lord Brahma—is over 311 trillion years. Of this, the Vedas describe that little over half is over.

Lord *Brahma* lives for 100 of his years, and he has completed 50 years, 6 *manavantara*, 6 *sandhi*, 27 *chaturyugi*, 9 *yuga*, and 5114 years in the *kali-yuga*. The current age of the universe is over 155 trillion years.

DURATION NAME	UNITS ELAPSED	YEARS ELAPSED	
BRAHMA YEARS	50	155,520,000,000,000	YEARS
MANAVANTARA	6	1,840,320,000	YEARS
SANDHI	6	10,368,000	YEARS
CHATURYUG	27	116,640,000	YEARS
YUGA	9	3,888,000	YEARS
KALIYUGA		5114	YEARS
TOTAL AGE		155,521,971,221,114	YEARS

Table 23: The Age of the Universe

By modern scientific estimates, the universe is 13.7 billion years old, and scientists estimate that time will end in another 5 billion years. Both these estimates are way off according to Vedic cosmology. The universe is 155 trillion years old, which is more than 10,000 times greater than the scientific estimates. And the universe will continue to exist for roughly the same amount of time, which is 30,000 times greater than the current scientific estimates. While science does not speculate about when the universe will be recreated, we can estimate that after its annihilation, the universe would be recreated after 311 trillion years. Of course, the concept of a "year" estimated through the movement of a Sun would not be possible because the Sun itself would not exist, and therefore we cannot "measure" how time is passing because the clock of that measurement itself doesn't exist. The only way to know how much time is remaining before the creation is reinitiated is to depend on the breath of Lord *Mahā Viṣṇu*. Like *prāna* in our body maintains the biorhythms, similarly, God's *prāna* keeps His biorhythm of creating and destroying the universe.

12

Principles of Vedic Astrology

Although fixed in His abode, the Personality of Godhead is swifter than the mind and can overcome all others running. The powerful demigods cannot approach Him. Although in one place, He controls those who supply the air and rain. He surpasses all in excellence.

—Śri Īśopanisad, Mantra 4

Three Descriptions of Space

Before we begin to understand astrology, we must comprehend the different ways in which types are used in Vedic cosmology, and how these gradually manifest into the phenomenal world we observe:

- Space has an absolute definition in terms of a coordinate reference frame of four directions (north, south, east, and west), which remain invariant across different individuals. This reference division can be used to define the universe as a house, and its divisions into various parts can therefore be viewed analogously to the divisions within a house[1] such as kitchen, bedroom, dining, study, bathroom, etc.
- The reference space is overlaid with the events that will occur in this space. These events have two components—space and time—that define where and when that event will occur. The events also span across our subtle body experiences, gross body changes, and the body of *prāna* which connects these two bodies. These events, as we have seen, are produced by

time in two forms: Lord *Ananta* in the *Garbhodaka Ocean* and Lord *Saṅkarṣaṇa* in the Causal Ocean.

- The description of events, however, does not define the participants in those events. The participants connect a succession of events as their personal life stories, and they are analogues of *trajectories* in science. An object joins the event-states in a scientific theory, and similarly, an actor joins the succession of events in a life story. The description of events must therefore be complemented by a description of the trajectories that join or sequence these events.

We have already discussed the first two of these stages at length, and this chapter is devoted primarily to describing the third. We can call these three typed divisions the *stage* (which is the absolute division of space, and creates a reference frame for everything else), the *play* (which comprises a story being depicted on the stage, together with the roles, although without the actors), and the *actor* (which represents the individuals or objects living or placed inside the role-based division). These represent the incremental stages of the enactment of a play. In a typical play, the same actor can play many different roles, and a particular role may alternately be played by different actors. Thus, the play can remain invariant, although the actors can change. If the play is all the events that will occur, and it is defined by the working of time, then the universe is deterministic in the events, although indeterministic in the actors.

Indeed, this is how the universe is described in Vedic cosmology—deterministic in the events but indeterministic in the actors. The periodic occurrences of the ages, and their characteristics, indicate that the events are fixed. Similarly, the predictions of the future in texts such as *Bhaviśya Purāna* entail that the events are predetermined, down to the names of the individuals who will perform those actions, or those who will participate in them. And yet, despite this determinism of events, there is still free will by which a person can choose to play a different role. The choice of a role by an actor does not change the events in the play or the roles themselves. They are however akin to an actor choosing to play a different role in the fixed play. When an actor chooses to play a different role, he or she wears the attire expected of the character and behaves just as the character is expected to behave. From the external perspective, therefore, we cannot make out that the actor behind the façade is different. To that extent, whichever actor chooses to play a role in a drama would be indistinguishable from the observable phenomena. But there is still a sense in which there is a different person enacting a specific role.

Astrology is about the study of the extent to which a person can change his or her role in the play, and its understanding involves the discussion of how individuals are selected to enact a part in the cosmic play. Clearly, this selection is based on some of our *capabilities* or *desires* to play a certain part, which are represented through the *prakriti* or *guna*. But they are also equally defined by the manifestation of *karma*.

Our *guna* are habits of enjoyment, perception, and action acquired during previous lives. The *karma* is the consequences of those habits. While our habits push us in different directions, they can ultimately be conquered and modified through free will. In that sense, everything that happens in the subtle body can be changed with free will. Since *karma* limits or restricts our desires and habits, when the habits and desires are changed, this limitation still acts, although on a changed habit or desire. For instance, a person's good *karma* would result in material successes, although these successes can be in relation to different desires. For instance, if someone's primary interest is business, then good *karma* can entail success in business. However, if this interest is modified into politics, then good *karma* will create opportunities for success in politics.

The causes in astrology are structured in a hierarchy at the root of which lie our *guna* or habits and desires. The *guna* are present in the coverings of the universe, and they are gradually manifest into a subtle body whereby these unconscious desires and habits become conscious. The manifestation of the desires into the subtle body gradually evolves with time due to the effect of internal time, and thereby different desires are manifest in different lives. All desires, however, are manifest only in the subtle body unless they are permitted by *karma*, which is when they also manifest in the gross body, and its various activities. Certain things that are not desired by us can also happen in the gross body, but these are things that exist in someone else's subtle body, and they manifest in our gross body due to the actions of other individuals, because of the *karma* and desires of the other individuals. In between the gross and the subtle bodies lies a realm of *prāna* which converts the subtle into gross.

The relation between the subtle body, the gross body, and *prāna* represents three different descriptions of an object. Consider an object such as a car. This object embodies a *concept* called the car, which corresponds to its subtle body. Of course, something would not be a car, if it did not work like a car, and therefore to *prove* that something is a car, it must also act like a car. This action is *prāna* which demonstrates the concept. But this demonstration would not be observable by the senses if the activity was not occurring in gross matter. To make this activity observable, there must also be material properties such as sight, taste, sound, touch, and smell, due to which we can actually *prove* that the activity is real. Thus, the subtle body is a conceptual description of an object; the *prāna* is the evidence of that concept in terms of activity; and the gross body is the evidence of the activity. Since the lower tiers of reality are produced as evidence for the higher tiers, the lower tier depends on the higher tier. Furthermore, in trying to provide the evidence, the subtle must also be elaborated into details. This, as seen earlier, creates an inverted tree.

Since the gross is produced as an evidence for the subtle, sometimes when the evidence is absent, we conclude that the subtle is absent. And when the evidence is presented, we don't treat it as the evidence of the subtle, but as the only reality that exists. Material science has been produced by treating the observables as the reality itself, rather than a proof or demonstration of the existence of the subtle, while Vedic science and cosmology only treat these as phenomena indicating a deeper reality.

Prāna is part of the subtle body in the sense that we can control it through free will. In fact, it is the grossest part of the subtle body, and the preliminary practices of *yoga* involve the practice of *prānayāma* which helps control the mind. As the mind is controlled, the expression of the mind into the gross body is controlled, and gradually the mind is also controlled. If, however, the *prāna* is not controlled, then the expression of the mind into the gross body is curtailed by *karma*. First, this *karma* acts in the production of the senses, then the sensations, and then the sense objects. The subtle body is therefore the trunk of the tree of causality. From this trunk, many branches of subtle activity are produced. And from this activity, many objects are produced. The production of the senses and their objects are controlled by *karma,* but the other higher levels of matter can be controlled by free will, and they are therefore purely *guna.*

The *guna,* the *prāna* and the *karma* cannot be manifest unless there is an event in the universe occurring, and therefore the events are even more fundamental than *guna*. Due to *guna* we may desire to take up a role or perform an action that is already about to occur due to the determinism of events. However, even if we did not desire, nature will arrange a suitable alternative individual who will grab such an opportunity[2].

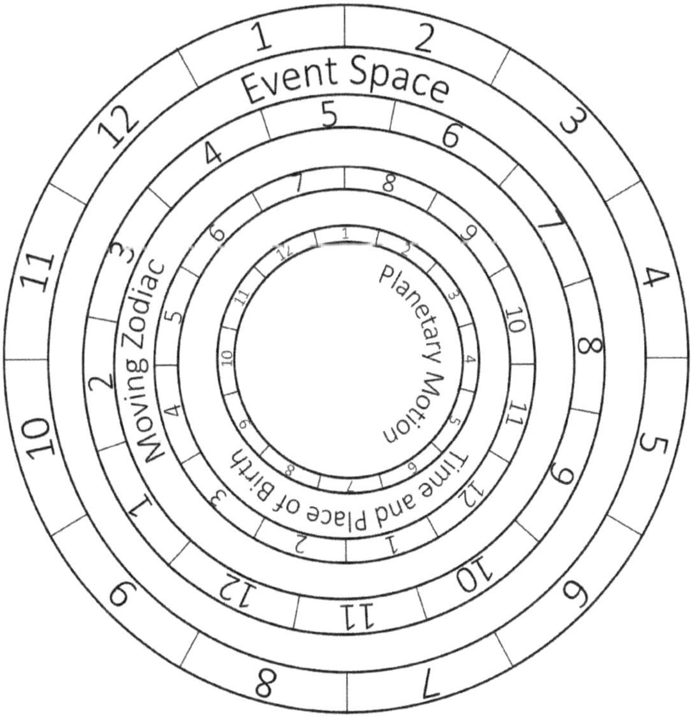

Figure-45 The Four Tiers of Causality

The resulting hierarchy of causes is shown in Figure-45. The basis of all causes lies in the cosmic time that produces a subset of all possible events. A subset of these events is desired by us, due to our *guna*. Only a subset of our desires is converted by the *prāna* into the actions of the senses, and only a subset of the actions culminate into the intended results, due to *karma*. Each successive layer of manifestation is controlled by time, by defining the extent to which an event is converted into gross matter. For instance, at certain times, the only possible events are desires, and we can then dream about the past or the future, but never convert it into action of the senses. At subsequent times, we can have the desires as well as the necessary power to perform some actions, although they will not produce the intended outcomes. Finally, sometimes, we can desire, act, and achieve the results, because they are permitted by cosmic time.

Those who don't understand this hierarchical model of causality attribute success to their power of thinking and acting, due to which they achieved some results. They might forget that our imagination, desire, or sensual power is inadequate without the necessary *karma* and time.

Vedic astrology considers these tiers of causality, although much of the understanding about the true nature of causality has been lost in modern times. The rotation of the zodiac, which represents the evolution of our *guna* or desires, is also said to denote *sidereal time*. This time presents a description of our life in terms of the changes in mind, intellect, ego, and *mahattattva*. At a certain point in sidereal time, an individual is born in the world, initiating the flow of the *prāna* in the body. The event of birth (the place and time of birth), which defines the origination of our *prāna* is denoted by the astrological houses, and they represent the description of our life as the activities of the *prāna*. The houses are said to describe different aspects of our 'life', and this 'life' should be understood as *prāna*. Finally, the conversion of these activities into the gross body is controlled by the motion of planets, which manifest the *karma* of the living being. The three key elements of astrology—zodiac, houses, and planets—are thus representations of three tiers of our material existence.

It should be noted that the *karma* to be manifest during the entire life is already present with the living being at the time of birth. The *karma* is not 'received' or sent anywhere. It is like a book that is in our hands, although we haven't read it yet. As time passes, the pages of this book are automatically flipped, and the effects on the gross body are manifested.

Astrology works by drawing maps of the relation between the zodiac, the location of the houses, and the positions of the planets. In this description, the effect of cosmic time is already taken for granted through the motion of planets and that of the zodiac. That is, we assume that the planets and the zodiac will continue moving just as they have been moving previously, and these fixed periods and rates of movement are borrowed from astronomy, generally without a good understanding of why the planets and the zodiac are moving. However, if such an assumption has been made, and the relation between the zodiac, the houses, and the planets are understood as the distinction between the subtle, the *prāna*, and the gross bodies, then a good understanding of astrological predictions can be developed. If, however, this relationship is not established or understood, then the cause-effect relationships remain obscure, and sometimes we erroneously consider an effect to be a cause, and a cause to be an effect.

Ideally, a particular absolute location is suited for a particular type of event; an event is suited for a particular character; and a character is suited for a particular type of actor. However, this ideal matching of the stage, the drama, the role, and the actor is not necessarily true in all situations, and many imperfect situations are created due to a semantic mismatch. For instance, as the zodiac signs move into different spatial locations, they create different types of incompatibilities between the *guna* of the living being and the ideal activity to be performed at a location. As the houses are moved into different zodiac signs, they create incompatibilities between the characteristics of a role and the sensual capabilities needed to enact that role perfectly. Finally, as planets move into different houses, they create incompatibilities between the capabilities expressed in the senses, and the results obtained from those actions, and we see that sometimes little action produces many results, and at other times a lot of action produces no results. Or that some incapable person is very successful, while a very capable person languishes in obscurity. These incompatibilities enhance or diminish the effects of the zodiac sign, a particular house or a specific planet:

the effects are enhanced when the compatibility is high and reduced when the compatibilities are low.

Astrology is the study of these interactions, what they represent, and how their mutual influences enhance or curtail the effects. To understand the causality in astrology, we must understand the *hierarchy* in the causality. The fact that causes flow in a hierarchy has already been discussed earlier. Some elements of this hierarchy too have been discussed previously in great detail, but other elements are either new or inadequately described earlier. This chapter will discuss these elements in detail.

The Nature of the Sun and the Moon

In Vedic astrology, the Sun represents the intellect and the Moon represents the mind. The role of the mind is in producing meanings, while the intellect performs judgments. In perception, the intellect plays a crucial role in deciding whether the cognition is true or false, employing the memory of past experiences, and it produces a cognition of the nature of reality, by judging it to be true. Thus, for instance, when we read a book, the senses indicate that the objects being perceived have some color, shape, size, etc. The mind divides these sensations into groups, thereby forming words, sentences, paragraphs, etc. and attaches meanings to these objects. The intellect then judges if these meanings are true by comparing them to other meanings, which may be retrieved from memory.

The mind of a materially conditioned soul is habituated to discard many facts in perception. A scientist may, for instance, look at a planet and discard its shape, size, color, etc. and simply model it as a point particle. Or, these properties may be considered, but the planet is never associated with a meaning. The intellect too is habituated to accept these false perceptions as truths, because over time we have become so accustomed to these falsities that they remain prominent in our memory and are unquestionably accepted as truth. The result of these false perceptions is that a *karma* is created which can correct these misperceptions in the future by bringing into focus the failure of the misconceptions due to which the soul may be compelled to revise his wrong conceptions.

This *karma*—produced as a result of a misperception in the intellect or a mistaken idea in the mind—becomes the cause of our future experiences. These experiences are manifest to us through the sensations and sense-objects, which have five varieties: taste, touch, smell, sound and sight. The light that we see from the planet is only one of the sensations: the sensation of sight. This light should be understood not as a physical object, but as an *effect* produced by *karma*. That is, we see certain things when the *karma* manifests. We don't see things when the prerequisite *karma* necessary to produce an experience is missing, or the *karma* exists but is not currently manifest. Since *karma* is produced from the misunderstanding of meanings, and a misjudgment of their truth, the Sun and the Moon, which are representations of the intellect and the mind, have an important role to play in the production and delivery of *karma*.

The light that we see is the part of the *karma* that is being manifest and which is being *absorbed* as knowledge. There can also be light that is discarded from our perception: e.g., our eyes can see something, but the mind or the intellect doesn't accept it as being real. The production of *karma* therefore has two parts: (1) the knowledge that is experienced and absorbed, and (2) the knowledge that is available although discarded. The latter part of *karma* manifestation produces a new *karma* which would be again manifest at a later time, and then it can again be absorbed or discarded. Only when light is completely absorbed, we can say that knowledge is completely accepted and no new *karma* is created.

Thus, when the Sun enlightens the world by imparting its light, and we neglect some parts of the world available for observation, the light in the Sun (which is a manifestation of the previous *karma*) is divided into two parts: (1) the part we perceive, and (2) the part we do not perceive. The part that we do not perceive is reconverted into a *karma* for the future, while the parts that we perceive become the (partial) results of the earlier *karma*. So long as we continue to misperceive reality, some part of the *karma* is again transformed back into new *karma*. Since the parts that we discard depend on the soul's *guna*, the new *karma* created depends on the type of the *guna* that was acquired due to previous habits. In a sense, the Sun is lighting up the world, but that light has two parts: (1) as something that is revealed, and appears as information we perceive, and (2) that which is hidden and stored for revelation at a later point in time.

We can say that the light perceived by the observer is 'absorbed', while the light that is discarded from our perceptual process is 'reflected'. Both the absorption and the reflection of light should be treated semantically and not physically. For instance, in the physical view, for light to be reflected, it must first be received by our body, then absorbed, and then emitted. This physical view of the world results in the notion that there is a lot of information being received that is 'redundant' to us; we might call it the 'spam' that we don't need. In a semantic understanding of nature, however, a message is sent only when the receiver is capable of receiving it[3]. The Sun does not, therefore, 'spam' us with light, some of which we absorb while the other goes to waste. Rather, a source and destination have to be 'entangled' before light is transmitted, and this entanglement entails that the information that we cannot process will never be sent. The information that we don't process produces new *karma.*

The Moon plays an analogous role to the Sun, although the Sun performs this role during the day, while the Moon does it during the night. Effectively, during daytime, *karma* flows through the intellect while during the night it flows through the mind. The intellect is rational, organized, and judgmental, while the mind is sensual, creative, and social; the Sun represents the intellect, while the Moon represents the mind. The tendencies of the intellect and the mind thus predominate during the day and the night: the intellect is stronger in the day, and in turn controls the mind. During the night, the mind is stronger, and the intellect is weak. Rational and organized activities are thus better performed during the day, and creative activities are better done during the night.

Of course, if the mind is not under the control of the intellect, 'creativity' will only produce illusions, and nights are thus not recommended for any activity because the intellect is weakened due to the setting of the Sun. However, we can see that most creative people—e.g., artists, writers, poets, and even scientists—are very active during the night, allowing their minds to freely create new ideas. During dreams too, the mind and the senses are very active, while the rational judgments are weakened.

The Sun and the Moon are key planets because they play such an important role in transacting the *karma*. When both the Sun and the Moon are absent (e.g., on a moonless night called *Amavasya*), the *karma* is transacted through the polestar, and on such nights, everyone is advised to worship Lord *Viṣṇu* who resides on the polestar, to directly surrender the results of our activities to Him. All the planets in Vedic cosmology are 'hooked' to the polestar through 'ropes of wind' which means that the information going between these planets is being converted from Fire to Air. The 'rope' is the path on which the information between planets travels. In modern science, these 'ropes of air' are modeled as force fields[4].

The Meanings in the Zodiac

The mind and the intellect, however, don't operate on their own; rather, they are paired with two other entities: the solar and the lunar zodiacs. The solar zodiac represents our moral values, which work with the reason and judgment of the intellect. As we have earlier noted, *mahattattva* and the intellect are both judgments, but they are judging in different ways: the intellect judges by comparison of facts (including the memory of prior facts) while *mahattattva* judges by our innate values. Two facts may seem consistent with each other, and we may judge them to be true based on this consistency, but if they don't match our values, both would be rejected as logically consistent although untrue. The zodiac of the 12 signs and the Sun therefore cooperate to arrive at judgments of truth based upon two different considerations: the facts of the world, and our values.

Similarly, the lunar zodiac represents our intentions, which must be paired with the meanings in the mind to create knowledge. The meanings in the mind include ideas such as table and chair[5]. While perceiving an object, these perceptions are attributed to the observer, whereby we suppose that this is *my* experience. Philosophers have called this the *intentionality* of experience. Similarly, when propositions about the world are formulated, the intended object is referred by a *name*. For instance, we might say that 'the Earth is round' such that 'Earth' is a name, while 'round' is a concept. The words sometimes denote a concept, and at other times names. These two uses of words correspond to the mind and the ego, respectively. The term 'ego' arises because all experiences involve an 'I' which is a name for the self. However, the use of references is not limited to the self but exists commonly in all languages as names.

The lunar mansions (called *Nakṣatra*) represent our intentional system due to which the mind attaches its ideas to certain types of things and becomes preoccupied with those things. For instance, the mind's creativity can be applied in many domains like art or politics, and these domains associate with the mind to create intentions. These mansions are therefore governors of the working of the mind and the tendencies of the mind are modified through their application to a specific object outside the self. When the object becomes the self, the person becomes preoccupied with himself, and such a person is generally considered selfish because this attachment of the mind to self-interest is still material. The *Nakṣatra* in which the Moon is situated, therefore, represents the intentionality of the mind, by its attachment to a certain type of external object. This sign of the placement of the Moon is called the *rāshi* in Vedic astrology and many predictions can be made simply based on this *rāshi*.

The zodiac, the *Nakṣatra*, the Sun and the Moon thus represent our subtle body comprised of morality, ego, intelligence, and the mind. In *Sāñkhya* these elements precede the gross body, and they are thus representations of our *guna* or past habits. These habits can be modified by our free will, and therefore the subtle body can be controlled by free will, although fighting our habits by the force of free will is sometimes very hard, if the habits are very strong, and push the mind to act in a certain way. The subtle body is under the control of internal time, therefore, with the passing of this time, the mind, intellect, ego and morality can be automatically modified. These changes are seen when a person's personality is altered during life, and new interests are automatically aroused.

A common mistake often made in understanding these elements is to confuse them with 'consciousness' which is a misconception at two levels: (1) consciousness is different from these material elements, and exists even when the element doesn't exist, and (2) when the elements exist, consciousness may not be aware of their existence. The subtle body is therefore not to be equated with consciousness, and not everything in the subtle body is also conscious *experience*. The crucial distinguishing factor here is that we may never be aware of lots of things present in the subtle body. A classic example of this fact is that the gross body is produced from the subtle body, but we aren't aware of this production.

It should be noted that the Sun, the Moon, the zodiac, and the *Nakṣatra* represent *guna* rather than *karma*. *Karma* acts on the *guna* in the subtle body to produce the gross body, and, therefore, *karma* has to pass through the Sun and the Moon. However, this doesn't mean that the Sun and the Moon themselves are representations of *karma*.

We can understand this distinction through an everyday example. Suppose a person is born with a deep interest in music. Is that inclination their *guna* or their *karma*? Many astrologers tend to attribute this to *karma* which is incorrect, because *karma* determines not our inclinations but whether those tendencies will be realized through the senses, and whether they will be successful in relation to other living beings. For instance, you might have a great musical talent, but you may never be able to become a successful musician. Alternately, you may have great musical success, although your musical talent is quite mediocre. The subtle body of the living being—*mahattattva*, ego, intellect, mind, and senses—denotes their *guna*, while the elements manifested from these, namely, sensations, and sense objects, are produced from *karma*. All living beings have *guna* although the gross body depends on their *karma*. If a person is deaf, the sense of hearing is present, although the body is incapable of hearing. Thus, deafness is due to *karma* although you may have a great musical talent due to your *guna* (Beethoven is an example of this).

There is, however, an even more profound reason for separating *guna* and *karma*, which concerns free will. If our minds and intellects were defined by *karma* then we couldn't have any control over our thoughts, we couldn't learn things by our effort, we couldn't develop new interests, and we couldn't interpret the world differently. That would mean that we are machines governed by the previous *karma* and have no choice; indeed, some mistaken views of astrology see it as a fatalistic approach to life, where everything is determined by the past, and you cannot choose anything. They must, of course, realize that if there is no natural system for deciding the reward or punishment for actions, then there is no need for morality; we may try our best to beat the system of ethics created by humans. Both positions—namely, fatalism or freedom without responsibility—are problematic. The resolution to this problem is that the mind can be free (although it is governed by past habits, which must be overcome by will), but the body is governed by the past *karma*.

Since the body is manifested from the mind, it carries the habits of the past, the free will of the soul, as well as the control of *karma*. The soul can change the *guna* through its will, while *karma* acts on the *guna* to produce the body. Thus, the soul is the highest, the habits in the mind are lower than the soul, and the body is even lower than the mind. If this hierarchy of causality is understood, many confusions are resolved. The 27 lunar mansions therefore represent the domains that direct the mind, and the 12 solar signs represent the morals that direct the intellect. The *karma* that produces the gross body essentially limits the mind or the intellect, but we must understand the distinction between the substrate and its modification, which gives us the causal hierarchy.

The Meaning of the Five Planets

In Vedic philosophy, the activities of the mind do not produce *karma*. For instance, if you dream having killed someone, the violence does not create *karma*. Similarly, if you think about cheating, but never express that thought into action (perhaps because the thought is arrested by the judgment of wrongness in the intellect), there is no *karma*. The production of *karma*, thus, depends upon the expression of the mental states into the modification of the external world, which in Vedic philosophy is described as the five elements: Earth, Water, Fire, Air, and Ether. Similarly, the consumption of *karma* only applies to the gross body. This is another reason to separate the domains of *guna* and *karma* because if our mental states were consequences of *karma* (rather than *guna*) then all mental activities, judgments, etc. would also produce *karma* even though they are not expressed in the activities of the gross body. Thus, while illusion exists in the subtle body, unless this illusion is manifest in a wrong activity, *karma* is not created. All misperception, therefore, has to be understood as the neglect of one of the five elements by the mind or the subsequent acceptance of this misperceived reality by the intellect.

The resulting *karma*, which will eventually produce one or more of the five elements, therefore must be associated with those elements. Since these elements are produced by the manifestation of *karma*, the *karma* must exist objectively until it is manifested. In the unmanifest state, the *karma* is the potential for becoming one of the five elements, but this potential cannot be observed by the senses. This is one of the key reasons that modern atomic theory can never solve the problem of observation until *karma* is invoked, because the reality being observed exists objectively as *karma* although it cannot be observed until it really manifests during a measurement. When *karma* manifests, it produces one of the five elements, which are then perceived by the observer. Until then, *karma* lies dormant, as something that was created in the past.

Karma is the past that exists in the present due to its causal influence, although we just cannot see it until it produces an effect. *Guna* is also habits and impressions created in the past, and we cannot know their existence unless they produce an effect. The difference between the two is only in the part of our material existence that is altered by the existence of this past: the subtle body by *guna* and the gross body by *karma*.

When *karma* is created, it must be stored in a form which can later produce the states of the five elements. This *karma* exists with the living being all the time, although it is manifested gradually, thereby producing the gross body from the subtle body. We have earlier discussed how *karma* goes through unmanifest, about to manifest, and manifest stages; the manifest stage is the visible state of *karma* produced from two other invisible states. The conversion of the *karma* from unmanifest to manifest state is determined by the motion of the five planets (Jupiter, Mars, Mercury, Venus, and Saturn), and these planets are therefore understood to be the places where the *karma* exists while in its unmanifest state.

It is notable that the idea that *karma* exists with the living being, and in one of the five planets, are not contradictory notions, because our lives are perspectives on the demigod lives. In a sense, the five planets are representations of *karma* that gradually produces the five elements. We might say that when *karma* is produced, it is absorbed by the five planets, where it lies dormant until the time for its manifestation arrives[6].

The five planets that absorb and emit *karma* are identified with the five gross material elements, namely, Earth (Saturn), Water (Venus), Fire (Mars), Air (Mercury), and Ether (Jupiter)[7]. This identification is instructive but its significance is generally missed in modern astrology: the import is that these planets control the manifestation of the subtle body into the gross body. In *Sāñkhya*, gross matter is manifested from subtle matter; for instance, Ether is created from the Mind, Air from the Ether, Fire from the Air, etc. When the five planets control the *karma* responsible for creating specific kinds of elements, they regulate when, where, and how the subtle body is converted into gross effects. For instance, Jupiter represents the Ether and Moon denotes the Mind. If Jupiter is strong (in the sense that *karma* that can convert the Mind into Ether exists), then the ideas in the Mind would be proficiently expressed as words. If Jupiter is well placed, but Mercury is not, then the further manifestation of sound would be arrested: one can express their ideas ardently as speech, but these ideas will not bring about a 'tangible' change in the world.

If Jupiter, Moon, and Mercury are well placed but Mars is hindered, then the changes can be touched but their impacts will not be visible[8]. Each planet thus curtails the effects of the previously higher planets, by diminishing the extent to which they are being manifested in matter. If a higher planet is debilitated but a lower planet is exalted, then the effects at the gross level may still be minimized because the manifestation process is hindered previously. The process of *karma* manifestation should be viewed as a critical chain in which the weakest link fails first.

Karma is defined as being of two types: good and bad. The good *karma* is produced from the mode of passion (*rajo-guna*), bad *karma* is produced from the mode of ignorance (*tamo-guna*), and under the mode of goodness (*sattva-guna*) neither bad nor good *karma* is produced. When good *karma* exists, the planet is 'strong' and when bad *karma* is present, the planet is 'weak'. These strong and weak planets essentially denote the extent to which the subtle can be expressed into gross. Thus, for actions performed under *rajo-guna*, the resulting *karma* is good, and the living beings who perform such actions enjoy their *guna* in the future because these *guna* are manifested into gross matter. Similarly, bad *karma* produced from *tamo-guna* hinders the fulfilment of our *guna* or produces incidents and events contrary to our *guna*. The living entity suffers because what the mind thinks, or the intellect judges to be true, or the ego desires, or the moral sense considers to be righteous, cannot be manifested into the gross body and its activities, or things contrary to the thoughts, judgments, intentions, and morals are forcibly manifest.

The planets representing the more subtle elements (in the order of Jupiter, Mercury, Mars, Venus, and Saturn) are therefore more important, although any debilitated planet affects the results produced by other planets, by restricting the manifestation of *guna* at a grosser level. Of course, no planet is completely hindered, and the strength of some planets can overcome the weakness of other planets, although the ill effects of a debilitated planet would still be manifest. The successive planets act as *filters* that curtail the expression of *guna*. We should realize that the planet itself is actually not weakened, but our *perspective* on the cosmic situation is hindered, due to which the same cosmic situation appears better or worse to us. Our *guna* and the *karma* produce our perspective, and whether our state is therefore caused by the *guna* and *karma*, although we can study this state through the motion of planets because the *guna* and the *karma* are both unmanifest to our ordinary sense perception.

At different points in time, different types of *karma* manifest for different people. For instance, I might be losing money due to the effect of Saturn, while someone else is gaining money due to the effect of Mars. This transfer of money between two people comprises many different parts of *karma* since the manifestation of the gross object can be curtailed by the missing *karma* in the subtle parts. If, however, this transfer occurs, the different parts of *karma* should be understood as having moved from one part of the planet to another. For instance, the *karma* that produces Ether would be moved within Jupiter, the *karma* that produces Air would be moved within Mercury, etc. This motion of *karma* should be understood as the transfer of light from one location to another within a planet. The living beings on these planets are also participants in this exchange, and when Air is moving from one part of Mercury to another, we should view this as a living being in Mercury giving Air to another living being. The living beings on *bhūloka* share the bodies with the demigods, although the demigods and the *bhūloka* residents have different perspectives on this sharing: the demigods partake in all the elemental exchanges of a certain type, while we partake in a small subset of all elements.

The Cosmic Chandelier

We have seen earlier how information must go up and down a semantic tree, and not directly, because the *path* of information exchange is through the branches of the semantic tree. Even in the case of material exchanges, information must disappear at one location and appear in another. This disappearance doesn't mean that the information is lost, and the appearance doesn't mean it has been gained. Rather, information becomes subtle and travels up the tree, and then becomes gross and travels down the tree. The number of nodes traversed in this up and down travel depends on the semantic difference between the sender and the receiver of information; the greater the difference, the higher up the information must travel; similarly, if the difference is minimal, the information needs to travel only a fewer nodes. Sometimes, therefore, the information will simply move within a planet. At other times, however, the information exchange must traverse through the other planets. For instance, the information from Saturn (which represents Earth) can go up the semantic hierarchy to pass through one or more of the five planets. It can even pass through the Moon, the Sun, the stars in the zodiac or the *Nakṣatra.*

When information passes through multiple nodes, we should view it as light being exchanged between the planets, or between the planets and the stars (depending on how high the information travels upwards). When our mental states or intellectual judgments are manifest in the body, we should understand that the *karma* from one of the five planets is passing through the Sun and the Moon. Similarly, when new *karma* is created due to the misperception of the mind or the misjudgment of the intellect, it must go from the Moon and the Sun, respectively, to one of the five planets. When the *karma* is produced due to a wrong attribution of phenomena to actors, the *karma* would flow from the *Nakṣatra*, and if it is produced due to a mistaken morality, it would flow from the zodiac. There are thus 'roads' in space on which the *karma* travels, and these roads connect the different planets, the zodiac, and the *Nakṣatra*.

All these roads are said to pass through the polestar, on which Lord *Kṣīrodakaśāyī Viṣṇu* resides, because all *karma* is ultimately tied to the soul, and not the material body or any of the subtle body elements. Lord *Viṣṇu* on the polestar is also called the *Paramātma* (the Supersoul) who is said to 'observe' the living being 'eat' the 'fruits' of the material tree. The choices that produce *karma* and their consequences which produce material changes, are therefore, always observed by Lord *Viṣṇu*. This observation is achieved because all the actions of the living beings traverse through the polestar. Even if *karma* is exchanged within two parts of a planet (and it doesn't travel up and down the hierarchy), it must still pass through the polestar. In that sense, Lord *Viṣṇu* is involved in every activity in the universe, as the observer of that activity, and nothing goes unnoticed by Him. He is said to be present everywhere, although He is situated on the polestar, because He becomes aware of all interactions since the causality of these interactions always flows through Him. Just like planets partake in many material exchanges of a certain type of element, similarly, Lord *Viṣṇu* partakes in *all* exchanges of *all* the types. His awareness of every part of the universe is not due to His physical presence in all the parts, but because all causality flows through His approval.

Thus, when a living being's *karma* has to be delivered by any planet, the information will be sent to the polestar, where it must be 'approved' like a letter going overseas has to be stamped at the outgoing post office, before being sent to its destination. Due to this approval process, Lord *Viṣṇu* can mediate and terminate the effects of any *karma* and His worship is the only worship that needs to be done to mitigate *karma*. Essentially, Lord *Viṣṇu* only has to disapprove the manifestation of any *karma* and the information flow would immediately terminate. The object that had moved upstream, and had therefore disappeared from our vision, would never appear again, because the exchange is terminated.

The five planets are the repositories of the collective *karma* of all living beings. This subtle information is stored until it has to be manifested. The motion of the planets continually manifests *karma* and new *karma* is also created, if the living beings are misperceiving reality. The cause of this misperception is the *guna* that dominate in the subtle body, but its effect is the changes produced in the gross body. This causality in nature cannot be understood unless we recognize that our mental states are producing consequences which would be reaped at a later point in time.

Thus, when light is received from the Sun, and only a part of it is used as knowledge, while the other parts are discarded, the discarded part of light is transmitted and stored in subtle form in the five planets (Jupiter, Mercury, Mars, Venus, and Saturn), until the time to retrieve it has arrived. When this time arrives, the five planets emit their light which then enlightens the world to produce the phenomena by which we can correct the mistakes in the past. But, of course, whether the soul perceives the phenomena suitably, and corrects the past mistakes of perception in the process, is not up to the planets, but to the soul's free will.

The outcome of the above information flow is that all the planets must transact through the polestar, which now becomes the 'root' of the inverted *Sisumāra* tree. As shown in Figure-46, all planets are connected to each other through the root (the polestar) and not directly, implying that light between these planets does not go in straight lines between these planets. Rather, if a leaf node has to send light to another leaf, then it must first send it to the polestar, which must then 'approve' the transaction, before the information is passed to another node. The system of stars and planets thus appear to be like a cosmic chandelier; the zodiac rotates at a constant *angular* rate, while the planets rotate at a constant *linear* speed. These two motions create the luminary combinations.

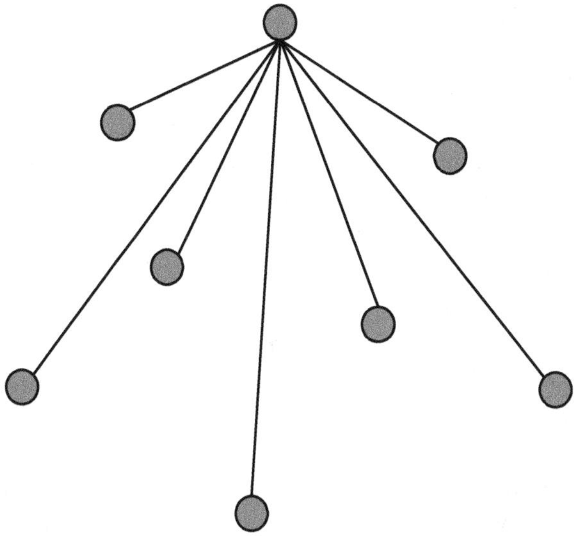

Figure-46 The Cosmic Chandelier

This model of the *Sisumāra* creates difficulties when compared to the physical view of light. For instance, if all light comes to us through the polestar (or via other planets such as the Sun and the Moon), then we should only see the light of the object from which light was sent, not those of the planets or stars which originated this light. After all, if the light has been delegated to the Sun, and it is being received through the Sun, how would we know that it was 'originally' sent by another planet? Similarly, if the light is passing through the Sun and the Moon, we should not see the other stars, including the polestar. This clearly contradicts our ability to see all the planets and the stars and requires an explanation. How are we seeing all stars and planets, if the light is hopping through nodes?

The Vedic view of the cosmos cannot be understood in the physical view of light because all light will be 'projected' in a straight line backwards, and we would only see the last hop. Similarly, in the physical view, there is no reason for light to travel up and down; it would simply travel in a straight line. Thus, unless a different view of light is developed, the Vedic view will remain incomprehensible, or would be misinterpreted.

Light and Meanings

The semantic view of light is that it constitutes a proposition, like a sentence, which comprises of two things: a subject and an object. The subject is denoted by a name, and the object is denoted by a concept. For instance, in the proposition 'the Sun is yellow', 'Sun' is the name, and 'yellow' is a concept. Or, we may say 'the day is sunny', in which 'day' is a name and 'sunny' is a concept. One of the problems in modern mathematics (which is an exemplar of formal linguistics) is that a word can be used to denote a name and a concept, and if we treat these two physically, we can easily produce logical contradictions[9] due to which all formal systems become either inconsistent or incomplete. The solution to the problem is that *names* and *concepts* are two distinct things, denoted by the same word. A Mr. Barber is not necessarily a barber, and if we confuse the name with the concept, we can create contradictions, as Bertrand Russell's Barber's Paradox shows[10]. The solution therefore requires the ability to distinguish between names and concepts, and every proposition must be able to *represent* names and concepts differently, to avoid logical paradoxes.

The name is what the proposition *refers* to while the concept is what it says about the reference. Thus, if we said that 'the Sun is yellow' the reference is the Sun, and yellow is what we are saying about the reference. As we have discussed, names and concepts are present in our body as ego and mind, respectively. All information must carry these two types, because otherwise we can be speaking about something, but not saying anything, or saying something, but not speaking about anything.

In the case of light too, there is a name and a concept. The name indicates the places from where the light is coming from, and the concept carries a meaning. Light from Jupiter can say 'good *karma* from Jupiter', which will then be superimposed on the *guna* in the mind, to convert the ideas in the mind into a sound symbol. The light thus carries two kinds of information: (1) a name such as Jupiter, and (2) a meaning such as good or bad. When this light is received, the ego determines that the light is coming from Jupiter[11]. Of course, this is a simplified caricature of the process; a more refined picture is that the name is not simply Jupiter, but 'Jupiter at location X', where the location itself is a type given by its presence in a particular type of a zodiac sign. Jupiter in Aquarius is therefore not the same as Jupiter in Gemini, and depending on its location, the name of Jupiter is modified. This means that the name of Jupiter also has to be defined hierarchically (Jupiter followed by a location). When this information is applied to the subtle body, a sensation is produced where the senses perceive a certain location of the planet, but the image that we see is actually a construction from the information received. Of course, the message may be misunderstood if the ego is not purified of misconceptions, which would then produce a mistaken position. However, this is no different than any other kind of sensual misperception.

The message from Jupiter is like a letter addressed to the end-destination (i.e., a living being) but instead of being sent directly to the living being, it is sent to a post office (the polestar), which then puts its stamp on the letter. The post office then forwards this letter to another post office (one of the planets), and depending on the destination address, the letter is delivered to the correct mind or intellect, which then produces a sensation. The process of forwarding the letter to the Sun or the Moon is identical to that of sending to a specific mind or intellect, because our minds and intellects are *parts* of the Sun and the Moon. Like a letter is received at a destination city post office, which then delivers it to a citizen in that city, similarly, when the Sun or Moon receive the message, they deliver it to a part or place within their 'city' which is semantically identical to our mind or intellect. When the message is delivered to that location in the Sun or the Moon, it appears in our mind or intellect, because our minds or intellects are of the same *type* as parts of the Sun or the Moon. Since the message has the name of the sender, the material mind or intellect know where it is received from, which is then used to decide the outcome. For instance, the message from Jupiter will manifest sound (due to Ether), while the message from Mercury will manifest touch (due to Air).

In the physical description of nature, light is believed to have been absorbed by the body before being delivered to the mind, whereas in the Vedic view, the message is first delivered to the mind, and then manifests in the body. When the message is first delivered to the mind, we remain unaware of its existence due to lack of mental development. Only when this message is manifest in the body, we become aware of its existence, and we believe that the light was actually absorbed by the eye, and then delivered to the mind, when actually it was first sent to the mind.

Recent experiments in neuroscience have affirmed the inverted process of perception. In Benjamin Libet's experiments[12] (and others after him), for instance, it has been observed that the electrical impulses in the brain are seen several milliseconds *before* the observer reports a perception. The materialists interpret this fact as entailing that our minds are produced from the brain processes, because the brain activity precedes the conscious report of sensation by several milliseconds. This is, however, a problem of our conscious development, not a problem of consciousness per se. We are so engrossed in the experiences of the senses, that we cannot perceive how *karma* is acting on our minds to produce the body. Due to considering ourselves the body, we have developed a mistaken notion that the mind is produced from the body, when actually the mind produces the body. The fact that the brain registers electrical activity before we report seeing something affirms that *karma* has already acted, and we are simply reporting this activity as an afterthought.

The key point is that the light coming from the planets is not coming as vision. It is rather coming as *karma* which is used to produce a vision. Since our perception is not advanced to see that subtle cause, we believe that we are receiving light rather than *karma*, when that light is an effect and not a cause. When light is defined as a subtle object (i.e., a message with meaning), it would be understood as carrying a name and a concept. The name would *refer* to its source (e.g., Jupiter) and the concept will indicate the meaning (e.g., good or bad). When this message is used to create an effect (e.g., a sensation), the *cause* is the source of the message. If we want to find the source, then we have to map the *name* of the object to a location in space, which means that spatial locations must denote names. In modern science too, we identify material objects by the coordinate numbers, which are names given to objects. Similarly, in a semantic theory, all objects have names, imprinted on their messages, as the address of the sender. The reason we are seeing the planets, therefore, is that we are converting the sender's address into a location in space, even though the message is delivered through a particular post office.

The Vedic viewpoint cannot be understood unless a deep appreciation of the underlying notions of causality is grasped. The latter requires an understanding of the problems in atomic physics; for instance, why a photon is a symbol of meaning, rather than just a frequency of vibration, and how its properties denote both names and meanings, which we cannot decode in current physics, resulting in incomplete theories[13].

The Role of Astrological Houses

The motion of the zodiac and that of the planets is common for all living beings in the universe, but the individual living beings still have different *guna* and *karma*. This difference is represented by *placing* each living being at a certain location in this movement. This placement is determined at the time of birth, which effectively decides the *manifestation* of different *guna* and *karma* at these times. The manifestation is of course different from the evolution, because as we undergo the events in our lives, our *guna* and *karma* are modified by our choices and/or by the manifesting *guna*. Thus, while the zodiac and the planets move in a fixed way, their effects on the different living beings are different due to their different placement in relation to these motions. The placement is defined by the 12 astrological houses or *bhāva* that denote different aspects of our lives such as finances, family, health, education, profession, spirituality, etc. Through this placement, the qualities in the *guna* and the consequences from the *karma* are manifest in different aspects of our lives.

For instance, the house of finances can coincide with the star sign that represents a warrior, and that would indicate that a person would have the tendency to earn money through war. Whether this tendency is successful and the extent to which it is successful is then determined by the *karma*, which modifies the five elements. The tendencies in the subtle body are therefore not manifest uniformly across all aspects of our lives. Similarly, good or bad *karma* is not manifest uniformly across all aspects of our lives. Whether the *karma* is good or bad, its effects are not visible in all aspects of our life. For instance, a person may be a good speaker at the workplace, but his speech may be hindered in the family. Or, one might have the *karma* for creative expression in writing and speaking, but the same type of creativity could be missing in one's personal relationships. The overlapping between the *bhāva* and zodiac signs creates a correspondence between our life values and the values of the zodiac signs on which the *bhāva* exists. For instance, if our life value is austerity, and the *bhāva* overlapping with it represents our family life then this life becomes a source of austerity. If, on the other hand, this value maps into finances, then one will undergo austerities to earn money. Whether or not that hard work produces desired outcomes, however, is not given by the *bhāva* placement in a certain sign; it rather depends on the planetary positions in those *bhāva* and whether they express good or bad *karma*. Sometimes, therefore, there can be results after much hard work, and at other times, there are no results in spite of hard work.

The result of these facts is that the effect of planets is not uniform across all aspects of our life. Rather, *karma* is differently manifested in different aspects, accelerating some aspects and hindering the others. This placement thus determines two aspects of causality: (1) the type of *guna* and *karma* that is manifest in our lives, since this manifestation is caused by the motion of the zodiac and that of the planets, which is common for all living and a placement is therefore needed to distinguish between the living beings, and (2) which specific aspects of our lives would be affected by this *guna* and *karma* since all aspects are not equally affected. The placement thus decides both the type and the aspect.

Every living being has the same aspects in life, and therefore there is a fixed arrangement of the 12 astrological houses with well-defined meanings. Therefore, ultimately, the aspects themselves are not being determined by this placement; only the type of *karma* manifesting in a specific aspect. As we have earlier noted, the aspects of our lives are like parts of a machine, such as a car. Quite like the car has different types of parts, which are sourced from different regions of a car factory, similarly, the aspects of our lives are parts of our life sourced from the types of the demigods. The placement of the houses therefore decides which *part* of the zodiac and planet our life is placed in. This placement is semantic in the sense that simply by a different placement, the parts become different types, and the locations in this placement therefore have meanings.

The placement of the astrological houses is decided by the time and place of birth, which effectively produces our *perspective* of the cosmic situation. The cosmos is the same for everyone, but our perspectives of it are different. Thus, for instance, the Sun produces both good and bad intellects, the Moon produces both good and bad minds, the *Nakṣatra* produce all varieties of intentional domains, and the solar zodiac produces all variety of moral values. Similarly, the other five planets produce both good and bad *karma*, and what is good or bad may be relative to our mind, intellect, intention, and morality. Our perspective on this situation is a specific combination of all the material elements due to which we experience some parts, while we remain unaware of many other parts. Thus, while the planetary and star movement creates the collection of all possible tendencies and activities, a specific perspective on this production constitutes the experiences of a particular individual in the cosmos.

The placement of the living being in the cosmic situation is defined by *prāna*, which is more abstract than the gross body, and less abstract than the subtle body. In one sense, the *prāna* lies between the gross and subtle bodies. In another sense, this *prāna* defines the position of the living being in the cosmic situation and thereby which qualities and activities are produced as a consequence of this placement. When a living being dies, the *prāna* 'carries' the living being to another perspective in the cosmic situation, which is another location and time of his birth.

Based on this three-fold division of our material existence, the Vedas have recommended the use of three different kinds of methods for spiritual advancement. Those interested in the activities by the gross body can perform their duties without desire for rewards in return, and this is called *karma-yoga*. Those interested in the activities of the subtle body can develop advanced knowledge of reality, and this is called *jnana-yoga*. Finally, those who can understand the workings of the *prāna* are advised to practice *dhyāna-yoga* or *astānga-yoga* to develop the perspective of God, and become detached from its workings, quite like God.

We have seen how *prāna* represents the trajectories of change, and we can now illuminate this idea even further: the trajectory of the observer represents their changing reference frame or perspective from which they view the world. The time of birth fixes the start of this reference frame, but subsequently the *prāna* carries the person to newer perspectives of experience. Since every living being is experiencing new phenomena at every moment in time, their states are defined by their trajectories, which represent the context or situation into which they are carried. The movement can be controlled by free will, although a person's habits generally force how they are carried forth by the force of time. To change our path, we must overcome our previously acquired habits. Unless these habits are overcome, the path is predetermined. If, however, habits are changed by free will, then the path can also be altered.

In that sense, the *prāna* is subordinate to the *guna* or the subtle body, because it only magnifies the abstract objects into detailed objects. But if we were to think of the individual's placement in relation to the gross world of objects, then that location is defined by the trajectory. By changing the *guna*, one changes one's character, which then alters the role that the person is playing in the cosmic drama. As a person becomes situated in a different role, the *karma* that produces events is also altered, since that *karma* is based on a perspective on the planetary motions. This doesn't mean that the *karma* is destroyed; it only means that some *karma* will not be manifested immediately and would be manifested later.

The astrological houses are the only new thing in the description of Vedic cosmology, which already covers the motion of the zodiac and the planets. However, this addition is very valuable because it connects the cosmic motions to the lives of individuals, and how this motion constrains our lives, although does not fix it. The presence of free will also entails that the positioning of the houses cannot be fixed, if indeed a person alters their character and habits through the application of free will. This process of modification is generally very slow, and overcoming the past habits is not easy, since these habits have been acquired over numerous previous lifetimes. Nevertheless, any time spent in this modification is worth the effort, since it is the only way to escape the determinism of the motion of the zodiac and the planets. These motions entail a trajectory for the individual, but free will can be used to change the trajectory. When such changes happen, then astrology based on a fixed location of the houses would become ineffective. Rather, the astrologer must be competent to draw a new placement of houses, after assessing the kinds of changes a person has brought about through their free will, which could not have been anticipated simply from the birth chart.

The System of Divisional Charts

The placement of the houses fixes our trajectory and perspective of the world, but this perspective is semantic, and therefore described in many ways, which constitutes the system of computing divisional charts, called *śodaśvarga* which is a system of 16 different charts employed to estimate different aspects of our lives. The divisional chart system achieves a far greater accuracy in terms of the placement of the planets. However, in a semantic scheme, the point is never to obtain an infinite accuracy, but only the relevant type of accuracy through a specific type of division.

For instance, if the chart is subdivided into three parts, then the division represents the states of the three *guna*. If the chart is divided into four parts, it represents the states of different values in the *mahat-tattva*. If the chart is divided into 7 parts, it represents the stages of the seven layers of matter (*mahattattva*, ego, intelligence, mind, senses, sensations, and sense-objects). If the chart is divided into 5 parts, it represents the states of the five elements (Earth, Water, Fire, Air, and Ether). If the chart is divided into 6 parts, then it will represent the 6 properties in nature (beauty, knowledge, renunciation, power, wealth, and fame). We can also combine two or more such divisional types and arrive at more complex methods of division. So, there are many ways to divide the chart, depending on which *aspect* of system we are interested in. Even if undertake a particular type of division, the perspective thus produced is always incomplete, because the other types of divisions have been contextualized. No division thus produces a complete picture, and all the divisions taken separately paint an inconsistent picture. When this inconsistency arises, the macro picture must be taken as the broad trend, and the detailed picture as the refinement of the macro picture. Only when these pictures are combined into a single larger picture of how the subdivisions are produced, can we obtain the completeness and consistency necessary.

The issue in these divisions isn't that they are possible, but what they *represent*; i.e., what meanings must we attach to the symbols produced by dividing? These questions can only be answered when we begin to see the world in terms of meanings and types[14]. Thus, if the six-fold division represents the types of meanings in nature, then the contrast between the divisions is that between the six qualities. Similarly, if the four-fold division denotes the parts of *mahattattva*, then by creating a four-fold division we are signifying the differences in moral values. If the division is seven-fold, then it refers to the seven layers of material manifestation. If the division if five-fold, then it refers to the five gross elements.

When the chart is divided in different ways, more and more accurate placements of the planets can be obtained. If previously the planet happened to be in the 7th house, after this subdivision, the planet can be seen in the 12th house. The relationships between the planets can now be seen in a new light, and the interpretations of this positioning change, even though neither the planets nor the star signs, nor the time and place of birth have actually changed. The divisional chart system is therefore a magnification of a specific aspect of our perspectival relationship to the cosmos. Once we magnify a specific aspect, we also neglect other aspects. This might give us some specific insights, while also obscure the other insights, quite like if we see things under a microscope, we might lose the big picture. The expert astrologer is therefore expected not just to look at the detailed picture, but also to synthesize the many possible detailed pictures within the bigger abstract picture. This is not always easy.

When the chart is divided into smaller parts, the effects of their location is determined based on the nature of space in the immediate proximity, rather than in the wider neighborhood. The process of division implies that the nature of the proximity differs from the nature of the neighborhood, quite like the properties of a branch are different from the properties of the leaves or fruits. The strength of a planet depends on the nature of space in which it is located, and if the space is divided into smaller and smaller parts, and the parts have different types, then their effects on the planets must differ too. The question really is: How small must we divide to assess the type interactions? The point of the divisional chart system is to associate a certain level of proximity with a certain aspect of our life. For instance, the division by 7 describes the effect on a person's relationships which is a coarse-grained effect relative to the division by 24 which governs the effect on a person's education. This means that the effect on a person's education changes very rapidly with the change in a person's time of birth (which changes planetary positions), while the effect on relationships changes slowly in comparison. Alternately, a person's education is affected by the nature of space in the immediate vicinity, while relationships depend on the nature of space in the broader neighborhood. The divisional chart system thus also constitutes a hierarchy of broader neighborhoods and immediate vicinities in space.

The divisional chart system comprises of five tiers in which the first tier begins with division by 1 (D-1) and ends in division by 12 (D-12). Similarly, the second tier begins in D-13 and ends in D-24. The system supports a maximum division by 60 which represents the D-1 chart of the past life. Thus, if the time of birth is known accurately, then it is possible to draw a chart of the past life, and from that chart, through a division by 60, it is possible to know the charts of the successive previous lives. Of course, the accuracy of these charts depends upon the accuracy of the time of birth. If the birth time is inaccurate, then even many divisional charts (which locate the planets in increasingly accurate locations) would be inaccurate, and the charts of previous births (which require increasing amounts of accuracy in the time of birth) would also be inaccurate.

In modern astrology, the knowledge about why divisions signify a specific aspect of life has been lost, and astrologers tend to use these divisional systems somewhat mechanically. To properly understand the astrological tools, we thus need to grasp the key principles of Vedic astronomy, which in turn needs a deeper appreciation of Vedic philosophy.

The principle underlying the relationship between spatial divisions and life aspects is intimately tied to the nature of atomic reality and is observed in quantum slit experiments as illustrated in Figure-47. In these experiments, the reality being measured is the same. However, this reality is viewed through an increasing number of slits, which produces a different *representation* of the same reality. With two slits, there are fewer number of broader bands. But, as the slits are increased, the width of the bands decreases, and their peaks increase. When this phenomenon is interpreted semantically, we can see that a different number of slits denote different ways of describing the same reality, and the peaks of measurement denote the symbols observed in that description. The meanings of the symbols is given by two things: (1) the number of slits being used, and (2) the locations of space on which the peaks occur. Essentially, with a different number of peaks, the same location in space is given a new meaning, and particles at that location become symbols of a different kind of meaning. The order of particle arrival now represents the succession of symbols which denotes semantic propositions.

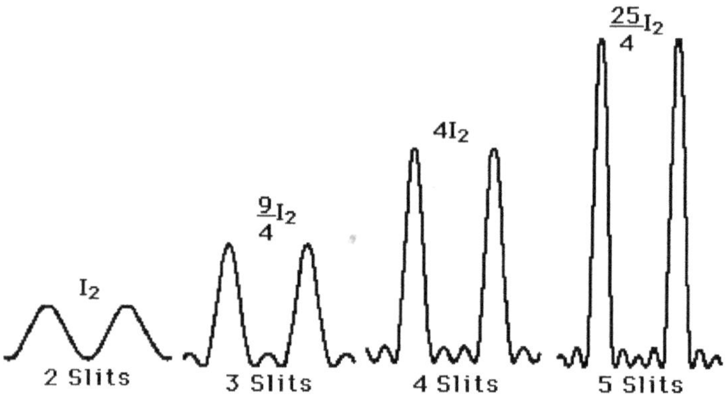

Figure-47 Division of Space Emphasizes Meanings

The subdivisions in the divisional chart system are analogues of the number of slits through which we are seeing the same reality. As space is divided into smaller parts, the frequencies of the symbols don't remain the same. Rather, some symbols become very prominent, while the other symbols are suppressed. Which symbols are enhanced and which others are suppressed depends on how space is subdivided into parts. Thus, different subdivisions are used to denote the different life aspects. The behaviors of slits shown in Figure-47 are for a uniform radiation spectrum (the so-called Bell Curve distribution).

And the peaks and troughs are accordingly symmetrical. If, however, the reality being measured is not uniform, then the peaks and troughs will also not be symmetrical. This asymmetrical distribution will then represent the relative strengths of the different symbols that arrive at these locations. A symbol that arrives frequently (with a high peak) represents a type of light that is strong, and a symbol that arrives infrequently (with a low peak) denotes a type of light that is weak. When these lights are given meanings, then it will be understood as arriving from different planets, and hence indicate the relative strengths and weakness of the planets, and thus their effects.

The key point is that the tools underlying astrology have a deep scientific significance which is inadequately understood currently because the science of types (for objects, space, and time) is unknown. When this science is properly understood, then the astrological tools will be technological devices, quite like measuring instruments in modern science.

The Viṁśottarī Daśā System

The motion of the zodiac, and those of the planets, create different types of clocks, which are summarized into a single clock called the *daśā* system. There are several *daśā* systems, of which the *Viṁśottarī daśā* system is prominently used in modern times. All such systems divide time into types (similar to how space is divided into types in the divisional chart system), which have different durations. The periods of cosmic change and their durations are shown in Table 24. Each *Nakṣatra* undergoes the same type of clock, but they are at different points in the clock: the time through which two *Nakṣatra* are passing is never the same. Rather, each *Nakṣatra* shows a different time. The clocks are all identical; however, each clock tells a different time, quite like clocks in different time zones on Earth can be identical, although they show different times. The implication of this type of clock is that if a child is born with the Moon at the beginning of the *Ketu* cosmic cycle, then the first 7 years of his childhood would be governed by the motion of Ketu, the next 20 years by the motion of Venus, the subsequent 6 years by the period of the Sun, etc.

Graha	Mahādaśā (Years)	Lord of Nakṣatra		
Ketu	7	Ashwini	Magha	Mūla
Venus	20	Bharani	Pūrva Phālguni	Pūrva Ashādhā
Sun	6	Krittika	Uttara Phālguni	Uttara Ashādhā
Moon	10	Rohini	Hasta	Shraavana
Mars	7	Mrigashīra	Chitra	Dhaniśtha
Rāhu	18	Ardra	Svāti	Shatabhisha
Jupiter	16	Punarvasū	Vaisakha	Pūrva Bhādra
Saturn	19	Pushya	Anurādhā	Uttara Bhādra
Mercury	17	Ashlesha	Jyeshta	Revati

Table 24: The Vimśottarī Daśā System

There are two confusing aspects of this scheme. First, the durations of different types of intervals are not identical. Second, it is hard to correlate the intervals to the periodic motion of the planets. Typically, we expect the clocks to measure equal intervals of time, but the *Viṁśottarī daśā* system divides time unevenly. The periods in the *Viṁśottarī daśā* system (each period is called *mahādaśā*) are also not the rotational periods of the planets themselves. For instance, Saturn has a *mahādaśā* of 19 years although Saturn's revolution is approximately 29 years in both Vedic and modern calculations (these calculations are listed in Table 11). Similarly, the Sun's *mahādaśā* period is 6 years, although the Sun goes around the Earth once per year. These periods, therefore, cannot be related to the periods of the planets, although they are certainly related to their movement. Then, how should we understand these periods?

The *mahādaśā* system adds up to a period of 120 years, which repeats three times in the zodiac cycle. The zodiac has 360^0, and there are 9 planets, each of which occupies 3 *Nakṣatra*, therefore the pattern of planet occupation must be repeated 3 times in 360^0. Every year in this cycle corresponds to a 1^0 per year motion, which does not correspond to the motion of any luminary. However, this cycle is identical to the lifetimes of the demigods, because a demigod year equals to 360 of the Earthly years. The *Viṁśottarī daśā* system can therefore be correlated to the manner in which the lives of the demigods are passing, rather than to how our lives are passing. The lifetime of the demigods is 36,000 years of the solar cycle, and the *Viṁśottarī daśā* system divides the time into 360 parts, although there are other ways of dividing this time as well.

Each breath of our life is measured as a *prāna* which is described as 4 seconds. 360 *prāna* of our life constitute a *ghatika* (24 minutes of our time), which is then a *prāna* of the demigods, and the *ghatika* system is frequently used in the calculation of planetary motions. The essence of this scheme is that when we have completed a full breath, the demigods have completed 1^0 in that cycle. Since our breaths are parts of the demigod breaths, the phase of their breath influences our lives too.

The key remaining question is why the phases of *mahādaśā* are not equal. That is, why is the period of the Moon longer than that of the Sun? If we correlated these changes with the periods of planets, then the period of the Sun would be longer than that of the Moon (since the Moon undergoes more revolutions in the same duration). The answer to this quandary is that these times are not related to the planetary movement but are described *analogously* in terms of the types represented by the planets. This, in one sense, simplifies the vocabulary in astrology, since a fewer numbers of terms (houses, zodiac signs, and planets) are used. In another sense, to demystify the resulting confusion, we must realize that we aren't actually speaking about the motion of planets, but simply about a *quality* in the time that predominates at a certain given time.

This quality in time, however, would be seen even in the spatial division. Table 25 illustrates the types in time by using the spatial divisions[15]. The scheme divides the zodiac into 120 parts as follows. First, each *Nakṣatra* is divided into 4 parts using the 12 signs of the zodiac producing 27 x 4 = 108 divisions. Second, the 12 zodiac signs are added to these divisions. Then, each of the divisions is associated with the quality of the planets. The intersection of the *Nakṣatra* and the zodiac results in different qualities, which, when correlated with the qualities of the planets, creates the 'dominance' of that planet (although there is no planetary motion involved in this division). When these qualities are added up, we find the same kind of ratios as that seen in the *Viṁśottarī daśā* system.

	Nakṣatra Name	Zodiac Name	MERCURY	KETU	VENUS	SUN	MOON	MARS	RAHU	JUPITER	SATURN	
1	Ashvinī	Aries				1						
		Taurus	1									
		Gemini	1									
		Cancer					1					
2	Bharani	Leo								1		Aries
		Virgo							1			
		Libra	1									
		Scorpio							1			
3	Krittika	Sagittarius								1		
								1				
		Capricorn							1			
		Aquarius							1			
		Pisces			1							
4	Rohini	Aries								1		
		Taurus			1							Taurus
		Gemini							1			
		Cancer					1					
5	Mrigashīra	Leo							1			
		Virgo									1	
					1							
		Libra			1							
		Scorpio	1									
6	Ardra	Sagittarius									1	
		Capricorn							1			
		Aquarius							1			Gemini
		Pisces			1							
7	Punarvasū	Aries				1						
		Taurus			1							
		Gemini									1	
			1									

		Cancer					1					Cancer
8	Pushya	Leo								1		
		Virgo									1	
		Libra									1	
		Scorpio								1		
9	Ashlesha	Sagittarius								1		
		Capricorn							1			
		Aquarius							1			
		Pisces								1		
							1					
10	Magha	Aries				1						Leo
		Taurus					1					
		Gemini	1									
		Cancer					1					
11	Pūrva Phālguni	Leo								1		
		Virgo									1	
		Libra			1							
		Scorpio						1				
12	Uttara Phālguni	Sagittarius								1		
						1						
		Capricorn							1			Virgo
		Aquarius							1			
		Pisces	1									
13	Hasta	Aries	1									
		Taurus					1					
		Gemini							1			
		Cancer					1					
14	Chitra	Leo	1									
		Virgo							1			
			1									

		Libra			1							Libra
		Scorpio	1									
15	Svāti	Sagittarius	1									
		Capricorn							1			
		Aquarius							1			
		Pisces			1							
16	Vaisakha	Aries	1									
		Taurus			1							
		Gemini									1	
					1							
		Cancer		1								Scorpio
17	Anurādhā	Leo		1								
		Virgo									1	
		Libra									1	
		Scorpio						1				
18	Jyeshta	Sagittarius								1		
		Capricorn						1				
		Aquarius									1	
		Pisces								1		
								1				
19	Mūla	Aries				1						Sagittarius
		Taurus			1							
		Gemini		1								
		Cancer					1					
20	Pūrva Ashādhā	Leo		1								
		Virgo	1									
		Libra			1							
		Scorpio									1	
21	Uttara Ashādhā	Sagittarius								1		
										1		

		Capricorn						1				
		Aquarius									1	
		Pisces			1							
22	Shraavana	Aries		1								
		Taurus			1							Capricorn
		Gemini	1									
		Cancer		1								
23	Dhaniśtha	Leo		1								
		Virgo									1	
											1	
		Libra			1							
		Scorpio	1									
24	Shatabhisha	Sagittarius									1	
		Capricorn							1			
		Aquarius							1			
		Pisces			1							Aquarius
25	Pūrva Bhādrapadā	Aries								1		
		Taurus			1							
		Gemini									1	
											1	
		Cancer					1					
26	Uttara Bhādrapadā	Leo				1						
		Virgo									1	
		Libra			1							
		Scorpio						1				Pisces
27	Revati	Sagittarius								1		
		Capricorn	1									
		Aquarius									1	
		Pisces			1							
										1		
			17	7	20	6	10	7	18	16	19	120

Table 25: The Viṁśottarī Daśā Year Calculation

It is worth noting at this point that the above method of calculating is illustrative of the type of approach we must take in understanding time divisions but is not entirely accurate. For instance, if this scheme is applied literally, then beginning with Aries, we will anticipate a year of Sun, followed by two years of Mercury, followed by a year of Moon, then a year of Jupiter, and then a year of *Rāhu*. This is certainly not how the periods are calculated. Furthermore, in the *Viṁśottarī daśā*, the entire zodiac is divided into 360 parts while the above scheme divides into 120 parts. To be accurate, each *Nakṣatra* must be divided by the 12 zodiac signs. Also, the *Viṁśottarī daśā* system is hierarchical in the sense that the *mahādaśā* period is divided into *antardaśā* periods, which is then divided into *pratyantardaśā*, etc., each time following the same proportions.

The scheme in Table 25 is not accurate, but I have illustrated it because it is indicative of the kind of approach needed to understand the differences in *mahādaśā* periods. The key point is that when time is described semantically, then the durations of various types are not equal, as different qualities will dominate for different durations. Similarly, when space is divided into parts, the degrees of the qualities are not equal, although we attribute the star signs and *Nakṣatra* equal degrees. The reason for this is the *Sāñkhya* theory of mode interaction in which two modes don't sit side-by-side. Rather, when two modes are mixed, one mode goes higher and becomes the abstraction, while the other mode details it.

This fact has important implications for *Viṁśottarī daśā*, which is that the durations allocated to different planets cannot be constant for all times. Rather, these durations are themselves byproducts of the mode mixing, which changes during the different *yuga* and different parts of the *yuga*, and the scheme being used right now (for computing the *durations* of *mahādaśā*) is only a temporary phenomenon. The scheme will have to change as time passes. The result of mode mixing would not be the same as the modes go over and under. The consequence of that change would be that all the planetary periods would no longer be the same.

As we have seen, the internal time controlled by Lord *Saṅkarṣaṇa* manifests the mode domination, and this time is represented in the universe by the rotation of the zodiac. The signs in the zodiac are representation of the modes, as are the planets. However, as time passes, some of these modes will be overwhelmed by other modes. Correspondingly, some star signs will be naturally become strengthened over time while the others become weak. As these signs are subdivided by further modes, sometimes the divisor will overwhelm the divided, and sometimes, the divisor would be totally overwhelmed by the divided. Which mode dominates will therefore decide the result of mode combination, and the planetary slots that are assigned a value in Table 25 would change over time as the undercurrent becomes the overcurrent, or vice versa.

The process of division by 120 can be intact forever, although the *result* of this division, as longer and shorter durations of the planets will change with time. To calculate the new durations, we would have to take into account not just the periodic motion of the planets which always remains constant, but also how this motion is now passing through a different *age* such as *Satya-yuga*, *Tretā-yuga*, etc. or even a different *manavantara*. While all the principles of astrology remain unchanged, all the *tools* being used to make predictions such as methods of computing the effects of planetary aspects, or the relative domination of planets, or how long or short a planetary period lasts in the *Viṁśottarī daśā*, would changc.

Only when astrologers are spiritually inclined, understand the theory of material mode domination, and have the insight to measure the effect of this mode domination, can they keep evolving the tools of astrology suited for a specific time. If this understanding is discarded, or if the tools are used mechanically over long periods of time without revising them with the passing ages, the resulting predictions would be useless. As a result, over time, astrology will itself disappear as a tool for making accurate predictions if this understanding is lost and would have to be reestablished through a proper understanding of the principles.

The Nature of Rāhu and Ketu

Vedic cosmology is unique in that it describes two luminaries called *Rāhu* and *Ketu*, which are absent in modern astronomy and therefore also missing from Western astrology. When the Western astrologers study Vedic astrology they try to interpret the nature of *Rāhu* and *Ketu*, but rather than recognizing them as separate planets, they are simply treated as "lunar nodes" —the node being the point at which the Moon's orbit around the Earth intersects the ecliptic or the Sun's orbit around the Earth.

The fact is that *Śrīmad Bhāgavatam* describes that *Rāhu* lies 10,000 yojana below the Sun, and the Sun is itself 200,000 yojana below the Moon. While the Sun and the Moon move slightly up and down, this movement is not so great as to cause an intersection between the orbits of the Sun and the Moon, although this intersection appears to occur from the *bhūloka* standpoint because both the Sun and the Moon are "above" *bhūloka*. There is, hence, no intersection between the orbits of the Sun and the Moon, and there is no reason to associate a celestial entity with the intersection. Through that association, *Rāhu* and *Ketu* become fictitious entities.

Furthermore, the eclipses of the Sun and the Moon are attributed to *Rāhu* and *Ketu* and these are not just earthly appearances, as the modern astronomical explanations claim. Rather, when the Sun and the Moon are eclipsed, they are eclipsed all over the universe. The eclipse thus pertains to the Sun and the Moon rather than to our *vision*. In the modern explanation, the Sun and the Moon are eclipsed in our vision, but they continue to shine in the universe. In Vedic cosmology, the eclipse is attributed to the Sun and the Moon themselves, and not just to our vision of these planets. Therefore, to understand the eclipses, and how they are caused by *Rāhu* and *Ketu,* a completely different kind of explanation is required.

To understand the nature of *Rāhu* and *Ketu*, we must clarify the meaning of *Graha*, which is to grab or hold, and all the nine planets are called *Graha*. When the Sun and the Moon have eclipses, the phenomenon is called *Grahana*, which means that the Sun and the Moon have been grabbed or held. But all the planets are actually *Graha*, so the eclipses share some facts common with the other planets, which are presently not so well understood. When an eclipse is attributed to *Rāhu* or *Ketu*, we tend to view this as an activity unique to these two planets rather than to all the other planets. Before we understand how a *Grahana* is caused, therefore, we must understand what is actually meant by the word *Graha.*

The common view of why we see the planets is that some light is *reflected* by them, but in practice we also know that they absorb the light. The phenomenon of reflection is thus a combination of two phenomena: absorption and emission. If the planets were simply reflecting the same light received from the sun, then all the planets would appear to have the same color—i.e., the color of sunlight. The reason that light from different planets has different colors is that they are actually not reflecting the light, but first absorbing it, and then emitting it. The absorption and emission are different, and they don't occur simultaneously. Each *Graha* thus 'holds' some light, before emitting it. Due to this holding, the planet is called *Graha*[16]. The Vedic explanation of light emission is *karma* under the influence of time. All objects are thus *Graha* because they receive, hold, and transmit information. However, the planets are primary *Graha* because the other transactions are parts of the information exchange between the *Graha*. Thus, the planets are absorbing and emitting light, and this should be viewed as absorption and emission of *karma.*

The uniqueness of *Rāhu* and *Ketu* is that unlike the other planets which absorb and emit, these two only absorb light. They are thus 'accepting' information but not 'giving back' information, and duc to that reason, we can never see them, because all sight is caused when an object emits light[17]. *Rāhu* and *Ketu* should be seen as *sinks* of material information. The issue in understanding *Rāhu* and *Ketu* is why some material entities are sinks of information: Why does information disappear?

In a physical view of nature, matter is always conserved; i.e., it is never created or destroyed, although it may be transmuted from one form to another. In a semantic view, matter isn't the reality; information is reality, which can be created, conserved, and destroyed. Information is always created as *karma*, conserved as *karma*, and then destroyed as *karma*. The source of all this information is the Sun, and this information is created when our judgment about the nature of reality goes wrong, producing *karma*. One of the five planets (Jupiter, Mercury, Mars, Venus or Saturn) stores this *karma*, and later manifests it. However, with all the other planets, the light exchange is a two-way phenomenon: you give some and you receive some. With *Rāhu* and *Ketu* it is a one-way phenomenon.

Rāhu and *Ketu* are sinks of *karma*: they absorb but never emit.

When the light is stored, and then retrieved, to create an experience, the information is conserved. This conservation appears as light coming from the Sun to us, by which we see certain things, but it is actually the *karma* coming from the planets through the Sun. The energy that was previously reflected to the planets, and then stored in them, is later emitted and transmitted to the Sun. The Sun transmits a part of it to us (the part that we can perceive) and the rest is reflected back to the planets, thus creating new *karma* from the old *karma*. The essence of this process is that we can learn a lesson in life provided we are ready to learn. If we are not prepared to see what the planets are showing us, the lesson would be archived for later education, which then represents the new *karma*.

However, there are also times when *karma* is destroyed, because it has performed its role of revealing something that wasn't previously revealed to us. This type of *karma* is light going from the Sun (or the Moon) to *Rāhu* and *Ketu*, which simply absorb the light, and never emit it again. We cannot see *Rāhu* and *Ketu* because they never emit the information that they have previously absorbed. In other words, if we completely learn the lesson being taught, then all the information is 'absorbed' and none is reflected. Since nothing is reflected, we cannot see, and that inability to perceive is the absorber disappearing from our vision.

We can say that when such enlightenment occurs, the person is under the influence of *Rāhu* and *Ketu*, and their effect obscures the affected person from the vision of other people. That is, other people think that this person may not be intelligent or has no ideas; as the body is produced from the mind, their impact on the world will dramatically reduce, and they will be 'eclipsed' from the world's vision. The information loss can thus be good and bad depending on how we view it; for instance, these planets in Vedic astrology are associated with liberation, detachment, and separation, which can be understood positively or negatively.

The cosmic eclipses are times when everyone's life is slightly obscured from the vision of others because there is less light in the world, and thus no one can see the other person clearly. The effect of an eclipse is that many of the informational transactions between the living beings on Earth, that could have transpired otherwise, would now be blocked, and they will surreptitiously fail. Living beings are thus advised to avoid any major activity during eclipses because they are likely to fail.

Besides these cosmic eclipses are 'eclipses' occurring in an individual's life although not in everyone's life[18]. These are the times when individuals are gradually liberated from illusion because they can see more than they were earlier seeing, and the light coming to them is being absorbed because of *Rāhu* or *Ketu*. While other people may think that the person has become hidden, the affected person is actually learning.

In an absorption, we gain an insight, although since our effort does not produce a new outcome to be reaped later, this effort can be (mistakenly) considered 'wasted', presuming that all effort is performed for obtaining some material benefit. The loss or gain is thus subject to what we consider the goal of all effort to be. We might be ridding ourselves of unwanted baggage, without creating new baggage, but if that baggage is wanted (due to other planets) then you will view this as a loss.

Unlike modern science, therefore, where matter is never created or destroyed, in Vedic cosmology, information is created, conserved, and destroyed. When *karma* is created, our destiny is created. When *karma* is conserved, the destiny manifests as an experience. When *karma* is destroyed, the experience is over, and no new destiny is created. *Rāhu* and *Ketu* are therefore planets that represent the possibility of liberation from material existence. Their effect is that they reveal something new that causes a change in *guna* due to which some of the illusions that previously existed are destroyed. Of course, new illusions are constantly being created due to new experiences being produced by the other planets. So, a living being may become partially enlightened due to the effect of *Rāhu* and *Ketu*—or at least an opportunity to be enlightened is presented (which may be rejected as a false notion due to the effect of the other planets)—and then forget it due to the effect of the other planets.

The Locations of Rāhu and Ketu

The problem in understanding *Rāhu* and *Ketu* stems from the fact that we cannot observe them and measuring their positions and effects is hard. Furthermore, unlike the position of *Rāhu*, which is said to be 10,000 yojana below the Sun's orbit in the *Śrīmad Bhāgavatam*, *Ketu*'s position is not clearly described. We therefore cannot easily infer their radii, heights, and periods. How will we then determine their effects? Fortunately, there is a reference to *Rāhu* and *Ketu* in *Śrīmad Bhāgavatam* in which *Rāhu* is described as a single individual while there are 100 *Ketu*. From this we can infer that unlike *Rāhu*, which is a single planet, and its position is described like the other planets, *Ketu* is 100 planets.

> *In his wife Siṁhikā, Vipracitti begot one hundred and one sons, of whom the eldest is Rāhu and the others are the one hundred Ketus. All of them attained positions in the influential planets. [SB 6.6.37]*

There is also an incident about the churning of the Milk Ocean by the demigods and the demons in which *Rāhu* sits between the Sun and the Moon (pretending to be a demigod) to drink nectar from *Mohini*—a form of Lord *Viṣṇu*. When the Sun and the Moon point out that *Rāhu* is not a demigod, *Mohini* cuts the head of *Rāhu* and his body then becomes *Ketu*. Since that time, *Rāhu* and *Ketu* are thus said to be inimical to the Sun and the Moon. These descriptions appear contradictory, because in one case there are 100 *Ketu*—which are said to be sons (and therefore full-fledged individual living beings)—and in another *Ketu* is the body of one demon, whose head is *Rāhu*. The *Purāna* are filled with narrations that have occurred in different *yuga* or *manavantara*. The planets *Rāhu* and *Ketu* are places in the universe which can be ruled or controlled by differing living beings, quite like the demigods too are roles or positions in the *svarga*. The living beings entering these positions change from one age to another, and their positions are impermanent. The living beings that occupy a specific planet, and the reason they occupy that position, is therefore not of direct importance to why that position itself exists in the first place.

Therefore, associating *Rāhu* and *Ketu* with a narration about how a living being obtained that position isn't crucial. What is crucial is that these positions exist in the universe, and will be occupied by a living entity, who will perform the activities expected of that position. In that sense, we can separate these narrations from the philosophical and scientific rationale of how these positions operate in the universe.

The scientific rationale for the existence of *Rāhu* and *Ketu* is that sometimes *karma* as light is absorbed and modifies the *guna* of the person. As we have earlier seen, the *guna* exist as seven coverings of the universe, while *karma* exists as the 'water' covering of the *brahmanda*. Inside this 'water' covering, two parts are created—*loka* and *āloka varṣa*—and the *āloka varṣa* is the 'inside' part of the various globes because the light never enters the inside; in a semantic representation, the inside of the globe goes outside the *loka varṣa*. The unmanifest *karma* is therefore deep inside the planets, and it gradually comes up to the surface of the planet, to the point where it is automatically 'evaporated' or 'emitted' from the planet's surface. Similarly, the newly created *karma* goes deep inside the planet. As a living entity is born into a new body, this *karma* begins to come up to the surface of the planet, and when the correct time arrives, this *karma* is ejected as light from the planets, transferred to the Sun or the Moon, and then delivered to the living entities. When the universe is annihilated, the entire *brahmanda* is merged into the 'water' covering, which means that all the matter at the 'surface' of the planets has been exhausted, and the inner core of the planet is no longer manifest by time. All experiences therefore disappear. Thus, the *loka varṣa* merges into the *āloka varṣa* which then merges into the 'water' covering, which then merges into the successive layers of material illusions, and everything merges back into the pores of the body of Lord *Mahā Viṣṇu*.

The light being destroyed through *Rāhu* and *Ketu* thus enters these planets (which is *āloka varṣa*), crosses the 'water' layer, and enters one of the seven layers of material coverings, causing a change to them. In one sense, the light has escaped the *brahmanda* but in another sense, it causes changes to the layers of *guna*, positioning the soul into a new perspective about the universe, from which things that were previously unseen could now be seen. In other words, the energy that is disappearing, is actually causing a change to the state of the living being's illusion. In that sense, the energy never disappears, although it changes its form from *karma* to *guna*. Thus, when this light disappears from our sensual and mental perception, it has become a new kind of 'potential energy' in the seven coverings, from which a new type of *karma* may be created in the future.

In modern times, the eclipses are explained through an entity that comes in the 'path' of light to the Earth, when paths are defined as straight lines. Many interpreters trying to explain *Rāhu* and *Ketu* also think of these as lying in a straight-line path. This is a mistake because as we have noted earlier, light doesn't have to travel in a straight line from our physical perspective. The planets *Rāhu* and *Ketu* are certainly moving but they don't need to be in a straight line to the Sun or the Moon, just like the other planets delivering the *karma* aren't in a straight line. In a semantic science, we will see that the effect of a cause can be predicted based on the change in meanings that results. When the change in meaning is such that all light can be absorbed, the light travels to *Rāhu* or *Ketu*. When some of the light is 'reflected' then the light travels to the other planets. They key issue therefore is the time that these changes occur, and when *Rāhu* and *Ketu* become as dominant as to absorb all the light.

This time is already known as the intersection of the orbits of the Sun and the Moon. Beyond this, we cannot sensually observe their motion, although with advanced perception, it may be possible to correlate the effect of *karma* on *guna* and by those effects, it will be possible to assign them a position. In other words, the positions of *Rāhu* and *Ketu* require an understanding of the changes they are causing to *guna*. Since this change occurs in the seven coverings of the universe, which are far more subtle than anything that can be sensually observed, understanding the positions of *Rāhu* and *Ketu* itself requires a view of matter that transcends the world of *vaikharī* and *madhyamā* into *paśyanti*.

Earlier in the book we discussed how the light of the Sun goes to all parts of a universe, but when we compared the sizes of the universe given in *Śrīmad Bhāgavatam* and *Surya Siddhānta*, we found that the latter's sizes are many orders of magnitude higher than given in the former. I showed how this difference is because the total universe is covered by the seven layers of matter, each ten times bigger than the previous. However, this interpretation implies that the light of the Sun must go even into the coverings of the universe, and that it must enter *āloka varṣa* which is not lighted, and then the 'water' layer, which is also said to be dark. How the light of the Sun passes through these layers then becomes a mystery. This mystery can now be understood: the light escaping the *brahmanda* into the outer coverings is escaping through *Rāhu* and *Ketu*. This light should be understood as *karma* which is converted into a change to our *guna*. The light that goes out to the seven coverings is not what we see through our eyes. In fact, since the light goes through subtle and gross parts of the universe, we cannot define it simply as that which causes heat or fire, although these phenomena are manifestations of light.

While we cannot cover all the details of Vedic astrology here, we can see two things: (1) that there is a deep causal connection between *Sāñkhya*, *karma*, and time, on the one hand, and the predictions of astrology on the other, which is often misunderstood in modern times, and (2) the practice of astrology is scientific if this connection is grasped.

Uranus, Neptune, and Pluto

Vedic astrology includes nine planets, ignoring Neptune, Pluto, and Uranus. It is sometimes argued that these planets have been recently discovered and were unknown earlier and therefore Vedic astrology did not include them. This argument is preposterous because so many other planetary systems (lower and upper) are included, which still remain unknown. The Vedic descriptions are not based on empirical observation. They are rather based on a theory of the cosmos based on types and perception of these types by higher sensual faculties and revelations. Neptune, Pluto, and Uranus are indeed celestial objects, but we don't know which planetary system they are part of, unless their semantic properties are known. Furthermore, as we have earlier noted, the parallax method of observation (which tells us the distances to the planets) is based on a particular theory of light, space and time which is not accepted in Vedic cosmology. Therefore, whether these planets are indeed as far out as they are currently measured to be through parallax, need not be true. The fact is that the distances to these planets go beyond the *loka varṣa* and if the modern distances are taken on face value, then these planets would lie in *āloka varṣa*, which as we have previously discussed is impossible, since the *āloka varṣa* does not exchange information with *loka varṣa*.

That these planets are seen rotating doesn't mean that they are part of the same *system* as the other planets. In Vedic cosmology, there are many planets that go around the *Sumeru Mountain* but they are not considered parts of the *Sisumāra*. The observation of these planets indicates a fact that we don't understand. We can envision several possibilities:

- Neptune, Pluto, and Uranus can be part of the distant 'islands' of *bhūloka* such that they are in *loka varṣa*, and the parallax distance is misleading as far as going to these planets is concerned,
- They could be a part of a higher planetary system, and they become visible due to information exchanges with the Earth,
- They may be the four cities on the *Lokāloka Mountain* in the four cardinal directions, and another planet is yet to be discovered[19],
- They may not be planets but stars, which are dimmer than the other stars as they exchange lesser information with the earthly planets and are thus conflated with the planets in the solar system.

The key point is that there are many explanations possible for the same phenomena, which differ from the currently offered explanation. Just because Vedic astronomy doesn't describe these planets should not, therefore, be taken to mean that these planets were simply not known earlier. It should, however, mean that the inclusion of these planets in the astrological system is flawed. Certainly, since they are being seen, they are exchanging information with Earth, but unless the *type* of information is understood, its effect, and thereby the nature of the source cannot be described. This shortfall need not be anything more profound than the lacunae in understanding the billions of other luminaries.

The Modern Practice of Astrology

An understanding of the causalities underlying astrology is missing in the modern practices; astrology has become a tool in helping people solve their day-to-day material problems without a profound understanding of a living being's entanglement in the material creation. This results in many difficulties, and both the practitioners and their clients remain ignorant about what is really happening. Moreover, many false ideas from Western astrology have been inducted into Vedic astrology, to the point that even the Vedic practitioners sometimes use them heuristically.

In the modern determination of an astrological chart, the zodiac is considered fixed, and only the motion of planets is employed. This picture is not entirely accurate, because the zodiac is also moving in Vedic astronomy, which then causes the changes in the relative predominance of the three modes, which then alters the durations of *Viṁśottarī daśā* and the effects of planetary combinations. Since the science of mode domination, and how this domination inverts mode relationships is unknown in modern times, and the effect of time in calculating mode dominance is discarded, astrologers rely most only heuristics of astrological tools, without a deeper insight into the cosmic principles. For instance, the system of divisional charts (called *śhodaśhvarga*) is commonly employed in modern times, but a proper holistic integration of these charts is difficult. Due to different charts, the accuracy of predictions on one hand is increased due to a more detailed assessment of the type interactions and decreased on the other due to the separation of the charts. Finally, the combinations of various planetary positions (called *yoga*), which represent auspicious or inauspicious meanings, are also harder to decode in many cases because the science of type interactions is not known, and how these combinations have to be interpreted is not always well understood.

Another key problem in modern astrology is the inability to distinguish between subtle and gross matter. Owing to this, the role of planets in influencing different aspects of our existence is misunderstood. For instance, Jupiter is frequently associated with a person's intelligence, same as the Sun. Similarly, the Moon is associated with love and feelings, same as Venus. Then, the Sun is called a fiery planet, and often treated in similar ways as Mars. Since Mercury is associated with a fickle nature, it is sometimes compared to the Moon which is also changeful as the mind. Perhaps only Saturn is unique, because it is not compared to any other planet!

Everything in the material world is comprised of the three modes of nature, so every planet has all the three modes in different proportion. We can always find the property produced by a particular mode in any planet and compare it to similar properties produced by the same mode in other planets. Thus, water and mind can be compared, and the fire and intellect can be compared, because one is hot and the other is cold. These comparisons are not wrong, but they miss the point: words like 'hot' and 'cold' are used analogously to describe both subtle and gross matter. Our feelings, emotions, and attachments are considered 'watery', while analytics, detachment, and argument are considered 'fiery'. Both water and fire can be contrasted to 'airy' things which are moving and changing. Everything in the universe comprise these three qualities, but the proportions vary, and accordingly, they affect different aspects of our existence. The gross objects can affect the subtle objects because the subtle exists in the gross. Similarly, the subtle objects can influence the gross, because the gross is produced from the subtle. Supposing these influences is therefore not incorrect, although if we misunderstand the manner in which this influence occurs, we will mistake the causality.

The astrologers largely rely on a physical representation of a semantic system, and the meanings you derive from these symbolic representations often depends on the expertise of the astrologer, similar to how one may decode different meanings from the same text. Unlike the *śabda* process of interpreting scripture, where the scriptures are fixed and the knowledge descends from master to disciple, and masters have written commentaries on the key scriptures, in the case of astrology, deciphering horoscopes is very difficult given that every individual has a unique horoscope. In many cases, even expert astrologers tend to go wrong.

The problem of interpreting astrological charts is actually the problem of deciphering meanings from physical symbols. This problem is not new and has been previously encountered in the interpretation of Vedic scriptures themselves. Various *Purāna*, for example, describe different aspects of Vedic philosophy, and while all of them are true, their relative *importance* can be misjudged by the reader, *if* you take only that *Purāna* into account. If, however, you try to interpret the collection of all the scriptures collectively, the amount of information that needs to be assimilated is so enormous that the human mind is unable to comprehend the complexity. The remedy to this issue is following the disciplic succession of masters who have received this knowledge from God Himself.

The problem exists in modern science as well, with regard to the interpretation of observations. Should we describe an observation according to thermodynamics, classical mechanics, quantum theory, general relativity, quantum field theory, or something else? Depending on which theory you use, you can articulate a radically different view of causality, and thereby a different prediction. Science has learnt that all theories don't explain all the phenomena equally well, and therefore, with *hindsight*, we have also learnt to selectively apply different theories to different phenomena, although in actuality we know that this separation of theories is hiding some key features of reality that we don't understand.

Modern astrology suffers from the problem of interpreting symbols into meanings. Which astrological tool should be used to explain and predict which phenomenon is not always clear, although if you know the outcomes, then in hindsight you could find the right explanatory tools, similar to the problem of interpreting in modern science where we find the correct theory to describe a phenomenon *after* we determine which theory accurately predicts the phenomenon. The variety accepted by astrology is considerably higher than in modern science, and therefore the ambiguity arising from different astrological tools also becomes higher.

By no means am I trying to apologize for the shortcomings of modern astrology. All I'm trying to insist upon is that these shortcomings arise from a deficit in our knowledge of types and the theory of their interaction. When this deficit is overcome by employing more tools that seem to work for different scenarios, then the choice of a particular tool itself precludes some facts out of the predictive process, thereby creating new limitations. The key point is that astrology is not *theoretically incomplete* as any physical description is. However, to see the value in that description, we must develop a sound understanding of the types in nature, and how they interact. It is fair to say that the modern Vedic astrology needs a sophisticated science of type causality and effort should be directed in understanding the simple concepts of space, time, matter, and causality, before these are applied for the purpose of making actual predictions.

The Theory of Perspectives

In present practices of astrology, the understanding of how planets affect the lives of living beings is missing. That our minds, intellects, and bodies are 'ruled' by various planets is not grasped, because how can an object 'rule' over another? Understanding this causal model needs a revision to our understanding of matter, in which our minds and bodies are *parts* of the planets, due to their semantic similarity, and if a planet changes position, it affects us, depending on which *part* of the planet we are in.

As we have previously discussed, the demigods are not just on the planets; they are also in our bodies. More correctly, our lives are parts of the demigod lives, and demigod lives are part of our lives. These two kinds of lives are created as two distinct kinds of perspectives, which as we saw earlier, can be understood through the example of a vehicle factory. The material universe is slightly different from this analogy of a car factory in the sense that the creators of the parts create each part in a somewhat different manner. All the cars, therefore, have an engine, chassis, steering, etc. but these parts are not identical, and they, in effect, produce different cars. If one person is driving a sedan, the other is riding a truck. This difference is created because the demigods produce many kinds of parts that are instances of a certain type of part, although not identical. In a semantic view, these instances are different locations in a different type of space—the planet on which the demigod resides.

Parts of our bodies therefore exist in the demigod planets quite like the steering of a car was manufactured in a certain part of the car factory. However, we are not fully in the demigod planet because other parts of our body were produced in a different part of the car factory. The space in which the cars exist is different from the spaces in which the parts of the car exist. Every living being is therefore in two spaces: (1) a space of disaggregated parts, and (2) a space of an aggregated mechanism. The space of the demigods is the space of disaggregated parts, as they rule over different parts of our lives. Our space, on the other hand, is the space of the aggregated mechanism. Our life depends on the parts of our mechanism working properly, and in that sense, we depend on the demigods. But a factory that manufactures parts is required only when there are some consumers of cars; in that sense, the demigods depend on us. There is, hence, a mutual dependence between ordinary living beings and demigods. However, given that there is only one car factory in the entire universe, and there are many car consumers, those who run the factory have a monopoly and hence an upper hand in controlling the production of cars. The demigods, hence, have a much superior situation; they control the production of the parts, which we need to create our journey.

The demigods, of course, are not independent. They are supervised by a factory owner—Lord *Viṣṇu*—who ensures that all workers do what is expected of them. The supervisor defines the roles of workers and supervises the activities. The demigods are, therefore, different parts of a factory supervised by Lord *Viṣṇu*. The components they produce are assembled into different mechanisms, which the other beings use. Ordinary living beings thus see the cosmic situation defined by demigods from their perspectives. Similarly, the demigods see the cosmic situation defined by Lord *Viṣṇu* from their perspectives. To understand astrology, we need to understand how demigods see God from a different perspective, and how we see the sum of all the demigod perspectives from our perspective. The relation between our life and those of the demigods is established by our perspective (space-time location) of demigods while the lives of the demigods are defined by their perspective (space-time location) in relation to God. There is one reality—God—but subsidiary realities are created by generating perspectives on that reality. The demigods are semantically parts of God's body because they *see* God from a different perspective. Similarly, we are semantically parts of the demigod bodies because we *see* the demigods from different perspectives.

Ideally, astrology should be constructed in two tiers: (1) the demigod perspective of God, and (2) our perspective of the demigods, implying that our material existence is under the control of the demigods, who are themselves under the control of God. The worship of demigods is emphasized in several parts of the Vedas, which obscures the worship of God, because the material causality is indeed governed by the demigods. But, if a devotee only worships God, then he can also take care of his material life because God in turn controls the demigods. In this latter form of worship, there is causality from the devotees to God, and from God to the demigods, without the devotees directly worshipping demigods.

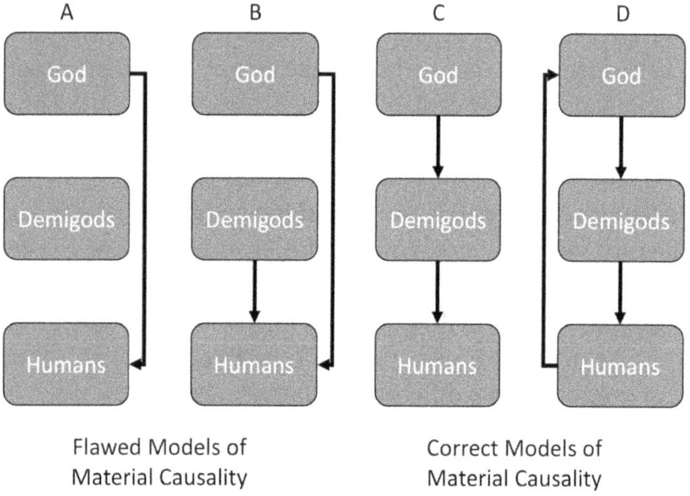

Figure-48 The Four Models of Material Causality

There are (at least) four models of causality in religions, as shown in Figure-48. The first model only considers a direct relationship between God and the soul and considers demigods a religious heresy. This viewpoint predominates in Abrahamic religions, which reject astrology on philosophical grounds. The second model views our lives as being governed by the zodiac and the planets, and disregards how the demigods are controlled by God; this model underlies much of modern astrology, where astrologers make predictions based on charts and then *separately* profess allegiance to some form of God without understanding how God is involved in every action of the demigods, and therefore the control of nature. The third model is the correct Vedic materialistic model in which God controls the demigods, who then control the humans, and forms the basis of most ritualistic practices, which have detracted people from the direct worship of God. The fourth model is the spiritual model in which a devotee only worships God, and the demigods are happy to serve such a devotee of the Lord and facilitate his spiritual advancement through good or bad material situations. The devotee in such situation may superficially appear to suffer, but that suffering is in effect the grace of God, who tries to purify the devotee and bring him into His service. This suffering (or enjoyment) should not be compared to those of the other living beings who are simply reaping the results of their previous activities and waiting to be reincarnated into another type of material body.

In the first model the devotee considers God to be his order supplier and expects Him to provide all the necessities of his life, while in the fourth model the devotee considers himself the servant of God, and only asks for things essential for His service. Thus, in the spiritual model, the devotee has no expectation that worship enriches material life, or that material sufferings would be reduced. In fact, in this model, the devotee never even expects liberation from the material world; he only asks that whichever material form he is born into, he can keep rendering service to God. This kind of devotion is the ultimate perfection of life.

Perspectives and Coordinate Transforms

The semantic view defines our lives as a perspective on reality, not reality itself. The events occurring in the cosmos are reality. By changing our perspective on reality, we see different parts of reality, without changing reality. In one sense our change of perspective changes nothing in material reality. In another sense, our change of perspective alters our lives. If in changing our life we had to change reality, then it would entail some violation of the laws that govern reality. However, if our life is a perspective on reality, then changing that perspective entails no such violation. The only difference is that the predictions made by astrology about the entire sequence of events in our lives would be amiss. The astrological predictions should therefore not be seen as precluding free will. Rather, free will can overcome the predictions of astrology without violating any fundamental principle in nature, or the evolution of reality itself.

The key principle is that our experiences are perspectives on reality, and this perspective is a misconception about the nature of God and our relationship to Him. We can go through our entire life without changing that misconception and if we do so, we haven't changed our perspective despite having moved into a lot of different places and times. The misconception in that sense is not in the universe; it is rather the covering of the soul, and lies in the seven coverings of the universe, and the soul has a 'position' or 'location' within these seven coverings. The change in perspective is when the living being either gradually removes some of the layers of ignorance and moves 'outward' towards the edges of the seven coverings or falls deeper into ignorance by entering even more 'inward' or deeper forms of ignorance. The events in our lives can change our perspective of reality, but that change is governed by free will. If a living being keeps neglecting God, he falls deeper and deeper into ignorance, resulting in lower and lower forms of life. If, however, he begins to understand God, then he emerges from ignorance and attains higher planetary systems. A perfection of this understanding results in transcending the seven layers of illusory understanding covering the consciousness.

Astrological predictions would therefore fail when a soul increases his acceptance of God and emerges from ignorance, or if he further rejects God and falls deeper into ignorance. Our lives should not be seen as statically defined at the time of birth, but by an evolving free will that has the ability to change our future, and even the present life. Of course, the emergence from illusion or falling deeper into illusion are slow processes, as they are unconscious, and have been built over many lifetimes, and changing them is not a rapid process. But that such rapid evolution can occur if the soul wills it, is always an undeniable possibility.

In one sense, our destiny is completely in our hands, but the mechanism of that destiny is not by trying to change the things in the world. It is rather changing our *perspective* about those things. The things in the world cannot be changed, and they are already predetermined by the space-time structure. Our perspective, however, can be changed, and the consequence of that change would be that we will enter a different part of the cosmic experience. Nothing in the world would have changed, except our experience. Contrary to the dominant view that astrology entails a denial of free will, the understanding of astrology helps us see when astrological predictions will fail, and what this failure really means. The point of failure is that our perspective about reality is given at our time of birth, but that perspective isn't fixed. As we go through life experiences, some of these perspectives change—both in terms of the experiences we have, and the lessons we derive from these experiences. The lessons we derive from the experiences are particularly unpredictable if one utilizes their free will to update their understanding of reality. If this free will is not used, then the predictions of astrology hold good. But if we use free will to change our understanding, then the extent of change would indicate the extent to which astrological predictions would be violated.

One of the key difficulties in understanding this viewpoint is that we have become convinced that all perspectives are equally good. So, no perspective could be objectively preferred over another. For instance, the modern theory of general relativity arose from the idea that all observer perspectives on reality are *equivalent*. That is, we cannot distinguish between these perspectives because the *theory* of nature would hold equally well in all the perspectives, even though we might construct different *models* of this reality from different viewpoints. General relativity in fact implies that there are infinitely many distinct models of reality that can be constructed from any observation. For instance, if you feel a backward pull on your body, that effect might be caused either by your forward acceleration, or by the presence of large amounts of matter behind you. This inadequacy itself implies that we cannot know the real structure of the universe, because all our observations are consistent with infinitely many matter distributions. Since all these distributions are consistent with both the *theory* and the *observation*, we cannot distinguish the real structure of the universe based on neither. The principle of equivalence should have signaled the end of cosmology, but it hasn't, because cosmologists don't take the indeterminism arising from equivalence very seriously, although they consider the theory of relativity true.

These issues can be addressed only if we discard equivalence. That is, we must acknowledge that all perspectives on reality are not equivalent. The laws of nature can be true in all perspectives, but that doesn't entail that all perspectives are equivalent, if the law takes into account our perspective about reality. The reality in Vedic cosmology is God, and the perspectives on this reality produce our experiential phenomena. The law of nature is that the perspectives produce different outcomes of future experiences, given by the *gap* between reality and our understanding of it, until the perspective is perfected, at which point, the law ceases to exist because the gap between reality and perception is nil. The law of nature can therefore hold true in all material situations, because the law measures the gap between perception and reality. But that doesn't mean that all perspectives are equivalent, because their *consequences* differ.

Our perspective is a coordinate frame, and the soul is covered by seven layers of matter, of which space and time are two coverings. This space and time is the counterpart of the idea of a coordinate frame in science, which 'covers' our viewpoint in the sense that it places us at a particular point in space and time. However, this space and time is not physical, as science treats it. It is rather semantic and represents our *ideology* about reality. This notion can be easily understood via an example.

Suppose we are seeing the Eiffel Tower from different angles, distances, and heights. In each of these viewpoints, we have a particular position in space and time due to which we get a different experience of the Tower. These viewpoints produce a partial understanding of the Eiffel Tower, because, fundamentally, we are *outside* the Eiffel Tower. If we *became* the Eiffel Tower, then we could know the entire tower from within, quite like we can experience all parts of our body simultaneously.

Similarly, if a soul is 'outside' God, and tries to view His existence like we try to see the Eiffel Tower from the outside, thereby forming different perspectives of it, the experience is always incomplete. If instead the soul becomes a part of God's experience, then it would be possible to know the entire reality at once, and although it would still be from a particular perspective, that perspective would not hide any part of reality. This idea can be easily understood by visualizing two observers—one inside and the other outside a cube. The observer outside the cube has a perspective on reality and that perspective entails seeing only a part of reality: one face of the cube is visible, while the other faces are invisible. The observer on the inside, however, still has a perspective, but he can see all of the inside: all the faces of the cube are visible, although a different observer at a different point inside the cube will see all the faces differently.

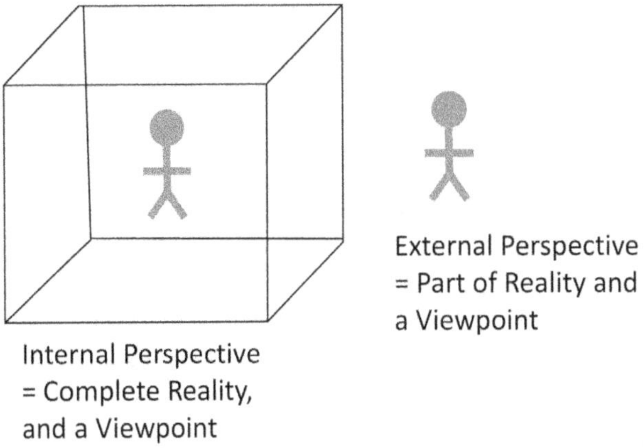

Figure-49 Internal and External Perspectives

The material vision of the world is like seeing a cube from the outside such that we cannot see all its parts, and our 'location' denotes a perspective on reality. Clearly, all perspectives are not equivalent, although the law of nature can hold everywhere. The *niyati* and *kāla* coverings of the soul (and the universe) represent the space and the time of an observer's coordinate frame, and the observer can see only a part of reality, because he is 'outside' reality. By changing his position in *niyati* and *kāla*, the soul will see something else, and while the law of nature will still measure the difference between reality and our perspective, the experiences of that reality obtained from a new perspective would be different.

If an observer goes closer to the cube, at some point he can become identical to the surface of the cube. At that point, he cannot see anything inside or outside but since he is part of the cube's surface, all perspectives are destroyed, and this stage of experience corresponds to the *Brahman* stage of God realization when the soul has merged with the body of God but is not actually part of His experience. Such souls are said to be in the bodily 'effulgence' of God, which is the boundary between the outside and the inside. As the observer further enters the cube, he can gain a complete understanding of the whole, although from a perspective, and this corresponds to the *Bhagavān* realization of reality, where the experiences are recovered although the complete reality is known from within.

Thus, the material world is called the *bahiranga* or 'external' energy, the spiritual world is called the *antaranga* or 'internal' energy, and the *Brahman* effulgence where the soul sees nothing but itself (and which lies 'between' the internal and external energies) is called the *taṭasthā* or 'marginal' energy (the term *taṭasthā* means 'situated on the shore'). One must be cognizant that internal, external, and marginal, are not different substances; they are only *perspectives* on the same substance—God. Like we can be inside, outside, or on the surface of a cube, the soul also can be inside, outside or on the surface of God. All outside experiences are incomplete, and the law of nature creates *karma* from this incompleteness. All surface experiences are devoid of any knowledge, except that of the self. And all internal experiences represent complete knowledge, although from a particular perspective within God's experience.

Thus, all perspectives are never equivalent, although the laws of nature are always true. It is unnecessary to equate all perspectives with the universality of laws, and this idea can be discarded without violating the general application of universality. Once this equivalence has been discarded, it becomes possible to conceive new laws by which our perspective on reality can be understood as creating new consequences.

In Vedic cosmology, the living beings are indeed in different coordinate frames of their *guna* and *karma* which produce the subtle and gross bodies, although these frames exist outside the visible or manifest part of the universe. These frames are the 'goggles' that a living being wears to perceive God, and the resulting experience is an outcome of the goggles as much as it is an outcome of perceiving God. By free will, the soul can change his goggles, which corresponds to a space-time transformation into a new coordinate reference frame, which is then another type of goggles, and hence another location in the covering of the universe, until all such goggles are discarded, and the living being exits the coverings of the universe, then exits the material pleasure, then crosses the boundary of *Brahman* and finally becomes part of God's own experience.

The semantic coordinate transformation is also a type of motion, although it occurs in the 'space' outside the *brahmanda*. It is the space of all possible perspectives, called *niyati* and *kāla*. We can think of this space as that of all reference frames. These frames of space and time are in turn produced from deeper kinds of reference frames of knowledge, ability, desires, and personalities, because the reason we adopt a particular perspective on reality is because we have a desire to know and express ourselves in a particular manner, which stems from a deeper notion of our personality—or who we are. All these ingredients are ultimately material, because no matter what viewpoint an observer adopts, he would be outside reality, and will always derive a limited perspective on it, which will then cause the evolution of perspectives and experiences.

The difference in the coordinate frame in modern science and Vedic cosmology is that science treats these frames logically and not materially. The fact that an observer has a particular perspective is never identified with something that exists 'within' that observer, and the reference frame is just viewed as a point with three axes point in some particular direction. This reference frame, in Vedic cosmology, is a type of subtle matter. In fact, before the manifest world is created, the reference frame of observation—i.e., the goggles of vision—is created. And even before these goggles of vision, there are even more subtle desires of knowledge and activity, stemming from an even subtler material personality.

The 'place' and 'time' in which the soul is born is therefore not in the *brahmanda*. It is in the covering of the *brahmanda*, which defines the googles of space and time, which limit what we see. These goggles are covered by the goggles of *karma* which further limit our desires, and thus what we can see. And under the goggles of space and time are even deeper goggles of desires arising from a material personality that define what we want to know and express ourselves as. Once all these goggles have been worn, then the material experience is produced like the virtual reality of seeing some phenomena by peering into the kaleidoscope.

The phenomenal space and time used in astrology (which measures the latitude, longitude and clock time of birth) is not the true causal picture of our bondage in the material vision. In fact, this phenomenal picture is somewhat misleading because it gives the impression that we are 'inside' the material body, when the soul actually never enters matter. The soul only observes matter from the outside, wearing many layers of goggles, which cover his vision of Lord *Saṅkarṣaṇa* turning the wheel of time in the ocean of material pleasure created by Lord *Mahā Viṣṇu*.

All the individual horoscopes can be—in a semantic understanding of space and time—viewed as coordinate transforms of an absolute space-time, which then result in imperfect scenes, roles, and actors. Accordingly, our lives also become imperfect, because we become actors in imperfect scenes and roles. The irony of an imperfect horoscope is that the depicted storylines, roles and actors are actually produced from a perfect story—the life story of *Garbhodakaśāyi Viṣṇu*—who oversees the universe.

Astrology and God

Astrology indicates the existence of a person with the perfect horoscope in which the role and the actor are perfectly defined. This person is called *Garbhodakaśāyi Viṣṇu* who originates and terminates each universe. His life is the story of the universe He inhabits, parts of His body are the functional divisions in the universe, identified with the roles of the demigods who control the different aspects of the universe, and His persona is the key controller of the demigods who perform the various functions.

The horoscope of *Garbhodakaśāyi Viṣṇu* begins with the origin of the universe and ends with the universe. Each universe, thus, also has a horoscope, and the events in this horoscope are defined by the horoscope of *Garbhodakaśāyi Viṣṇu*. These events can be understood from the space-time structure, when science has sufficiently advanced to understand the nature of the material creation, which will then help us understand the horoscope, and ultimately the personality of *Garbhodakaśāyi Viṣṇu* also called *Hiranyagarbha*. The study of the material world, therefore, can also be viewed as the study of God, when this study has been perfected.

The irony of the material creation is that no part is perfect—since these parts are produced from *māyā*—but the whole is still perfect. Each individual part produces an incomplete understanding of the whole; specifically, the fact that these parts are produced from God is not easily understood from the study of the parts because the parts are only obfuscating this primordial reality. The knowledge of the whole is practically very difficult since as observers we are incapable of knowing everything at all times in the universe. Nevertheless, if an observer's perception is purified, the whole is seen in every phenomenon because the phenomenon is produced from the perfect reality by illusion obfuscating that reality.

The participants in each universe only see parts of the whole, and they might consider their lives imperfect. If, however, they saw the universe from the standpoint of *Hiranyagarbha* they would find that even the material creation is perfect, when taken as a whole. In essence, if you take a play, and selectively study only the lines of a specific actor, these lines by themselves may make little sense, unless seen in relation to every other actor's lines. The storyline remains unclear, and the reason why someone says something cannot be explained unless correlated to every other actor's lines, which then span across numerous "scenes".

When we cannot comprehend why something is happening in our lives, the confusion is because we don't understand the complete play, and why we are playing a certain role. When a living being is freed from the influence of the *guna*, the obfuscation ends. He now sees the world as seen by *Hiranyagarbha*. As the perception is purified, the soul is freed of suffering, even though each manifest phenomenon individually is imperfect. The perfect understanding of these phenomena is not how they hide different parts of reality, but that they are produced from a reality through obfuscation. If one focuses on individual differences, the knowledge is imperfect. If, however, one focuses upon what is common across all the phenomena, then each phenomenon is seen perfectly.

Epilogue

Throughout this book we encountered several new ideas that differ from modern thinking and form the foundations of Vedic cosmology:

- We saw why Euclid's first postulate is incorrect and leads to a straight-line motion of light, which then leads to the parallax method, which measures cosmic distances in the same way that we measure depth with our eyes. This view of light becomes false when space and time are viewed conceptually rather than physically.
- We saw how force collapses in modern science because this force only leads to a stationary state, not a state of motion. In Vedic philosophy, the cause of motion is a separate kind of entity called *prāna,* which is different from matter and exists even when material objects do not exist. All ideas about force as the cause of moving objects need to be replaced by a new kind of mechanism of change.
- We saw how the zodiac drags the Sun, which then drags the other planets, in what was compared to the motion of an ant on top of a potter's wheel, moving in opposite directions. The deferent and epicycle rely on the notion that the zodiac and the Sun influence planets not via force but by dragging the space in other objects.
- We discussed how the universe is 'real' at many levels, not necessarily at the lowest detail of reality. This results in the existence of higher and lower planes of existence, and the vertical dimension in space is treated as different levels of abstraction. In physical space, all locations are identical, and any coordinate transformation can be done in space. If coordinate transforms will convert abstractions into details, then

these abstractions can't be permitted.

- We noted how the universe has to be understood as different kinds of number domains and why there are entities at the bottom of the universe which can represent the entire state of the universe at any given time. We also discussed how the universe is created from possibility rather than matter, when time selects one of the possibilities. That process of selection injects a central role for consciousness even in the process of creating the material phenomena.
- We saw how the nature of causality is not just cause and effect, but also cause and consequence. That consequence depends on how we *interpret* the world, and the law of nature is designed to correct that interpretation and align it with reality. We saw how knowledge can never be perfected unless a natural process assists this knowledge discovery and guides us into situations where false theories can be disproven, and correct theories can be formulated.
- We discussed why the space within the universe and in between the universe has to be treated differently, because locations in this space denote different kinds of meanings (the space between the universes denotes types of pleasure desires, while that within the universe represents conscious events described semantically).
- We discussed spherical vs. flat geometries and how the conversion of spheres to flat structures results in the lotus form; the petals of this lotus represent *directions* which indicate the existence of different types. We noted the meaning of light and dark regions as knowledge and ignorance, what they represent informationally.
- We also discussed how space itself can change parity causing a flip in direction and the lighted parts become dark, and the dark parts become lighted. We discussed how this basic principle underlies the phenomena of changes in seasons, and the phases of planets.
- The causality in these shifts is the influence of the Sun on other planets as it goes up and down vertically. The vertical motion of the Sun is caused by its motion in the signs of the

> zodiac. Ultimately, therefore, 'ups' and 'downs' are caused by the interaction between types. The interaction between types was described as something that is based on the compatibility between an actor, role, and a stage.

Just as a chair kept near a table transforms the nature of both the chair and the table as a study chair and table, or a dining table and chair, similarly, physical proximity when combined with a conceptual understanding of the world produces a new causality that is missing in current science. The world, when modeled through that type of causality, brings many changes in our model and theory of the cosmos. The intuitive basis of this new kind of causality exists in our everyday observation. The notions of hierarchical space and cyclic time also exist in our everyday experience. And yet, these have been systematically neglected in modern science. To interpret the observations correctly, we need a new theory of space, time, and matter. That this theory will present a consistent and complete description of nature, that it will predict new phenomena that current science cannot, and that it will explain the so-called "dark" realities, is only the beginning. The deeper impacts it will have on our own understanding and place in the universe are even more profound.

In the beginning of this book I described the differences between *models* and *theories*. In modern astronomy, models of the universe are constructed empirically through observation: e.g., we find that there are many planets, planetary systems, universes, etc. But the model constructed is incorrect if we use the parallax method because it assumes a flat space-time. These models then have to be explained through a theory, which must predict *why* there are only these planets, planetary systems, and universes, but that explanation is impossible in modern science because of the *matter distribution problem* where the theory of the cosmos is consistent with many possible matter distributions, and hence it can never predict which of these distributions is real. To some extent, modern science is able to predict the motion of planets based on gravitational theory, but that prediction in turn depends on the existence of specific planets, with specific radii, which in turn depend on their masses, which cannot be predicted. Ultimately, therefore, modern science works only when we are able to input a set of initial and boundary conditions into the mathematical equations, but how nature came to be in those specific initial and boundary conditions remains impossible to know because the theory of nature allows infinitely many possible initial and boundary conditions.

This fact underscores an important difference between Vedic and modern astronomy because Vedic astronomy tries to explain not just the motion of the planets, planetary systems, and universes, but also why certain types of celestial entities even exist. In the former sense, Vedic astronomy is similar in its goals to modern astronomy. In the latter sense, however, Vedic astronomy surpasses modern astronomy. We might say that modern astronomy is a combination of empiricism and rationalism, and it uses empirical evidence to construct *models* and uses scientific *theories* to explain these models. The theory, however, does not explain or predict why the universe is a particular type of model, which Vedic astronomy does. In that sense, the Vedic system is entirely rationalistic because it not only tries to explain how the universe evolves, but also why the universe has a particular structure—planets, planetary systems, and universes. Observations and experiences are simply used to confirm the truth of the theory and the model, not used to formulate a model, which cannot then be predicted by the theory. However, even this confirmation requires one to find the path on which an object will be transformed rather than merely change its location without changing its properties.

The gaps between the scientific model and the theory have significantly grown in recent times because we are now required to postulate additional forms of matter such as "dark matter" and "dark energy" to explain the gaps in prediction based on what we can actually observe. These new forms of matter are *models* although not yet *theories*. It is obvious that if the universe is 96% "dark" then the theory of reality that incorporates these forms of matter would have to undergo a substantial revision. That revision is nowhere in sight today. It is also well-known that modern physics describes different kinds of natural phenomena through three main kinds of theories which are mutually inconsistent: quantum theory, general relativity, and thermodynamics, whose unification and resolution of contradictions is itself nowhere in sight today. The most dominant approach to the unification of these theories today is String Theory, which postulates 10 to 26 dimensions, which cannot be empirically detected in any foreseeable near future. Furthermore, these theories today don't explain the existence of dark energy or dark matter.

The physical picture of nature is in a huge disarray because: (1) all the theories put together only explain 4% of the observable universe, (2) these theories present mutually inconsistent descriptions of nature, and therefore cannot be reconciled, (3) the attempts at reconciliation postulate space-times that have so many dimensions that they can never be empirically confirmed, even if a theory could be formed, and (4) all these attempts do not incorporate an explanation of "dark" matter and energy, so even the empirically unconfirmable theoretical reconciliation would still only explain 4% of the universe. If you thought that science has brought us to a perfect view of the universe, you are mistaken. Even if you thought that our theories are imperfect, but we can close the gap between what we know and what we don't, you would be wrong again.

I discussed throughout this book the key reason why a physical theory *must* always be incomplete: the reason is that nature is both matter and meaning; meaning is also material, although not in the same sense as the material objects in modern science. To understand this new kind of matter, we cannot just slap another layer of material reality on top of the present one, because any such addition creates the mind-body interaction problem. To add meaning into the picture of nature, we must change our theories about material objects in a very fundamental way: (1) objects are symbols, (2) symbols are produced from meanings, and (3) both meaning and matter must be described as types, rather than quantities. This model of description leads to a change in our theory of space and time from open, linear, and flat, to closed, cyclic, and hierarchical. All meanings and objects are nodes in a hierarchical space-time structure; the gross objects that we can perceive are "hanging" on the branches created by subtle objects; the subtle objects are themselves hanging on the invisible trunks of *guna* and *karma* which become manifest only under the influence of time, and cannot be observed unless they are manifest.

The study of the cosmos is that of the structure of the semantic tree: i.e., how it is divided into trunks, branches, twigs, leaves, and fruits, and how it loses its leaves and fruits during some "seasons" and then grows them again during other "seasons" with the passing of time. In one sense, the study of the cosmos is very straightforward because at a high level, we can clearly understand its structure and how it evolves with time. In another sense, the structure is enormously complicated, and since it comprises various forms of material entities, which can only be thought, judged, intended, and valued (rather than being sensed) it requires advanced forms of perception for it to be known. If we don't have this type of perception, how can we hope to understand the cosmic structure?

The problem of science, the nature of its solution, the resulting structure of space and time, followed by the cosmic structure this space and time produce are all within the domain of science provided two things can happen: (1) we can give up our current materialistic approach to nature and incorporate meanings into science, and (2) we can develop advanced forms of perception to perceive the subtle material realities that exist but can never be seen by the senses, although their effects can be seen. If, therefore, someone prefers to follow a rational-empirical approach to nature, he too can, in principle, understand the nature of the cosmos by widening the rationality and deepening the empiricism to include meanings. I am quite certain, however, that practically no scientist today is capable of this kind of broadening and deepening.

We therefore turn to the Vedic description to find those answers that can help us broaden and deepen our rationality and empiricism. This shift is only in lieu of our ability to find the answers within our current forms of rationality and empiricism. Our capitulation to scripture is not intended to replace reason and experience with faith. It is rather to broaden our reasoning and experience by the use of knowledge that we don't possess right now and can only be obtained via teachers who had this knowledge in the past, and to listen to these teachers, we must have the prerequisite faith in them, similar to the fact that even to learn science you must trust the teachers in science if you wish to learn anything.

Science has reached a point where even the specialists can only grasp a very small part all that is being said by the practitioners of science. Physicists rarely understand chemistry, chemists rarely delve into biology, biologists rarely comprehend the advances in mathematics and computing, and practically no one cares about the philosophical issues involved in perception, conception, and theory formation. As a result, despite all this complexity, science is nowhere near explaining our most immediate questions concerning the nature of sensation, meaning, language, intentionality, happiness, and free will. Even more worrying is the fact that scientists often lack honesty and humility in recognizing the numerous intractable and hard problems that science currently faces. When challenged with these questions, most scientists would tell you about their track record of having delivered progress in the past.

Modern science is not just fueled by its method of reason and experience, but also fed by a sense of morality in which ignorance is not a crime: so long as you don't know the nature of truth, you haven't committed a felony. In Vedic philosophy, the methods of reason and experience remain intact, but the sense of morality is altered through its theory of *karma*: ignorance is a misconduct. When ignorance is a crime, then continuing on the ignorant path is also immoral and science becomes immoral if it remains on the ignorant path. When you remain immoral, you also do deeds which only bring unhappiness and suffering to everyone who follows, teaches, practices, and takes pride in this ignorance.

The difference between Vedic and modern approaches is not that one relies on faith and the other one on reason and experience. The difference is that science thinks that ignorance is not a crime, which then leads to a sense of complacency in the search for truth. If you knew that not knowing the truth is the cause of your suffering, you would be looking for the fastest path to truth, rather than whatever path you are currently on.

Vedic cosmology is more scientific than anything that science has created because its theories explain and predict the models. In fact, they explain and predict far more than any individual scientific theory, and all of the mutually contradictory theories put together. No scientific theory, for instance, can predict what will happen to society in a few million years, nor does it tell us how society worked in the past. Vedic theories make those predictions. They explain when the universe was created, and when it will be destroyed. They predict the existence of life forms that are different from our life form, and types of planets and planetary systems where far greater pleasure than ours exists. They also tell us how and why our place is different than those places. Unfortunately, since we don't have the necessary perceptual advancement, and because we have fallen into the delusion that if we cannot see something with our senses then it must not exist, when presented with this information, we imagine that it must only be the outcome of the ancients' fertile imagination.

We are gluttons of the illusion that modern science represents "progress" of knowledge that never existed in the past. The fact is that far more sophisticated information about the universe existed in the past, and a fragment of that knowledge is still available for those who are truly interested in learning about it. This book is by no means a complete description of Vedic astronomy and cosmology. It is merely an introduction to some of the key concepts which I hope can be used to better understand how the Vedic cosmological system is far superior to the modern one. Since the conceptual basis of the Vedic system has been lost over time, it needs to be rediscovered and investigated in much the same way that modern scientific investigations are conducted. I invite readers to take up this study for their own sake, and for everyone else's.

Endnotes

PREFACE

1. The term 'planetary system' is used differently in Vedic cosmology than in modern science. The term, for instance, does not denote a 'solar system' because there is only one Sun, and the stars are said to reflect the light of the Sun, rather than generate their own light (quite like the Moon or other planets in the modern solar system). The Sanskrit terminology for planetary system is *loka* and, as we shall see during the course of the book, in a semantic space different locations are also of a different type.

1. STUDYING VEDIC COSMOLOGY

1. This is the essence of Einstein's General Theory of Relativity in which if you feel a backward pull on your body, the cause of that pull might be your own forward acceleration or a massive object behind you. Whether you are accelerating or whether there is a massive object behind you, are two distinct models, generated by interpreting the same observation. These are, in fact, not the only possible alternatives. It is also possible to conceive many other models in which the pull you experience is a combination of numerous massive objects and your own acceleration. The General Theory of Relativity thus permits an infinite number of models which will explain the observations equally well and you have no way of knowing which of these models is true.

2. The problem of underdetermination cannot be overcome in a physical theory, but I will later show how it is overcome in a semantic theory. In brief, you can spread a bottle of ink on paper in many ways, which will conserve the total ink, and the only way to know which pattern of spreading is real is if you can associate each spreading pattern with a meaning. The

problem of underdetermination is therefore overcome by the induction of meanings in the physical world.

3. There are many recent studies on Vedic cosmology such as those done by Richard L. Thompson. I haven't discussed their work in detail in this book, although one key difference between their work and this book is the illustration of why *Sāṅkhya* entails a different theory of space, time, matter, and light, before this theory is used to understand Vedic cosmology. In particular, we will see during the course of this book, that common assumptions such as the idea that space is linear (rather than hierarchical) and that light travels in a straight line are inconsistent with the Vedic theory of matter. These assumptions are employed in the calculation of distances, trigonometric calculations of angles and declinations, and phenomena such as the passing of seasons are explained based on these assumptions. This book, however, shows why the use of trigonometry based on a linear space-time theory is clearly inadequate for understanding Vedic cosmology.

4. Dalela, Ashish (2015). "Signs of Life: A Semantic Critique of Evolutionary Theory". Shabda Press.

5. A detailed discussion of this problem will take us beyond the scope of the present book, and so the interested reader may refer to *Moral Materialism: A Semantic Theory of Ethical Naturalism.*

6. The reader is referred to two of my previous books *Six Causes* and *Is the Apple Really Red?* for a detailed discussion about the various forms of God in the material creation, and the different roles they play by taking on different functions, and becoming their observers.

7. The role of *prakriti* and how it comprises the three modes of nature called *sattva*, *rajas* and *tamas* is discussed later. The observer's perception and material objects are both created from *prakriti* and therefore the qualities in terms of which we perceive (e.g., sound, taste, sight, smell, and touch) are also the properties of material objects. This is an important aspect of Vedic philosophy, which I have discussed at length in my previous book *Sāṅkhya and Science*.

8. Dalela, Ashish (2014). "Quantum Meaning: A Semantic Interpretation of Quantum Theory". Shabda Press.

2. AN INTRODUCTION TO SĀṄKHYA PHILOSOPHY

1. There are other definitions of numbers that do not explicitly count to a particular number, but all those definitions still suffer from the same problem. For instance, one recent definition of numbers begins with the idea of zero defined as an empty set denoted by two braces as {}. The next number, one, is defined as a set that contains this empty set and is therefore depicted as {{}}. Successive numbers are similarly defined by adding more braces. To know a particular number, therefore, we must count the number of braces. In particular, to define zero, we must count two braces, when the number two hasn't yet been defined.

2. Wigner, Eugene (1960). "The Unreasonable Effectiveness of Mathematics in the Natural Sciences". Communications on Pure and Applied Mathematics, vol XIII, 001-14(1960). New York University.

3. THE VEDIC VIEW OF CAUSALITY

1. This is a difficult point here, but it stems from an understanding of quantum theory in which all particles remain in 'stationary states' also called 'eigenstates'. Unlike classical physics where particles were always in a state of motion or dynamics, quantum theory shows that particles would remain in stationary states unless energy is absorbed or emitted. How this energy can be absorbed or emitted, however, can never be explained or predicted in current quantum theory. As we have seen above, this collapse of causality in all motion or change is filled in the Vedic view by the notion of *prāna* which causes changes.

2. It has been observed that leaders of modern terrorist organizations don't come from the unintelligent, impoverished, or hungry demographic. In fact, they are often financially well-off, run charitable organizations such as educational institutions or homes for the poor, and they read from scriptures. Often times, they are also well-educated. They thus have a lot of mode of goodness in them, due to which they become respected in societies

where goodness is generally lacking. However, since the mode of ignorance predominates, this goodness is used to systematically instantiate the ignorance of crime, violence, and terror. The Vedas too describe how demons such as *Rāvana* and *Hiranyakasipu* performed severe austerities, were well educated, and were born into the families of elevated sages. Due to the presence of the mode of goodness, they became very powerful, and yet, since the mode of ignorance dominated, all this goodness was employed in terrorizing the living beings. The presence of goodness is thus not sufficient. Rather, the domination of goodness is more important, and a person should be judged not just by their good or bad qualities, but by which quality predominates. With a slight change in domination, the effects are inverted, and this is one of the reasons that astrologers often go wrong in making predictions, because they cannot assess the actually dominating mode.

3. This point will be elaborated in detail in a later chapter where we will see that in Vedic cosmology there is a realm of subtle matter that exists as the possibility of the events in the universe and is called the *Garbhodaka Ocean.* From this realm, time creates the state of the entire universe as a whole, rather than the states of each object individually. Once the state of the universe has been determined, the objects (observers) are chosen to *fit* those events according to their *guna* and *karma*. In that sense, the choice of the events *precedes* the selection of observers, so the observers are not the cause of those events, although they participate in those events, and therefore become responsible for them.

4. This is an important point for the different religions of the world, or even atheistic materialistic theories, because in all these viewpoints, there is an element of truth, which might appear to contradict the truths in other theories or religions. The contradictions in various viewpoints is produced by covering different parts of the ultimate truth, like the five blind men who touch different parts of the elephant and argue amongst themselves by believing their limited perceptions to be complete truths.

4. PROBLEMS IN MODERN COSMOLOGY

1. Hammond, Richard (2008). "The Unknown Universe: The Origin of the Universe, Quantum Gravity, Wormholes, and Other Things Science Can't

Explain". Career Press.

2. Leighton, Robert; Sands, Matthew (1965). "The Feynman Lectures on Physics", vol. 3, Addison-Wesley, pp.1.1-1.8.

3. This topic is less frequently discussed in standard text books on quantum physics, and the fact that the quantum wavefunction can be *represented* through many distinct *basis functions* is taught mathematically although its correlation to the number of slits is described less often. The fact is that the quantum wavefunction is a reality that is divided differently depending on the number of slits used in measurement. Therefore the components of the wavefunction, and what we measure in an experiment depends as much on the wavefunction as a whole, as it does on the number of slits (i.e., the method of measurement).

4. Dalela, Ashish (2014). "Quantum Meaning: A Semantic Interpretation of Quantum Theory". Shabda Press.

5. FUNDAMENTAL PRINCIPLES OF VEDIC COSMOLOGY

1. Inelastic dynamics refers to a type of physical interaction in which colliding bodies can result in a different number of bodies due to these objects splitting or merging. If the theory of nature describes the motion of an individual object, then through splitting or merging, the total number of equations that govern the system must change. As a result, the system as a whole must become indeterministic.

2. Jameson, Celia. "The Short Step from Love to Hypnosis: A Reconsideration of the Stockholm Syndrome". Journal for Cultural Research, 14(4):337-355. Taylor & Francis.

3. The list of galaxies at https://en.wikipedia.org/wiki/List_of_galaxies associates the galaxies with the constellations in which they are found.

4. There are many methods employed in modern cosmology for objects at varying distances. These methods form the Cosmic Distance Ladder: Howard, Sethane (2011). "Cosmic Distance Ladder". Journal of the Washington

Academy of Sciences.

5. The inverse square law states that the intensity of light reduces with the inverse square of the distance. Thus, if an object is twice as far from us, then its intensity must be 1/4th of the intensity of the closer object. "Inverse Square Law". Science Direct website. Retrieved at: https://www.sciencedirect.com/topics/engineering/inverse-square-law

6. THE STRUCTURE OF A UNIVERSE

1. A phase space is used to represent the complete state of a system, as opposed to simply its motion or position. In classical physics, the phase space has six dimensions (three each of position and momentum). For more details, please refer to: Nolte, David (2010). "The Tangled Tale of Phase Space". Physics Today, vol 3(4), p.33. Retrieved at: http://www.physics.purdue.edu/nlo/NoltePT10.pdf.

2. A fuller treatment of this topic is present in *Quantum Meaning: A Semantic Interpretation of Quantum Theory*, and the interested reader may refer to it, in case there is interest in understanding the implications of semantics for atoms.

3. Shannon's Information Theory distinguishes between signal and noise; the signal is that which is of interest to us, noise is which is uninteresting or cannot be comprehended. The theory argues that there are limits to how much information we can transmit in a channel, given that all channels are noise limited. That is, they will inject something that we cannot process, and we must find ways to overcome this effect by symbol repetition (or other mechanisms called 'encoding', which are refinements of the repetition process). If information has to be repeated, then the total unique information that can be passed through a channel becomes naturally limited (most of the bandwidth of the channel is consumed for symbol repetition). Modern wireless technologies have reached close to Shannon's limit, and therefore to send information faster and faster, more and more wireless spectrum has to be allocated. The Shannon's limit essentially represents our sensual limits to processing details, due to which we are forced to discard a lot of information as noise, when there is actually no noise in nature. Noise is said

to be created when a signal interacts with other objects, which modify the signal. In essence, the signal we receive carries information about all the objects it has interacted with, but we have no way of understanding that information because it is so detailed we just don't know how to process it. If our senses were advanced, we would not just decode the original signal but also how it was modified through numerous interactions. In other words, if you are talking to someone over a phone, and the phone had the ability to decode the incoming 'noise', it would present not just what the other person is speaking, but also the exact environmental conditions in which he or she is speaking. For instance, if the person is sitting under a tree, or walking on the street, information about their surroundings would naturally be available to the phone as well. The demons therefore are far more advanced because they can decode far more information from the signal, while we discard most of it as noise. As we go lower down in the universe, there is more and more signal and less and less noise. As we go higher up in the universe, there is more and more noise and less and less signal. The spiritualist therefore discards all the details of the world, and becomes detached from all the happenings, grasping only its essence.

4. "Duodecimal". MathWorld website: Retrieved at: https://mathworld.wolfram.com/Duodecimal.html

5. The Standard Model of current physics speaks about 6 quarks and 6 leptons, with an equal number of antiparticles. There are thus 12 fundamental particles, and another 12 fundamental antiparticles. The combination of particles and antiparticles make a total of 12 quarks and 12 leptons

6. The semantic representations are different from the physical ones in the sense that a symbol that represents that number has the properties of that number. A physical representation does not have the properties of the numbers. Thus, for instance, a material object that denotes the number 5 will 'resonate' or become semantically 'entangled' with other objects that comprise this number.

7. The higher life forms are called *prajāpati* in Vedic cosmology, and they reside in the two higher planetary systems called *Maharloka* and *Janaloka.* Vedic cosmology describes 14 *prajāpati* who are called *Daksha, Prachetā,*

Pulaha, Marīchi, Kaśyapa, Bhrigu, Atri, Vaśiśtha, Gautama, Angiras, Pulastya, Kratu, Prahlāda, and *Kardama.* As we have noted earlier, *Maharloka* and *Janaloka* are representations of the mind and intellect, respectively, and we will see later how these two material elements are denoted by the Moon and the Sun, respectively. The *prajāpati* create the specific type of mind and intellect, and they are therefore the progenitors of all the species of life, which are, in the Vedic view, manifest from a type of mind and intellect. The Sun and the Moon are deliverers of the *karma* which in turn modifies which of the propensities in the mind and intellect will be manifest or curtailed. The different members of the species are thus outcomes of two things—*guna* or types of species produced by the *prajāpati* and the individual members of the species from the Moon and the Sun. Their different members of the species are expanded from the forms created by the *prajāpati*, by successive generations preserving and expanding the meanings established by their predecessors. These form the famed *Chandra Vanśa* and *Surya Vanśa* dynasties of living beings. While this book isn't about the Vedic genealogy, this genealogy is always covered in detail in all descriptions of Vedic cosmology, thereby integrating the cosmic descriptions with the historical creation of life forms.

7. THE PRESENT UNIVERSE

1. In Buddhism the four basic judgments are called *chatuśkoti* and they represent the judgments of (1) true, (2) false, (3) both true and false, and (4) neither true nor false. Aristotelian logic is based upon three principles—identity, non-contradiction, and mutual exclusion. Non-contradiction implies that something must either be false or true, and cannot be both; (3) violates this principle because something is both true and false. Mutual exclusion entails that every statement must be either true or false, and it cannot be anything else; (4) violates this principle as something is neither true nor false. The principles of Aristotelian logic are sacred in material logic, but they are not applicable to other domains beyond matter. In these domains, it is possible to choose the opposites simultaneously or not make a choice at all between the opposites. Only when logic is seen as a function of choice, rather than of matter, these possibilities are realized.

2. The senses can perceive objects but not their absence. If we see empty

space, for instance, we cannot say that this emptiness represents the lack of a table or a chair. All senses thus perceive the presence of properties not their absence. Nevertheless, modern physical theories (due to reasons of time symmetry) require the properties and their opposites to exist equally. The absent properties are therefore sometimes interpreted as properties moving in negative time. This negative time has a semantic interpretation which I will discuss subsequently.

3. The word 'passion' has a negative connotation in modern times, and often people misunderstand what this mode means, equating it to hedonism. The mode of passion or *rajo-guna* actually represents what we commonly consider 'good' in the material world. Thus philanthropy, altruism, familial love, social camaraderie, affection to children, leading a healthy life, material education, etc. all fall under mode of passion. The mode of ignorance or *tamo-guna* is the opposite of the mode of passion, while *sattva-guna* is freedom from both opposites.

4. Just as the false ego creates the subtle sense objects, Mahārāja *Bharata* created five sons in the womb of *Pañcajanī*, his wife. These sons were named *Sumati*, *Rāṣṭrabhṛta*, *Sudarśana*, Āvaraṇa and *Dhūmraketu* [SB 5.7.2]. Destiny fixed the time for Mahārāja *Bharata*'s enjoyment of material opulence at one thousand times ten thousand years. When that period was finished, he retired from family life and divided the wealth he had received from his forefathers among his sons. He left his paternal home, the reservoir of all opulence, and started for *Pulahāśrama*, which is situated in Hardwar. The śālagrāma-śilās are obtainable there. [SB 5.7.8]

5. In Vedic sacrifices performed in India, the worshipper is located hierarchically by the words: *jambudveepe, bharatkhande, aryavarte*, where India is referred to as *aryavarta* or the land of Aryans. In this method of addressing, *Bhārata-varṣa* is called *Bharatkhand* but the positioning of the worshipper doesn't stop at this, and goes on to mention *aryavarta*. It is obvious therefore that India is neither *Jambudvīpa* nor *Bhārata-varṣa* but referred to as *aryavarta*. The method of addressing also indicates that *Bhārat-varṣa* (sometimes also called *Bharat khanda*) is part of *Jambudvipa*, and *aryavarta* is part of *Bharat khanda*.

6. One recent example of this type of interpretation is seen in the work of Richard L. Thompson in his work *Vedic Cosmography* which equates the *bhūloka* with the planisphere representation of the Earth, and visualizes a correspondence between the modern solar system and the different *dvīpa* in *bhūloka*.

7. "Pangea". Encyclopedia Britannica website: Retrieved at: https://www.britannica.com/place/Pangea

8. The 33 demigods are in addition to the three primary deities in the universe: namely, *Viṣṇu*, *Brahma*, and *Śiva*. If these deities are added to the 33 demigods, the total deities are 36, of which *Viṣṇu*, *Brahma*, and *Śiva* are the primary deities. The number 36 is produced by dividing 12 by 3, and the first deity in this division is divided into the three primary forms *Viṣṇu*, *Brahma*, and *Śiva*, which are said to be representations of the 3 modes of nature, while the remaining 11 deities divided by 3 create the 33 demigods. *Viṣṇu*, *Brahma*, and *Śiva* are primary because they represent the first or the original deities, and they are therefore often called *Bhagavān* which is a term generally reserved for the Supreme Person of the spiritual world. The nomenclature misleads many people because different Vedic texts call the different deities as *Bhagavān*, and a literal reading of this address suggests that these deities are indeed the supreme creators, when they are only the primary deities within a particular context.

9. Complex numbers enter physical theories while modeling atomic objects in which two properties—position that represents objects and momentum that represents activities—which were previously treated as separate dimensions in classical physics had to exist in the ordinary space because both these properties were to be derived from the same *wavefunction* which was possible only when we made the wavefunction complex valued. The complex numbers therefore represent the fact that we are trying to represent a combination of two things: (a) an object, and (b) the procedure by which it was constructed, as part of the same entity. The definition of an object is incomplete without the procedure, and the procedure is incomplete without the object. Only a combination of the two represents a complete description; however, this complete description requires a complex number representation.

10. Vedic texts describe three forms of God's self knowledge, namely, God as He is, as He is not, and as He may be. The material universe is a product of God's self-knowledge as He is *not*. In that sense, the universe is produced from God's self-knowledge, and is unlike Him, and therefore called *māyā* (that which is *not*). The knowledge of what God is not exists during the universe's existence, but is not permanent. The knowledge of what God is, is permanent. The interested reader may refer to *Six Causes: The Vedic Theory of Creation* for a detailed discussion of this topic, and how creation is an outcome of self-knowledge.

11. There are two kinds of *karma* which I will elaborate later. First, that which appears as our abilities (or limitations), and which constrains our desires. This kind of *karma* can be, to some extent, controlled by our desires. For instance, if I have the ability to write, I can choose not to write. The desire of writing must therefore appear before the ability to write can be utilized. Second, there is a type of *karma* which doesn't depend on our choices, and would be inflicted even when we don't want it. The *karma* I am discussing here is of the first type; I will revisit this point again later when we are better equipped to understand the differences and relationships between these two types.

12. Some *Vaishnava Ācharyas* have called this water covering *ghanodaka* which if literally translated means 'dense water'. It is water because it is not differentiable just like we cannot distinguish between parts of water. It is dense because it is even harder to differentiate, because when density increases, the parts are placed even closer, which makes it even harder to distinguish between them. Unlike the *brahmanda* which is differentiable in our experience, and the āloka *varṣa* which is not differentiable but is about to manifest, the water covering beyond the āloka *varṣa* is even less differentiable. These are degrees of difficulties in knowing unmanifest, about to manifest, and manifest *karma*.

8. THE MOTION OF LUMINARIES

1. Readers interested in this topic, and the general relationship between atomic theory's problems and semantics, can refer to *Quantum Meaning: A Semantic Interpretation of Quantum Theory.*

2. The water of the Celestial Ganges was brought to *bhūloka* on the request of King *Bhaghiratha* whose ancestors were burnt due to the curse of Sage *Kapil*, and the King was advised to bring Ganga to the *bhūloka* on the advice of Lord Brahma to immerse the ashes of the ancestors in its water, so that they can be liberated from the curse. Following this Ganga is also called *Bhaghirathi* and there is a tradition even amongst modern day Hindus to immerse the ashes of dying ancestors into the river Ganga. When Ganga descended from the *svargaloka* (on top of the *Sumeru Mountain*) *Lord Śiva*, who resides in the *Ilāvṛta-varṣa* at the center of *Jambudvīpa*, bore the force of the falling water of His head, and then divided the water into several rivers that flow on the *bhūloka*. Lord *Śiva* is thus always worshipped on the *bhūloka* with the water of the celestial Ganges on His head. One form of this worship is bathing His deity with the water of Ganges.

3. Later in the book I will discuss how light is *karma* and the fact that we see certain things due to sunlight is due to the *karma* we have created. If the *karma* doesn't exist, we will not see the phenomena. On the dissolution of all *karma*, therefore, the material experiences themselves cease, because these experiences are only produced by *karma*.

9. THE THEORY OF LANGUAGE

1. Classical physics recognized three key properties of space and time which were called momentum, angular momentum, and energy. These respectively corresponded to the homogeneity of space, the isotropicity of space, and homogeneity of time. In quantum physics, another property called spin has been added, which relates to the direction of time, and with the discovery of antiparticles, we can call this isotropicity of time. These four properties are the basic conceptual foundations of modern science, because they are *conserved*. It is notable that only those properties which are conserved are considered physically real. Other properties (such as the number of particles) is not conserved, and therefore not considered physically real. Of course, as we know, the use of these four properties in quantum physics does not overcome the uncertainty and indeterminism, and this is for two main reasons: (1) the properties themselves have to be viewed semantically rather than physically, and (2) these aren't the only properties.

2. Magnus, Margaret (2010). “Gods in the Word: Archetypes in the Consonants”. CreateSpace.

3. Köhler, Wolfgang (1929). “Gestalt Psychology”. Liveright.

4. While we generally understand the nature of relationship to others, the nature of relationship to ourselves in the sense of knowing who we are, our self-interest which results in desire for pleasure, and expression of our personality, are the foundations of any relationship. If this foundation is neglected, and a person enters a relationship without truly knowing who he or she is, or if this knowledge exists but is not properly understood by the others in the relationship, the relationships fail. The relationship to the self is therefore the foundation of all other relationships, even though we don’t often treat it as a relationship.

5. The theorem that proves that there is no largest prime number is called Euclid’s Theorem (https://mathworld.wolfram.com/EuclidsTheorems.html). Since the numbers are treated physically in number theory, each number is not associated with a meaning. Similarly, the search for larger prime numbers (https://mathworld.wolfram.com/LargePrime.html) has no relationship to the question of whether these numbers can be realized in nature in terms of the smallest and largest possible divisions. In a sense, mathematics has detached itself from the real world, because of this physical treatment of numbers. In a semantic theory, numbers would be related back to meanings, and only those meanings which can be experienced and represented would be possible numbers.

6. Dalela, Ashish (2014). “Gödel’s Mistake: The Role of Meaning in Mathematics”. Shabda Press.

7. The *Pancharātra* texts are also considered *Tantra* although they are described as *Vaishnava Tantra* rather than *Shaiva* or *Shakta Tantra*. Texts such as *Sātvata Tantra* are often quoted by *Vaishnava Acāryās*, and they describe the four forms of *Viṣṇu* previously discussed.

10. THE VEDIC THEORY OF TIME

1. Every material object can be, in Vedic philosophy, be inhabited by a consciousness, including houses. In fact, there are Vedic practices that involve the 'installation' of house by doing *bhūmi puja* by which a *vāstu puruṣa* is installed before the construction of the house. The house is also constructed step by step, manifesting the 'body' of this living being. What we consider inanimate objects presently—such as mountains or rivers—are actually living beings in Vedic philosophy. The entire universe is also a house, inhabited by the consciousness of *Garbhodakaśāyī Viṣṇu*. Similarly, every implement in the spiritual world—e.g., a toy, a pot, or a house—is inhabited by a consciousness. This, of course, does not mean that all objects in the material world are conscious, because they aren't necessarily produced through a process of incarnating a living being into a material body. If this process is correctly followed, all material objects will also be living beings.

2. In Vedic philosophy, there is indeed a material property called *karma* which causes the manifestation of observations. However, *karma* is not like ordinary material objects which can be observed; in fact, it is property that can only be observed *after* it has manifested. Therefore, this problem of missing causality in science should be viewed as the inability to find a measurable or observable entity, and the problem is solved by the notion of *karma* which lies dormant or unmanifest.

3. This is a very simplified description of the problem in epistemology. Readers interested in exploring this problem may refer to *Uncommon Wisdom: Fault Lines in the Foundations of Atheism*, which explores the flaws in the modern rationalistic and empiricist approaches to knowledge, and shows why knowledge of the world needs a much bigger space and time than that of the real universe to store all the false notions before they can be eliminated either by experience or reason.

4. Resnick, Robert (1968). "Supplementary Topic B: The Twin Paradox". Introduction to Special Relativity. John Wiley & Sons, Inc.

5. "Progeria". Encyclopedia Britannica website. Retrieved at: https://www.britannica.com/science/progeria

12. PRINCIPLES OF VEDIC ASTROLOGY

1. In our everyday world, space is divided into parts and these parts are accorded functional meanings. For instance, the space inside a house is divided into a kitchen, bedroom, study, bathroom, etc. *Vāstu-Shāstra*—which is the science of auspicious space planning, stipulates the correct and incorrect functional divisions of space. For instance, within a house, ideally the temple must be at the north-east, the main bedroom in the south-west, the kitchen in the south-east, and the guest-room in the north-west. If you don't plan the house in this way, you will still have a functional division of space, but that division may not be *auspicious*. Of course, not everyone has to plan the space in the same way, and whether the house should have an entrance on the north, south, east, or west, depends also on the nature of the person living in the house. For some people a south facing house can be more auspicious, while for others a north facing house will be better. Accordingly, the functional divisions of the house—such as the location of the kitchen, the dining room, the bedroom, the place of entertainment, the study and the bathrooms—can also change. When a certain closed space is not planned well, *Feng Shui* (a Chinese practice similar to *Vāstu-Shāstra*) recommends how to "fix" the problems in that plan by placing additional objects into that space which alter the nature of that space—compensating for its ill-effects. Similarly, Vedic astrologers recommend a person to wear gems, beads, or eat specific kinds of food to counteract ill effects. The physical properties of an object naturally make it capable of certain types of behaviors or activities. However, when the object is embedded in a space that modifies its meaning, these behaviors may be suppressed, enhanced, hidden, or revealed. All properties in an object are not always visible, and they may become visible in different contexts.

2. Sometimes, when there is no suitable individual who can perform a role, Lord *Viṣṇu* himself incarnates to perform that role. These forms of God, which advent to perform a specific function, are called śaktyāvesha avatar.

3. This is a profound scientific point which arises when quantum physics and thermodynamics are unified; rather than explaining it here, I would refer the curious reader to *Moral Materialism: A Semantic Theory of Ethical Naturalism* for a detailed discussion of his topic, and why some of profound problems of irreversibility in thermodynamics can be understood if matter

was treated semantically.

4. The idea of force originated as the notion of 'push' and 'pull', and this pushing and pulling involves the act of coming in contact with another object, which is called 'touch' or *sparsha* in *Sāńkhya*. All push and pull effects are therefore manifestation of the element of air, which symbolizes its meaning as 'touch'. Even the 'heat' of radiation is perceived by the skin, as a sensation of touch. Therefore when modern science speaks about motion caused by radiation, that effect is also air. All forces in modern science are therefore variations of the properties of air. Even radiation is air, although sometimes when this property is detailed, it appears as light. When this detailed information is left behind, and the abstraction is transferred, the information is transferred as air. The fire element in *Sāńkhya* is said to have heat and light, but the heat cannot be seen, although it can be touched. Therefore, the import of saying that fire has heat and light is that it carries the element of air (which represents touch), and a grosser manifestation of this touch as light (which represents sight).

5. When we perceive sensations, such as red, round, and sweet, the meaning of the sensations is perceived to be an apple. The apple is a conceptual object which is not perceived by the senses, although its existence is inferred by the mind. This inference may not be true, and therefore, the intellect must assess the inference by comparing to other similar inferences in the past, drawn from the memory of past experiences, when such experiences have worked. Thus, the mind perceives meanings, and the intellect judges them to be true.

6. The planets are described in *Sāńkhya* to have three aspects: *ādidaivika*, *ādiatmika*, and *ādibhautika*. In the case of the Sun, for instance, the deity in the Sun who controls all the activities of the Sun, is *ādidaivik*a. We can say that this deity is the concept or the 'mind' of the Sun. All the living beings in the Sun planet, and therefore the planet as a whole, is *ādiatmika*—the *prāna* of the Sun, which converts the will in the Sun's mind into physical activity. This activity is the motion of the Sun in a specific orbit, with a specific period. This orbit and period is the *evidence* of the existence of the mind. Without this motion, the idea of the Sun exists, but is not evidenced to any living being except the Sun deity himself. The effect of the Sun on

other parts of the universe is *ādibhautika* which appears to us as the heat and light from the Sun. The unmanifest *karma* therefore lies in the Sun as the unmanifest body of the living being. When this unmanifest is manifest, it becomes the perceived heat and light. The manifestation is caused by the periodic motion of the Sun, and in that sense we say that the light is coming from the Sun, or the planet is the cause of experience. This causation, however, is due to our own *karma,* which lies dormant.

7. There are sometimes differing opinions in this regard, especially about whether Mercury represents Air or Earth. This difference can be resolved by the story from several *Purāna* in which Moon begets Mercury in the womb of the wife of Jupiter, Tara. The Moon is the mind, which represents ideas. Jupiter is the Ether in which these ideas are objectified by *prāna*. Sound is the property of Ether, and can be called the 'wife' of Ether. When the Moon begets a child in the womb of sound, the idea that originally existed in the mind is objectified as the element Air. Mercury is thus a child of Jupiter, because Air is manifested from Ether, and also a child of the Moon because this manifestation is caused when the ideas from the mind are objectified. There are many such stories in the *Purāna* which appear mythical or allegories, but they are actually quite scientific. An important thing to note here is when the Moon begets Mercury, the reference is not to the planets, but to a particular ruler of that planet who lives for a certain duration. Not every ruler may be the child of the Moon, because as the time changes, the properties of these elements are also altered slightly. The proper understanding is that Air is manifested from the Ether by the mind, but this could be the mind of another deity, not the Moon per se.

8. The visibility can be understood as the experimental demonstration of ideas. Thus, for instance, when ideas in the mind manifest in the Ether, a theory is propounded. When this theory is widely propagated and understood, then it begins to bring about changes, such as some people start trying to experimentally demonstrate its truth. When the theory is experimentally proven it is converted into Fire. When the experimental demonstration is converted into "proof of concept" technology, it is converted into Water. When the early technology is adopted by everyone in their day to day life, it becomes Earth.

9. Readers interested in this understanding this problem further can refer to *Gödel's Mistake: The Role of Meaning in Mathematics.*

10. Russel, Bertrand (1940). "The Philosophy of Logical Atomism". Routledge.

11. The ego here is not conscious. It is a material element interacting with *karma*. To a living being with advanced perception, the interaction is visible. But to other people, it remains unconscious. This fact is further elaborated shortly.

12. "Benjamin Libet". The Information Philosopher website. Retrieved at: https://www.informationphilosopher.com/solutions/scientists/libet/

13. A detailed discussion of the problems in atomic theory, and why they necessitate a semantic view is out of scope here. The interested readers may refer to *Quantum Meaning: A Semantic Interpretation of Quantum Theory* which describes why the present theory of atomic objects is incomplete, and what that incompleteness means. Essentially, in current atomic theory, messages are treated as objects. If you think that the words in this book are not symbols of meaning, then the *order* in which they appear would be quite mysterious. You may try to explain the order of the words by computing some probabilities (e.g., the word 'what' appears with probability X and the word 'probably' appears with the probability Y) but you can never predict the exact order, because that order is given by the meaning, which is *expressed* through words, but cannot be *reduced* to the words. The problem of atomic theory can be solved if atomic objects are viewed as symbols of meaning, because then we can explain why the words occur in a specific order. However, when we interpret the physical phenomena as symbols of meaning, then some physical properties themselves have to be seen as signs of meaning. For instance, the position of an object is no longer a physical state, but a meaning. The position of a planet like Jupiter should therefore be described in relation to the constellation Aries or Gemini as a different *type* of location, rather merely as a certain angle, declination, or degree. This doesn't mean that the numerical position cannot be described. It only means that we can never understand the real causality in nature if we only employ these numbers. Sitting in the bathroom and sitting in

the study room are not just degrees. They are different kinds of positions. Similarly, the planetary positions have to be understood as different types of places, rather than just numbers, because that numerical approach cannot help us understand how the planets cause changes. Alternately, numbers too can be understood as different types, such that 30^0 has a different meaning than 60^0. Readers interested in a typed view of numbers can refer to *Gödel's Mistake: The Role of Meaning in Mathematics,* which discusses the relation between numbers and meanings.

14. These types can be related to the typed based view of numbers expressing two interpretations of numbers: cardinal and ordinal. For instance, if we are dividing color into numerous types of color, there are two ways to understand types: (1) the type of color, and (2) the instances of the types such as red, blue, or green. The former represents the semantic view of *cardinals* while the latter denotes the semantic view of *ordinals.* The type 'color' therefore is also a number, just as the types 'green', 'red', and 'blue' are types. However, in a given context, the same number can denote an abstract or a contingent idea. Unless these numbers are treated as types, and the types are understood in their proper context, a quantitative view of numbers results in a confusion of what the number really represents, which then leads to problems of incompleteness, and sometimes even inconsistency.

15. This scheme is based on an article written by Jugalkishore Kalani, which can be accessed at the following: https://www.scribd.com/doc/111118078/How-mahadashas-period-calculated.

16. This fact is no longer a mystery after the advent of quantum theory where all objects absorb light, and 'rise' to a higher quantum state. Subsequently, they may also emit the light and 'fall' back to the original state. This absorption and emission cannot be predicted in quantum theory. The reason for this inability is that the cause of absorption and emission is the manifestation of *karma,* which is not a physical entity until it has manifested. Once it manifests, we can speak about its existence, but until it does, we cannot measure it. In quantum physics, this fact is modeled by a probability wave which is not a material object, but it is said to 'collapse' to create

an observation. Since this 'collapse' cannot be predicted by a law, quantum physics remains incomplete and indeterministic.

17. In effect, they are similar to what modern cosmology terms a 'black hole' which only absorbs light but never emits it, although the modern notion of a black hole involves extreme densities of matter. Some key issues arise in the understanding black holes, such as the disappearance of information. For instance, how can a black hole endlessly absorb light and matter? Where does all this information disappear after being absorbed? Can a black hole actually gobble up an entire universe?

18. According to the *Viṁśottarī daśā* system, a horoscope can undergo a period of 18 years of *Rāhu* and 7 years of *Ketu*. There are also cases when a horoscope has a '*sarpa dosha*' caused by *Rāhu* and *Ketu*.

19. In popular imagination, such a planet is called Planet X, and idea of such a planet has been mooted for at least a century to account for discrepancies in the orbits of outer planets. There are many arguments for and against such a planet, including whether Pluto is a real planet. In some viewpoints, for instance, Neptune is considered the last planet in the solar system, while Pluto is classified as a "dwarf planet".

Index

www.ingramcontent.com/pod-product-compliance
Lightning Source LLC
Chambersburg PA
CBHW060232100426
42742CB00011B/1514
9789385384066